Collective Action and Property Rights for Poverty Reduction

This book is published by the University of Pennsylvania Press (UPP) on behalf of the International Food Policy Research Institute (IFPRI) as part of a joint-publication series. Books in the series present research on food security and economic development with the aim of reducing poverty and eliminating hunger and malnutrition in developing nations. They are the product of peer-reviewed IFPRI research and are selected by mutual agreement between the parties for publication under the joint IFPRI-UPP imprint.

Collective Action and Property Rights for Poverty Reduction

Insights from Africa and Asia

EDITED BY ESTHER MWANGI, HELEN MARKELOVA,
AND RUTH MEINZEN-DICK

Published for the International Food Policy Research Institute

University of Pennsylvania Press
Philadelphia

Published by
University of Pennsylvania Press
Philadelphia, Pennsylvania 19104-4112
www.upenn.edu/pennpress

Library of Congress Cataloging-in-Publication Data

Collective action and property rights for poverty reduction : insights from Africa and
Asia / edited by Esther Mwangi, Helen Markelova, and Ruth Meinzen-Dick. — 1st ed.
     p.   cm. — (International Food Policy Research Institute)
   Includes bibliographical references and index.
   ISBN 978-0-8122-4392-5 (hardcover : alk. paper)
    1. Poverty—Africa.   2. Right of property—Economic aspects—Africa.
   3. Community organization—Economic aspects—Africa.   4. Poverty—Asia.
   5. Right of property—Economic aspects—Asia.   6. Community organization—
   Economic aspects—Asia.   I. Mwangi, Esther.   II. Markelova, Helen.
   III. Meinzen-Dick, Ruth Suseela.   IV. Series: International Food Policy Research
   Institute (Series)
   HC800.Z9P62413   2011
   362.5'561095—dc23   2011032478

Printed in the United States of America on acid-free paper
10 9 8 7 6 5 4 3 2 1

Contents

Figures

Tables

Boxes

Foreword

During the past three decades, major advances have been made in understanding the structure and function of community organizations and the origins and evolution of property rights and access to natural resources. Both local organizing and property rights and access to natural resources have been demonstrated to have profound implications for whether resources such as forests, fisheries, water, and pastures will be sustainably used and managed. Public policy has advanced along with this growing understanding. Similar progress has been made in poverty studies, and we now have a better understanding of the origins, dynamics, and multidimensional aspects of poverty. Policy communities at global, regional, and national levels have renewed and strengthened commitments to poverty reduction in response to findings that economic growth imperatives may leave some people behind.

Despite these advances in research, policy, and practice, contemporary thinking has yet to sufficiently bring the significant lessons from institutions in the natural resources sector to bear on the understanding of poverty and how it can be alleviated. The central focus of this edited volume is the interface between institutions and poverty. This book represents an effort to apply broad lessons and thinking from the vast collective-action and property-rights literature to poverty reduction, in order to provide a deeper understanding of processes and practices relevant to the global poverty-reduction agenda.

The work presented in this book underlines some basic findings. First, the diverse institutions crafted by the rural poor at local levels make possible different forms of organizing. These forms of organizing help the rural poor to manage shocks, reduce vulnerability, or do both; access previously unreachable markets for their products; and facilitate equitable access (including for women and marginalized ethnic groups) to natural resources and to extension services, thus countering elite capture. Second, assets, including property rights to those assets, can limit the rural poor's ability to participate in collective organizing, even as collective organization provides one way of acquiring assets that would be difficult on an individual basis. Third, community organizing on its own is insufficient. Cooperation among communities and between communities and external actors, including government officials, can support community action by lowering the costs of organizing, providing access to new information and opportunities, and promoting the adoption of policies and practices that enhance community efforts. These policies and practices can, in turn, be sensitized to local needs and priorities.

This book will be a useful "handbook" for policymakers and practitioners and students and researchers in a wide range of disciplines, including public policy, sociology, anthropology, and development economics. It should be viewed as part of a wider research program on understanding the role of institutions in society. The studies presented here, individually and collectively, contribute to our knowledge of an increasingly urgent policy problem and inspire new research efforts.

Shenggen Fan
Director General, International Food Policy Research Institute

Acknowledgments

This book is the product of the decade and a half of collaborations, networks, and friendships built among a wide range of stakeholders in the Systemwide Program on Collective Action and Property Rights (CAPRi), a program of the Consultative Group on International Agricultural Research (CGIAR).

The volume itself is the product of collective action among researchers at CGIAR research centers, German universities, and national universities and agricultural research centers in seven countries. Without the work of each of the contributors and their respective research teams, this volume would not have been possible. They organized and participated in numerous research meetings to discuss the conceptual framework for the book and to draw common lessons from the case studies' findings. Those with field experience often challenged the design of the research so as to make it more relevant for policymakers and practitioners. We thank all of them for their perseverance in the research for and preparation of this volume. Their names and affiliations can be found in the list of contributors at the end of the book, and the longer-form versions of their chapters can be found in the CAPRi working paper series (http://www.capri.cgiar.org/pubs.asp).

Of special importance were the people who assisted in different ways in putting the research into book form. Stephan Dohrn was a helpful assistant during the earlier part of the research that informs this book. Chelo Abrenilla and Betsy Pereira were invaluable in keeping track of research, documents, and manuscript revisions. Patty Arce held us all together by streamlining project administration and financing. Three anonymous reviewers helped us to improve the text, while IFPRI's Publications Review Committee ensured that the volume met high standards and Corinne Garber provided invaluable support to the whole process. In the later stages of the book's production we benefited enormously from John Whitehead's management of the production process.

This work was done with the financial support of the German Federal Ministry for Economic Cooperation and Development, to which we are very grateful. We owe our deepest thanks to rural men and women, policymakers, and practitioners in all seven countries for their generosity in sharing their time, information, and stories. All of them contributed to our understanding and inspired us in our work.

Acronyms and Abbreviations

AARC	Areka Agricultural Research Center
AHI	African Highlands Initiative
APL	*areal penggunaan lain* (areas for other uses)
APN	agricultural production network
ATT	average participation effect (average treatment effect on the treated)
AVA	Awash Valley Authority
BPN	national land agency
CAPRi	Systemwide Program on Collective Action and Property Rights
CDD	community-driven development
CF	community facilitator
CIFOR	Center for International Forestry Research
DPC	*Musyawarah Perencanaan Pembangunan* (*musrenbang;* development planning consultation)
DU	developmental unit
ERHS	Ethiopia Rural Household Survey
FRG	farmer research group
HKm	*Hutan Kemasyarakatan*
IAD	Institutional Analysis and Development
ICRISAT	International Crops Research Institute for the Semiarid Tropics
ICT	information and communication technology
IFPRI	International Food Policy Research Institute
IIC	internal institutional capacity
IMC	internal mobilization capacity
IV	instrumental variable
IWM	integrated watershed management
KADLACC	Kapchorwa District Landcare Chapter
LEC	local environmental committee
MAADE	Middle Awash Agricultural Development Enterprise
MDG	Millennium Development Goal

NGO	nongovernmental organization
NRM	natural resource management
NRPC	natural resource protection committee
OLS	ordinary least squares
PA	peasant association
PAR	participatory action research
PIA	project implementing agency
PMG	producer marketing group
PRONA	Program Nasional Agraria
PSM	propensity score matching
PSNP	Productive Safety Nets Programme
PTF	policy task force
REDD	reduced emissions from deforestation and degradation
RGC	Royal Government of Cambodia
RIMCU	Research Institute for Mindanao Culture
RTRWK	Rencana Tata Ruang Wilayah Kabupaten (District-Level Land Use Plan)
RTRWP	*Rencana Tata Ruang Wilayah Provinsi* (Provincial-Level Land Use Plan)
SLA	sustainable livelihoods approach
TGHK	*Tata Guna Hutan Kesepakatan* (Forest Land Use by Consensus)
TLU	total livestock unit
UWA	Uganda Wildlife Authority
WA	watershed association
WC	watershed committee

Collective Action and Property Rights for Poverty Reduction

PART I

Introduction and Conceptual Framework

Part I includes Chapters 1 ("Introduction and Overview") and 2 ("Property Rights and Collective Action for Poverty Reduction: A Framework for Analysis"), which set the stage for the rest of the volume. Chapter 1 introduces readers to what the book is about: the role of institutions, especially those focused on collective action and property rights, in contributing to poverty reduction. It explains how the book fits into the existing literature on poverty by uniting the natural resource management (NRM) literature with the non-NRM poverty studies, cross-pollinating the vast knowledge on institutions of the former with a focus on the poor and their assets of the latter. The chapter also provides brief highlights of each of the case studies and explains how they were chosen for inclusion in the collection. It introduces the main themes of the volume:

- Risk and vulnerability to shocks
- Market access for smallholders
- Natural resource governance and access to resources
- Conflict and postconflict development
- Poverty, power, and elite capture

Then the chapter elaborates on the contributions of the case studies to the existing literature on these topics as well as their overall importance for poverty reduction.

Chapter 2 is the conceptual backbone of the volume. It presents the framework that guided the research projects that served as the bases for the case studies. The elements of the framework are discussed in detail to show how, together, they help researchers to understand how institutions of collective action and property rights can be vehicles for poverty reduction and how, in turn, these institutions are influenced by the other elements of the framework, such as assets, risks, and governance structures. The chapter also offers potential research questions that can be generated using the framework to investigate various aspects of poverty. The design of the framework is aimed to show the complex and dynamic nature of poverty reduction, and application of the institutional lens captures the interactions between various actors that shape certain poverty-related outcomes.

1 Introduction and Overview

ESTHER MWANGI, HELEN MARKELOVA,
AND RUTH MEINZEN-DICK

Poverty reduction has been at the forefront of global discussions for several decades but has recently gained fresh momentum, with various parties urgently pushing for policies and programs that would enhance the well-being of the world's 1 billion poor.[1] The United Nations' Millennium Development Goals (MDGs) adopted in the 1990s provide a normative framework and specific targets for poverty reduction efforts. On the other hand, Poverty Reduction Strategy Papers (comprehensive country-based strategies for poverty prevention), which are based on consultative processes with a wide range of stakeholders, provide an instrumental road map for achieving the MDG targets. Embedded in these global policy efforts is a crucial need to better understand the manifestations of poverty and the factors affecting it in order to inform policy and practice.

Poverty-related research has shown that despite their low asset endowment and vulnerability to shocks, the poor employ various strategies to improve their well-being, which in some cases have proved effective in addressing some of the vital needs that poor households face (Moser 1998; Krishna et al. 2004). However, the success of these strategies is highly dependent on the socio-political and legal environments in which the poor live (Uphoff, Esman, and Krishna 1998). Therefore, to make poverty reduction policies and programs effective in reaching the poor, it is necessary to understand what existing mechanisms the poor use and how these can be strengthened through various measures, whether via direct interventions in the form of well-designed and well-targeted programs or indirect ones in terms of favorable pro-poor policies.

More attention has recently been given to the value of institutions in poverty reduction. Although the role of institutions and their development has been widely recognized in natural resource management (NRM) studies (see Ostrom 1990, 2005; Agrawal 2001; and James Acheson's 2006 review), their importance for broader poverty reduction efforts is now gaining more attention (Narayan 2002; Ellis, Kutengule, and Nyansulu 2003). The institutions of collective action and property rights have particularly been identified as essential for enhanc-

---

1. World Bank estimates for 2001.

ing the livelihood options of the poor because the most vulnerable and marginalized rural groups often lack access to resources because they do not have secure property rights and find participation in collective action too costly in terms of time and resource constraints (Ostrom 2000). The United Nations Office of the High Commission for Human Rights defines poverty as "a human condition characterized by the sustained or chronic deprivation of the resources, capabilities, choices, security and power necessary for the enjoyment of an adequate standard of living and other civil, cultural, economic, political and social rights."[2] For many of the world's rural poor, property rights are part and parcel of economic rights and entitlements, and their ability to engage in collective action is an essential choice, capability, and source of power.

Property rights to natural resources are the key institutional assets on which rural people build their livelihoods. Secure property rights, both individual and communal, provide not only an income stream today but also incentives to invest in productive technologies and sustainable management of the resources for the future. The rural poor are usually those with the weakest property rights; thus, secure rights over land, water, trees, livestock, fish, and genetic resources are fundamental mechanisms for reducing poverty (Carter 2003). However, many government programs are implemented without an understanding of the complexity of property rights and have actually reduced tenure security for poor and marginalized groups, for example, by allowing elite capture of property. A better understanding of how the poor can protect and expand their access to and control of resources can make a powerful contribution to poverty reduction.

There is also growing recognition of the importance of collective action as a valuable asset for poverty reduction. Through formal and informal groups, smallholders can work together to overcome limitations of wealth, farm size, and bargaining power. Collective action is also needed to adopt many NRM technologies and practices that operate at the landscape level (Meinzen-Dick et al. 2002). In addition, collective action can contribute to poverty reduction through mutual insurance, sustainable management of natural resources, increased opportunities for income generation, and improved provision of and access to public services (Bebbington 1996, 2007; Dercon 2002; Meinzen-Dick et al. 2002). As in the case of property rights, the poor and women are often at a disadvantage when it comes to collective action because of social exclusion, lack of time to participate in meetings and activities, lack of education, lack of confidence to speak at meetings, and domination by local elites; however, there is heterogeneity in terms of access to these resources among women as a group (Agrawal 2001; Thorpe, Stewart, and Heyer 2005).

Although these two areas of institutions research may seem disconnected at the first glance, they intersect in many areas essential to the livelihoods of the

---

2. <www.unhchr.ch/development/poverty> (accessed September 15, 2006).

poor. Both rights to vital resources and various forms of collective action (such as that of groups and networks) are important assets for the well-being of poor households and communities. On the other hand, the poor often do not have access or use rights to vital resources, and they are unable to secure or protect these rights individually. Collective action can help to overcome these barriers (for example, through microfinance programs) and enable the poor to negotiate their rights collectively. Moreover, the often-present ambiguity over property rights creates incentives for people to organize and act together to secure access to resources and to negotiate joint management of resources. These linkages between collective action and property rights, especially in the realm of NRM (see Mearns 1996 and Adhikari 2005 for examples) uniquely position them to be analyzed concurrently by the same poverty-oriented research project.

To examine the role of the institutions of collective action and property rights on poverty reduction in both NRM and non-NRM areas, the Systemwide Program on Collective Action and Property Rights (CAPRi) of the Consultative Group on International Agricultural Research commissioned a global research project with study sites in seven countries across Africa and Asia: Ethiopia, Kenya, Uganda, Cambodia, Indonesia, and the Philippines. The main goal of the project was to contribute to poverty reduction efforts by identifying effective policies and practices that enhance the ways that collective action and property rights are (and can be) used to build secure assets and income streams for and by the poor. The project aimed to provide policymakers, nongovernmental organizations (NGOs), and community groups with knowledge of the factors that strengthen the rights of the poor to land and water resources and lead to more effective collective action by the poor. The portfolio of case studies under this global project includes both NRM and non-NRM-related research, so by presenting the findings from the global research project, this volume sits at an interesting intersection between NRM and non-NRM poverty research.

The extensive literature on NRM (for reviews, see Ostrom 1990, 1999, 2005; Baland and Platteau 1996; and Agrawal 2001) has described in detail the factors that influence sustainable NRM, including the importance of collective action institutions and secure tenure rights. However, looking at individual factors can lead to a somewhat mechanistic approach to institutional development and resource governance, disregarding the complexity of the interactions among the various factors affecting institutions in NRM. Moreover, this body of research has not necessarily focused on the very poor, who may not have access to natural resources; although it has contributed important findings on what leads to effective collective action and property rights, this literature has not paid much attention to the poverty–power–vulnerability nexus.

The non-NRM poverty research, on the other hand, has achieved great strides in understanding poverty, including its dynamic aspects (Hulme and Shepherd 2003; Barrett and Swallow 2006) and has paid some attention to the issues of inclusiveness by studying power relations and vulnerability (Chambers 1997;

Narayan 2000). However, its understanding of and attention to institutions has not been as well developed as that for NRM. For example, collective action is often portrayed as a naturally emerging response of poor people to the injustices they face (see, for example, the accounts of social movements in Escobar and Alvarez 1992 and Tarrow 1998), without critically examining the factors behind the emergence of cooperation, its sustainability, or reasons behind the failure of some group approaches, as in the case of the failed agricultural cooperatives (Coulter 2007). The studies of the community-driven development (CDD) projects also highlight the benefits of group approaches for targeting, public service delivery, and project sustainability, and some even touch on the issues of elite capture (see Mansuri and Rao 2004 for a review of these studies). However, they admittedly lack the detailed analysis of institutions underlying cooperation around CDD activities. The microfinance literature has made strides in examining not just the economic benefits of group lending but also the determinants of cooperation based on demographic and other characteristics of group members, including contributing to the debate on the relevance of group homogeneity for its success, which is widely discussed in the NRM literature (Sharma and Zeller 1997; Zeller 1998; Karlan 2007; for an example of this discussion in NRM, see Adhikari and Lovett 2006).

As for property rights institutions, much of the non-NRM poverty literature considers only individual property rights and looks at them primarily in terms of their economic value, for example, in terms of increases in investment and agricultural productivity and the adoption of commercial crops and improved farming practices (Besley 1995; Field, Field, and Torero 2006); some studies go further and highlight the increased bargaining power and increased security of tenure as a result of titling and certification programs (for example, Banerjee, Gertler, and Ghatak 2002; Deininger, Ayalew Ali, and Yamano 2008; Deininger et al. 2008). However, there are multiple studies, mostly in the NRM realm, that have demonstrated that property rights systems around the world are complex and dynamic, are based on multiple sources beyond a title deed, and fulfill multiple functions in the lives of the poor (Schlager and Ostrom 1992; Deere and León 2001; Meinzen-Dick and Mwangi 2009). Moreover, common property resources are rarely considered in the non-NRM poverty studies, although there is mounting evidence of their vital importance in the livelihoods of the poor around the world (Cousins 1999; Beck and Nesmith 2001).

Thus the valuable lessons learned from the NRM literature about institutions, including ones related to collective action and property rights, have not been widely applied to other poverty-related topics. The Institutional Analysis and Development (IAD) framework developed by Ostrom and colleagues (2005), which has been useful in studying NRM institutions, has not been adopted by other poverty researchers working in non-NRM areas. This framework and the work by other NRM scholars on the creation of sustainable institutions can offer valuable lessons applicable to other poverty-related topics. For example, Markelova et al. (2009) show how similar factors that influence collective action for the management of natural resources can be applied to group marketing. Therefore, there is broad unexamined scope for the interaction between the two bodies of research in order to understand and create institutions that would facilitate poverty reduction across sectors.

Elinor Ostrom, the 2009 Nobel Prize winner in economics, has drawn attention to the need to go beyond the traditional solutions to problems facing socioecological systems (resource degradation, and so on) and develop a more refined understanding of how institutions develop and operate. She calls for a more nuanced method that identifies combinations of variables that affect the incentives and actions of actors (Ostrom 2007). For example, both the NRM and other poverty literature would benefit from a more nuanced understanding of the issue of elite capture, especially in the context of decentralization reforms, where the fiscal and decisionmaking authority across various sectors, including resource distribution and management, is being handed over to the lower levels of state agencies. Many scholars and practitioners recognize elite capture as a central dilemma in decentralization processes and offer ways to develop effective strategies for avoiding or countering it (Bardhan 1997; Ribot 2003; Barrett, Mude, and Omiti 2007). However, there is still considerable scope for identifying the factors that lead to elite capture and how elite capture conditions certain poverty outcomes, which goes beyond what has been covered in detail by NRM and other poverty literature.

What Is Unique about This Volume?

This volume lies at the confluence of the streams of literature on NRM and poverty reduction. Building on the understandings of the institutions of collective action and property rights that have been developed in studies of NRM, it goes one step further to examine how and to what extent these institutions can contribute to poverty reduction. It proposes a conceptual framework that expands on Ostrom's IAD framework to include poverty research in non-NRM areas and facilitates analysis of the complex interactions among various aspects of the reality of the poor. The book examines institutions, especially those of collective action and property rights, in terms of the factors that influence their formation and dynamics and studies the contributions that these institutions make to poverty-related outcomes in light of the actors and the interactions between actors, adding a dynamic aspect to poverty analysis. It discusses power issues, including elite capture, in terms of their origins and their effect on poverty outcomes. In doing so, it does what Elinor Ostrom (2007) proposed: it goes beyond offering panaceas for a simplistic understanding of poverty and solutions for its reduction to a careful examination of the role of institutions in facilitating certain poverty outcomes for the poor.

The chapters in this volume report on the case studies that were part of the global research project mentioned earlier, exploring how the institutions of collective action and property rights may affect the well-being of the poor. The studies achieved this by employing various research traditions, spanning different settings, and examining several cross-cutting themes that illustrate the important role that institutions can play in poverty reduction efforts. The studies provide a unique opportunity to compare findings across settings and to draw generally applicable as well as context-specific implications for policy, practice, and research. They vary across poverty-related themes such as coping with risk, accessing scarce natural resources, participating in markets, and dealing with postconflict reconstruction, which allows them to teach generalizable lessons on the role of collective action and property rights institutions in each specific area as well as to compare and contrast the findings across the themes. By focusing on the role of institutions in both NRM (resource access and conflict around resource access and use) and non-NRM areas (risk management and market access), the volume unites these development domains, which in many cases have been viewed and treated as disparate by policy, research, and practice.

Bridging the gap between NRM and risk management and market access is especially valuable and has not been widely discussed in the past but presents important synergies, especially in the application of collective action institutions in a broader policy perspective. The importance of these institutions' acting together to gain access to resources and to manage them effectively, equitably, and sustainably has been well discussed in the large body of NRM literature, and a number of important lessons on the applicability, sustainability, and impacts of collective action have been drawn. To date, these lessons have not been widely applied in many of the other poverty-related domains, with the exception of microfinance. The collection of studies in this volume allows for the cross-pollination of these findings from NRM cases to the non-NRM cases and demonstrates the relevance of collective action institutions for wider poverty reduction efforts. It must be noted, however, that although the case studies in this volume covered a wide range of topics related to collective action, such as its role in enabling market access for smallholders, facilitating access to resources, and insuring against shocks, this is not an exhaustive description of how these institutions may contribute to poverty reduction. Social and political movements, as examples of large-scale collective action that are important for the livelihoods and empowerment of the poor, fall beyond the scope of this volume and are covered elsewhere.[3]

A common framework (Chapter 2 of this volume) was drawn up at the inception of the project to inform the diverse case studies. The framework drew

---

3. For example, good accounts of this form of collective action are presented in Branford and Rocha's (2002) description of the Brazilian landless movement and in Bebbington's (2007) overview of the potential role of social movements in poverty reduction.

on the IAD framework that has been widely applied in natural resource management (for example, in Ostrom 2005) and broadened it out to address other aspects of poverty as well. It outlined key variables and relationships essential to an inquiry into the links between poverty and the institutions of collective action and property rights. It also showed how initial conditions (assets, vulnerability to shocks, and the legal or political environment) affect the ability of the rural poor to create institutions that mediate interactions and lead to certain welfare outcomes. This conceptual framework did not limit one to a particular method or research question but rather encouraged the application of multiple approaches. The individual studies (including the research questions and methods) were undertaken using different kinds of research designs. Each covered part (but not all) of the framework, with emerging results fed back in an iterative process of framework and case study development. For example, the Philippines and the Ethiopia–*iddir* studies examined hypotheses generated from the framework that communities facing uncertainty are disadvantaged in terms of welfare and use collective action institutions as a way to deal with shocks. On the other hand, the Ethiopia–Somali and Ethiopia–Afar cases highlighted that the action resources held by pastoralists and state authorities shape their patterns of interactions and the poverty-related outcomes of these interactions. Similar relationships can be found among the elements of the framework and other chapters, each focusing on several elements of the framework, with the central attention given to the ways that collective action and property rights are being used by the poor themselves or in collaboration with their external allies to overcome various constraints—and the limitations that are faced in these processes.

Table 1.1 presents a brief description of each study. Four case studies relied primarily on quantitative methods, two used mainly qualitative techniques, two were based on the participatory action research approach, and one combined qualitative methods with experimental games. These various methods are different not only in terms of the instruments they use (surveys, focus groups, trust games, negotiation processes, and so on) but in terms of their overall approach to the current situation (status quo) at the research site. For example, participatory action research is an iterative process embedded in local communities and internalized by them (German and Stroud 2007). It focuses on the collaborative identification of priorities and promotes subsequent steps to initiate the change in the status quo (that is, examining and doing "what is to be"), whereas most other empirical approaches identify strengths and challenges in the status quo (that is, analyze "what is") and at best recommend change to be implemented by a third party. Because each methodological approach gives a specific insight on the nature and causes of poverty (Kanbur and Shaffer 2007), the variety of methods across these studies exposes the true multidimensionality of the topic and provides different lenses through which one can examine the complex reality of the poor. This is especially important because many poverty-related studies narrowly focus on only the economic or quantita-

TABLE 1.1 Overview of case studies

Case study	Country/site	Lead institution	Main research method	Main research theme	Main research question
Risk management and market access					
Ethiopia–*iddir*	Ethiopia (nonpastoral areas)	International Food Policy Research Institute (IFPRI)	Quantitative and some qualitative	Vulnerability and risk	Role of group membership in shock mitigation and risk mitigation
Philippines	Philippines (Mindanao)	IFPRI	Quantitative and some qualitative	Vulnerability and risk	Role of membership in formal and informal groups in risk management
Kenya	Semiarid areas of eastern Kenya	International Crops Research Institute for the Semi-Arid Tropics (ICRISAT)	Quantitative	Markets	Role of membership in producer organizations in dealing with market imperfections
Natural resource governance and access to resources					
India	India	ICRISAT	Quantitative	Natural resource management	Impact of collective action on poverty reduction and resource improvement outcomes
African Highlands Initiative (AHI)	Ethiopia (Ginchi and Areka) and Uganda (Kabale and Kapchorwa)	AHI	Participatory action research and other qualitative techniques	Natural resource management and governance	Approaches to facilitate equitable collective action and negotiated natural resource management solutions

Indonesia	Indonesia (Jambi Province)	Center for International Forestry Research	Participatory action research	Natural resource governance	How collective action can be catalyzed among various stakeholders to enhance local people's access to resources and policy processes
Ethiopia–Afar	Ethiopia (Afar)	Humboldt University, Berlin	Qualitative and some quantitative	Conflict	Impact of changing property rights regimes on collective action institutions and livelihoods
Ethiopia–Somali	Ethiopia (Somali)	Humboldt University Berlin	Qualitative and some quantitative	Natural resource management, conflict	Impact of changing property rights regimes on welfare and wealth distribution via access to water resources
Cambodia	Cambodia (Kampong Thom and Kampong Cham Provinces)	Philipps University, Marburg	Qualitative and experimental games	Natural resource management, postconflict rebuilding	Impact of formal and informal institutions of collective action and property rights on socioeconomic change and poverty reduction

SOURCE: Authors.

NOTE: *Iddir* are burial societies.

tive measures of poverty; however, several of the studies in this volume also reflected on the empowerment aspects of poverty reduction, the examination of which goes beyond numbers. Moreover, the conceptual framework and the cases drew on a variety of disciplines, including economics, sociology, anthropology, and political ecology, which contributes to the disciplinary richness of this volume.

In addition to representing a broad range of methodologies, the studies in this volume touched on several themes that are important for poverty reduction efforts. Despite the broad range of methods, sites, and research questions, the topics that were investigated in the case studies seemed to coincide, suggesting their relevance and importance in the lives of the poor. These common themes are

- Risk and vulnerability to shocks
- Market access for smallholders
- Natural resource governance and access to resources
- Conflict and postconflict development
- Poverty, power, and elite capture

What unites these themes is the particular way that they were examined in the case studies: an institutional lens was applied in each case to highlight the central role that institutional arrangements play in all these poverty-related areas. By *institutions* we understand "the rules of the game in a society or, more formally, the humanly devised constraints that shape human interaction" (North 1990, 3). They are not equated with organizations, although the latter are part of institutional arrangements (Meinzen-Dick et al. 2004). Many years of poverty reduction efforts have provided evidence that programs that simply transfer technologies, capital, or funds to the poor are not sufficient to deal with structural causes of poverty or ensure equitable distribution of resources (Barrett, Carter, and Little 2006). It has been shown that creating appropriate institutional structures that enable the poor to take advantage of such programs as well as strengthening the capacity of existing traditional institutions is necessary for positive welfare outcomes (Meinzen-Dick et al. 2002; World Bank 2002).

Among all institutions, this research effort aimed to investigate collective action arrangements and property rights regimes to learn more about their effects on poverty and their potential for poverty reduction. As a result, all the case studies undertook analyses of various factors that contribute to poverty and can lead to poverty reduction in light of their interaction with the institutions of collective action and property rights. The findings showed that these institutions are important and prominent in all the themes listed earlier, offering ample evidence that both access rights and cooperation are vital for the livelihoods of the poor, whether for mitigating shocks, dealing with market imperfections, ensuring equitable access to key resources, or addressing the consequences of sociopolitical conflict. Chapter 2 provides the conceptual underpinnings of the mechanisms by which these interactions occur; the case studies (Chapters 3–11) illustrate these mechanisms in concrete settings. In the next section we present synopses of the case studies before returning to themes that are interwoven through the cases.

The studies in this volume also covered a variety of contexts within Africa and Asia, providing opportunities to look further into the nature of poverty between and within countries. The African Highlands Initiative (AHI) and Indonesia cases highlighted the similarity of resource governance–related issues between Africa and Asia. The Ethiopia–*iddir* and Philippines studies showed that the poor in both countries are vulnerable to similar shocks and employ similar strategies to mitigate them. The Ethiopia–Afar, Ethiopia–Somali, and Cambodia cases presented similar accounts of the pernicious effects of government policies on local institutions and livelihoods.

Several additional features of these case studies should be noted. First, they were selected by an independent and multidisciplinary panel through a competitive application process. Thus they do not represent a comprehensive geographic spread but rather provide a unique collection of thematically and geographically diverse studies from which to draw insights on the nature of poverty and on how collective action and property rights might enhance welfare. Second, all studies relied heavily on collaboration with local and international research institutions as well as some local NGOs and government authorities. Overall, the global project was carried out by linking with 49 partners, which generated opportunities for enhancing local capacity for poverty-related research, creating awareness of relevant issues among various stakeholders, and building new networks as well as strengthening existing ones. It also enabled the research teams to share with policymakers, NGOs, and community groups knowledge of the factors that strengthen the rights of the poor to critical resources, enhance their abilities to cope with shocks, improve their input into decisions, and enable them to more effectively engage in collective action, with expectations that such information will influence decisionmaking.

This book is intended for a diverse audience. The wide representation of research methods and empirical case studies would be of use to researchers, academics, and development students. Practitioners and policymakers, whether in government or NGOs, can learn about potential limitations to or conditions supporting specific policies. Finally, all parties will be better informed about the key roles played by institutions of collective action and property rights in the lives of the rural poor.

Overview of the Case Studies

The nine cases included in this volume spotlighted seven countries: five were from Africa (Ethiopia, Kenya, and Uganda), and four were set in Asia (Cambodia, India, Indonesia, and the Philippines). All nine dealt with the issues of collective action, and four also examined property rights, mostly in conjunction with collective action. It must be noted that these studies were designed not to provide ex post impact assessments of certain interventions but rather to develop an understanding of the processes involved. Several of the studies were actually written as the institutions of collective action were being developed and property rights regimes were being changed and clarified. The order of the case studies in the volume follows the non-NRM and NRM distinction, and they are grouped together according to their respective main themes, gradually progressing from the non-NRM studies to the ones that dealt with natural resources. In Part II ("Risk Management and Market Access"), Chapters 3 and 4 focus on the application of collective action institutions to risk management, and Chapter 5 examines collective marketing. Part III ("Natural Resource Management") presents studies that dealt with various aspects of NRM. Chapter 6 looks at collective action for watershed management. Chapters 7 and 8 examine the role of collective action institutions in securing access to resources and services. Both case studies presented used the participatory action research approach and complemented each other in providing an understanding of this methodology as well as its application to the development of sustainable collective action. Chapters 9 and 10 deal primarily with the theme of the transformation of collective action and property rights institutions around land and water management in the traditionally conflict-ridden areas of Ethiopia. However, they also provide insight into the role of these institutions in dealing with political risks, thus extending the insights on the topic of institutions of risk management highlighted in Chapters 3 and 4. The final case study, in Chapter 11, investigated the role of collective action institutions in postconflict rebuilding. Even though the case studies in Part III focused on different topics within the resource management arena, the accounts of them are positioned in a way that allows their lessons to build on each other and shows the reader a variety of issues within the NRM realm. Following is a brief description of each study.

Burial Societies (Iddir) *in Ethiopia*

Adverse shocks have numerous malign effects on the poor. The study presented in Chapter 3 examined how an indigenous means of collective action, burial associations, or *iddir,* influences households' abilities to deal with adverse events. The study found that in rural Ethiopia, drought and health-related shocks have the worst impacts on household welfare. Using econometric analysis, the authors show that membership in *iddir* can help smooth household consumption for idiosyncratic shocks but not for covariate shocks. This quantitative analysis is complemented by qualitative research that examines how these burial societies overcome the informational problems typically associated with the provision of mutual help for health shocks. *Iddir* providing health insurance are homogeneous along some dimensions (geography and, to a certain extent, religion) but heterogeneous with respect to age. They impose membership restrictions that reduce the cost of obtaining information and restrict assistance to an observable component of illness shocks (medical expenditures) that can be verified; further, they limit the extent of their assistance so that the provision of assistance does not come at the cost of financial sustainability. The main conclusion made by the authors is that forms of collective action such as *iddir* can serve as an insurance mechanism during shocks but have limitations in mitigating widespread shocks.

Local Groups and Migrant Networks in the Philippines

The case study reported in Chapter 4 used a rich longitudinal dataset and qualitative studies from Bukidnon, Philippines, to examine the impact of shocks on household consumption and how these impacts differ across household types. The authors also look at the determinants of membership in groups and informal networks. Similar to the Ethiopia–*iddir* case, this study found that illness, death, and drought were the worst shocks. The impact of these shocks varies with asset ownership. Drought had the worst impact on landless households, whereas the death of a household head negatively affected families with more land and assets. Joining groups and networks appears to be one way that households respond to shocks. However, better-off households are more likely to participate in formal groups, especially economically oriented associations such as credit groups. The poorer households, however, are as likely as their wealthier cohorts to participate in burial societies as well as in civic and religious groups. Heterogeneity with respect to location was found to be important in insuring against covariate shocks: migrant networks serve an insurance function through remittances, especially those received from migrant daughters.

Producer Marketing Groups in Kenya

Drawing on data from communities, producer marketing groups (PMGs), and farm households in semiarid eastern Kenya, the study recounted in Chapter 5 investigated the potential of farmer organizations to remedy market imperfections in rural Sub-Saharan Africa. The analysis shows that although the functioning of markets is constrained by high transaction costs and coordination problems along the supply chain, PMGs provide new opportunities for small producers through vertical and horizontal coordination of production and marketing functions. Group effectiveness is determined by levels of participatory decisionmaking, member contributions, and their initial start-up capital. The likelihood of membership in PMGs is negatively associated with per capita farm size, indicating that the incentive for membership is higher for small and medium farmers, who face high transaction costs, than for large farmers with higher levels of marketed surplus and lower transaction costs. The benefits of membership, however, are directly related to the amount marketed through groups; hence farmers with larger amounts of marketed surplus gain greater benefits. The overall success of PMGs is constrained by the lack of access to credit.

Watershed Management in India

Community watershed programs have received substantial investment, but their effects on poverty have not been clear. This study reported in Chapter 6 investigated the institutional and policy issues that limit effective participation in community watershed programs and identified key determinants of the degree of collective action and its effectiveness in achieving economic and environmental outcomes. Based on empirical data from a survey of 87 watershed communities in semiarid Indian villages, the study used factor analysis to develop aggregate indexes of collective action and its effectiveness. Regression methods were then employed to test the effects of certain policy-relevant variables and to determine the potential effects of collective action in achieving the desired poverty reduction and resource improvement outcomes. The authors found that collective action had a positive and highly significant effect on natural resource investments but found weaker positive evidence of its effect on household assets and poverty reduction outcomes. They attribute these findings to longer gestation periods for realizing the indirect effects of collective natural resource investments and the lack of institutional mechanisms to ensure the equitable distribution of such gains across the community, including to the landless and marginal farmers.

Natural Resource Management in the AHI

To generate working solutions to problems facing rural communities in their efforts to manage their natural resources in the highlands of Ethiopia and Uganda, the study presented in Chapter 7 integrated empirical and action research methods. Using four study sites (two in each country), the research team led the communities through four primary steps: situation analysis, stakeholder workshops, action research, and impact assessment. During these activities, the main natural resource management problems were identified and sustainable solutions to these problems were negotiated. The authors present findings on the existing forms of collective action at the study sites and discuss the influence of local and external institutions on economic development. The results of the action research process showed positive livelihood outcomes in the form of improved natural resource management, increased bargaining power of the communities, greater access to technologies and extension services for women, and enhanced overall equity through participatory crafting and enforcement of bylaws.

Access to Forest Resources in Indonesia

The case study recounted in Chapter 8 looked at the role of collective action in securing access rights to forests in the context of decentralization in Indonesia. Using participatory action research, the research team worked in parallel with local community groups, on the one hand, to clarify their goals regarding property rights and productive activities, negotiate with district authorities and representatives of the private sector, and increase their self-confidence and capacity to interact with external groups. At the same time, a similar process of participatory action research was initiated with government officials, who strengthened their abilities to analyze local situations, learned something of the value of listening to communities, and gained skills in cooperation, conflict management, and negotiation with both higher and lower levels. In addition, efforts were undertaken to avoid elite capture by private companies and village heads. Although the processes started through the project are ongoing, the outcomes of the project include strengthened local capacity and learning, creation of multilevel coalitions, and increased awareness and discussions of sensitive issues such as rights over forestlands and gender. The authors found that although local collective action can be effective in enhancing the rights of the poor to forest resources, it benefits greatly from institutional support from more powerful stakeholders.

Changes in Pastoral Livelihoods in Afar, Ethiopia

The study reported in Chapter 9 analyzed the changes that have occurred among the pastoralists in the Afar Region of Ethiopia as a result of shifting property rights systems. Although the traditional landholding arrangements were based on communal ownership with access for different user groups, these systems are changing based on external and internal pressures. The authors distinguish between coercive changes (state expropriations and sedentarization policies) and noncoercive shifts (decisions to cooperate around farming activities). They found that changes caused by government policies resulted in inequality in access to land and subsequent livelihood options, especially marginalizing women and the poor. On the other hand, the decision to farm collectively was seen to be more prevalent among the poorer community members, suggesting that it served as a coping strategy in the face of recurrent droughts and an adaptation strategy in response to state programs promoting farming.

Changing Property Rights and Collective Action in Somali, Ethiopia

The study presented in Chapter 10 investigated current practices of collective action and how these are affected by changing property rights in the pastoralist and agropastoralist economies of three selected sites in eastern Ethiopia. The authors describe forms of collective action in the management of water resources (wells, cisterns, and ponds) and pasturelands to analyze how changing property rights regimes affect incentives for cooperation around management of these resources. They show that incentives for collective action in managing water artifacts depend on economic cost–benefit considerations and social norms. Further, exclusion of nonmembers is difficult to enforce, which reduces the incentives to contribute to collective action in maintaining these resources. Recent state policies have created opportunities for elite capture that increase economic inequalities within clans. In its analysis of access to pastures, the study highlighted that interclan relationships are guided by kinship and principles of reciprocity; however, these arrangements are breaking down as a result of spreading private enclosures and shrinking communal lands.

Socioeconomic Changes in Postwar Cambodia

The final case study, reported in Chapter 11, investigated how formal and informal institutions of property rights and collective action influence poverty reduction in rural Cambodia. It focused on emerging endogenous mechanisms of cooperation as well as on the role of external actors and instruments in forming or enhancing collective action institutions and enforcing use and ownership rights among the rural poor. Findings indicate that access to and use of natural resources still contribute significantly to rural incomes. Access to natural resources, however, is defined by multiple and overlapping rights, both private and common, which are in turn governed by formal and informal patterns of cooperation. Collective action also contributes to improved livelihoods, but there are differences in the degree of participation based on asset endowments. The authors emphasize that due to Cambodia's recent history of genocide, forced collectivization, and resettlement, property rights regimes have been severely affected, remain contested, and are re-established only slowly with mutual trust.

Key Themes

As mentioned earlier, the key themes of this volume include

- Risk and vulnerability to shocks
- Market access for smallholders
- Natural resource governance and access to resources
- Conflict and postconflict development
- Poverty, power, and elite capture

Although each case study focused on a particular theme as its main focus, several of the case studies encompassed a number of the key themes, thus allowing the reader to examine these themes in a comparative way, especially between the NRM and non-NRM cases. The theme of poverty, power, and elite capture is found across most of the case studies, especially those presented in Part III. By studying these themes in light of the institutions of collective action and property rights, the case studies introduce a new dimension to the understanding of poverty reduction in the areas of risk and vulnerability, market access, natural resource management, and postconflict rebuilding.

Risk and Vulnerability to Shocks

The Ethiopia–*iddir* and Philippines cases add to the body of knowledge on risk management by the poor. Although they confirm the importance of various types of networks for managing shocks as previously noted in the literature (see Dercon 2002), they also look in depth at group membership and functioning and show that those who are better off have larger networks than the poor and are thus better able to deal with shocks. This finding is also important for other studies of collective action because it shows that the poor may be disadvantaged in their access to certain forms of collective action. The Ethiopia–Afar chapter builds on the literature about how pastoralist communities deal with shocks through livelihood diversification (Little et al. 2001). It shows that the institutions of collective action facilitate the transition into farming, which is a response to both sociopolitical shocks (government policies causing uncertainty in property rights relations) and natural shocks (recurrent droughts). Moreover, the Ethiopia–*iddir* study highlights the limitations of collective action in dealing with covariate shocks, a finding with an important policy implication regarding the necessity of social safety networks to deal with large-scale shocks such as droughts.

Market Access for Smallholders

The role of collective action in enabling poor people to access markets has been gaining more attention in recent years as donors and governments have continued to promote commercialization of small farmers as a development strategy (Dorward et al. 2004; Bernard and Spielman 2009). The Kenya case study shows that farmer groups can indeed help farmers to overcome market imperfections but that the incentives for cooperation around marketing activities are dependent on farmers' opportunity costs and the transaction costs they face. This result, along with the policy recommendation of public investment in complementary institutions for effective smallholder marketing, echoes the findings by Markelova et al. (2009) that collective action in marketing is a valid approach but needs certain factors in place to succeed as well as the support of the public and private sectors and civil society.

Natural Resource Governance and Access to Resources

Five of the case studies address aspects of natural resource management, with a special focus on rights to resources. The Indonesia case study provides a unique look at how the poor can use collective action in the form of negotiating processes in order to secure their rights to forest resources by enabling poor forest communities to simultaneously negotiate with more powerful actors such as state authorities and representatives of the private sector. Through these processes, facilitated by the participatory action research (PAR), the poor were able to make strides in clarifying their resource rights, illustrating the important links between collective action and property rights. The AHI study (Chapter 7) shows the importance of bylaws in natural resource management, which is an emerging issue in NRM research (Markelova and Swallow 2008). Through various steps outlined by the PAR methodology, the authors illustrate that in order for these rules to lead to pro-poor outcomes such as equitable resource use and access to technology, they must be created in a participatory way involving various stakeholders, based on the institutions of collective action.

Conflict and Postconflict Rebuilding

Case studies related to this theme are also centered on natural resources. The Ethiopia–Somali case study dissected the nature of the local conflicts in the Ethiopian pastoral areas to show the unclear access rules to both land and water resources and how government actions promoting sedentarization disturb the traditional interclan reciprocity arrangements and lead to disputes and further income differentiation between the poor and better-endowed households. This study is a valuable addition to the burgeoning literature on the importance of customary institutions in preventing conflict and sustaining collective action. It confirms previous findings on the importance and effectiveness of the endogenously crafted institutions in delineating rules of resource access and use as well as maintaining the quality of resources, especially resources held under customary or communal tenure arrangements (Agrawal and Ostrom 2001; Haro, Doyo, and McPeak 2005; Nkonya and Markelova 2009). The Cambodia case provides a look at the local institutional environment surrounding natural resource management in the complex postconflict context. It shows that despite years of dictatorial regime that systematically destroyed traditional social networks, there is still a variety of collective action institutions, such as mutual help groups, religious groups, and small-scale associations at the local level, even though their activities are limited by low degrees of trust, which is crucial for effective functioning of groups (Pretty and Ward 2001).

Poverty, Power, and Elite Capture

Cross-cutting all these case studies that relate to the themes outlined, the theme of asymmetric power relations and asymmetrical access to power emerges as an underlying logic across all studies. Several of the case studies (especially the Indonesia, Cambodia, Ethiopia–Afar, and Ethiopia–Somali studies) highlight the power dynamics between various groups: the central government, district-level authorities, the private sector, wealthier community members, farmers, pastoralists, women, and so on. As shown in these studies, these relationships, some of which are "invisible" without an in-depth inquiry, condition the outcomes of policies and programs for the poor and influence the institutions of collective action and property rights. Undoubtedly, the issue of power is a sensitive one; examining and addressing it requires sensitivity, caution, and courage (Chambers 1997; Alsop 2004). The studies in this collection attempted to uncover some of the principal trends in power relations to reveal their impact on poverty and, in some cases, like the Indonesian and AHI cases, carefully instigated change in the dynamics of such relations in favor of the poor. As a result, this volume as a whole stresses the need to look beyond the usual factors that are considered in poverty studies (assets, income streams, and so on) to the underlying currents of power that significantly contribute to shaping the poverty context.

The Structure of the Volume

The volume is organized in a way that aims to take the reader from an understanding of the central concepts examined in all the studies (poverty reduction, property rights, and collective action) to the application of these concepts in different contexts by means of various research methods. Part I ("Introduction and Conceptual Framework") sets the stage with an introduction and Chapter 2, which provides a description of the conceptual framework and identifies the key research questions that are important when examining the institutions of collective action and property rights in poverty studies. Part II ("Risk Management and Market Access") includes the Ethiopia–*iddir,* Philippines, and Kenya studies, the non-NRM case studies on collective action for risk management and market access. Part III ("Natural Resource Management") includes Chapters 6–11, which deal with various aspects of resource management and access, as well as postconflict rebuilding. Part IV ("Synthesis and Conclusions") synthesizes the findings of the case studies and reflects on the role of collective action and property rights in poverty reduction (Chapter 12), then points out the potential implications of these findings for policy, research, and practice (Chapter 13).

References

Acheson, J. 2006. Institutional failure in resource management. *Annual Review of Anthropology* 35: 117–134.

Adhikari, B. 2005. Poverty, property rights and collective action: Understanding the distributive aspects of common property resource management. *Environment and Development Economics* 10 (1): 7–31.

Adhikari, B., and J. Lovett. 2006. Institutions and collective action: Does heterogeneity matter in community-based resource management? *Journal of Development Studies* 42 (3): 426–445.

Agrawal, A., 2001. Common property institutions and sustainable governance of resources. *World Development* 29 (10): 1649–1672.

Agrawal, A., and E. Ostrom. 2001. Collective action, property rights, and decentralization in resource use in India and Nepal. *Politics and Society* 29 (4): 485–514.

Agarwal, B. 2001. Participatory exclusions, community forestry, and gender: An analysis for South Asia and a conceptual framework. *World Development* 29 (10): 1623–1648.

Alsop, R., ed. 2004. *Power, rights, and poverty: Concepts and connections.* Washington, D.C.: International Bank for Reconstruction and Development / World Bank and Department for International Development.

Baland, J. M., and J. P. Platteau. 1996. *Halting degradation of natural resources: Is there a role for rural communities?* New York and Oxford, U.K.: Food and Agricultural Organization and Clarendon Press.

Banerjee, A., P. Gertler, and M. Ghatak. 2002. Empowerment and efficiency: Tenancy reform in West Bengal. *Journal of Political Economy* 110 (2): 239–280.

Bardhan, P. 1997. Corruption and development: A review of issues. *Journal of Economic Literature* 35 (3): 1320–1346.

Barrett, C., and B. Swallow. 2006. Fractal poverty traps. *World Development* 34 (1): 1–15.

Barrett, C., M. Carter, and P. Little. 2006. Understanding and reducing persistent poverty in Africa: Introduction to a special issue. *Journal of Development Studies* 42 (2): 167–177.

Barrett, C. B., A. G. Mude, and J. M. Omiti. 2007. Decentralization and the social economics of development: An overview of concepts and evidence from Kenya. In *Decentralization and the social economics of development: Lessons from Kenya,* ed. C. B. Barrett, A. G. Mude, and J. M. Omiti. Cambridge and Wallingford, U.K.: CABI.

Bebbington, A. 1996. Organizations and intensifications: Campesino federations, rural livelihoods and agricultural technology in the Andes and Amazonia. *World Development* 24 (7): 1161–1177.

———. 2007. Social movements and the politicization of chronic poverty. *Development and Change* 38 (5): 793–818.

Beck, T., and C. Nesmith. 2001. Building on poor people's capacities: The case of common property resources in India and West Africa. *World Development* 29 (1): 119–133.

Bernard, T., and D. Spielman. 2009. Reaching the rural poor through producer organizations? A study of agricultural marketing cooperatives in Ethiopia. *Food Policy* 34 (1): 60–69.

Besley, T. 1995. Property rights and investment incentives: Theory and evidence from Ghana. *Journal of Political Economy* 103 (5): 903–937.

Branford, S., and J. Rocha. 2002. *Cutting the wire: The story of the landless movement in Brazil.* London: Latin America Bureau.

Carter, M. 2003. Designing land and property rights reform for poverty alleviation and food security. *Land Reform, Land Settlement and Cooperatives* 2: 44–57. Rome: Food and Agriculture Organization of the United Nations.

Chambers, R. 1997. *Whose reality counts? Putting the first last.* London: Intermediate Technology Publications.

Coulter, J., 2007. *Farmer groups enterprises and the marketing of staple food commodities in Africa.* CAPRi Working Paper 72. Washington, D.C.: International Food Policy Research Institute.

Cousins, B. 1999. Invisible capital: The contribution of communal rangelands to rural livelihoods in South Africa. *Development Southern Africa* 16 (2): 299–318.

Deere, C. D., and M. León. 2001. *Empowering women: Land and property rights in Latin America.* Pittsburgh, Penn., U.S.A.: University of Pittsburgh Press.

Deininger, L., D. Ayalew Ali, and T. Yamano. 2008. Legal knowledge and economic development: The case of land rights in Uganda. *Land Economics* 84 (4): 593–619.

Deininger, K., D. Ayalew Ali, S. Holden, and J. Zevenbergen. 2008. Rural land certification in Ethiopia: Process, initial impact, and implications for other African countries. *World Development* 36 (10): 1786–1812.

Dercon, S. 2002. Income risk, coping strategies, and safety nets. *World Bank Economic Observer* 17 (2): 141–166.

Dorward, A., J. Kydd, J. Morrison, and I. Urey. 2004. A policy agenda for pro-poor agricultural growth. *World Development* 32 (1): 73–89.

Ellis, F., M. Kutengule, and A. Nyansulu. 2003. Livelihoods and rural poverty reduction in Malawi. *World Development* 31 (9): 1495–1510.

Escobar, A., and S. Alvarez. 1992. *The making of social movements: Identity, strategy, and democracy.* Boulder, Colo., U.S.A.: Westview Press.

Field, A., E. Field, and M. Torero. 2006. *Property rights and crop choice in rural Peru, 1994–2004.* MTID Discussion Paper 100. Washington, D.C.: International Food Policy Research Institute.

German, L., and A. Stroud. 2007. A framework for the integration of diverse learning approaches: Operationalizing agricultural research and development (R&D) linkages in eastern Africa. *World Development* 35 (5): 792–814.

Haro, G., G. Doyo, and J. McPeak. 2005. Linkages between community, environmental, and conflict management: Experiences from Northern Kenya. *World Development* 33 (2): 285–299.

Hulme, D., and A. Shepherd. 2003. Conceptualizing chronic poverty. *World Development* 31 (3): 403–423.

Kanbur, R., and P. Shaffer. 2007. Epistemology, normative theory and poverty analysis: Implications for Q-squared in practice. *World Development* 35 (2): 183–196.

Karlan, D. 2007. Social connections and group banking. *Economic Journal* 117 (517): F52–F84.

Krishna, A., P. Kristjanson, M. Radeny, and W. Nindo. 2004. Escaping poverty and becoming poor in 20 Kenyan villages. *Journal of Human Development* 5 (2): 211–226.

Little, P., K. Smith, B. Cellarius, D. L. Coppock, and C. Barrett. 2001. Avoiding disaster: Diversification and risk management among East African herders. *Development and Change* 32 (3): 401–433.

Mansuri, G., and V. Rao. 2004. Community-based and -driven development: A critical review. *World Bank Research Observer* 19 (1): 1–39.

Markelova, H., and B. Swallow. 2008. Bylaws and their critical role in natural resource management: Insights from African experience. Paper presented at the 12th Biennial Conference of the International Association for the Study of the Commons, Cheltenham, England, July 15–18.

Markelova, H., R. Meinzen-Dick, J. Hellin, and S. Dohrn. 2009. Collective action for smallholder market access. *Food Policy* 34 (1): 1–7.

Mearns, R. 1996. Community, collective action and common grazing: The case of postsocialist Mongolia. *Journal of Development Studies* 32 (3): 297–339.

Meinzen-Dick, R., and E. Mwangi. 2009. Cutting the web of interests: Pitfalls of formalizing property rights. *Land Use Policy* 26 (1): 36–43.

Meinzen-Dick, R., M. DiGregorio, and N. McCarthy. 2004. Methods for studying collective action in rural development. *Agricultural Systems* 82 (3): 197–214.

Meinzen-Dick, R., A. Knox, F. Place, and B. Swallow, eds. 2002. *Innovation in natural resource management.* Baltimore: Johns Hopkins University Press.

Moser, C. 1998. The Asset Vulnerability Framework: Reassessing urban poverty reduction strategies. *World Development* 26 (1): 1–19.

Narayan, D. 2000. *Voices of the Poor: Can anyone hear us?* Washington, D.C.: World Bank.

———. 2002. *Empowerment and poverty reduction: A sourcebook.* Washington, D.C.: World Bank.

Nkonya, E., and H. Markelova. 2009. *Looking beyond the obvious: Uncovering the features of natural resource conflict in Uganda.* CAPRi Working Paper 95. Washington, D.C.: International Food Policy Research Institute.

North, D. 1990. *Institutions, institutional change, and economic performance.* New York: Cambridge University Press.

Ostrom, E. 1990. *Governing the commons: The evolution of institutions of collective action.* Cambridge, U.K.: Cambridge University Press.

———. 1999. Design principles in long-enduring irrigation institutions. In *Polycentric governance and development: Readings from the workshop in political theory and analysis,* ed. M. McGinnis. Ann Arbor, Mich., U.S.A.: University of Michigan Press.

———. 2000. Collective action and the evolution of social norms. *Journal of Economic Perspectives* 14 (3): 137–158.

———. 2005. *Understanding institutional diversity.* Princeton, N.J., U.S.A.: Princeton University Press.

———. 2007. A diagnostic approach of going beyond panaceas. *Proceedings of the National Academy of Sciences* 104 (39): 15181–15187.

Pretty, J., and H. Ward. 2001. Social capital and the environment. *World Development* 29 (2): 209–227.

Ribot, J. 2003. Democratic decentralization of natural resources: Institutional choice and discretionary power transfers in Sub-Saharan Africa. *Public Administration and Development* 23 (1): 53–65.

Schlager, E., and E. Ostrom. 1992. Property rights regimes and natural resources: A conceptual analysis. *Land Economics* 68 (3): 249–262.

Sharma, M., and M. Zeller. 1997. Repayment performance in group-based credit programs in Bangladesh: An empirical analysis. *World Development* 25 (10): 1731–1742.

Tarrow, S. 1998. *Power in movement: Social movements and contentious politics.* Cambridge, U.K.: Cambridge University Press.

Thorpe, R., F. Stewart, and A. Heyer. 2005. When and how far is group formation a route out of chronic poverty? *World Development* 33 (6): 907–920.

Uphoff, N., M. Esman, and A. Krishna. 1998. *Reasons for success: Learning from instructive experiences in rural development.* West Hartford, Conn., U.S.A.: Kumarian Press.

World Bank. 2002. *World Development Report 2002: Building institutions for markets.* New York: Oxford University Press.

Zeller, M. 1998. Determinants of repayment performance in credit groups: The role of program design, intra-group risk pooling and social cohesion. *Economic Development and Cultural Change* 46 (1): 599–620.

2 Property Rights and Collective Action for Poverty Reduction: A Framework for Analysis

MONICA DI GREGORIO, KONRAD HAGEDORN,
MICHAEL KIRK, BENEDIKT KORF, NANCY MCCARTHY,
RUTH MEINZEN-DICK, BRENT SWALLOW,
ESTHER MWANGI, AND HELEN MARKELOVA

This chapter presents a conceptual framework for examining how formal and informal institutions of property rights and collective action can contribute to poverty reduction, including through external interventions and action by poor people themselves. The past two decades have witnessed an increased understanding of the role of institutions in natural resource management (Ostrom 1990; Baland and Platteau 1996). The insights on the role of formal and informal property rights and collective action institutions in improving well-being can assist both research and policies for poverty reduction. They shed light on issues of governance, power relations, and ideological factors that keep people in poverty.

The rural poor are usually those with weakest property rights and the least secure rights to resources. Understanding how the poor can protect and expand their access to and control of resources can contribute to poverty reduction and improvement of government programs, which have sometimes produced unwanted effects, such as the reduction of tenure security for poor and marginalized groups, for example, by weakening customary rights or allowing elite capture of property.

There is also growing recognition that collective action allows people to overcome limitations linked to lack of resources, power, and voice. Collective action also underpins many community-driven development programs for service delivery, such as those for water supply, healthcare, and agricultural extension (Nitti and Jahiya 2004). As in the case of property rights, the poor and women are often at a disadvantage with regard to collective action because of social exclusion, lack of resources, and domination of meetings by local elites.

The United Nations Economic and Social Council (2001, 2–3) defines poverty as "a human condition characterized by the sustained or chronic deprivation of the resources, capabilities, choices, security and power necessary for the enjoyment of an adequate standard of living and other civil, cultural, economic, political and social rights." For many of the world's rural poor, property rights are part and parcel of economic rights and entitlements, and their ability to engage in collective action is an essential choice, capability, and source of

25

power. In many cases, overcoming poverty requires transforming power relationships that keep people poor.

Poverty is complex in its manifestations and causes, which differ across different contexts. The conceptual framework presented in this chapter offers a way in which we can identify the contextual factors that underlie poverty. But although structural conditions are important, poverty is not static. Thus, the framework provides a basis for examining how property rights and collective action can contribute to poverty reduction, including both external interventions and action by poor people themselves. The case studies reported in this volume use this framework to explore various aspects of these relationships, and in the synthesis presented in Chapter 12 of this volume we review the findings and insights they provide for policy and practice to reduce poverty.

After a brief definition of the concepts of property rights and collective action, the first part of this chapter examines the initial conditions of poverty, highlighting the role of assets, risks and vulnerability, and governance structures and power relations. The latter part investigates the decisionmaking dynamics of actors—both poor and nonpoor—and how they can use the tangible and intangible resources they have to shape their livelihoods and the institutions that govern their lives. The chapter concludes with a discussion of how this framework can improve the understanding of outcomes in terms of changes in well-being.

Property Rights

We can define *property rights* as "the capacity to call upon the collective to stand behind one's claim to a benefit stream" (Bromley 1991, 15). Strength and security of property rights therefore depend on relationships between individual rights holders, others who have duties to respect those rights, and the institutions that back up those claims.

The fact that property rights do not necessarily imply sole authority over resources is especially relevant to poverty studies. The claim to a benefit stream can refer to a number of different "bundles" of rights: rights to access and withdrawal (use rights) and to management, exclusion, and alienation (decision-making rights) (Schlager and Ostrom 1992). Different individuals, groups, or the state often hold overlapping use and decisionmaking rights to resources. As we move from access to alienation, the potential benefit flows generally increase. Nonetheless, rights with low benefit flows are crucial, especially for poor people who might not hold other property. Security is given by the interplay of breadth, duration, and assurance that a right will be respected (Place, Roth, and Hazell 1994);[1] the last of these is the most important determinant of security. Assur-

---

1. *Breadth* refers to the number of bundles held. Access rights have less breadth than do access and management rights together.

ance is in part due to the recognition and legitimacy provided by governance structures that enforce rights and duties through supervision, sanctioning, and provision of forums for dispute resolution. The presence of multiple legal orders, referred to as legal pluralism (Griffiths 1986), indicates that rights can be backed by diverse institutions such as state, customary, and religious laws or other normative principles. The effectiveness of these claims depends on recognition of rights through internalized legitimacy or external enforcement. In some cases, state institutions may be very strong and traditional laws weak, while in others, customary or religious institutions hold much stronger sway.[2]

When backing institutions are weak, increased uncertainty about benefits and the inability to defend rights in case of disputes make the poor particularly vulnerable. People relying on customary institutions for enforcing claims on resources, where the state has claimed ownership, might presently enjoy benefits streams, but they also face the possibility that the state may exert various rights to their detriment in the future.

Collective Action

Collective action can be understood as an action taken by a group to achieve common ends (Marshall 1998). Collective action can be voluntary or obligatory for specific persons,[3] and members can act directly on their own or through an organization. Much collective action occurs informally through social networks or even through people's temporarily coming together for short-term purposes. The mere existence of an organization is not sufficient for collective action to occur.

Collective action can contribute to poverty reduction in several ways. In communities throughout the world, people work together to provide local goods and services. Self-help groups and mutual risk sharing substitute for imperfect credit markets, and microfinance groups allow people to access credit, sometimes helping poor people to build their own assets. Collective action can provide the poor with the opportunity to access services and protection claims and to increase their bargaining power. Finally, collective action is often essential to regulate the access, use, and maintenance of common pool resources, including devising rules, monitoring use, devising enforcement mechanisms, and implementing sanctions (Ostrom 1990).

---

2. *Formal property rights* often refers to state-recognized rights, while *informal rights* generally refers to rights that are neither recognized nor protected by state authorities. Note, however, that many such customary rights are highly formalized.

3. However, we exclude hired labor, corvée (obligatory unpaid labor), and forced labor from our analysis of collective action because the incentive structure for each is very different.

A Conceptual Framework

The conceptual framework presented here is adapted from the Institutional Analysis and Development (IAD) Framework (Ostrom 2005), highlighting the role of property rights and collective action in poverty reduction. It provides an analytical tool that can help to guide empirical research on institutions and poverty reduction and can inform policy decisions, as illustrated by the case studies in this volume.

The property rights of the poor affect their initial conditions, especially their asset base, exposure to shocks, and position in power relations. Collective action affects their ability to make use of resources in decisionmaking and action situations. To conceptually move from conditions of poverty to strategies for poverty reduction, we need a dynamic framework that shows the processes by which property rights and collective action can contribute to building people's asset bases. Such a framework is presented in Figure 2.1.

In the first box in Figure 2.1, the context represents the initial conditions that people face, which shape the initial opportunity set of possible actions. The context includes physical, technical, socioeconomic, and policy and governance conditions. In this chapter we focus on two particular aspects related to physical, technical, and socioeconomic conditions of particular relevance to the poor: asset endowments and vulnerability to shocks. In addition we look at the basic governance structure, the legal and political system. Each of these shapes the nature of the existing institutions of property rights and the capacity for collective action. The second part of the framework, the action arena, helps us to illustrate how people themselves, the state and other entities, and different actors together can make use of institutions of property rights and collective action as well as change institutions to reduce poverty. While the context represents the initial conditions that affect people's actions, people's agency (the actions themselves) and their interactions with other people or actors shape their future. The action arena represents possible action situations, for example, a decision about investing resources, negotiating among different interest groups, or making collective efforts to maintain a local irrigation system.

Decisionmaking rules are particularly important in the action arena, because they represent the "authority relationships that specify *who* decides *what* in relation to *whom*" (Oakerson 1992, 46, emphasis in the original). In the action arena parties act independently, wait for the actions of counterparts, cooperate, discuss, negotiate, challenge each other, and so on. They exchange resources, devise new rules, and demand action from other parties. Our interest in this volume is in highlighting how action, and specifically cooperation among the poor, can bring about change.

Over time specific actions create patterns of interaction that may, in turn, affect the initial conditions for the next round. *Patterns of interaction* refers to the regularized and observable behavioral outcomes of actors acting within a

FIGURE 2.1 Conceptual framework for the role of property rights and collective action in poverty reduction

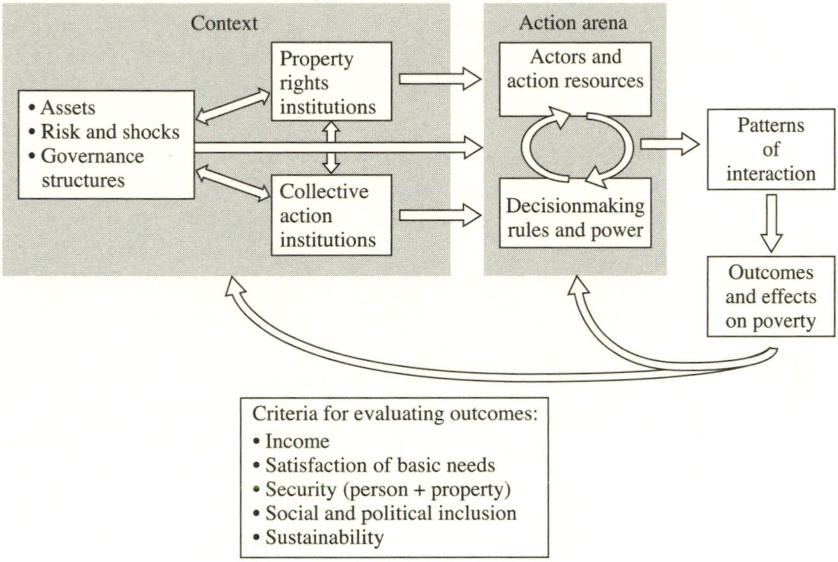

SOURCE: Authors' adaptation based on Ostrom (2005).

specified set of rules. In these interaction processes, actors reinforce existing institutions or create new institutions. Existing (a priori) institutions delineate the socioeconomic space and the rule-boundedness within which actors make their choices and take action. For example, often rules and norms constrain women's voice and their ability to assert claims. On the other hand, although institutions constrain, allow, and affect actions a priori, actions may alter institutions a posteriori (Giddens 1984), thus changing the initial conditions (see feedback arrows in Figure 2.1). One example is that of concerted and sustained action over time increasing women's rights.

Finally, actions and patterns of interaction lead to outcomes. Outcomes are as varied as the action situations; they can be direct effects on well-being, such as an increase in income due to a good harvest, or changes in institutions themselves, such as the strengthening of collective action capacity and the re-design of property rights arrangements. Actions geared toward social and political structural changes (as opposed to more immediate outcomes) generally require a longer time frame to realize and thus necessitate a long-term analysis. A number of feedback loops from patterns of interaction and intermediate outcomes back to the action arena and the context might be needed before institutional changes will affect the lives of the poor, for instance, through improved social and political inclusion, income, health, security, and sustainability or reduced vulnerability. These final indicators can serve as final criteria for evaluating outcomes in terms of poverty reduction.

The Context

Assets

Most of the poverty literature has focused on income and consumption. Here we want to highlight the importance of assets for the poor as a means of not only providing increased income but also facilitating accumulation of additional assets over time.

Poverty-related research has moved beyond simple income–expenditure measures of well-being to consider a more holistic approach that takes into account people's assets and capabilities (Bebbington 1999). The sustainable livelihoods framework outlines five basic types of assets that are essential for the livelihoods of the poor: human, physical, natural, financial, and social (Scoones 1998). This traditional "asset pentagon" has been expanded by identifying public capital and political capital, which are also considered essential for the institutional environment of the poor. Public capital is defined as access to public goods and services, which include a range of services and infrastructure such as health posts, roads, and electrification (Winters et al. 2002). Political capital can be understood as the political resources held by individuals and communities that can be used to influence policy processes to achieve desired outcomes (instrumental political capital) as well as the structure of a political system that shapes actors' access to instrumental political capital (structural political capital). Examples of instrumental political capital include electoral leverage or interest groups, while state fiscal capacity and internal organization of the state are examples of structural political capital (Birner and Wittmer 2003). Although the links between assets and collective action or property rights are illustrated by one arrow in Figure 2.1, theory does not predict a single relationship between assets and these institutions. One could argue that assets are either a necessary complement or a substitute for collective action. Clearly we need to look in more detail at the particular types of assets and their context. Table 2.1 presents examples of assets and possible hypotheses regarding their linkages with collective action and property rights. This list is by no means exhaustive but is intended to show how all seven types of assets have implications for the institutions that are of interest to the studies in this volume. For each type of asset, it is possible to identify more detailed hypotheses regarding how they would increase or decrease the likelihood of institutional arrangements that include or exclude the poor. Indeed, the case studies on *iddir* in Ethiopia (Chapter 3), social networks in the Philippines (Chapter 4), producer marketing groups in Kenya (Chapter 5), watershed management in India (Chapter 6), and collective action in Cambodia (Chapter 11) performed quantitative tests of how different types of assets affect the likelihood of engaging in collective action. Although

TABLE 2.1 Assets and their links with institutions

Type of asset	Examples	Links to collective action (CA)	Links to property rights (PR)
Human	Education, health, labor supply	Education expands vision for CA; poor health restricts participation in CA.	Education helps secure statutory rights; labor can secure "sweat equity."
Physical	Agricultural technologies, tools, houses and other buildings	Cell phones and vehicles facilitate CA; CA is needed to acquire some technology.	Buildings require land but can also secure land rights.
Natural	Land, water, trees, biodiversity, environmental services	Landscape planning and many environmental services require CA.	PR mediate use and benefits of natural resources.
Financial	Credit, savings, remittances	Microfinance groups use CA as collateral and social networks for remittances.	Financial capital is necessary to acquire property; PR serve as collateral for loans.
Social	Kinship and other support networks, marketing groups	Social capital is a stock that enables the flow of CA.	Social capital helps secure group PR.
Political	Collective representation, interest groups, political parties	CA can increase political voice.	Political capital helps in lobbying the state for secure PR.
Public	Roads, water connection, communications infrastructure	CA can provide some public infrastructure when the state does not.	Lack of PR can be a barrier to accessing some public assets, such as water connections.

source: Authors.

it is also possible to generate and quantitatively test hypotheses about how various assets affect property rights (for example, whether credit availability increases property rights to land), many of these linkages are not straightforward, especially if we look beyond property rights as narrowly defined by titles and full ownership. Thus, many of the linkages between assets and property rights in this volume are explored qualitatively as, for example, in the Indonesian case (Chapter 8), where social and political capital were used to strengthen the land rights of forest communities.

The link between available assets and ability to choose is widely recognized (Sen 1997). Asset endowments include not only physical assets, but also bundles of rights to resources (the right to collect firewood from forest or graze common pastures), personal skills gained through education or experience, and social networks based on trust and reciprocity.[4] Current endowments generally depend on intergenerational transmission of assets, past investments in health and education, and past policies (Adato et al. 2003).

Individuals and households hold diverse assets that can be combined to provide different livelihoods; alternatively, certain assets may be leveraged to gain access to yet more assets. Assets are often complementary and partly substitutable. Human capital—for example, agricultural knowledge and experience—improves returns to land assets. Similarly, access to complementary inputs such as credit, input and output markets, transportation, and storage improves the value and productivity of land. Secure property rights to land can provide the collateral required to access financial capital. Similarly, rights to one asset may provide substitutes for missing assets, as when people gather food from common lands if crops fail. It is thus advantageous to hold a diverse portfolio of assets, especially to reduce vulnerability during periods of hardship.

The literature on poverty traps emphasizes the importance of thresholds in transforming assets into income, which constrain accumulation of capital goods that would allow higher returns (Dasgupta 2003). Security of property rights or redistribution can substantially improve the ability to satisfy basic need thresholds, improving human capital development and thus increasing future earnings (Strauss and Thomas 1998). The second major threshold, the inability to undertake lumpy investments for more productive livelihood strategies, is compounded by poor access to financial markets (Barrett and Swallow 2005). Even small investments (for example, in goats) may be prohibitive for poor households that barely meet their subsistence needs and cannot borrow from formal or informal credit markets. Collective action can allow pooling of resources among the poor to invest in what would be prohibitive for one person alone.

Insecure property rights imply a high risk that benefits from investments will be lost or appropriated by others. Together with subsistence requirements, which also put more value on the present than the future, insecure property

---

4. Asset endowments are the pool of resources or assets available to an individual or household.

rights contribute to holding the poor in low-yielding livelihood strategies. This is particularly relevant when returns to investments accrue only long after the investment is made.

Poverty and poverty traps can be exacerbated by lack of access to public services such as safe water and health facilities. Access to these can also dramatically increase the productivity of individually held assets. Although who benefits from improvements in public services depends on various conditions, in general, public education and public health should have at least mildly progressive impacts on the poor.

In the absence of effective public services, the poor may opt for collective action to produce local public goods. The likelihood that people will mobilize resources depends on their capacity to undertake collective action and on the specific incentives structure—expected benefits and expectations about others' behavior (Sandler 1992). Here, social cohesion and the history of cooperation and trust contribute to the capacity of a group to pool together resources for the provision of public goods and services.

Collective action is also a means for the poor to secure access to benefit streams derived from resources. Property rights are only as strong as the institutions that back them up, and collective action can provide the collective support to secure claims, even transforming informal claims into formal rights. Recognition of indigenous rights to resources and requests for improvement of public service provision are two recurring examples. Leadership and capacity to cooperate are key to successful acknowledgment of rights.

Risk and Shocks

Poverty and well-being are determined not only by households' assets and income but also by their degree of vulnerability to shocks over time, which pushes them into greater impoverishment and often perpetuates poverty (Jalan and Ravallion 1999). Shocks come from multiple sources, affect whole communities (covariate) and individual households (idiosyncratic), influence one or more livelihood sources at a time, and demand multiple responses, creating large variations in income over time (Dercon 2002; Fafchamps and Lund 2003). The vulnerability of a household has three components: (1) exogenous characteristics of the risks faced (for instance, distribution of rainfall), (2) the extent to which a household engages in ex ante risk management, and (3) the extent to which it can engage in ex post risk coping.

The impact of risk and uncertainty on subsistence farmers has long been recognized (Moscardi and de Janvry 1977). In the absence of perfectly functioning insurance markets (formal and informal), producers tend to favor less risky subsistence crops (Fafchamps 1992) and, despite a higher concentration of subsistence crops, greater diversification (Walker and Ryan 1990). Greater vulnerability also leads to smaller investments (Skees, Hazell, and Miranda 1999), less adoption of new technologies (Antle and Crissman 1990), and ultimately to a higher likelihood of remaining trapped in poverty (Barrett and Swallow 2005).

Here we consider three categories of risk: natural, economic, and socio-political. In each category, some of the risks occur frequently, meaning that people's understanding of the probability that different outcomes will occur is likely to be quite high. Other risks occur only sporadically, and people generally have more difficulty in estimating the probability of their occurrence. Yet other events occur with such infrequency that there is simply no basis on which to assess their probability. Table 2.2 gives illustrative examples of these types of risk for each category, acknowledging that certain risks might change categories depending on the location. The case studies in this volume explore some of these shocks in greater depth. For example, illness and death of family members are major concerns in Chapters 3 and 4, price fluctuations in Chapter 5, pest infestations in Chapter 7, policy changes in Chapters 8–11, and drought in Chapters 9 and 10. The Cambodian case study in Chapter 11 dealt with risks ranging from illness to flooding, civil war, and genocide.

As in the case of assets, we cannot formulate a simple hypothesis regarding the likely effect of risk on collective action and property rights. Rather, we need to look at the likely effects of each type of risk.

It is difficult for anyone to directly insure against rare events, but wealthier households are more able to build up generic savings to insure against many risks. Without access to government or donor relief, we would expect that poorer households would need to sell productive assets sooner and would be more likely to move into chronic poverty. Evidence suggests that in crisis situations even external aid is often neither efficiently nor fairly distributed (Keen

TABLE 2.2 Risks and their occurrence

Type of shock	Frequent, with well-known probability	Less frequent, with imprecise knowledge of probability	Rare events, with probability unknown
Natural	Seasonal rainfall Hail Endemic pest infestations Frost	Droughts Floods Morbidity and mortality	Earthquakes Forest fires Epidemic disease outbreaks Global climate change
Economic	Seasonal prices Input availability Informal loan rates	Formal-sector interest rates Inflation Real estate values	Asset bubbles and stock market crashes "Revolutionary" technologies (computers)
Sociopolitical	Elections	Personal security Property security Ethnic discrimination	Changing regulatory frameworks Warfare and revolutions Genocide

SOURCE: Authors.

1994). Additionally, whereas governments and donors often act in response to natural disasters, responses to economic crises are themselves highly variable, and responses to sociopolitical shocks are even less predictable.

Because their individual and household savings are lower and access to formal insurance markets nearly absent, the poor not only tend to be more exposed to various risks but are also more likely to lose productive assets. A shock that results in asset reductions below a crucial threshold level may change a household's status from being temporarily poor to being trapped in chronic poverty (Barrett and Swallow 2005).

One potential option for reducing vulnerability is to increase the security of access (property rights) of the poor to various resources. Often the use of common or state-controlled resources provides a safety net in times of extreme need. Such access functions as an ex post mechanism to smooth consumption or maintain the asset base (for example, livestock). Flexible access can help to absorb many shocks, including climatic, economic, and, in certain cases, sociopolitical upheavals. Informal systems supporting these access claims can be exercised regularly to offset idiosyncratic but regularly occurring events such as seasonal rainfall and also to offset potential losses from less frequent but locally specific events such as floods and droughts (Goodhue and McCarthy 1999).

However, flexible access rights may be seen as less secure and thus quite costly in terms of lower investment in and management of these resources. Additionally, in times of generalized shocks (for example, widespread and prolonged drought), flexible, informal property rights systems may perform very poorly as insurance mechanisms, possibly leading to the dramatic increase in conflicts. This highlights the potential link between formal and informal land tenure systems: formal land tenure policy should recognize the inherent strengths of informal systems in managing idiosyncratic risks but also provide a formal framework to manage conflict or provide relief during generalized crises.

Another key dimension of shocks is how widespread their effects are: whether they vary from individual to individual (idiosyncratic) or whether the same shock is felt by a larger social group (covariate). In many cultures, local people rely on social networks that function as insurance networks (for instance, funeral societies) to deal with individual (idiosyncratic) shocks. These networks range from informal to highly formal organizations. Empirical work highlights the capacity of local networks and collective action to smooth consumption (Kurosaki and Fafchamps 2002). However, local insurance mechanisms are also often unable to buffer households from large-scale, long-lasting (covariate) shocks (Skoufias and Quisumbing 2003), offering an opportunity for more formal insurance mechanisms to link to informal insurance networks so that each source of insurance is complementary and synergistic. Social networks that link rural households to urban economies and labor markets may be more effective than local social networks in helping households to cope with generalized shocks, such as Thailand's financial crisis of 1997–98 (Geran 2001).

Major natural disasters such as earthquakes or widespread drought may exceed even the capacity of countries to buffer and insure against them, calling for international coordination.

This classification of risks can be used to generate hypotheses regarding the effects of different types of risks on the capacity of collective action to provide some form of insurance mechanism: for instance, that collective action is more likely to reduce people's vulnerability to more predictable, idiosyncratic risks than to unpredictable, covariate risks (see Chapters 3 and 4). One might hypothesize that infrequently occurring risks whose probability is imprecisely known are likely to lead to flexible property rights arrangements, whereas more predictable risks lend themselves to more fixed private property systems (see the report of the Ethiopia–Somali case study in Chapter 10). One might also form hypotheses regarding the links among assets, risks, and collective insurance mechanisms, such as that greater assets allow one to self-insure and opt out of collective action for mutual insurance.

These examples highlight a small part of the role of property rights and collective action in reducing vulnerability. Informal tenure and collective action are often extremely important in managing idiosyncratic risks. However, there remains a very real need to forge links with formal-sector insurance, especially with respect to generalized shocks. Even within the informal sector, the poorest are often excluded from these reciprocity-based networks, implying that there are opportunities for more formal government programs.

Governance Structures

Legal, political, and power structures strongly affect the distribution of property rights, the extent of collective action, and resulting poverty levels (see Table 2.3 for a summary). They determine if rights to income streams are in fact accessible to the poor, how rights are negotiated, and if collective action will contribute to income and increased participation.

In the past decade market integration, privatization, democratization, and the transparency-enhancing revolution in information technology have allowed far-reaching reforms of legal systems, power, and governance structures (Bardhan and Mookherjii 2000). Some of these changes helped to economically integrate the poor, increase their voice, protect their rights, and make politics accountable. However, even countries that have embraced reform underestimate the challenge of transforming norms, law, and power into an enabling institutional environment for the poor (Alden Wily 2003). To understand the reasons for this variability, it is important to look at the nature and capacity of the state, the degree of its legal pluralism (the relative strength of customary and statutory systems), the extent of its decentralization, and the strategies that organizations (especially state agencies) employ in dealing with communities. Each of these has particular relevance to collective action and property rights, as summarized in Table 2.3.

TABLE 2.3 Key aspects of governance structures

Aspects	Implications for collective action	Implications for property rights
Nature and capacity of the state	Democratic and authoritarian states have different policies on supporting or restricting collective action. The capacity of a state affects the need for collective action in service delivery.	Different political systems have different types of support for private, state, and common property. Weak states have less capacity to keep records and enforce property rights.
Legal pluralism	Strong customary systems are often built on collective action and social capital. Dominant statutory systems may crowd out collective action.	A high degree of legal pluralism may create property rights conflicts between statutory and customary claimants.
Decentralization	Decentralization can create spaces for community organizing to strengthen rights and access new opportunities, for instance, participate in budgets.	Decentralization creates insecurities when associated processes and structures are unclear and can allow for elite capture but can also strengthen local rights.
Organizational strategies	Extension agents and others work with individuals, decreasing opportunities for collective action.	The complexity of land registration procedures favors those with more education, time, and mobility, leading to elite capture of property rights.

SOURCE: Authors.

The nature and capacity of the state plays a fundamental role in shaping many other institutions. Democratic and authoritarian political systems have very different approaches to the poor (and the wealthy). We can hypothesize that democratic governments are more likely to tolerate and even encourage voluntary collective action; totalitarian governments may collectivize or extract corvée but suppress voluntary associations that the state does not control. Respect for rule of law will affect the security of property rights. It is not only the type of government and the intent of the state that matters but also its capacity to deliver on its policies. Where the state is weak, collective or private action may be the only option for securing services—whether delivery of water or education or even policing. Similarly, property rights are only as strong as the institution that stands behind them. We can therefore hypothesize that if the state is weak, government-issued titles will not be as meaningful as where the state has capable record keeping and legal enforcement of property rights.

Legal pluralism is ubiquitous; the coexistence of statutory, religious, customary, and even donors' law is more the rule than the exception (Meinzen-

Dick and Pradhan 2002). Any rigid conception of statutory law frequently ignores secondary use rights, sometimes reducing access by the most vulnerable to key assets and sources of livelihood. But the relative strength of statutory and customary systems and the degree to which they are harmonized or in opposition will vary. We can hypothesize that strong legal pluralism is likely to favor collective action and polycentric governance, whereas dominant statutory systems may repress collective action. In the realm of property rights, legal pluralism may create ambiguities, but these can work either in favor of or against poor or disadvantaged people, giving them access to resources even where they are not able to secure formal ownership.

Decentralization of legal, administrative, and political structures can change power relations further by engaging the disenfranchised in the political process (Bardhan 2002). In this context, the state should act as a catalyst in mobilizing people and neutralizing local oligarchies. If not, poor villagers can neither use their "voice" to vote out incapable politicians (because the politicians are their landlords), nor can they exit by moving to other jurisdictions (because they are bound in interlinked contracts) (Litvack, Ahmad, and Bird 1998). However, decentralization may be misused by a state to reduce its budget obligations, further discriminating against the poor (Ngaido and Kirk 2001). Any successful decentralized delivery of public services depends on the accountability of decisionmakers, implying that there are public debates on their work performance and sanctioning.

Despite lower information costs to identify the poor in decentralized systems (Galasso and Ravallion 2001), capture of benefits by local elites, often associated with high poverty levels and weak political institutions, might undermine the reform benefits (Bardhan and Mookherjii 2000). Moreover, in newly decentralized structures with insufficient accountability, public spending is often channeled toward the nonpoor (Litvack, Ahmad, and Bird 1998). Participation through collective action is often regarded as a silver bullet to break the vicious cycle of power imbalances and recurrent poverty. Cross-country data show that participatory political regimes are associated with significantly lower levels of economic instability and that participation helps to moderate social conflicts (Hadenius and Uggla 1996). However, participation requires investments of time or money, both of which the poor lack, plus a critical mass of activists. Besides involving possible free-riding problems, participation may be weak as long as the right to unite and form coalitions cannot be enforced at the local level (Litvack, Ahmad, and Bird 1998).

Organizational strategies refer to regularized plans within the structure of incentives produced by rules, norms, and expectations of the behavior of others (Ostrom 2005). Although mostly applied at the individual level in the IAD framework, the strategies of organizations are an important aspect of governance structures that influences the likelihood that poor people will be able to engage in collective action and property rights. Does an organization employ participatory approaches and seek to accommodate people with little educa-tion? For example, an extension agency may work either with "contact farmers" (usually local elites) or through group-based approaches; we can hypothesize that the latter approach fosters collective action, while the former is more likely to lead to elite capture of knowledge. Similarly, we would anticipate that agen-cies with complex, formal approaches to land registration can lead to elite cap-ture of property rights. Strategies of participatory land-use planning can lead to the accumulation of natural capital and stronger property rights for certain groups as rights to graze or harvest firewood are clarified.

Property Rights

In the conceptual framework presented in Figure 2.1 we have identified prop-erty rights and collective action institutions as part of the context but have put them in separate boxes to highlight their particular relevance in this volume. Secured land access and control contribute to livelihoods through farm income, food security, and buffering against economic shocks, as well as through accu-mulating other forms of assets. Securing property rights to productive resources and enabling their transfer can help the poor to escape from poverty traps (Deininger 2003). Redistribution of land rights may be necessary to overcome deeply rooted inequality in assets, break the power of oligarchies, and bring resources into the hands of the more productive. Whether the market alone can accomplish this or an active role for the state is needed remains contested (Deininger 2003). Moreover, simply redistributing land to the poor is not enough; providing economic prospects to beneficiaries is as vital (Deininger and Kirk 2003). What is often ignored when comparing the costs and benefits of re-distributive policies is the substantial positive spillover effect in terms of enlarg-ing the stake of the poor in the political system by strengthening local democracy (Bardhan 2002): the capture strategies of local elites lose their momentum if land can be mortgaged through titling and new external credit sources are opened.

Collective Action

Collective action can shape norms as well as legal and power structures. First, it can serve as a lobbying instrument because groups can more easily protect their interest vis-à-vis others competing for a limited piece of the "cake" (Had-enius and Uggla 1996). Second, collective action can be the foundation for organizations, from informal groups up to service cooperatives. It can also help to disseminate information on the shortcomings of policy reforms (Litvack, Ahmad, and Bird 1998).

However, experience has shown that collective action at the local level often remains limited in its impact if it is not backed by external support (Meinzen-Dick, Knox, and Di Gregorio 2001). In addition, vertical links from local collective action institutions to civil society and political arenas are neces-sary to reach higher policy levels and to create forceful countervailing power.

Many of the hypothesized links between property rights and other aspects of the context of collective action have already been identified. We should note that we also postulate a link between property rights and collective action institutions, such as, for example, when land ownership is a criterion for membership in a group (such as a water users' association) or when collective action to patrol boundaries strengthens a group's exclusion rights. The hypothesized roles of collective action and property rights in poverty reduction in different contexts are discussed in the following section.

The Action Arena

We now turn from an examination of the context to an analysis of the dynamics of the action arena. This encompasses the actors, the action resources on which they draw, and the factors that lead to changes in material conditions and institutions themselves. This is, in the first place, a positive view that can become the basis for a normative approach dealing with the process of creating and changing institutions. It exemplifies the mechanisms by which tangible and intangible assets (which are part of the initial condition) are mobilized for individual and collective action, often through bargaining and negotiation processes by actors mediating different interests. Rules are supplied by the legal and institutional setting, but at times action can also occur outside of conventional institutionalized rules (for example, in protest actions). The action arena shows how initial conditions contribute to action dynamics.

Actors and Action Resources

Actors may be individuals, citizens of a state or community, or collective entities such as organizations, government departments, private companies, or NGOs. Each actor will have specific action resources and possible choices about strategic behavior. There can be both internal and external actors. Internal actors are those who are to follow the specific rule system that emerges from institutional bargaining, while external actors may influence the bargaining processes of institutions that define rule systems for other actors and may act as benevolent agents or as opportunistic rent seekers. Once major actors are identified, we can look for specific change agents, those that can influence other actors. They can have positive or negative influences, which may be intentional or unintentional, and their clout may change over time. A variety of individual or collective behavioral theories can be applied to actors in our framework, including rational choice and bounded or situational rational choice.

Action resources are intangible and tangible assets that give actors the capability for agency. Agency includes the ability to exercise livelihood choices, to participate in collective action at various levels, to influence other actors' agency choices, and to get involved in political processes.

All assets can potentially become action resources, but their value depends on the specific action situation and the rules that are applied. For example, kinship networks (social capital) are more important in some societies than in others. A car (physical capital) is more important as an action resource for accessing services where there are good roads than where roads are poor or missing. The ability to mobilize labor to clear land (one form of human capital) can be an important action resource to enable someone to acquire property rights under customary tenure in swidden agriculture (shifting cultivation), whereas formal education and knowledge of the legal systems (other forms of human capital) become an action resource that enables people to gain secure property rights when tenure systems are formalized.

We have seen the importance of access to and control of tangible resources; here we present some less tangible but equally important action resources.

Information and knowledge are key action resources (Schlüter 2001) that enable powerful actors to change the perceived values of the different alternatives (Young 1995). Because access to information is costly and often spreads through networks, the poor can be at a particular disadvantage if excluded from these networks. Also, social functions often give higher value to knowledge of modern global phenomena than to tacit, traditional knowledge.

Cognitive schemata, or mental models, define the borders of what is imaginable to actors in terms of their understanding (knowledge) and normative perspective and thus provide the limits of what actors can perceive as feasible in their lives. According to bounded rationality theories, the borders of what is imaginable to an actor are delimited by mental models (North 1990) that define the knowledge base and the normative perspective of an actor. Cognitive dissonance, the difference between mental models and reality, affects how an actor processes actual events and legitimizes group solidarity.

Social standing within a community or social group is another important action resource, one that derives from two sources: the habitus of an actor and the embeddedness of the actor in social networks (Bourdieu and Accardo 1993). The habitus actors demonstrate in the public and private realms is essential to how they can gain recognition as a leader in public discourse and collective action. How do actors behave, what clothes do they wear, what confidence and cultural knowledge can they show in public? This is often rooted in mental models, constantly molded by social interaction. The embeddedness of an actor in social networks can refer to both formal and informal networks that reach outside the local community. Horizontal social networks provide space to combine forces and to increase relative leverage in order to reinforce identities and self-confidence. Vertical political networks are an important source of benefit streams that affect the capabilities of individuals and groups. Recognized membership in specific organizations may be a necessary entry point to the public arena where collective action is negotiated. For example, many irrigation associations allow only landowners or heads of households to be members. Wives or heads of landless households are not included and hence do not participate in public discourses over collective action for managing the irrigation, although they are affected by the decisions of the group (Meinzen-Dick and Zwarteveen

1998). At the same time, formal membership may not be sufficient to give one a say because relative bargaining power also depends on other action resources. Both the habitus of local actors and their ability to draw on social networks influence the recognition they receive from outside the immediate community. Hence, they provide the space for networks with powerful actors on a higher spatial level than the village. In many clientele societies, these "political assets" are an important source of benefit streams, for example, in the form of employment, welfare benefits, and so on. These may affect the capabilities not only of individuals but also of groups.

Time itself is an action resource that allows people to engage in collective or individual action to further their interests. A significant disadvantage of the poor, especially poor women, is the high opportunity cost of their time. However, the costs are not constant: for example, wage laborers may be able to participate in collective action in times of unemployment. Thus, the rules that define when interactions take place will shape the action resources available to different groups.

There are important interactions among different types of action resources. In most societies, tangible assets also convey status and increase options, because "income only maintains consumption, but assets change the way people interact with the world. With assets, people begin to think for the long term and pursue long-term goals. In other words, while income feeds people's stomachs, assets change their minds" (Sherraden 1991, 13). In many agrarian societies wealthier households have better access to information and collective resources. Even within households, control of assets influences the bargaining power of individuals; for instance, women with control of assets have more influence in intrahousehold decisionmaking (Quisumbing, 2003).

Decisionmaking Rules and Power

Collective action takes place in the action arena. Within the action arena, we can envision different decisionmaking mechanisms and resulting rules, such as strategic negotiation, democratic deliberation, social bargaining, and coalition building, all of which include forms of collective action at some level.

In a strategic interaction scenario, action resources of individuals or collective actors determine their bargaining positions. Power includes the ability to change other players' choice sets, preferences, mental models, and constraints. Strategic behavior is affected by two types of power, positional power and sanctioning power.

There is a strong interaction between power and decisionmaking rules in use. In general, democratic deliberation works best when power is relatively evenly distributed, or less powerful actors have specific guarantees that their rights will be protected. Strategic negotiations might be more effective in situations of strong power disparities (Fung and Wright 2003).

In an institutional game, bargaining success is a function of the ability to produce credibility for strategic actions. Players with more action resources may be able to forgo present benefits for future ones, wait until a new round of negotiation starts, or recruit coordination alternatives (Hanisch 2003). Also, the resources they control might provide credibility to specific strategic behavior.

The actual bargaining power, then, depends on the initial asset endowment an actor disposes of and on the specific interaction. The latter is determined by the remaining contextual factors, such as risk and uncertainty, as well as the normative legal setting, the identities of the other actors, and their context. These conditions shape how actors make credible commitments or threats. Thus, the specific interaction determines which action resources actors can use and how effectively these resources can be transformed into power endowments.

Understanding the action arena has important implications for poverty reduction. We can hypothesize that the poor are disadvantaged by lack of action resources or by decisionmaking rules that call for resources that the poor do not have. The first is relatively easy to test, at least for tangible or quantifiable assets such as education, as indicated in Chapters 3, 4, and 11 of this volume. Because of the huge range of rules that can be found, testing hypotheses regarding how decisionmaking rules do or do not disadvantage the poor and how they favor one type of action resource over another generally requires more in-depth qualitative work, such as that done in the Indonesia case (Chapter 8).

By identifying the key action resources or rules that disadvantage the poor, internal or external actors who want to address poverty can either build up the critical action resources that poor people lack or shift the rules to favor other resources that the poor do have. For example, where poor people (especially women) cannot obtain credit because they lack land titles or other forms of conventional collateral, one approach would be to strengthen the property rights of the poor or women; another would be to develop alternate rules for loans that use forms of collateral that poor people are more likely to have—as has been done in microfinance programs, which use groups and social capital as collateral.

Patterns of Interaction

The actors, their action resources, and the applicable rules all delimit the space within which actors make choices and take action in a specific action situation. The action situation is shaped by the asset endowments and action resources of the actors, their relative positioning, and the a priori rules defined by the initial condition. Accordingly, different actors will have different limits and opportunities within any single action situation. In the action arena, parties act independently, wait for the actions of counterparts, cooperate, discuss, negotiate, challenge each other, and so on. They exchange resources, devise new rules, and demand action from other parties. Repetition of these bargaining processes leads to interaction as regularized and observable behavioral outcomes. In these interaction processes, actors reinforce existing institutions and create new ones.

These patterns of interaction gradually form social relationships and structures, which can reduce or reinforce poverty and lessen or increase social inequality and exclusion as well as cooperation or conflict. As these patterns of inter-action affect the constitutional level of rules, we find societies shaped by patron–client relations, neopatrimonialism, ethnic antagonisms, caste differen-tials, or democratic decisionmaking. These patterns of interaction also transfuse the very nature of the state and how the state acts and develops its own admin-istrative and political structures. In this sense, the institutional outcomes con-stitute the outcomes of prior social bargaining that reflects the unequal action resources of different social actors.

In turn, patterns of interaction produce outcomes. If outcomes are positive for all those involved, the actors will maintain the structure of the situation. When outcomes are not positive for all actors or for some of the actors, they will try to change their strategies. Negotiations in action situations often have to do with distributional aspects related to expected outcomes.

Outcomes and Effects on Poverty

Outcomes from the action arena can be evaluated in terms of how the poor and the nonpoor fare with regard to all the critical aspects of poverty: the ability to secure basic needs, the level and distribution of income, the degree of social and political inclusion, opportunities, and vulnerability. Starting from initial conditions and the subsequent dynamic interactions, a variety of poverty out-comes are possible from changes in both formal and informal property rights and collective action institutions. In addition to direct outcomes in terms of the welfare of individuals, what happens in the action arena affects the initial condi-tions and institutions of successive interactions. It is important to keep in mind that property rights systems are dynamic: the distribution of rights as well as how they are interpreted and enforced will change over time. Some of the change is driven by changing material conditions, but shared mental models, normative and cognitive frames, and power in particular also play major roles in changing property rights. Collective action is, by definition, dynamic, and it changes over time even when institutionalized through an organization.

Poor people may be able to influence change in these institutions in their favor, but based on the framework, we would hypothesize that their lower level of action resources, especially power, makes such outcomes more difficult to achieve. External change agents, including the state, can assist in such processes, but the complexity of institutional change means that favorable outcomes are not automatic, even if external agents are genuinely interested in reducing poverty.

Conclusion

Research on natural resource management shows us the importance of property rights and collective action for self-organization and improved livelihoods. The poverty literature highlights the importance of asset thresholds and poverty traps, as well as the central importance of the agency and capabilities of all people, including poor men and women. We attempt to bridge the domains of the natural resource and poverty literature so that an understanding of what enhances the outcomes of collective action and property rights institutions can lead to more effective poverty reduction by poor people themselves and by external agencies.

Three characteristics of the initial conditions of the poor are particularly relevant in understanding the constraints and opportunities they face. These include their assets, the sources of the risk and uncertainty that cause their vulnerability, and the power constellation created by legal and governance structures. Power plays an important role in the process of change and is the most critical for poverty reduction. Both the broad power structure of a society and the one specific to an action arena affect outcomes. The poor, with few power resources, are often at a disadvantage. Although human agency certainly plays a major role in these outcomes, the options available to men and women are strongly conditioned by their material conditions and the institutional environment in which they live. But people's actions and interactions can also shape both the physical and institutional environments in which they operate.

Understanding these effects can provide insights into how policies and programs can improve the choices of poor people and their capabilities to pursue their goals. Providing specific examples can help build understanding of these concepts. The following chapters of this volume present individual case studies that explore relationships among particular elements of the conceptual framework. Each case focuses on aspects that are most relevant to the situation and research questions of that case.

Some used formal hypothesis testing through quantitative measures; others were more exploratory, using qualitative measures and action research to gain a more complete understanding of the interactions among different groups and individuals. Through the accumulation of evidence from different approaches, we hope to get a more complete picture of the factors that facilitate or constrain the development of collective action and property rights institutions that will enable poor people to strengthen their bargaining power in a range of action arenas, establishing more equitable and less volatile patterns of interaction as well as improved outcomes for environmental sustainability and poverty reduction.

References

Adato, M., T. Benson, S. Gillespie, D. Gilligan, L. Haddad, S. Harrower, J. Hoddinott, S. Kadiyala, J. Maluccio, A. Murphy, A. Quisumbing, M. Sharma, K. Simler, F. Yamauchi, and Y. Yohannes. 2003. *Pathways out of poverty: A proposal for a global research program.* Washington, D.C.: International Food Policy Research Institute.

Antle, J. M., and C. C. Crissman. 1990. Risk, efficiency, and the adoption of modern crop varieties: Evidence from the Philippines. *Economic Development and Cultural Change* 38 (3): 517–537.

Alden Wily, L. 2003. *Governance and land relations: A review of decentralization of land administration and management in Africa.* London: International Institute for Environment and Development.

Baland, J. M., and J. P. Platteau. 1996. *Halting degradation of natural resources: Is there a role for rural communities?* New York: Food and Agriculture Organization and Clarendon Press.

Bardhan, P. 2002. Decentralization of governance and development. *Journal of Economic Perspectives* 16 (4): 185–205.

Bardhan, P., and D. Mookherjii. 2000. Capture and governance at local and national levels. *American Economic Review* 90 (2): 135–139.

Barrett, C. B., and B. M. Swallow. 2005. Dynamic poverty traps and rural livelihoods. In *Rural livelihoods and poverty reduction policies,* ed. F. Ellis and H. A. Freeman. London: Routledge.

Bebbington, A. 1999. Capitals and capabilities: A framework for analyzing peasant viability, rural livelihoods and poverty. *World Development* 27 (12): 2021–2044.

Birner, R., and H. Wittmer. 2003. Using social capital to create political capital: How do local communities gain political influence? A theoretical approach and empirical evidence from Thailand. In *The commons in the new millennium: Challenges and adaptation,* ed. N. Dolsak and E. Ostrom. Cambridge, Mass., U.S.A.: MIT Press.

Bourdieu, P., and A. Accardo. 1993. *La misère du monde.* Paris: Editions du Seuil.

Bromley, D. W. 1991. *Environment and economy: Property rights and public policy.* Cambridge, U.K.: Blackwell.

Dasgupta, P. 2003. *World poverty: Causes and pathways.* Cambridge, U.K.: Cambridge University Press.

Deininger, K. 2003. *Land policies for growth and poverty reduction.* Washington, D.C.: World Bank and Oxford University Press.

Deininger, K., and M. Kirk. 2003. Land policy, poverty alleviation and sustainable rural development. *Agriculture and Rural Development* 10 (2): 44–47.

Dercon, S. 2002. Income risk, coping strategies, and safety nets. *World Bank Economic Observer* 17 (2): 141–166.

Fafchamps, M. 1992. Solidarity networks in pre-industrial societies: Rational peasants with a moral economy. *Economic Development and Cultural Change* 41 (1): 147–174.

Fafchamps, M., and S. Lund. 2003. Risk-sharing networks in rural Philippines. *Journal of Development Studies* 71 (2): 261–287.

Fung, A., and E. O. Wright. 2003. *Deepening democracy: Institutional innovations in empowered participatory governance.* London: Verso.

Galasso, E., and M. Ravallion. 2001. *Decentralized targeting of an antipoverty program.* Washington D.C.: World Bank.

Giddens, A. 1984. *The constitution of society: Outline of the theory of structuration.* Berkeley, Calif., U.S.A.: University of California Press.

Goodhue, R. E., and N. McCarthy. 1999. Fuzzy access: Modeling grazing rights in Sub-Saharan Africa. In *Property rights, risk, and livestock development in Africa,* ed. N. McCarthy, B. M. Swallow, M. Kirk, and P. Hazell. Nairobi, Kenya, and Washington, D.C.: International Livestock Research Institute and International Food Policy Research Institute.

Geran, J. 2001. Coping with crisis: Social capital and the resilience of rural livelihoods in northern Thailand. Ph.D. dissertation, University of Wisconsin, Madison, Wisc., U.S.A.

Griffiths, J. 1986. What is legal pluralism? *Journal of Legal Pluralism* 24: 1–55.

Hadenius, A., and F. Uggla. 1996. Making civil society work, promoting democratic development: What can states and donors do? *World Development* 24 (10): 1621–1639.

Hanisch, M. 2003. *Property reform and social conflict.* Aachen, Germany: Shaker.

Jalan, J., and M. Ravallion. 1999. Are the poor less well insured? Evidence on vulnerability to income risk in rural China. *Journal of Development Economics* 58 (1): 61–81.

Keen, D. 1994. *The benefits of famines: A political economy of famine relief in South-Western Sudan, 1983–1989.* Princeton, N.J., U.S.A.: Princeton University Press.

Kurosaki, T., and M. Fafchamps. 2002. Insurance market efficiency and crop choices in Pakistan. *Journal of Development Economics* 67 (2): 419–453.

Litvack, J., J. Ahmad, and J. Bird. 1998. *Rethinking decentralization in developing countries.* Washington, D.C.: World Bank.

Marshall, G. 1998. *A dictionary of sociology.* New York: Oxford University Press.

Meinzen-Dick, R. S., and R. Pradhan. 2002. *Legal pluralism and dynamic property rights.* CAPRi Working Paper 22. Washington, D.C.: International Food Policy Research Institute.

Meinzen-Dick, R. S., and M. Zwarteveen. 1998. Gendered participation in water management: Issues and illustrations from water users associations in South Asia. *Agriculture and Human Values* 15 (4): 337–345.

Meinzen-Dick, R. S., A. Knox, and M. Di Gregorio, eds. 2001. *Collective action, property rights, and devolution of natural resource management: Exchange of knowledge and implications for policy.* Feldafing, Germany: Deutsche Stiftung für internationale Entwicklung / Zentralstelle für Ernahrung und Landwirtschaft.

Moscardi, E., and A. de Janvry. 1977. Attitudes toward risk among peasants: An econometric approach. *American Journal of Agricultural Economics* 59 (4): 710–716.

Ngaido, T., and M. Kirk. 2001. Collective action, property rights and devolution of rangeland management. In *Collective action, property rights, and devolution of natural resource management: Exchange of knowledge and implications for policy,* ed. R. Meinzen-Dick, A. Knox, and M. Di Gregorio. Feldafing, Germany: Deutsche Stiftung für internationale Entwicklung / Zentralstelle für Ernahrung und Landwirtschaft.

Nitti, R., and B. Jahiya. 2004. Community-driven development in urban upgrading. *Social Development Notes* 85: 1–6.

North, D. C., ed. 1990. *Institutions, institutional change and economic performance.* Cambridge, U.K.: Cambridge University Press.

Oakerson, R. J. 1992. Analyzing the commons: A framework. In *Making the commons work: Theory, practice and policy,* ed. D. W. Bromley. San Francisco: ICS Press.

Ostrom, E. 1990. *Governing the commons: The evolution of institutions for collective action.* New York: Cambridge University Press.

———. 2005. *Understanding institutional diversity.* Princeton, N.J., U.S.A.: Princeton University Press.

Place, F., M. Roth, and P. Hazell. 1994. Land tenure security and agricultural performance. In *Africa: Overview of research methodology,* ed. J. Bruce and S. Migot-Adholla. Dubuque, Iowa, U.S.A.: Kendall/Hunt.

Quisumbing, A. 2003. *Household decisions, gender, and development: A synthesis of recent research.* Washington, D.C.: International Food Policy Research Institute.

Sandler, T. 1992. *Collective action: Theory and applications.* Ann Arbor, Mich., U.S.A.: University of Michigan Press.

Schlager, E., and E. Ostrom. 1992. Property rights regimes and natural resources: A conceptual analysis. *Land Economics* 68 (3): 249–262.

Schlüter, A. 2001. *Institutioneller Wandel und Transformation: Restitution, Transformation und Privatisierung in der tschechischen Landwirtschaft.* Aachen, Germany: Shaker.

Scoones, I. 1998. *Sustainable rural livelihoods: A framework for analysis.* IDS Working Paper 72. Sussex, U.K.: Institute for Development Studies.

Sen, A. 1997. *Choice, welfare, and measurement.* Cambridge, Mass., U.S.A.: Harvard University Press

Sherraden, M. 1991. *Assets and the poor: A new American welfare policy.* Armonk, N.Y., U.S.A.: M. E. Sharpe.

Skees, J., P. Hazell, and M. Miranda. 1999. *New approaches to crop yield insurance in developing countries.* EPTD Discussion Paper 55. Washington, D.C.: International Food Policy Research Institute.

Skoufias, E., and A. Quisumbing. 2003. *Consumption insurance and vulnerability to poverty.* FCND Discussion Paper 155. Washington, D.C.: International Food Policy Research Institute.

Strauss, J., and D. Thomas. 1998. Health, nutrition, and economic development. *Journal of Economic Literature* 36 (2): 766–817.

United Nations Economic and Social Council. 2001. Substantive issues arising in the implementation of the international covenant on economic, social and cultural rights: Poverty and the international covenant on economic, social and cultural rights. Geneva. <http://www2.ohchr.org/english/bodies/cescr/docs/statements/E.C.12.2001.10Poverty-2001.pdf.> Accessed October 5, 2009.

Walker, T. S., and G. Ryan. 1990. *Village and household economies in India's semiarid tropics.* Baltimore: Johns Hopkins University Press.

Winters, P., B. Davis, and L. Corral. 2002. Assets, activities and income generation in rural Mexico: Factoring in social and public capital. *Agricultural Economics* 27 (2): 139–156.

Young, D. 1995. The meaning and role of power in economic theories. In *On economic institutions: Theory and applications,* ed. J. Groenewegen, C. Pitelis, and S. Sjoerstrand. Hants, U.K.: Edward Elgar.

PART II

Risk Management and Market Access

This part of the book features three case studies: two on the way that poor households use local institutions to cope with shocks (Ethiopia–*iddir* and the Philippines) and one on smallholder market institutions (Kenya). All three studies focus on collective action and its role in enabling smallholders to deal with certain constraints that they face in accessing insurance schemes and markets. These case studies are important because they spotlight the institutions of collective action in areas of poverty-related research other than natural resource management (NRM) in poverty areas and provide additional insights on various determinants of the effectiveness and sustainability of groups and networks that have been discussed in the NRM literature. For example, all three studies touch on the issue of group heterogeneity, showing that certain types, such as spatial and age diversification, may lead to more successful cooperation, whereas similarity in other characteristics between group members, such as wealth endowments, may ensure groups' financial viability.

The findings of the Ethiopia–*iddir* and Philippines case studies show that local forms of collective action have an important function in the livelihoods of the poor, including the role that groups and networks can play in reducing vulnerability to the negative effects of certain shocks, especially those related to health. The Kenya study highlights the role of producer groups in enabling smallholders to overcome market imperfections in selling their staples and achieving a higher price than they would by selling individually.

Both sets of findings are important because they show that collective action among the poor can be a useful vehicle for improving their well-being by increasing their resilience and enhancing their livelihood options, but it is not a panacea for poverty reduction. People cooperate when motivated by specific incentives, and not all poor people are able to participate in all forms of collective action. Although most of the poor belong to various groups and networks, the groups with higher economic returns may be available only to those with a certain level of asset endowments, precluding the participation of those below these thresholds.

The policy implications outlined by these chapters call for recognition of the importance of collective action in the lives of the poor and recommend policies and programs that would build on the established forms of cooperation to strengthen them to serve the poor even more effectively. At the same time, they advise those with decisionmaking power to proceed with caution. On the one hand, the trust and relationships built among group members can be easily broken by the heavy involvement of outsiders. On the other hand, policies and programs targeting the very poor may need to be realistic about the potential of collective action to bring people out of severe poverty.

3 Burial Societies in Rural Ethiopia

STEFAN DERCON, JOHN HODDINOTT,
PRAMILA KRISHNAN, AND TASSEW WOLDEHANNA

Collective action has both intrinsic and instrumental value. Being part of a group and participating toward meeting a common objective provides direct benefits to individuals. In the Ethiopian survey data used in this study, individuals who reported having larger networks also reported higher levels of happiness. Such correlations are not unique to Ethiopia. Using data from the World Values Survey, Helliwell and Putnam (2004) found that individuals who reported higher levels of individual and collective civic engagement also reported higher scores on measures of subjective well-being. Collective action is also a means to an end. For example, the joint management of irrigation canals, rangelands, and fisheries involves actions by groups that allow individuals to generate higher and more sustainable incomes. This chapter focuses on a specific, instrumental dimension of collective action: the role of groups and networks in helping households in poor communities manage their exposure to risks and cope with shocks to their livelihoods, which are identified as an important determinant of poverty and well-being by Di Gregorio et al. (this volume, Chapter 2).

In doing so, the chapter builds on research addressing how poor households respond to shocks; see Morduch (2005) and references therein, the review paper by Skoufias and Quisumbing (2005), and the recent collection edited by Dercon (2005). These show that in the face of shocks households can partially smooth consumption, but not perfectly; as might be expected, idiosyncratic shocks (for instance, low or late rainfall on household plots) are more likely to be insured collectively than are generalized shocks (such as low rainfall on most plots in the village). In most empirical studies of risk smoothing—for example, that of Townsend (1994)—the insurance unit has been assumed to be the village. Studies using Townsend's approach have often found that households are able to cope with idiosyncratic shocks but not covariate shocks, implying that local insurance mechanisms are inadequate to cope with aggregate shocks. More recent studies (for example, that of Munshi and Rosenzweig 2005) have begun to question the assumption that the appropriate unit of risk smoothing is the village. They suggest that consumption is smoothed within subcaste networks that extend beyond the village. Indeed, the literature on migration and remittances suggests that networks can cross geographic boundaries, with the formation of migrant networks at destination sites affected by shocks in the original locality (Munshi 2003).

There is also a subset of studies that has attempted to isolate the role of gift giving and informal loans in helping households to cope with shocks. The results indicate that households are not perfectly "altruistic"; the problems of asymmetric information and limited commitment mean that households are not likely to be fully insured (Foster and Rosenzweig 2000; Ligon, Thomas, and Worral 2000).[1] However, such analyses do not assess whether responses differ depending on the nature of the shock, and indicators for collective action and participation in different types of networks are generally either absent or rudimentary. There are some exceptions. Fafchamps and Lund (2003) differentiated among different types of risk, specifically addressing how different sorts of networks are used. They showed that risk sharing appears to occur mostly in very small networks of close friends and families—networks that may not have the heterogeneity required to efficiently share risk. In the case of Ethiopia, Dercon and Krishnan (2000) specifically addressed potential gender differences in terms of risk coping and found that poor women, particularly in one region, are less able to smooth consumption in the face of risks.

The collective action literature shows that the density of networks in general, and participation in more formal groups in particular, can lead to either more effective participation in community-based activities (White and Runge 1994; Isham and Kahkonen 2002) or higher household incomes (Narayan and Pritchett 1999; Pender and Scherr 2002; Haddad and Maluccio 2003). However, there is a lack of consensus on the impact of heterogeneity on collective action. In most empirical studies in which researchers have used various measures of heterogeneity to examine its impact on collective action or on household incomes directly, the impact of any type of heterogeneity has tended to be negative or not significant (Ahuja 1998; Alesina and La Ferrara 2000; Bardhan 2000; McCarthy and Vanderlinden 2004; Place et al. 2004), with the interesting exception of results reported by Grootaert (2001). It is often hypothesized that heterogeneity of any sort makes finding agreements mutually beneficial and acceptable to all more costly and that sociocultural heterogeneity in particular is likely to reduce trust among group members and also to reduce the efficacy of social sanctioning (Easterly and Levine 1997). On the other hand, much of the literature on group formation and networks highlights the added benefits to diversity (or heterogeneity) among members along any number of dimensions. Risk pooling is certainly more efficient when one's income is less correlated with that of other members of the groups, which implies that having members

---

1. However, Genicot and Ray (2003) show that with imperfect enforceability of contracts, stable insurance groups can exist above or below the village level.

with different agricultural activities and occupational structures is better for the insurance mechanism. Many networks exist to share information; clearly if everyone has the same background and the same current sociocultural and economic profile, there is little need to rely on networks to share information. Finally, there may be economies of scope in terms of information gathering—or accumulation of other assets, for that matter. In this case, economic heterogeneity also favors the pooling of resources to the benefit of all. Because there may be competing impacts of different types of heterogeneity on the functioning of groups, it becomes critical to examine which groups are able to harness the positive effects of heterogeneity and mitigate its negative effects.

Finally, if groups differ in terms of degree of heterogeneity and geographic dispersion, what kinds of enforcement mechanisms can be used to ensure compliance with network objectives and norms of behavior? Members of local networks are easier to monitor, but local networks are less able to insure against covariate shocks. Spatially diversified networks offer some protection against covariate shocks, but network members will be more difficult to monitor. If information and communications technologies are poor, more distant network members may not even be aware of a shock that occurred in their original communities.

Interest in these issues is more than just a matter of academic curiosity. Understanding these networks is as crucial to understanding the determinants of poverty and the policies necessary to move people out of poverty as understanding land tenure or access to financial capital. A misunderstanding of the roles of these networks can lead to policy changes that have unintended consequences on the functioning of the networks, with potentially damaging effects on the capacity of the poor to mitigate, and cope with, the effects of shocks. At the same time, a better understanding of such networks can lead to the identification of policies that complement networks that already serve the poor well and also to policies that can substitute for networks that simply are not reaching the poor.

In terms of the conceptual framework presented in Chapter 2, this chapter focuses on the impact of risks and shocks (especially natural shocks in the form of drought, death, and illness) on household well-being and the role of local collective action institutions in dealing with these risks. We show the impact of asset endowments (human and natural capitals, in particular) on the severity of these shocks, as well as on the composition of the groups and networks. We also discuss the size of collective action institutions and their scope to effectively contribute to poverty and vulnerability reduction. Using the language of the conceptual framework, the discussion focuses almost exclusively on the internal actors (*iddir* members) in the action arena, which is represented by the *iddir* (burial societies or funeral association). The patterns of interaction that emerge here are the innovative forms of cooperation (through cash transfers and loans given to *iddir* members to cope with a shock) and rules (governing that composition and operation of *iddir*) that allow poor households to achieve certain poverty-related outcomes, such as maintaining necessary levels of income and fulfilling basic needs, as well as sustaining these groups.

More generally, this chapter highlights the potential of local forms of collective action beyond economic groups (such as credit and savings associations) to enable poor households to cope with local shocks by overcoming the problems of moral hazard and adverse selection that the typical insurance schemes face. It provides an interesting bridge from the natural resource management (NRM) literature to the non-NRM poverty studies by showing how the same principles that apply to collective action for resource management (effective rules on membership, sanctions for noncompliance, and so on) can translate into non-NRM arenas and create conditions and incentives for effective group operation—in this case, for managing risks. It adds new insights to the discussion of the impact of heterogeneity on the effectiveness and sustainability of local groups and networks, which is of great interest and has long been debated in the NRM literature. By focusing on risks and their effect on household well-being, we contribute to an understanding of the complex and dynamic nature of poverty, which is of central interest to this volume.

In the material that follows, we address these issues by drawing on rich longitudinal and qualitative household and community data from Ethiopia. After describing these data in some detail, we examine the shocks these households face and their impact on living standards. We then look at the correlates of participation in groups and networks—both formal and informal—and the relationship between networks and access to other forms of capital. In the final substantive section, we pull this information together to assess how one form of collective action, represented by *iddir*, allows households to attenuate the impact of illness.

Data and Context

Ethiopia is a federal country divided into 11 regions. Each region is subdivided into zones and the zones into *woredas*, which are roughly equivalent to counties in the United States or the United Kingdom. *Woredas*, in turn, are divided into peasant associations (PAs), or *kebeles*, administrative units consisting of a number of villages. PAs were set up in the aftermath of the 1974 revolution. Our data are taken from the Ethiopia Rural Household Survey (ERHS), a unique longitudinal household dataset covering households in 15 areas of rural Ethiopia. Data collection started in 1989, when a survey team visited 6 PAs in central and southern Ethiopia. The survey was expanded in 1994 to encompass 15 PAs across the country, yielding a sample of 1,477 households. As part of the survey redesign and extension that took place in 1994, the sample was re-randomized by including the exact proportion of newly formed or arrived households in the sample, as well as by replacing households lost to follow-up with others considered broadly similar to them in terms of demographics and wealth by village elders and officials. The nine additional PAs were selected to better account for the diversity of the farming systems found in Ethiopia. The sampling of the PAs newly included in 1994 was based on a list of all households that was made with the help of local PA officials.[2]

The sample was stratified within each village to ensure that a representative number of landless households were also included. Similarly, an exact proportion of female-headed households was included via stratification. Consequently, as Dercon, Hoddinott, and Woldehanna (2005) show, the population shares within the sample were broadly consistent with the population shares in the three main sedentary farming systems—the plough-based cereal-farming system of the northern and central Highlands, the mixed plough-hoe cereal-farming system, and the farming system based around *enset* (a root crop also called false banana), which is grown in southern parts of the country. It should be noted that in 1994 the Central Statistical Office collected a dataset as part of the Welfare Monitoring System. Many of the average outcomes, in terms of health and nutrition, were similar to the results of the ERHS, suggesting that living conditions in our sample did not differ greatly from those found more generally throughout rural Ethiopia (see Collier, Dercon, and Mackinnon 1997).

For these reasons, the sampling frame for selecting the villages can be seen as one that was stratified by agroecological zones and subzones, with one to three villages selected per stratum. Further, sample sizes in each village were chosen so as to approximate a self-weighting sample, when considered in terms of a farming system: each person (approximately) represents the same number of persons found in the main farming systems as of 1994. However, we use this feature of the sample cautiously. It does not include pastoral households or urban areas. Also, the practical aspects associated with running a longitudinal household survey, when the sampled localities are as much as 1,000 kilometers apart in a country where top speeds on the best roads rarely exceed 50 kilometers per hour, constrained sampling to only 15 communities in a country of thousands of villages. So although these data can be considered broadly representative of households in nonpastoralist farming systems as of 1994, extrapolation from these results should be done with care.

Additional survey rounds were subsequently conducted in late 1994, 1995, 1997, 1999, and 2004. These surveys were conducted, either individually or collectively, by the Economics Department of Addis Ababa University, the Centre for the Study of African Economies, the University of Oxford, or the

---

2. The PA was responsible for the implementation of land reform following 1974 and held wide-ranging powers as a local authority. All land is owned by the government. To obtain land, households have to register with the PA, and thus lists are maintained of the households that have been allocated land. These household lists were a good source of information for the construction of a sampling frame.

International Food Policy Research Institute. Sample attrition between 1994 and 2004 was low, with a loss of only 12.4 percent (or 1.3 percent per year) of the sample over this 10-year period, in part because of the institutional continuity. This continuity also helped ensure that the questions asked in each round were identical, or very similar, to those asked in previous rounds and that the data were processed in comparable ways.[3] In addition, detailed qualitative studies were undertaken in the mid-1990s, the results of which were reported by Bevan and Pankhurst (1996). Smaller-scale qualitative studies have been carried out at selected survey sites on specific topics, including some on collective action; see "Networks, Groups, and Collective Action."

Table 3.1 provides descriptive statistics based on the 2004 survey round. Two features are immediately apparent. First, these households were very poor. Mean monthly consumption per capita was 106 birr, or about US$13 per person, and about 36 percent were below the poverty line. Second, agriculture was the dominant source of income for these households, accounting for two-thirds of household income.

Shocks in Rural Ethiopia

We define *shocks* as adverse events that lead to a loss of household income, a reduction in consumption, a loss of productive assets, or serious concern or anxiety about household welfare. The data used in this section are based on a household-level "shocks" module developed by Hoddinott and Quisumbing (2003). The module asked households to consider a list of adverse events and indicate whether the household was adversely affected by them. Ethiopian respondents were asked, "Has this household been affected by a serious shock— an event that led to a serious reduction in your asset holdings, caused your household income to fall substantially, or resulted in a significant reduction in consumption?"

Shocks were divided into a number of broad categories: climatic; economic; political, social, and legal; crime; and health. Climatic shocks included obvious examples such as drought and flooding but also erosion, frosts, and pestilence affecting crops or livestock. Economic shocks included problems in terms of access to inputs (both physical access and large increases in price),

---

3. We examined whether this sample attrition was nonrandom. Over the period 1994–2004, there were no significant differences between households that left the study and those that did not in terms of initial levels of characteristics of the household head (age, sex), assets (fertile land, all landholdings, cattle), or consumption. However, households that left the study were, at baseline, smaller than households that did not leave. Between 1999 and 2004, there were some significant differences by village; one village, Shumsha, had a higher attrition rate than others in the sample. Our survey supervisors recorded the reason why individual households could not be traced. Using these data, we examined attrition in Shumsha on a case-by-case basis, but could not find any dominant reason for households' attrition.

TABLE 3.1 Descriptive characteristics of the Ethiopian sample, 2004

Characteristic	Measure
Demographic	
Mean household size (persons)	5.7
Percentage of households that are female headed	30.3
Percentage of household heads with *any* education	23.1
Living standards	
Monthly consumption per capita, mean (birr)	106.2
Monthly consumption per capita, median (birr)	75.1
Percentage of households below poverty line	36
Income sources (percent)	
Crop income	67
Wage income	5
Self-employment	19
Transfers	8

SOURCE: IFPRI (2009).

NOTES: Monetary figures are in 2004 birr. At the time of the survey, the birr–U.S. dollar exchange rate was approximately 8 birr to the dollar. Self-employment income includes income from processing agricultural products (livestock, beer) and nonagricultural activities such as trading or selling firewood and charcoal. Transfers include both public and private transfers. For details on the construction of consumption and income aggregates and poverty lines, see Dercon, Hoddinott, and Woldehanna (2007).

decreases in output prices, and difficulties in selling agricultural and nonagricultural products. Political, social, and legal shocks included the confiscation of assets or arbitrary taxation by government authorities, social or political discrimination or exclusion, and contract disputes. Crime shocks included the theft or destruction of crops, livestock, housing, tools, or household durables as well as crimes against persons. Health shocks included both death and illness. We also considered miscellaneous shocks, such as conflicts and disputes with other family members, neighbors, or other village residents regarding access to land or other assets. Finally, in addition to these questions about specific shocks, households were also asked to enumerate the three most important adverse shocks that they had experienced over the previous five years.

As Table 3.2 shows, virtually all households in the Ethiopian sample (95 percent) reported a most important shock, 85 percent reported a second-most-important shock, and 62 percent reported a third-most-important shock. The most commonly reported "worst shocks" were drought (47 percent), death (43 percent), and illness (28 percent). When we disaggregated the responses by degree of importance of these worst shocks (not reported here), we see that these same three shocks were always listed as the most important adverse shocks experienced by these households. Input and output shocks, pests affecting crops, and crime were all reported by between 11 and 14 percent of households. Other shocks were less frequently reported. Strikingly, policy shocks (land redistribution, state confiscation of assets, resettlement, villagization or forced migration, bans on migration, forced contributions, or arbitrary taxation), which had featured so prominently in earlier rounds of the ERHS, substantially diminished in importance. Only 7 percent of households reported being adversely affected by such policy shocks, compared to 42 percent who reported being affected by these prior to 1994 (Dercon 2002, Table 1).

TABLE 3.2 Ethiopian household self-reports of the worst shocks experienced between 1999 and 2004

Worst shock	Percentage of households reporting each shock
Most commonly reported	
Drought	46.8
Death of household head, spouse, or another person	42.7
Illness of head, spouse, or another person	28.1
Inability to sell outputs or decrease in output prices	14.5
Pests or diseases that affected crops	13.8
Crime	12.7
Difficulty in obtaining inputs or increases in input prices	11.3
Policy or political shock (land redistribution, state confiscation of assets, resettlement, villagization, forced migration, bans on migration, forced contributions, arbitrary taxation)	7.4
Pests or diseases that affected livestock	7.0
Most commonly reported, by household-rated degree of importance	
Most important shock	
Drought	32.6
Death of household head, spouse, or another person	26.1
Illness of head, spouse, or another person	8.0
Second-most-important shock	
Death of head, spouse, or another person	14.8
Drought	13.6
Illness of head, spouse, or another person	12.3
Third-most-important shock	
Illness of head, spouse, or another person	12.2
Death of head, spouse, or another person	8.1
Drought	8.0

SOURCE: IFPRI (2009).

NOTES: Some 1,371 households reported information; in response to the question "What were the three most important shocks to affect this household?" 95 percent of households reported a most important shock, 85 percent reported a second-most-important shock, and 62 percent reported a third-most-important shock.

Although these data provide a detailed overview of the types of shocks experienced by households, it does not give us a quantitative sense of their consequences. Also, there are limits to cross-sectional analysis; it is difficult to tell whether, for example, conditional on location, wealth, and other observable characteristics, female-headed households in Ethiopia are more adversely affected by droughts than male-headed households. For these reasons, we summarize the results of Dercon, Hoddinott, and Woldehanna (2005), who reported an econometric assessment of the impact of these shocks on one measure of welfare, log per capita consumption.[4]

Log per capita consumption (*lnpcexp*) of household i in village v in time t is a function of two broad sets of household characteristics—household characteristics observed in the past (time $t - 1$) ($H_{iv,t-1}$) and shocks to households experienced between time $t - 1$ and time t ($S_{iv,t}$)—and community-level variables observed at time t ($X_{iv,t}$), such as the month or season of interview.[5] Vectors of parameters to be estimated are γ, β, and κ. In Ethiopia, log per capita consumption is measured from 2004, while past household characteristics from 1999 are used as regressors. Denoting $\varepsilon_{iv,t}$ as the white noise disturbance term, we write this relationship as

$$lnpcexp_{iv,t} = \gamma \cdot H_{iv,t-1} + \beta \cdot S_{iv,t} + \kappa \cdot X_{iv,t} + \varepsilon_{iv,t}. \tag{1}$$

Observable household characteristics are characteristics of the household head (age, gender, and schooling), demographic household characteristics (log size and dependency ratio), and household wealth (landholdings and livestock ownership, the latter expressed in livestock units). Also included are measures of households' networks and connections within the village that may also affect consumption levels: whether the household belonged to an ethnic or religious minority, whether it was related to anyone holding an official position in the locality, and whether a parent of the household head was an important person in the social life of the village. Because some shocks are relatively more com-

---

4. Consumption is the sum of food and nonfood consumption. For each food item, households were asked about the amounts they had consumed out of purchases, consumption out of their own stock, and consumption from gifts and in-kind wages in the previous week. In general, these consumption levels are valued using prices obtained from local market surveys fielded at the same time as the household survey. Nonfood items were limited to noninvestment goods, so we included consumables such as matches, batteries, soap, kerosene, and the like, as well as clothing and transport, but excluded investments in durable goods such as housing. Different recall periods were used for different items; for comparability, all results were changed into monthly (30-day) consumption rates and expressed in per capita terms. Dercon and Krishnan (2003) showed that earlier survey rounds, using various permutations of adult equivalency, did not fundamentally affect the analysis of the determinants of living standards.

5. In very loose terms, the specification of Equation 1 can be thought of as one in which, à la Friedman, consumption reflects the underlying asset base (which generates "permanent income") as well as transitory events that cause consumption to deviate from this level. We also include a vector that captures such potentially confounding factors such as the month in which the interview took place to capture seasonality.

mon than others, we aggregate the data we have on shocks into several categories indicating whether the household had experienced the following events that had led to a loss of household income, a reduction in consumption, or a loss of productive assets: a drought; too much rain; pests or diseases that affected field crops or crops in storage; pests or diseases that affected livestock; difficulty in obtaining inputs or increases in input prices; inability to sell or decreases in output prices; lack of demand for nonagricultural products; theft or destruction of tools, inputs, cash, crops, livestock, housing, or consumer goods; death of the household head, a spouse, or another person; and illness of the household head, a spouse, or another person. Finally, dummy variables are included for each village in Ethiopia. The implication is that shocks are identified by within-village (municipality) variation, which may make identification of covariate shocks difficult. However, even though covariate shocks were found in virtually all villages, even in the case of drought, there was no village in Ethiopia where all households indicated that they had been affected in the previous five years. This allows us to identify the impact of these relatively covariate events in our data.

The basic results from Dercon, Hoddinott, and Woldehanna (2005) are reported in Table 3.3. The striking feature of the results of the questions on shocks is how unimportant many of them seem to have been to those reporting them. Experiencing a drought at least once in the previous five years that lowered per capita consumption by approximately 20 percent and experiencing an illness that reduced per capita consumption by approximately 9 percent were the only shock variables that had a statistically significant effect on consumption. Other past shocks, controlling for a wide range of household characteristics, had no statistically significant impact on levels of consumption at the time of the survey (2004). Table 3.3, however, examines only the average effects of these shocks across all households in the sample. In Table 3.4 we extend this earlier work by disaggregating along three dimensions of preshock (1999) household characteristics —gender of household head, landholdings, and location—and explore the extent to which the impact of shocks differs across different household types. When we do so, some interesting differences emerge: drought shocks have a more severe effect on female-headed households and on poorer households as measured by landholdings, and illness shocks matter much more in survey areas south of Addis Ababa, where malaria is much more common. We return to this latter point later.

Networks, Groups, and Collective Action

Having described the broader environments in which our respondents lived and the effects of shocks on them, our next step was to consider the role of collective action in mitigating these.

Types of Networks and Groups

In the 2004 survey round, households were asked to provide details "about the five most important people you can rely on in time of need for support, both

TABLE 3.3 Impact of shocks and other covariates on (log) consumption per capita in Ethiopia, 2004

Covariate	Estimated coefficient	(1) t-statistic (absolute value)	(2) t-statistic (absolute value)
Shocks in prior five years			
Drought	−0.182	3.03*	2.49
Flood	0.025	0.59	0.28
Pests or diseases that affected field crops or crops in storage	−0.001	0.05	0.01
Pests or diseases that affected livestock	0.003	0.05	0.05
Difficulty in obtaining inputs or increases in input prices	0.058	1.00	1.11
Inability to sell outputs or decreases in output prices	−0.076	1.16	1.06
Lack of demand for nonagricultural products	−0.108	0.93	0.83
Theft or destruction of tools, inputs, cash, crops, livestock, housing, or consumer goods (crime)	0.051	0.96	0.71
Death of household head, spouse, or another person	0.025	0.59	0.63
Illness of head, spouse, or another person	−0.096	1.91*	1.68
Other controls			
Female-headed household, 1999	−0.024	0.45	0.39
Log age of household head, 1999	0.092	1.25	1.30
Some schooling for household head, 1999	0.082	1.39	2.19**
Log household size, 1999	−0.284	6.36**	8.43**
Dependency ratio, 1999	−0.033	1.92*	2.39**
Household in second land quintile, 1999	0.062	0.98	1.10
Household in third land quintile, 1999	0.140	2.29**	1.63
Household in fourth land quintile, 1999	0.143	2.27**	2.21**
Household in top land quintile, 1999	−0.036	0.49	0.42
Livestock units, 1999	0.035	4.05**	3.64**
Membership in ethnic minority	0.192	2.89**	2.94**
Membership in religious minority	0.064	1.11	0.79
Relative holds official position in a peasant association (PA)	0.124	2.99**	3.39**
Mother or father important in village social life	0.170	3.93**	3.18**
R^2	0.31		
Sample size	1,281		

SOURCE: Dercon, Hoddinott, and Woldehanna (2005).

NOTES: Standard errors are calculated using the Huber–White method (column 1) and clustered at the village level (column 2). * means significant at the 10 percent level; ** means significant at the 5 percent level. PA dummies are also included but not reported.

TABLE 3.4 Impact of shocks on (log) consumption per capita in Ethiopia, by household characteristics, 2004

Shock	Male-headed household	Female-headed household	Household in bottom three land quintiles	Household in top two land quintiles	Village located north of Addis Ababa	Village located south of Addis Ababa
Drought	-0.086	-0.433	-0.189	-0.152	-0.238	-0.295
	(1.21)	(3.77)**	(2.50)**	(1.55)	(3.63)**	(3.07)**
Flood	0.061	-0.097	-0.002	0.092	-0.094	0.086
	(0.89)	(0.77)	(0.03)	(0.95)	(0.88)	(1.17)
Pests or diseases that affected crops	-0.001	0.011	0.003	0.011	0.027	-0.037
	(0.02)	(0.10)	(0.04)	(0.12)	(0.29)	(0.58)
Pests or diseases that affected livestock	0.035	-0.037	-0.067	0.048	0.003	-0.021
	(0.56)	(0.22)	(0.85)	(0.53)	(0.03)	(0.30)
Difficulty in obtaining inputs or increases in input prices	0.084	-0.050	0.041	0.114	-0.062	0.099
	(1.37)	(0.32)	(0.56)	(1.20)	(0.53)	(1.34)
Inability to sell outputs or decreases in output prices	-0.063	0.068	0.042	-0.164	0.122	-0.098
	(0.93)	(0.36)	(0.56)	(1.56)	(0.58)	(1.47)
Lack of demand for nonagricultural products	-0.111	-0.270	-0.072	-0.358	*0.026	-0.317
	(0.91)	(0.97)	(0.50)	(1.75)	(0.11)	(2.09)**
Crime	0.010	0.204	0.010	0.118	-0.057	0.094
	(0.17)	(1.68)	(0.15)	(1.28)	(0.61)	(1.46)
Death of household head, spouse, or another person	0.057	-0.178	0.027	0.049	0.107	-0.027
	(1.20)	(1.92)*	(0.50)	(0.70)	(1.70)*	(0.46)
Illness of head, spouse, or another person	-0.076	-0.146	-0.058	-0.168	-0.003	-0.143
	(1.43)	(0.96)	(0.89)	(2.05)**	(0.04)	(2.17)**

SOURCE: Authors' calculations.

NOTES: Model specification, including covariates, as per Table 3.3. Standard errors are calculated using the Huber–White method. * means significant at the 10 percent level; ** means significant at the 5 percent level.

within the village and elsewhere." In addition, they were asked whether there were other people, beyond these five, on whom they could rely for help in time of need. We call such individuals a "network," and in this section we provide descriptive statistics on three dimensions of these networks: correlations between network size and observable household characteristics, characteristics of individuals within a household's network, and the degree of network heterogeneity.

Virtually all households—91 percent—reported that there was at least 1 person on whom they could rely for assistance. Figure 3.1 plots a density function for the size of networks reported by these households. The median number of people in a household's network was 5, with about a quarter of the households reporting that they had 2 or fewer people in their network and a smaller percentage (16 percent) reporting 10 or more people in their network. Further, there is some evidence that households do indeed call on these networks. Respondents indicated that they had received help from 86 percent of the individuals they listed as part of their network. There is also some evidence of reciprocity in these relationships: 75 percent of the individuals listed as being in a household's network had both given and received assistance in the past. Fewer than 10 percent of the individuals listed as part of a network had neither given nor received assistance.

Table 3.5 provides descriptive statistics on some of the characteristics of individuals found in these networks. Most individuals in the networks were neighbors (60 percent) or, although not neighbors, lived in the same village (27 percent). However, just over a quarter had at least one plot of land adjacent to a plot held by the surveyed household. Only 13 percent of individuals in households' networks resided outside the village. The most common relationship was

FIGURE 3.1 Network size, Ethiopia, 2004

Density

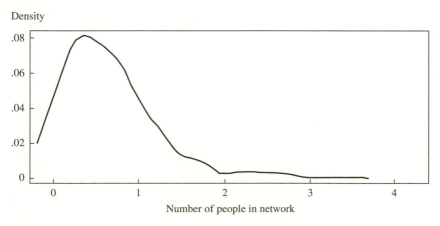

SOURCE: Authors' calculations.

TABLE 3.5 Characteristics of individuals in an Ethiopian household's network, 2004

Individuals who:	Percent
Are neighbors	60
Are not neighbors but are from the same village	27
Are not neighbors and live outside the village	13
Have plot(s) of land next to plots belonging to this household	28
Are members of the same *mehabir* (social group)	21
Are relatives	66
Belong to the same *iddir* (burial society)	57
Are neither relatives nor members of the same *iddir*	12
Are members of the same labor-sharing group	43
Are partners in a sharecropping or land-renting arrangement	6
Are partners in an oxen-sharing arrangement	23
Are members of the same *iqqub* (lending group)	7
Borrow or lend money	49
Do wage work	7
Buy or sell crops	4

SOURCE: Authors' calculations.

that of a relative or a member of the same *iddir;* indeed, only 12 percent of network members were neither relatives nor members of the same *iddir.* Many network members (49 percent) were individuals from whom the household had previously borrowed or to whom it had lent. They were unlikely to be individuals with whom the household sharecropped or from whom or two whom the household had hired in or hired out labor or bought or sold crops.

Were other network members similar or dissimilar to our respondents? We consider two dimensions: comparative measures of wealth and age. If we stratify the sample by landownership, we find that poorer households have relatively better-off households in their network, while richer households tend to have relatively poorer households in their network. However, when we compare them by oxen ownership, a different pattern emerges. Households with no oxen or only one animal tend to have similar households as network partners. Households with two or more oxen typically have other households with two or more oxen as network partners. Figure 3.2 graphs the distribution of the difference in age between the household head and other individuals in the network who are either relatives or members of the same *iddir.* The modal age difference for both is close to zero. However, although the distribution of age differences among *iddir* members is more peaked than that of relatives, both are characterized by a considerable spread around this mode.

Table 3.6 examines the associations between household characteristics and the likelihood that a household had a network as well as the size of that network. The first column reports the results of estimating a probit in which the

FIGURE 3.2 Age differences within networks, Ethiopia, 2004

Density

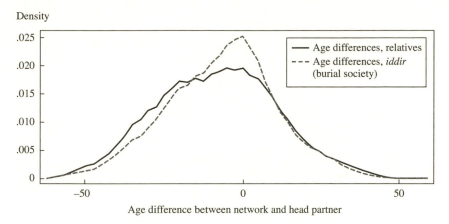

Age difference between network and head partner

SOURCE: Authors' calculations.

dependent variable equals one if the household has at least one person in its network, zero otherwise. To make the coefficients readily interpretable, we report the marginal effects of the regressors in column 1. In columns 2 and 3 we report the determinants of the size of the household's network. Because our estimates need to take account of the fact that the dependent variable is censored at zero, we use a tobit estimator, and the result is reported in column 2.[6]

There are few household characteristics that are associated with an increased or decreased likelihood that a household has at least one person in its network. The only statistically significant characteristics are whether the household's landholdings were within the second to fifth quintiles within the village and whether the father of the household head belonged to an *iddir,* which marginally increases (by 4.8 percent) the likelihood that the household had at least one person in its network. However, being wealthier, as defined in terms of landholdings, is associated with having a larger network. Households in the fourth and top land quintiles had one to two more people in their network than did the households in the bottom quintile of landholdings. Larger households and households in which the household head had some formal schooling had larger networks. Family background also plays some role in influencing network size. Having a parent who was an important person in the social life of the village, having a relative who held an official position within the village,

---

6. Because estimates derived from a tobit are suspect if the underlying disturbance terms are non-normally distributed, we also report the results of estimating Powell's (1984) censored least absolute deviations model. We report *t*-statistics based on bootstrapped standard errors; following Davidson and Mackinnon (2000), these are based on 1,000 replications.

TABLE 3.6 Correlates of the presence of networks in Ethiopia and their size, by household characteristics, 2004

Household characteristic	(1) Probit (dependent variable: household has at least one person in network)	(2) Tobit (dependent variable: number of people in household's network)	(3) Censored least absolute deviation (dependent variable: number of people in household's network)
Household in second landowning quintile[a]	0.032	0.039	0.607
	(2.28)**	(0.04)	(1.21)
Household in third landowning quintile[a]	0.040	0.527	0.685
	(3.15)**	(0.60)	(1.32)
Household in fourth landowning quintile[a]	0.050	1.904	1.856
	(3.67)**	(2.18)**	(3.97)**
Household in highest landowning quintile[a]	0.031	3.037	1.726
	(2.18)**	(3.07)**	(2.52)**
Log age of household head	−0.039	0.357	−0.114
	(1.81)*	(0.34)	(0.17)
Female-headed household[a]	−0.004	−0.938	−0.212
	(0.28)	(1.29)	(0.51)
Some schooling for household head[a]	0.024	2.081	0.951
	(1.55)	(2.57)**	(1.78)*

	(1)	(2)	(3)
Log household size	−0.008	1.302	0.443
	(0.64)	(2.15)**	(1.27)
Household head born in this village[a]	−0.003	−1.164	−0.682
	(0.20)	(1.59)	(1.57)
Mother or father important in village social life[a]	−0.007	0.814	0.977
	(0.60)	(1.24)	(2.52)**
Related to peasant association (PA) officials	0.020	1.378	1.111
	(1.62)	(2.22)**	(2.72)**
Father in an *iddir* (burial society)[a]	0.048	2.395	0.878
	(3.25)**	(3.38)**	(2.13)**
Household part of an ethnic minority in a PA[a]	−0.018	−0.582	0.309
	(0.73)	(0.60)	(0.52)
Household part of a religious minority in a PA[a]	0.002	0.988	0.100
	(0.11)	(1.22)	(0.20)

SOURCE: Authors' calculations.

NOTES: Results of the probit are presented in terms of the marginal effects of the regressors; dummy variables measure the marginal impact of switching from zero to one. In column 1, the absolute values of z-statistics are in parentheses; in columns 2 and 3, the absolute values of *t*-statistics are in parentheses. The standard errors in column 1 are heteroscedastic robust. The standard errors calculated in column 3 use a bootstrap with 1,000 replications. * means significant at the 10 percent level; ** means significant at the 5 percent level. PA dummies are included but not reported. The sample size is 1,124.

[a]Covariate is a dummy variable.

and having a father who belonged to an *iddir* all correlated with a larger mean number of persons in a household's network. Finally, households belonging to ethnic or religious minorities are not disadvantaged in terms of network size.

Iddir *and Their Role in Mitigating Shocks*

In this section we consider the role of one form of collective action—that provided by *iddir* (burial societies or funeral associations)—and their role in mitigating shocks in Ethiopia. Members of *iddir* typically meet once or twice a month, making a small payment into a group fund (1–2 birr per month). A striking feature of these organizations is their degree of formality; often there are written rules and records of contributions and payouts (Dercon et al. 2006). When a member dies, the *iddir* makes a payment to surviving family members in cash or in kind; the median amount paid out by the *iddir* to which the households we studied belong is 100 birr, although there is some heterogeneity in these payments.[7]

Outside of Tigray, *iddir* membership is widespread, with nearly 90 percent of households reporting that they belong to at least one *iddir*. Among households that report belonging to *iddir* (and again excluding Tigray, where *iddir* do not exist), just under 60 percent report belonging to one *iddir,* 21 percent belong to two, and another 20 percent belong to three or more. Very few households, around 4 percent of the sample, claim that they do not belong to an *iddir* because they cannot afford the monthly dues. Virtually all *iddir* (93 percent) are situated within the PA. Two-thirds of *iddir* appear to have had no restrictions on membership beyond paying the necessary dues and fees, 14 percent were restricted to members of the same church or mosque, 6 percent were restricted to women, and 14 percent had some other restriction. All villages had at least one *iddir* that was open to anyone.

Why are *iddir* of interest? In addition providing what is in effect a form of life insurance, a third of the *iddir* to which the households we studied belong provide cash payouts to their members when they have experienced other types of adverse shocks, and a quarter offer loans. As Table 3.7 shows, the most common form of assistance apart from paying for funerals is cash payouts in case of fire. In addition, 10 percent of *iddir* provide cash in case of illness, and 15 percent provide loans. However, the provision of some types of assistance is not found everywhere; for example, assistance in the case of illness is concentrated in four survey localities, all south of Addis Ababa. Noting this, we juxtapose the following observations: (1) after drought, households report that the two next-most-important types of shocks are illness and death (Table 3.2); (2) illness shocks have an especially large effect on consumption in villages located south of Addis Ababa (Table 3.4); (3) membership in *iddir* is widespread, and other *iddir* members are seen as individuals who can be called on in times of

---

7. One birr is equal to approximately US$0.12, so 100 birr is about US$12.

TABLE 3.7 Events for which Ethiopian *iddir* (burial societies) make payouts or offer loans, 2004

Event	*Iddir* will give a cash transfer (percent)	*Iddir* will give a loan (percent)
Funeral	100	9
Fire	20	9
Loss of oxen or other livestock	7	3
Destruction of house	6	4
Wedding	5	5
Illness	10	15
Harvest loss	3	2
Other event	6	1
Any event	34	25

SOURCE: Authors' calculations.

need (Table 3.5); and (4) in selected localities, some *iddir* provide assistance when illness shocks occur (Table 3.7).

Two questions arise: (1) does this provision of assistance when illness shocks occur—in effect a form of health insurance—reduce the impact of these shocks on consumption, and (2) if the answer to question 1 is affirmative, how do these *iddir* overcome problems of moral hazard and adverse selection that typically bedevil insurance schemes?

Answering question 1 is tricky, because households can choose the *iddir* to which they wish to belong. Because membership in *iddir* is endogenous, we cannot, for example, insert membership in *iddir* providing health insurance into question 1 to see how it modifies the impact of self-reported illness shocks; coefficients from such a regression would be biased and inconsistent. Instead, we take a different approach. We start by restricting the sample to villages south of Addis Ababa, where, in general, illness shocks have the largest effect on consumption. We separate these southern villages into two groups: those where *iddir* that provide health insurance are present and those where they are not present. Within these groups of villages, we estimate equation 1 using a modification of the specification reported in Table 3.3. Finally, we restrict the sample to households in the lowest three landholding quintiles to see if the availability of such insurance is particularly important for poorer households.

The results are reported in Table 3.8. These show that the illness shocks reported by poor households residing in villages where no *iddir* provide health insurance are associated with a large—20 percent—reduction in per capita consumption. In contrast, the impact of illness shocks on poor households in villages where *iddir* do provide health insurance is smaller and not statistically

TABLE 3.8 Impact of illness shocks on (log) consumption per capita in southern Ethiopia, 2004

Households residing in villages where:	Estimated coefficient	*t*-statistic (absolute value)
Iddir provide health insurance	−0.144	1.03
Iddir do not provide health insurance	−0.205	2.08**

SOURCE: Authors' calculations.

NOTES: Specification is a modified version of that reported in Table 3.3. Standard errors are calculated using the Huber–White method. * means significant at the 10 percent level; ** means significant at the 5 percent level.

significant. These results suggest that the availability of this health insurance attenuates illness shocks.

However, our household data have only limited information on how *iddir* manage the provision of health insurance. For this reason, we organized a small survey of *iddir* in four villages where the ERHS data indicated that *iddir* provided this form of assistance. The challenge in doing so was finding these *iddir*. There is no "official" list of *iddir*, let alone lists that describe which *iddir* provide which types of assistance. *Iddir* do not exist in a physical sense; for example, there is no *iddir* office. The names of *iddir* can be lengthy and are often shortened in different ways by different people. Leadership of *iddir* is, in many cases, on an elected basis, so the names of *iddir* leaders change over time.

Given all this, we organized the survey in the following fashion. Using the ERHS data, we generated a list of *iddir* in the four villages where *iddir* were known to provide health insurance. Enumerators were given a list of the names of 12 *iddir* that provided either cash grants or loans in the case of illness, along with identifying information such as alternate names, dates these *iddir* were formed, approximate numbers of members, and names of leaders such as the *iddir* chair. The enumerators were instructed to find at least eight of these *iddir*. Once they found an *iddir*, they asked if a small number of members would be willing to participate in a discussion about how this form of health insurance worked. The meetings included the *iddir* chair and, in nearly all cases, at least two other individuals knowledgeable about the functioning of the *iddir*, including the treasurer. Across all four villages, a semistructured questionnaire was administered to 33 *iddir*. Some questions were precoded (for example, Are members charged interest if they take a loan to cover health expenses?), while others were designed to encourage *iddir* members to explain how they functioned (for example, How do members go about requesting assistance?).

The successful provision of insurance revolves around the reconciliation of two forms of asymmetric information, adverse selection and moral hazard. In the context of health insurance, adverse selection arises because individuals who are less healthy than others have a greater incentive to seek insurance, but the healthiness of such individuals is difficult to observe by the insurer. Moral hazard occurs when, once insured, an individual does not bear the full consequences of actions that are (at least partially) unobserved by the insurer.

How do *iddir* deal with these problems of asymmetric information? One obvious way would be to impose restrictions on who can join and when they join. The household survey asked *iddir* participants if their *iddir* restricted membership in any way. In the four villages where health insurance is offered, most *iddir* (81 percent) described by respondents imposed some sort of membership restriction. As Table 3.9 shows, the most common restriction was geographic—all members had to live in the same PA. Other common restrictions included belonging to the same church or mosque or being open to women only. Membership restrictions based on clan, ethnicity, or youth were not common, and beyond these broad categories, no other restrictions were mentioned. *Iddir* that imposed certain types of membership restrictions—based on residing in the same PA or belonging to the same church or mosque—were more likely to provide health insurance than those that did not (see Table 3.9), even after taking into account other *iddir* characteristics, such as age of members, number of members, and location (Table 3.10). In the *iddir* survey, a number of respondents commented that this restriction existed largely because it was impractical for members to attend monthly meetings if they lived too far away, a point we return to later. In contrast, there did not appear to be restrictions on when individuals could join these *iddir*. In almost all cases, new members could join at any time, and only two *iddir* required that new members belong for a minimum length of time before they were eligible for assistance with health shocks. However, individuals who joined after the *iddir* was formed had to pay a membership fee (Dercon et al. 2006).

TABLE 3.9 Characteristics of Ethiopian *iddir* (burial societies) by provision of health insurance, 2004

| | | Percentage of *iddir* that: | | |
Membership restriction	Percentage of *iddir* with this restriction	Do not provide health insurance	Provide health insurance	Probit value on difference
Must reside in the peasant association	41.0	23.5	38.1	0.04**
Must belong to the same clan	4.0	28.3	57.1	0.10*
Must belong to the same church or mosque	24.9	26.2	39.5	0.10*
Must belong to the same ethnic group	4.0	28.5	50.0	0.19
Youth only	4.0	30.0	14.3	0.37
Women only	23.7	30.3	26.8	0.67

SOURCE: Authors' calculations.

NOTES: * means significant at the 10 percent level; ** means significant at the 5 percent level.

TABLE 3.10 Correlates of the provision of health insurance by Ethiopian *iddir* (burial societies) in selected survey areas, 2004

Covariate	Marginal effect	z-statistic (absolute value)
Membership restriction		
Must reside in the peasant association (PA)[a]	0.197	2.15**
Must belong to the same clan[a]	0.174	0.81
Must belong to the same church or mosque[a]	0.210	2.12**
Women only[a]	0.060	0.62
Log age of *iddir*	−0.074	1.58
Iddir in the second, third, or fourth quartile for size[a]	0.139	1.79*

SOURCE: Authors' calculations.

NOTES: Results of the probit are presented in terms of the marginal effects of the regressors. Dummy variables measure the marginal impact of switching from zero to one. Standard errors are calculated using the Huber–White method. * means significant at the 10 percent level; ** means significant at the 5 percent level. PA dummies are included but not reported. The sample size is 169.

[a]Covariate is a dummy variable.

All 33 surveyed *iddir* stated that members who wanted to request assistance should do so before they incurred any expenditure; only two would consider requests from members after expenditures had been incurred. Further, assistance was almost always limited to direct medical expenses: only one *iddir* would provide funds to pay for hiring workers to assist with agricultural tasks, only one would pay to hire someone to assist with domestic tasks, and none would compensate for loss of income as a result of illness.

The feature shared by these *iddir* was the way in which they addressed the problem of asymmetric information. Restricting membership geographically makes it easier to learn about members and to monitor their behavior. The same is true of the requirement of common church or mosque membership. Direct medical costs are observable. For example, one *iddir* reported of a member: "His neighbors serve as an informant. For example, if the member takes the money for medication and if he does not go to clinic/hospital, he will be asked to return the money." Other means of checking include going to the home of the member and asking to see receipts. In fact, about a third of the *iddir* surveyed stated that they had formal checks in place to make sure the funds provided were spent on medical costs. Second, a considerable number of *iddir* conducted background checks prior to approving a grant or loan, visiting the member at home or asking neighbors to confirm that assistance was needed. In contrast, compensation for income loss is much more problematic because it is difficult to determine how much of the income loss was directly ascribable to illness. The one informational asymmetry that these mechanisms do not address is that of adverse selection, cases in which individuals who might anticipate having to incur medical expenses in the future would join with the express purpose of accessing funds held by the *iddir*. Although *iddir* do not prevent this directly—recall that new members can join at any time, and very few *iddir* restrict new members' access to health insurance—the imposition of a membership fee for new members discourages such behavior.

In addition to these mechanisms for dealing with informational asymmetries, these *iddir* take a number of steps to reduce the likelihood that the provision of health insurance will lead to financial difficulties for the *iddir*. One is their age structure. As Figure 3.2 shows, there is considerable dispersion in the distribution of ages of *iddir* members. As a result, there is—in effect—health insurance across generations, because young members contribute to the *iddir,* whereas older members are more likely to have age-related illnesses. Another observation consistent with this argument is that youth-only *iddir* are less likely than other *iddir* to provide health insurance. A second mechanism is size. Preliminary work with the ERHS data suggested a nonlinear relationship between the size of *iddir* and the likelihood of providing assistance, with *iddir* in the second, third, or fourth quartiles, ranked by size, slightly less likely to provide health insurance (see Table 3.10). Third, what is especially interesting is that the amount of money provided to members, in the form of either cash or loans, is tied fairly tightly to the amount of money *iddir* collect each month. Figure 3.3 shows that the 33 surveyed *iddir* are fairly conservative in this regard. The median *iddir* providing cash grants provides an amount equal to one month's income, and the maximum cash grant of the *iddir* at the 75th percentile is slightly more than two months' income. Loans as a ratio of monthly income tend to be higher than cash grants. However, although few *iddir* (4/33) charge interest on

FIGURE 3.3 Ratio of cash grants and loans to monthly *iddir* (burial society) income, 2004

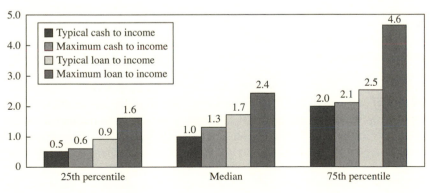

SOURCE: Authors' calculations.

these loans, about 75 percent require repayment within three months. In addition, most (82 percent) impose sanctions if members do not repay, either taking the individuals to local court or prohibiting them from making monthly contributions. The latter is especially effective because members who fail to make monthly contributions risk forfeiting their claim to their past contributions.

To summarize, health shocks have serious consequences for the consumption levels of rural Ethiopian households. In some localities, a form of collective action—that of *iddir,* or burial societies—provides a type of health insurance, and in these villages, illness shocks appear to have smaller effects on consumption. These *iddir* have managed to address problems of asymmetric information by imposing membership restrictions that reduce the cost of obtaining information, restricting assistance to an observable component of illness shocks, and using membership fees to discourage adverse selection. Further, they use a number of mechanisms to ensure financial sustainability: age structure, grant and loan size relative to income, and a series of mechanisms to ensure timely repayment of loans.

Conclusions and Policy Implications

Using longitudinal data and qualitative survey work, we have attempted to understand the role of groups and networks in determining how the poor manage their exposure to risks and cope with shocks to their livelihoods. In the Ethiopian villages where surveys were conducted, drought and illness have especially malign effects; for example, illness shocks reduce per capita consumption by 9 percent in regions where malaria is endemic. Nearly all households in the ERHS reported that they have a network of individuals on whom they can call for help. These networks consist largely of other households in the same village. This suggests that the scope for addressing covariate risks is likely to be limited, a supposition borne out by the observation made in "Shocks in Rural Ethiopia" that drought shocks lead to reductions in household consumption levels. Individuals within these networks would appear to engage in reciprocal assistance. Further, they typically have other ties; in particular, they are relatives, members of the same *iddir,* or members of the same labor-sharing group. Although these ties may convey benefits—for example, by providing multiple opportunities to observe other members, which limits opportunistic behavior—they limit the ability of members to cope with covariate shocks. Better-off households tend to have larger networks, as do households whose relations (parents or other relatives) had either status or connections within the village. Network heterogeneity is mixed: network members tend to be varied when measured by age or landownership but not in terms of ownership of oxen. *Iddir* providing health insurance are homogeneous along some dimensions (geography and, to a certain extent, religion) but heterogeneous with respect to age. They impose membership restrictions that reduce the cost of obtaining information and restrict assistance to an observable component of illness shocks (medical expenditures) that can be verified; further, they limit the extent of their assistance so that the provision of assistance does not come at the cost of financial sustainability. An attraction of such an approach is that it addresses the malign effect that asymmetries in information can have in the provision of insurance. A limitation is that some households are not able to fully insure themselves against health shocks.

Subsequent to the fielding of ERHS 2004, the Government of Ethiopia introduced a social safety net intervention, the Productive Safety Nets Programme (PSNP). It provides transfers of cash and food to food-insecure households in chronically food-insecure localities (Gilligan, Hoddinott, and Seyoum 2009). It is unclear how this will affect participation in networks and *iddir*. Although there are concerns that public interventions crowd out informal insurance arrangements, it is also possible that access to the PSNP will strengthen networks by providing a complementary source of resources for households. Further, given the positive association between wealth and network size, PSNP transfers may allow beneficiaries to increase the size of their networks. The impact of the PSNP on networks and informal insurance is a topic that awaits further study.

The present study looks in depth into the context "box" of the conceptual framework presented in Chapter 2 to show that risks from multiple sources affect poverty outcomes (for instance, by lowering consumption), but existing forms of collective action can be effective in mitigating the effects of the shocks to improve household welfare. Assets, especially human (age, ethnicity), natural (land endowments), and social (membership in religious groups) capitals, play a role in shaping the composition of burial societies and enabling their financial sustainability by creating rules regarding such things as sanctions, size of loans or grants, and membership fees (patterns of interaction) that address the problems of asymmetric information. Interestingly, both asset heterogeneity (age, land ownership) and homogeneity (religion) contribute to the sustainability of this form of collective action, but they also result in the exclusion of certain households from the insurance schemes offered by the *iddir*. These also highlight the importance of trust, a proven determinant of successful collective action in NRM, in creating incentives for lasting cooperation. Finally, these results show the limitations of local collective action. In turn, these results point to the following policy implications:

- Realism is needed in assessing the pro-poor benefits of support to collective action. Because wealthier and better-educated households tend to participate more in groups and to have larger networks implies that development practitioners need to pay more attention to identifying those barriers that prevent the poor—or other segments of the population—from participating in collective action. Not only because they have lower levels of wealth, but also because they participate less in risk-smoothing networks, the poor are more likely to be vulnerable to both covariate and idiosyncratic shocks.

- Realism is also needed in terms of the role of collective action in responding to shocks. Specifically, where households have limited ability to develop spatial networks, collective action has limited ability to respond to covariate (common) shocks. Direct public action is more appropriate in this area.

- Collective action may be more suitable for providing insurance in response to idiosyncratic (individual) shocks. Public action and policy that supports forms of collective action in this area must recognize, as exemplified by the *iddir* study here, that successful collective action
  - is based on norms of trust and reciprocity (because trust is easier to destroy than create, the principal of "do no harm" is important here, particularly when government actions are aimed toward existing collective action institutions),
  - has mechanisms for overcoming information problems, and
  - has mechanisms for sanctioning individuals who break the rules.

- *Iddir* providing health insurance exist in only some of the villages where illness shocks are prevalent and costly. Supporting the dissemination of examples of "good practice" across space—helping create "associations of associations" for example—would be valuable.

References

Ahuja, V. 1998. Land degradation, agricultural productivity, and common property: Evidence from Côte d'Ivoire. *Environment and Development Economics* 3 (1): 7–34.

Alesina, A., and E. La Ferrara. 2000. Participation in heterogeneous communities. *Quarterly Journal of Economics* 115 (3): 847–904.

Bardhan, P. 2000. Irrigation and cooperation: An empirical analysis of 48 irrigation communities in South India. *Economic Development and Cultural Change* 48 (4): 847–865.

Bevan, P., and A. Pankhurst, eds. 1996. *Ethiopian village studies*. Bath, U.K.: University of Bath.

Collier, P., S. Dercon, and J. Mackinnon. 1997. *Social Sector Review–Per II*. Ministry of Finance. Addis Ababa: Government of Ethiopia.

Davidson, R., and J. Mackinnon. 2000. Bootstrap tests: How many bootstraps? *Econometric Reviews* 19 (1): 55–68.

Dercon, S. 2002. Income risk, coping strategies and safety nets. *World Bank Research Observer* 17 (2): 141–166.

———, ed. 2005. *Insurance against poverty*. Oxford, U.K.: Oxford University Press.

Dercon, S., and P. Krishnan. 2000. In sickness and in health: Risk sharing within households in rural Ethiopia. *Journal of Political Economy* 108 (4): 688–727.

———. 2003. Changes in poverty in rural Ethiopia, 1989–1995. In *The new poverty strategies,* ed. A. Booth and P. Mosley. London: Palgrave Macmillan.

Dercon, S., J. Hoddinott, and T. Woldehanna. 2005. Consumption and shocks in 15 Ethiopian villages, 1999–2004. *Journal of African Economies* 14 (4): 559–585.

———. 2007. Growth and poverty in rural Ethiopia: Evidence from 15 communities 1994–2004. International Food Policy Research Institute, Washington, D.C. Photocopy.

Dercon, S., J. De Weerdt, T. Bold, and A. Pankhurst. 2006. Group-based funeral insurance in Ethiopia and Tanzania. *World Development* 34 (4): 685–703.

Easterly, W., and R. Levine. 1997. Africa's growth tragedy: Policies and ethnic divisions. *Quarterly Journal of Economics* 112 (4): 1203–1250.

Fafchamps, M., and S. Lund. 2003. Risk sharing networks in rural Philippines. *Journal of Development Economics* 71 (2): 261–287.

Foster, A., and M. Rosenzweig. 2000. Financial intermediation, transfers, and commitment: Do banks crowd out private insurance arrangements in low-income rural areas? In *Sharing the wealth: Demographic changes and economic transfers between generations,* ed. A. Mason and G. Tapinos. Oxford, U.K.: Oxford University Press.

Genicot, G., and D. Ray. 2003. Endogenous group formation in risk-sharing arrangements. *Review of Economic Studies* 70 (1): 87–113.

Gilligan, D., J. Hoddinott, and A. Seyoum. 2009. An analysis of Ethiopia's productive Safety Net Programme and its linkages. *Journal of Development Studies* 45 (10): 1684–1706.

Grootaert, C. 2001. *Does social capital help the poor? A synthesis of findings and recommendations from the social capital initiative.* Social Capital Initiative Working Paper 24. Washington, D.C.: Social Development Department, World Bank.

Haddad, L., and J. Maluccio. 2003. Trust, membership in groups, and household welfare: Evidence from KwaZulu-Natal, South Africa. *Economic Development and Cultural Change* 51 (3): 573–601.

Helliwell, J., and R. Putnam. 2004. The social context of wellbeing. *Philosophical Transactions of the Royal Society, Series B: Biological Sciences* 359 (1449): 1435–1446.

Hoddinott, J., and A. R. Quisumbing. 2003. *Data sources for microeconometric risk and vulnerability assessments.* Social Protection Paper 0323. Washington, D.C.: World Bank.

IFPRI (International Food Policy Research Institute). 2009. Ethiopia Rural Household Survey dataset, 1989–2004. <http://www.ifpri.org/dataset/ethiopian-rural-household-surveys-erhs-1989-2004>. Accessed February 28, 2011.

Isham, J., and S. Kahkonen. 2002. *Institutional determinants of the impact of community-based water services: Evidence from Sri Lanka and India.* Middlebury College Economics Discussion Paper 02-20. Middlebury, Vt.: Department of Economics, Middlebury College.

Ligon, E., J. P. Thomas, and T. Worral. 2000. Mutual insurance, individual savings, and limited commitment. *Review of Economic Dynamics* 3 (2): 216–246.

McCarthy, N., and J. P. Vanderlinden. 2004. Resource management under climatic risk: A case study of Niger. *Journal of Development Studies* 40 (5): 120–142.

Morduch, J. 2005. Consumption smoothing across space: Testing theories of risk-sharing in the ICRISAT study region of south India. In *Insurance against poverty,* ed. S. Derscon. Oxford, U.K.: Oxford University Press.

Munshi, K. 2003. Networks in the modern economy: Mexican migrants in the U.S. labor market. *Quarterly Journal of Economics* 118 (2): 549–599.

Munshi, K., and M. Rosenzweig. 2005. Why is mobility in India so low? Social insurance, inequality, and growth. Department of Economics, Brown University, Providence, R.I.

Narayan, D., and L. Pritchett. 1999. Cents and sociability: Household income and social capital in rural Tanzania. *Economic Development and Cultural Change* 47 (4): 871–897.

Pender, J., and S. J. Scherr. 2002. Organization development and natural resource management: Evidence from Central Honduras. In *Property rights, collective action, and technologies for natural resource management,* ed. R. Meinzen-Dick, A. Knox, F. Place, and B. Swallow. Baltimore: Johns Hopkins University Press.

Place, F., G. Kariuki, J. Wangila, P. Kristjanson, A. Makauki, and J. Ndubi. 2004. Assessing the factors underlying differences in group performance: Methodological issues and empirical findings from the Highlands of Central Kenya. *Agricultural Systems* 82 (3): 257–272.

Powell, J. 1984. Least absolute deviations estimation for the censored regression model. *Journal of Econometrics* 25 (5): 303–325.

Skoufias, E., and A. R. Quisumbing. 2005. Consumption insurance and vulnerability to poverty: A synthesis of the evidence from Bangladesh, Ethiopia, Mali, Mexico, and Russia. *European Journal of Development Research* 17 (1): 24–58.

Townsend, R. 1994. Risk and insurance in village India. *Econometrica* 62 (3): 171–184.

White, T. A., and C. F. Runge. 1994. Common property and collective action: Lessons from cooperative watershed management in Haiti. *Economic Development and Cultural Change* 43 (1): 1–41.

4 Shocks, Groups, and Networks in Bukidnon, the Philippines

AGNES R. QUISUMBING, SCOTT MCNIVEN,
AND MARIE GODQUIN

Because poverty and well-being are determined not only by households' assets and income but also by their vulnerability to shocks over time (Di Gregorio et al., this volume, Chapter 2), it is important to understand the nature and characteristics of risks and shocks, the extent to which a household engages in ex ante risk management, and the extent to which it can engage in ex post risk coping. Collective action, such as membership in formal groups and social networks, can help reduce vulnerability if such groups and networks also function as insurance networks.

This chapter examines the role of groups and networks in helping the poor manage their exposure to risks and cope with shocks to their livelihoods in the rural Philippines. It brings together two strands of the social capital literature: the literature that examines how social capital, variously measured, affects economic variables (for example, Narayan and Pritchett 1999; Haddad and Maluccio 2003) and studies that investigate the processes by which social capital formation, participation in networks and groups, and trusting behavior come about (for instance, Haddad and Maluccio 2003; Fafchamps and Gubert 2007). Specifically, the chapter attempts to answer the following questions:

- What kinds of shocks do rural households face? How do these shocks affect per capita consumption, and does the impact of shocks differ according to household characteristics?
- What kinds of formal and informal groups and networks do households join? Does exposure to risk encourage membership in such groups and networks?
- What are the returns to membership in formal and informal groups and networks?

Because groups and networks often bring together individuals who have different (and conflicting) preferences and objectives, the issue of heterogeneity is important. In this chapter we also attempt to understand how different types of heterogeneity affect network formation and how groups and networks use different mechanisms to enforce behavior in order to achieve their risk-smoothing objectives.

Households can invest in formal and informal social capital. The former is proxied by membership in groups and the number of groups to which one belongs, the latter by the size of trust-based networks. Both groups and networks can be local or spatially diversified. We do not restrict ourselves to local networks in light of recent studies (for example, Munshi and Rosenzweig 2005) that question the assumption that the appropriate unit of risk smoothing is the village (for instance, Townsend 1994). Munshi and Rosenzweig (2005) found that in India consumption is smoothed within subcaste networks that extend beyond the village, whereas the literature on migration and remittances suggests that networks can cross geographic boundaries. This literature is especially relevant to the Philippines given the importance there of both internal and external migration as a livelihood strategy (Quisumbing and McNiven 2005, 2010).

Problems of asymmetric information and limited commitment mean that households are not likely to be fully insured against adverse shocks (Foster and Rosenzweig 2000; Ligon, Thomas, and Worral 2000). However, social norms, such as norms of reciprocity, which are likely to characterize networks of close relatives, might be more effective in enforcing risk-sharing commitments compared to more formal agreements entered into by members of credit groups. In the Cordillera Region of the Philippines, for example, risk sharing appears to occur mostly in very small networks of close friends and families (Fafchamps and Lund 2003)—networks in which enforcement may be easier but there may not be the heterogeneity required to efficiently share risk.

Even though heterogeneity may be important for risk sharing, most empirical studies show a negative or insignificant impact of any type of heterogeneity on collective action or on household incomes (Ahuja 1998; Alesina and La Ferrara 2000; Bardhan 2000; McCarthy and Vanderlinden 2004; Place et al. 2004), with the interesting exception of results reported by Grootaert (2001) for studies in Bolivia, Burkina Faso, and Indonesia. As discussed by Dercon et al. (this volume, Chapter 3), heterogeneity may make finding agreements that are mutually beneficial and acceptable to all more costly, but it may also bring benefits that make risk pooling and information sharing more efficient.

This chapter attempts to address these issues as well as questions of enforcement and compliance using rich longitudinal data and qualitative studies from Bukidnon, Philippines. We first describe the data, the context, and the types of shocks faced by rural households. We then examine their impacts on log per capita consumption, as well as whether these impacts vary across different types of households. We next compare and contrast the determinants of membership in groups and in informal networks, focusing on the role of initial wealth and heterogeneity in the accumulation of social capital. We then examine the returns to membership in two types of groups—formal groups and migrant networks—on various indicators of well-being. We conclude with some reflections on the effectiveness of local and migrant networks in enabling asset accumulation and consumption smoothing.

In relation to the conceptual framework presented in Chapter 2, this study focuses on the role of collective action institutions in the form of formal groups and familial networks in helping households to insure themselves against shocks in order to maintain certain levels of consumption and meet their basic needs (poverty outcomes). It extensively examines the effect of assets on the ability to join groups and networks as well as on patterns of cooperation and mutual assistance (patterns of interaction) to draw conclusions about how the differences in asset endowments and patterns of interaction lead to differences in inclusion in various groups (another poverty outcome). The impact of asset heterogeneity on the severity of shocks' impact is also examined. The action arena here is represented by the social groups and networks, which facilitate accumulation of assets and provide insurance when shocks occur. The actors are mostly internal, represented by group and network members, but interestingly, the internal actors include both local and spatially removed network members. We exploit the spatial heterogeneity among network members to investigate whether local heterogeneity among group members can achieve the same results as spatially diversified members.

In terms of the themes that are of broader interest to this volume, the topic of the potential of collective action to insure against shocks and under what conditions is featured prominently here. The new insight that this chapter brings is our finding that there is a need to spatially diversify networks in certain cases, especially to protect against covariate shocks. In addition to highlighting the dynamic nature of poverty by showing how the welfare of the poor is affected by their exposure to various types of uncertainties, we also show that asset poverty can be manifested not only in low stocks of human, physical, or natural capitals but also in lower stocks of social capital, captured here by the quality and size of households' networks and groups. Although other studies have shown that social capital is often the main asset in the portfolios of the poor, this chapter shows that the poor are at a disadvantage in accumulating this type of asset.

Data and Context

Our data come from a longitudinal study conducted by the International Food Policy Research Institute (IFPRI) and the Research Institute for Mindanao Culture (RIMCU), Xavier University, of households residing in southern Bukidnon, a landlocked province in northern Mindanao comprising 20 municipalities and two cities, Malaybalay and Valencia. (See Figure 4.1, a map of the Philippines and the location of the study area.) The original survey in 1984–85 investigated the effects of agricultural commercialization on the nutrition and house-

FIGURE 4.1 Map of the Philippines indicating the study area

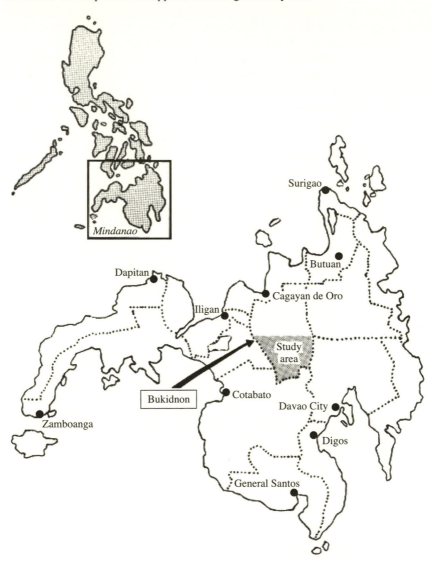

SOURCE: Bouis and Haddad (1990).

hold welfare of these rural families. The survey was fielded in four rounds at four-month intervals from August 1984 to December 1985, so each round corresponded to a different agricultural season. The survey included information on food and nonfood consumption expenditures, agricultural production, income, asset ownership, credit use, anthropometry and morbidity, education, and 24-hour food consumption recall. The initial sample included 510 households, although 448 households were interviewed in all four rounds. Bouis and Haddad (1990) provide a detailed description of the sample design and the survey area.

Following qualitative studies conducted in the study communities in early 2003, IFPRI and RIMCU returned to conduct two rounds of quantitative data collection using a survey questionnaire that closely reflected the one used in 1984–85. The first wave of data collection in the fall of 2003 included interviews of all the original respondents still living in the survey area. We were able to contact 311, or 61 percent, of the original respondents.[1] The respondents listed all children who lived away from home, providing contact information for non-coresident children. We sampled at random up to two non-coresident children living in or near the origin household's village, yielding 261 households.

The second wave of data collection began in April 2004 and ended in July 2004. In this wave the survey team interviewed any households formed by children who no longer lived in their origin *barangays* (villages).[2] These included a large group of households in three major urban areas in Mindanao (Valencia, the commercial center of Bukidnon; Malaybalay, the provincial capital; and Cagayan de Oro, the major metropolitan area in northern Mindanao), as well as many households in *poblaciones* (municipality seats) and other rural areas of Bukidnon. The sample from this migrant wave consisted of 257 households—about 75 percent of potential migrants to be interviewed. Although budgetary concerns did not allow us to interview all children, the survey nonetheless includes data on children who migrated to a variety of rural and urban locations. From the initial interview with the parents we obtained a basic set of information about all children, including location, educational attainment, and marital status. Obtaining this information from parents, plus assiduous follow-up of migrants and children residing in the community, avoided the common problem of sample selection bias if interviews were based only on residence rules (Rosenzweig 2003). The analysis in this chapter is based on 305 of the 311 parent households for which we have complete data (see Table 4.1).

Table 4.1 presents selected household characteristics of parents who were reinterviewed in 2003. The average household head was 55 years of age in 2003. Reflecting changes over the life cycle, household sizes had decreased from 6.8 persons in 1984 to 5.8 in 2003, and dependency ratios had markedly

---

1. Godquin and Quisumbing (2006) modeled the determinants of the probability of being reinterviewed in 2003. They found that older households were less likely to be reinterviewed. The percentage of households affected by peace and order problems contributed to the noninterview probability. However, households with a larger share of female working members in 1984 were more likely to be reinterviewed. Also, the percentage of households in a *barangay* that did not drop out of the study between the first and fourth survey rounds in 1984–85 was associated with higher reinterview probabilities. We have not found significant impacts of attrition on the coefficients estimated for the set of outcomes we consider (participation in groups).

2. Historically, *barangays* are relatively small communities of 50–100 families. Most villages have 30–100 houses, and their populations vary from 100 to 500 persons (Constantino 1975).

TABLE 4.1 Characteristics of parent households in Bukidnon, Philippines, 1984 and 2003

Characteristic	Parent households ($n = 305$)	
	Mean	Standard deviation
Age of household head		
1984	36.31	8.19
2003	54.67	7.63
Years of schooling of household head		
1984	5.73	3.14
2003	6.12	6.07
Household size		
1984	6.83	2.44
2003	5.84	2.74
Dependency ratio		
1984	1.66	0.84
2003	0.49	0.62
Percentage engaged in agriculture		
1984	0.91	0.28
2003	0.71	0.45
Area cultivated (hectares)		
1984	3.17	4.07
2003	3.09	7.27
Percentage with no land		
1984	0.33	0.47
2003	0.61	0.49

SOURCE: Authors' computations.

decreased, from 1.66 to 0.49. Agriculture seems to have become less important to parents as they aged: although 91 percent of parent households had been engaged in agricultural production in 1984, only 71 percent remained active in agriculture, many of them having divested themselves of land. Only 33 percent of parent households had had no land in 1984 (whether owned or rented), whereas 61 percent of parent households no longer had owned or cultivated land in 2003. This should not be interpreted as impoverishment of parent households, because parents typically bestow land on children when the latter marry, not when the parents die. The average area cultivated in 1984 had been 3.17 hectares; in 2003 it was 3.09 hectares.

Shocks in Bukidnon

Like Dercon et al. (this volume, Chapter 3), we define *shocks* as adverse events that lead to a loss of household income, a reduction in consumption, a loss of productive assets, or serious concern or anxiety about household welfare. The data used in this section are based on a household-level "shocks" module developed by Hoddinott and Quisumbing (2003). The survey modules and the classification of shocks we use are the same as in the Dercon et al. study (this volume, Chapter 3). The data on shocks are summarized in Table 4.2.

Drought was the most important shock reported by parents (38.7 percent of those reporting), followed by illness or disability (31.8 percent) and crop pests and diseases (27.5 percent). Death of the household head's spouse or other household member was also important—it was mentioned by 23.6 percent of households. Parent households also reported other weather-related factors (humidity, floods, high winds, and fires) (13.8 percent), as well as crime and peace and order shocks (12.8 percent), as among their worst shocks. Because reporting of shocks may have been subject to respondent bias (for example, wealthier people have more assets that can be stolen and thus may be more likely to report theft and crime shocks, and they have more livestock that can be affected by diseases), in the empirical work we used village-level measures of most shocks, except for illness and death shocks, for which we used household-level reports.

Shocks in the Rural Philippines: An Econometric Assessment

Although Table 4.2 provides a detailed overview of the types of shocks experienced by households, it does not give us a quantitative sense of their consequences or of whether these consequences varied depending on wealth, schooling, and other observable household characteristics. Di Gregorio et al. (this

TABLE 4.2 Household self-reports of the worst shocks experienced in Bukidnon, Philippines, 1984–2003

Type of shock	Percentage of parent households reporting
Drought	38.7
Crop pests and diseases	27.5
Illness or disability (including hospitalization) of household head, spouse, or other person	31.8
Death of household head, spouse, or other person	23.6
Other weather shock (humidity, flood, wind, fire)	13.8
Crime or peace and order shock	12.8
Input shock (lack of financing, high cost of inputs)	7.5
Livestock disease and death	5.6
Political shock (property rights or contract dispute)	5.3
Divorce or abandonment	2.0
Output shock (lack of demand for output) or unemployment	1.6

SOURCE: Authors' computations.

volume, Chapter 2) mention that the impacts of shocks on the poor may be more severe because they may be more exposed to risk and because they may also lose productive assets. For these reasons, we report an econometric assessment of the impact of these shocks on one measure of welfare, log per capita consumption, and examine how the impact of shocks may differ depending on the baseline human and physical capital of households.[3]

Log per capita consumption (*lnpcexp*) of household *i* in village *v* in time *t* is a function of two broad sets of household characteristics—household characteristics observed in the past (time $t - 1$) ($H_{iv,t-1}$) and shocks to households experienced between time $t - 1$ and time t ($S_{iv,t}$)—and community-level variables observed at time t ($X_{iv,t}$), such as the month or season of interview. Vectors of parameters to be estimated were γ, β, and κ. The dependent variable was measured in 2003, whereas the regressors were 1984 values of household characteristics. We used baseline household characteristics because 2003 household characteristics such as current assets, household composition, and levels of schooling of household members could have been affected by shocks in the intervening period and therefore would be endogenous. Denoting $\varepsilon_{iv,t}$ as the white noise disturbance term, we write this relationship as

$$lnpcexp_{iv,t} = \gamma \cdot H_{iv,t-1} + \beta \cdot S_{iv,t} + \kappa \cdot X_{iv,t} + \varepsilon_{iv,t}. \tag{1}$$

Observable household characteristics were characteristics of the household head (age, gender, and schooling), demographic household characteristics (log size and dependency ratio), and household wealth. We did not include gender of the household head in the regressions because none of the households were female headed in 1984. Household wealth was proxied by area cultivated in hectares and the value of net worth. Dummy variables for the household head's being Catholic (the dominant religious group) and having been born in Misamis Oriental were included. Having been born in Misamis Oriental, where the region's metropolitan center is located, may indicate better connections for business and commerce. Dummy variables were included for each surveyed municipality. The implication is that shocks are identified by within-municipality variation, which may make identification of covariate shocks difficult. Nevertheless, although covariate shocks were found in virtually all municipalities, there was no single municipality where drought affected all households unilaterally. Both factors

---

3. The consumption variable was constructed in the following fashion. Food and nonfood consumption were covered in separate modules in the questionnaire. For each food item, households were asked about the amounts they had consumed out of purchases, consumption out of their own stock, and consumption from gifts and in-kind wages in the previous week. With the exception of consumption of their own produce and gifts, which were valued using prices obtained from local market surveys fielded at the same time as the household survey, expenditures on purchased food were reported as they were. Nonfood items were limited to noninvestment goods, so they included consumables such as matches, batteries, soap, kerosene and the like, clothing, and transport but excluded investments in durable goods such as housing. Different recall periods were used for different items; for comparability all were changed into weekly (seven-day) consumption figures and expressed in per capita terms.

appeared to allow identification of the impact of these relatively covariate events in our data. These consumption regressions were estimated using ordinary least squares (OLS); note that although we have longitudinal data, we used past values as control variables instead of estimating a panel data model.

The shock data consist of dummy variables on each type of shock reported by each household—for example, whether the household experienced drought— and therefore do not indicate the severity of the shock. To minimize respondent bias and to obtain some indicator of severity of shocks, we aggregated common shocks into the following categories: the percentage of households in the village affected by a drought; too much rain or pests or diseases that affected field crops or crops in storage; pests or diseases that affected livestock; difficulty in obtaining inputs or increases in input prices; inability to sell outputs or decreases in output prices; and peace and order problems. We used the more general "peace and order shock" instead of "crime and theft shock" because the latter is more likely to be tainted by respondent bias. Illness and death shocks were disaggregated into illness of the household head or his spouse, illness of another household member, death of the household head or his spouse, and death of another household member.

Table 4.3 presents regression results showing the impact of shocks and other covariates on log consumption per capita in Bukidnon, controlling for household characteristics in 1984, and disaggregating on the basis of landholdings, net worth, and years of schooling in 1984. This allowed us to examine how initial physical and human assets mediate the impact of shocks. The percentage of households affected by drought—henceforth a drought shock, for brevity— decreased per capita consumption by 11 percent for all households. However, it is clear that the impact of shocks differed greatly across types of households.

Drought shocks had the greatest impact on households whose landholdings were below the median size, on households with below-median net worth of assets, and on households with greater than median levels of schooling. Crop and livestock pests and diseases significantly reduced the consumption of households without land in 1984 and households with landholdings below the median size but increased the consumption of households with land, households with above-median landholding size, and households with above-median net worth. Input shocks reduced the per capita consumption of those with less than median schooling but increased it for those with above-median schooling and those with no land in 1984. It is possible that these households were less likely to be engaged in agriculture and were in fact net suppliers of labor (in the case of those with no land) and other inputs (for those with above-median schooling, who could be engaged in nonagricultural occupations). Output shocks do not appear to have affected per capita consumption significantly.

Death and illness are shocks that are truly idiosyncratic. Both death and illness were disaggregated depending on whether the death (illness) was that of the household head or his spouse or of another household member. We found that the death of the household head or his spouse significantly reduced the log

TABLE 4.3 Impact of shocks on log consumption per capita in 350 parent households in Bukidnon, Philippines, 2003

Shock, 1984–2003	All households		No land in 1984		Had land in 1984		Below median land size, 1984	
	Coefficient	t-statistic	Coefficient	t-statistic	Coefficient	t-statistic	Coefficient	t-statistic
Shock affecting all households in village								
Drought	−0.11	−1.92**	−0.14	−1.38	−0.10	−0.90	−0.20	−3.90***
Excessive rain or flooding	0.10	1.38	0.06	0.60	0.05	0.43	0.12	1.67*
Crop or livestock pests or disease	0.04	1.18	−0.13	−3.15**	0.11	2.71***	−0.10	−3.98***
Input shock	0.03	0.09	1.17	3.03***	−0.41	−0.50	0.45	1.24
Output shock	0.16	1.04	0.32	1.36	0.10	0.48	0.05	0.33
Peace and order problem	−0.04	−0.54	−0.01	−0.05	−0.04	−0.19	0.05	0.52
Idiosyncratic shock								
Death of household head or spouse	−0.07	−0.67	0.35	1.24	−0.20	−2.11**	0.33	1.43
Death of another person	0.08	0.97	0.43	3.52**	0.01	0.04	0.19	1.64
Illness of household head or spouse	0.18	1.39	−0.04	−0.25	0.27	1.46	−0.03	−0.27
Illness of another person	0.10	1.45	−0.02	−0.11	0.09	0.71	0.09	0.52

SOURCE: Authors' computations.

NOTES: Regressions included control variables as of 1984: log of age of the household head, years of schooling of household head, log of household size, dependency ratio, net worth, area cultivated, whether household head was Catholic, and whether the household head was born in Misamis Oriental. Whether a household had land in 1984 refers to whether it had either owned or rented land. Median land size in 1984 was 1.75 hectares.

consumption per capita for households that had land in 1984 and for households above the median landholding size in 1984. Households that had more land were probably engaged in agricultural production, so their consumption was more vulnerable to the loss of an adult working member, particularly either the household head or his spouse. In contrast, the death of another person increased the per capita consumption of households without land. This may simply be an artifact of construction of the dependent variable: death reduces household size and therefore the denominator of the dependent variable. Illness did not significantly affect consumption in the aggregate or across household types.

Additional regressions that divided the shocks into two time intervals allowed us to investigate whether shocks have long-term and persistent impacts. Regressions not reported here (see Quisumbing, McNiven, and Godquin 2008 for details) indicated that for all households the 1987/88 drought had a larger and more persistent negative impact than the 1997/98 drought, indicating that

Above median land size, 1984		Below median net worth, 1984		Above median net worth, 1984		Below median schooling, 1984		Above median schooling, 1984	
Coefficient	*t*-statistic	Coefficient	*t*-statistic	Coefficient	*t*-statistic	Coefficient	*t*-statistic	Coefficient	*t*-statistic
−0.03	−0.44	−0.16	−2.28**	−0.04	−0.38	−0.05	−0.32	−0.27	−5.81***
−0.01	−0.07	−0.08	−1.54	0.12	0.68	−0.19	−0.67	0.20	1.60
0.10	2.73***	−0.06	−1.26	0.12	2.70***	0.08	1.95*	0.03	0.74
−0.35	−0.63	0.28	1.09	−0.56	−0.75	−0.96	−2.86***	1.27	3.60***
0.11	0.31	0.23	0.90	0.22	1.23	0.23	0.56	−0.09	−0.52
−0.25	−0.87	0.15	0.88	−0.20	−0.73	0.30	0.63	−0.13	−1.31
−0.30	−3.80***	−0.14	−0.85	−0.11	−1.03	−0.18	−1.49	0.03	0.18
0.01	0.04	0.13	1.28	−0.06	−0.56	0.09	0.87	0.08	0.60
0.36	1.42	0.05	0.50	0.08	0.36	0.06	0.66	0.36	1.60
0.20	1.29	−0.01	−0.07	0.27	1.38	0.10	0.83	0.11	0.88

Median net worth in 1984 was 7,580 pesos. Median years of schooling of household head in 1984 was 6 years. Standard errors were calculated using the Huber–White method. Municipality dummies were included but not reported. A constant term was estimated but not reported. * means significant at the 10 percent level; ** means significant at the 5 percent level; *** means significant at the 1 percent level.

drought response mechanisms may have improved in recent years. Not surprisingly, short- and longer-term impacts also differed across household types.

Groups and Networks in Bukidnon

If groups and networks perform an insurance function, we would expect past shocks to have increased membership in groups and networks. We tested this hypothesis using data on groups and networks observed in Bukidnon (see Godquin and Quisumbing 2006, 2008 for a more detailed exposition). Respondents in the 2003 round of the Philippine survey were asked about formal groups and informal networks to which they belonged. The group membership module asked the household members to list all the groups, associations, and cooperatives to which at least one household member belonged. Households provided information on a total of 689 groups, which were classified into production, credit, burial, religious, and civic groups. As a measure of social networks, each household was also asked about the number of persons to whom it can turn for help on specific occasions. Such events mobilize different aspects of social capital, such as trust, mutual insurance, information pooling, or copying (as in adopting neighbors' farming practices). Trust-related questions dealt with care of the house, care of children, and family problems, whereas questions related to economic networks were related to networks for coping with economic loss, receiving price information, and adopting technology. These questions were informed by discussions with Filipino researchers who were familiar with the local culture and were field tested by the authors.[4]

Households in the Philippines can count on various social and economic networks for support (Table 4.4). Membership in groups is widespread, with 76 percent of parent households belonging to at least one group. Parent households belonged to an average of 1.6 groups, with the proportion of households belonging to at least one group and the average number of groups to which a household belonged increasing steadily by asset quartile.

Religious groups were the most frequently mentioned groups, with 34 percent of the households belonging to at least one religious group. Civic groups were the least commonly mentioned type of group, with 15 percent of the households belonging to at least one such group. Household participation in religious, burial, and civic groups increased across asset quartiles but not steeply; however, participation in production and credit groups increased markedly as wealth increased. This suggests that lack of wealth may be a greater barrier to participation in economic versus noneconomic groups.

The types of groups to which households belong are quite diversified compared to other countries, such as Kenya and Senegal, where the most important groups are village women's or men's groups that engage in diversified activities (Kariuki and Place 2005). Godquin and Quisumbing (2008) investigated the determinants of men's and women's participation in groups. They found that although men and women have equal probabilities of participating in groups and belong to the same number of groups, men tend to belong to production and burial groups, women to civic and religious groups.

Households also belonged to a number of diverse networks dealing with social and economic matters. Table 4.4 presents information on the various networks on which households could rely for help in specific matters. The "all networks" variable was the sum of persons in all of a household's networks and could have overstated the size of the total network, because it is possible that the same person belonged to more than one trust-based network.[5] Across quartiles, virtually all households reporting had at least one person to whom they could turn for help on various matters, although this may have been an

---

4. See Godquin and Quisumbing (2008) for details and the exact wording of the questions.

5. Unlike in Ethiopia, we did not ask households to name the persons in their network, so we could not check whether the same person belonged to different types of networks.

artifact of the definition of this variable. Looking at various types of networks, 75 percent of households reported having a network to which to turn in case of economic loss, with the highest asset quartile the best insured with respect to economic loss (82 percent of households reported being able to turn to someone in case of severe economic losses in contrast to 71 percent of households in the lowest quartile). Only 48 percent of households reported having a network for technology adoption and copying, perhaps because farmers tended to rely on the formal extension system rather than their neighbors for information on new technologies. The study site was near an agricultural university that has active extension programs; also, the Department of Agriculture's extension agents conduct regular technology dissemination activities. On average, the number of persons to whom households could turn in case of important economic loss was larger than for the other scenarios.

Although it might seem that membership in groups and the sizes of a household's networks should have increased with asset ownership, these differences in means might also have arisen from characteristics of the households that also affected their propensity to join groups. Therefore, we explored the determinants of group membership and network size using econometric analysis. We investigated the impact of household physical and human capital as well as various aspects of village heterogeneity on membership in groups and networks, controlling for individual, household, and community characteristics. Among the community characteristics of interest are measures of heterogeneity at the village level, following Alesina and La Ferrara (2000). These are measures of ethnic, origin, education, and asset heterogeneity. We also included (from the community questionnaire) the cumulative proportion of households affected by peace and order problems since 1984 and by programs operating in the *barangay* during the previous year (2000–01).

Table 4.5 presents a tobit regression of the determinants of the total number of groups to which a household belonged. Both the human capital and the physical capital of the households were strongly associated with the accumulation of formal social capital. Whether the household head had completed secondary schooling and the percentage of household members with more than primary schooling positively and significantly affected the total number of groups to which the household belonged. Relative to the highest asset quartile, households belonging to the lower asset quartiles belonged to fewer groups. Catholic households also belonged to more groups, a result that was driven by membership in religious groups. Not surprisingly, distance from the town center reduced the total number of groups to which a household belonged. Consistent with our hypothesis that groups perform an insurance function, households that had experienced more negative shocks in the past belonged to more groups.

Group membership was lower in villages with higher ethnic diversity and higher asset heterogeneity, while education heterogeneity had a weak negative effect. Political unrest had a weak positive impact on the number of groups to which a household belonged, whereas the number of cooperatives had a strong

TABLE 4.4 Formal and informal networks of parent households in Bukidnon, Philippines, by 1984 asset quartile, 2003

Type of group	All parent households	Lowest quartile	Second quartile	Third quartile	Highest quartile
Formal groups					
Percentage of households participating in groups	0.76	0.56	0.75	0.80	0.84
Total number of groups to which a household belonged	1.57	1.00	1.41	1.53	2.05
Percentage of households with at least one member in a group, by type of group					
Production group	0.27	0.06	0.14	0.30	0.46
Credit group	0.21	0.15	0.19	0.21	0.27
Burial group	0.31	0.27	0.29	0.34	0.33
Religious group	0.34	0.29	0.41	0.34	0.30
Civic group	0.15	0.13	0.18	0.09	0.19
Networks					
Percentage of households with at least one person in a network, by purpose of network					
All networks	1.00	1.00	1.00	1.00	1.00

Specific-purpose networks

Care of house	0.53	0.52	0.48	0.50	0.60
Family problems	0.58	0.44	0.65	0.56	0.62
Child care	0.52	0.51	0.48	0.50	0.59
Economic loss	0.75	0.71	0.73	0.70	0.82
Price information	0.69	0.75	0.62	0.65	0.75
Technology adoption	0.48	0.55	0.40	0.44	0.54
Total number of persons in a household's network[a]	13.21	11.23	11.97	13.21	15.32
Size of specific networks (number of persons), by purpose of network					
Care of house	1.79	1.60	1.75	1.72	2.00
Family problems	2.33	1.81	2.19	2.50	2.56
Child care	1.66	1.54	1.66	1.68	1.73
Economic loss	3.38	2.79	2.89	3.06	4.41
Price information	2.40	2.29	1.93	2.49	2.68
Technology adoption	1.80	1.64	1.68	1.72	1.98

SOURCE: Authors' computations.

[a]Defined as the sum of persons across all networks.

TABLE 4.5 Determinants of the total number of groups in Bukidnon, Philippines, 2003

Variable	Tobit regression, all groups	
	Coefficient	*t*-statistic
Age of the household head, 2003	−0.015	−0.09
Age squared	0.000	0.14
Whether household head completed secondary schooling (10 years or more)	0.803	2.92***
Percentage of household members with at least 6 years of schooling, 1984	0.798	2.78***
Log household size, 1984	0.283	0.89
Dependency ratio, 1984	0.045	0.29
Asset quartile, 1984 (highest excluded)		
Lowest asset quartile	−0.825	−2.23**
Second asset quartile	−0.692	−2.50**
Third asset quartile	−0.786	−3.15***
Whether household was an agricultural producer in 1984	−0.169	−0.59
Whether household had a nonagricultural business in 1984	0.083	0.40
Whether household head was Catholic, 1984	0.743	2.28**
Distance to *poblacion* (town center), in kilometers	−0.186	−5.59***
Number of shocks, 1984–2002	0.134	1.99**
Barangay (village)–level variables		
Origin heterogeneity	0.682	0.82
Ethnic heterogeneity	−1.596	−3.15***
Asset heterogeneity	−0.759	−3.22***
Education heterogeneity	−2.436	−1.89*
Percentage of households affected by peace or order problems	0.004	1.86*
Programs operating in *barangay,* 2000–01		
Cooperatives	−0.674	−3.31***
Nongovernmental organizations	−0.159	−0.85
Government organizations	0.061	0.44
Mean of total value of nonland assets, 1984 (household excluded)	−0.002	−1.38
Constant	3.829	0.83
Sigma	1.462	20.85***
Number of observations	311	
Left-censored observations	75	
Uncensored observations	236	
Wald chi-squared (23 degrees of freedom)	142.62	
Probability > chi-squared	0.00	
Pseudo R^2	0.1281	

SOURCE: Authors' computations.

NOTES: * means significant at the 10 percent level; ** means significant at the 5 percent level; *** means significant at the 1 percent level.

negative effect. The unexpected impact of cooperatives on the number of groups can be explained by the negative reputation of the cooperative movement in the Philippines. Cooperatives have often been formed for political purposes, and the cooperative movement in the Philippines has risen and fallen depending on support from government officials.[6]

Do formal groups substitute for informal trust-based networks? Group membership can both increase the size of a household's network and be facilitated by a household's network if members of networks have better access to information or if membership in one group is restricted to acquaintances of current group members. Alternatively, membership in formal groups can substitute for informal networks if households turn to formal institutions to provide services—for example, risk sharing, credit, insurance—that were formerly provided through the households' informal social networks. To investigate this issue, we estimated a regression on the size of a household's network, defined as the sum of the number of persons to which the household could turn for help. As mentioned earlier, this variable may have overestimated the number of persons who could actually assist a household, because it would have double counted persons who provided help in different ways. To address the issue of double counting, we also estimated regressions separately for each type of network, but here we report the results only for total network size.

Household network density can be modeled as a function of household characteristics and village-level attributes. The household characteristics we included were the age and education level of the household head, household size, household demographic composition, asset position, and the number of shocks experienced since 1984. Because personal relationships may affect network formation more than economic considerations (Fafchamps and Gubert 2007), we included measures of kinship relationships within and outside the village: the number of sons and daughters living inside and outside the village. We also included the measures of village-level heterogeneity described earlier.

An underlying question is whether participation in groups increases network-based social capital. We treated participation in groups as endogenous, using as instruments variables that affected whether households joined groups but did not affect the size of the network. These variables were whether the household was a sugar producer, whether the household head was Catholic in 1984, *barangay* heterogeneity indexes in 1984, per capita expenditures on groups in 1984, and the mean number of groups in the *barangay,* excluding the household. Both OLS and instrumental variables estimates, in which group mem-

---

6. Cooperatives were encouraged during the Marcos regime, for example, especially for agrarian reform beneficiaries. Many of these cooperatives fell into disarray in subsequent years. The cooperatives movement paled in comparison to the rise of nongovernmental organizations during the Aquino administration but seems to have recovered with support from the Ramos administration.

TABLE 4.6 Determinants of the sum of all networks in Bukidnon, Philippines, 2003

| | Sum of all networks | | | |
| | Ordinary least squares | | Instrumental variable (IV) | |
Variable	Coefficient	z-value	Coefficient	z-value
Number of groups, 2003 (endogenous in IV)	0.015	0.07	0.080	0.13
Age of household head	0.121	1.22	0.116	1.23
Education of household head, 1984	0.394	2.61***	0.391	2.12**
Log of household size, 2003	0.286	0.18	0.236	0.16
Percentage of household members in 2003 who were				
Aged 0–14	0.295	0.13	0.603	0.28
Aged 15–19	−1.148	−0.45	0.988	−0.42
Aged 55 and over	2.706	1.01	2.873	1.18
Total household asset value in 1984	0.008	1.99**	0.008	2.24**
Other household characteristics				
Number of shocks, 1985–2003	0.465	1.65*	0.470	1.67*
Barangay (village) heterogeneity				
Origin heterogeneity	1.718	0.46	1.656	0.39
Asset heterogeneity (1984)	−2.004	−1.14	1.632	−0.83
Ethnicity of household head	0.001	0.64	0.001	0.76
Education of household head	0.115	0.29	0.068	0.18
Location of children living outside household				
Number of daughters living outside village	−0.539	−2.15**	0.538	−2.09**
Number of daughters living in village	0.060	0.09	0.105	0.16
Number of sons living outside village	−0.214	−0.70	0.206	−0.68
Number of sons living in village	0.925	1.38	0.866	1.34
Constant	1.672	0.24	1.902	0.28
Number of observations	304		304	
F (17, 29 degrees of freedom)	7.36		8.26	
Probability $> F$	0.00		0.00	
Centered R^2	0.13		0.13	
Uncentered R^2			0.79	
Root mean square error	7.20		6.98	
Test of exogeneity: H_0: Regressor is exogenous				
Wu–Hausman F-test (p-value)			0.022	0.88
Durbin–Wu–Hausman chi-squared test (p-value)			0.023	0.88
Instrumental variable diagnostics				
Shea partial R^2 test (F, p-value)			15.90	0.00
Anderson identification / IV relevance test (chi-squared, p-value)			59.77	0.00
Hansen J-statistic (overidentification test) (chi-squared, p-value)			9.71	0.21

SOURCE: Authors' computations.

NOTES: Regressions were estimated with attrition weights; standard errors are robust to clustering within *barangays*. * means significant at the 10 percent level; ** means significant at the 5 percent level; *** means significant at the 1 percent level.

bership was treated as endogenous, are presented in Table 4.6; exogeneity tests led us to accept the null hypothesis that the number of groups is exogenous.

Surprisingly, the total number of groups to which a household belonged did not affect the density of its networks. Human capital and physical capital contribute to the size of social networks: education of the household head and total asset value in 1984 both had positive and significant coefficients. There was some weak indication that networks perform a risk-smoothing function, because the number of shocks experienced since 1984 increased the number of persons to whom a household could turn for help. Interestingly, the number of daughters living outside the villages exerted a strong negative influence on the size of a household's local trust-based networks.

Do these results hold for different types of networks? Regressions not reported here examined the determinants of the size of three different types of social networks (those for care of house, dealing with family problems, and child care) and three types of economic networks (networks related to economic loss, price information, and technology information), with the number of groups as one of the regressors (treated as endogenous). What was remarkable in all these regressions was that the number of groups was almost always insignificant, indicating that the number of groups to which a household belongs does not significantly impact the formation of social and economic networks. Unlike in the regressions on group membership, very few variables related to the economic status of the household were significant in the economic network variables. Households that were wealthier, as indicated by total asset value in 1984, were slightly more likely to have larger networks that insure against economic loss, while the asset heterogeneity of the *barangay* reduced the size of these networks. Joining networks for price information may have been driven by risk-pooling considerations, with households experiencing more negative shocks since 1984 having larger networks for price information. However, a striking finding, similar to the findings of Fafchamps and Gubert (2007), was the importance of pre-existing personal relationships as drivers of economic trust-based networks. The larger the number of daughters living outside the village, the smaller were networks related to price information and new technologies. The size of networks for new technologies, however, was positively associated with the number of sons living inside the village but in separate households.

Our findings suggest that sons and daughters perform different functions in social and economic networks—a finding that can be traced to the different roles of men and women in Filipino society. Daughters are trained to be responsible and often play the role of insurers, migrating to towns and cities and then sending remittances to their origin households (Lauby and Stark 1988). The number of daughters living outside their origin village negatively affects the combined number of persons in all networks and the number of people in price information and technology adoption networks. Perhaps daughters living outside the village are a reliable source of information about price trends and new technologies. In contrast, sons who are living in separate households within the village are more likely to be engaged in agricultural production themselves and are a local source of technology information for parents.

Although the total number of groups does not capture differences in group objectives, which could have affected network density depending on the type of network, the results of regressions not reported here did not show that membership in a particular group consistently affected the size of a particular network.[7] In almost all cases, the coefficient of membership in a specific group was insignificant. We therefore conclude that different motivations drive participation in groups and social networks and that formal group membership neither substitutes for nor encourages the formation of trust-based networks. Because trust-based networks tend to be based on personal relationships (Fafchamps and Gubert 2007), economic factors are not the most important determinants of such networks.

Economic Returns to Groups and Networks in the Philippines

The regressions on group membership and on total network size suggest that negative shocks increase households' participation in groups and the size of their networks. In the present analysis, we do not provide definitive evidence that participation in groups and networks reduces the impact of shocks in the Philippines. Rather, we explore whether participation in groups yields economic returns in terms of increased per capita expenditures, the extent to which migrant networks form in response to shocks, and their possible impact on sending households.

To explore whether group membership generates economic returns, we estimated the impact of group membership—the total number of groups—on per capita expenditures using two-stage least squares to control for the potential endogeneity of group membership. As reported in the preceding section, we investigated whether the number of groups to which a household belonged had an impact on per capita expenditures. We regressed log per capita expenditures on human capital of the household head (age in 2003, whether the household head completed primary education, whether he completed secondary education), household demographics (log household size and dependency ratio in 1984), asset quartiles in 1984, the area of titled land in 2003, the *barangay* average of titled land in 2003 (excluding the household), and dummies for productive status.

Both OLS and independent variable (IV) estimates are reported in Table 4.7, with exogeneity tests leading us to accept the null hypothesis, that the total

---

7. In most cases, the first-stage diagnostics suggested that the instrument set was weak. Alternatively, where the Cragg–Donald statistics were in an acceptable range, we rejected the over-identification test.

TABLE 4.7 Impact of group membership on per capita expenditures in Bukidnon, Philippines, 2003

Variable	Ordinary least squares		Instrumental variable (IV)	
	Coefficient	z-value	Coefficient	z-value
Total number of groups (endogenous)	0.127	5.07***	0.163	3.99***
Age of household head	0.015	1.81*	0.015	1.87*
Log household size, 1984	−0.237	−1.55	−0.240	−1.68*
Dependency ratio, 1984	−0.143	−2.71***	−0.149	−2.81***
Household head has some elementary schooling	0.176	2.05**	0.170	2.07**
Household head has some secondary schooling or better	0.304	3.12***	0.267	2.50**
Asset quartiles, 1984 (highest excluded)				
Lowest quartile	−0.412	−3.19***	−0.380	−3.15***
Second quartile	−0.350	−3.54***	−0.328	−3.36***
Third quartile	−0.142	−1.41	−0.121	−1.28
Area of titled land, 2003	0.039	8.06***	0.039	8.33***
Barangay (village) average area of titled land (household excluded)	0.030	2.15**	0.034	2.46**
Agricultural household, 2003	0.005	0.11	0.002	0.04
Household had nonagricultural business, 2003	0.080	1.00	0.070	0.87
Constant	5.605	13.75***	5.560	14.08***
Number of observations	304		304	
F (13, 29 degrees of freedom)	57.90		42.53	
Probability $> F$	0.00		0.00	
R^2	0.44			
Test of exogeneity: H_0: Regressor is exogenous				
Wu–Hausman F-test (p-value)			0.94	0.33
Durbin–Wu–Hausman chi-squared test			0.99	0.32
Instrumental variable diagnostics				
F-test on excluded instruments (F-test, p-value)			21.38	0.00
Anderson canonical correlation likelihood ratio statistic (identification/IV relevance test) (chi-squared, p-value)			85.008	0.00
Hansen J-statistic (overidentification test) (chi-squared, p-value)			8.162	0.32

SOURCE: Authors' computations.

NOTES: Instrumental variables were estimated with attrition weights; standard errors are robust to clustering within *barangay*. Excluded instruments were as follows: whether the household was a sugar producer, whether the household head was Catholic in 1984. *Barangay* heterogeneity indexes in 1984 were as follows: origin, ethnicity, assets, education, per capita expenditures on groups in 1984, *barangay* mean number of groups (households excluded). * means significant at the 10 percent level; ** means significant at the 5 percent level; *** means significant at the 1 percent level.

number of groups can be taken as exogenous in a regression on per capita expenditures. The total number of groups to which a household belonged had a positive and significant impact on log per capita expenditures, while the signs of the other coefficients were as expected. However, the total number of groups might mask the impact of individual groups. Because participation in economically oriented groups might have a higher impact on per capita expenditures, we also explored alternative specifications in which group membership reflected membership in production, credit, burial, religious, and civic groups, respectively. These results, which are not reported here, suggest that membership in burial, religious, and civic groups had a significant positive impact on per capita expenditures.

We are unable to investigate whether social networks also yield economic benefits because we lack credible instruments that affect social networks but do not directly affect per capita expenditures. Insights from the qualitative work conducted among respondent households that experienced covariate and idiosyncratic shocks, however, suggest that local networks have only a limited ability to help households cope with shocks. Several respondents mentioned that they felt embarrassed to ask for help from their friends and neighbors, who were also poor and faced similar problems—even in the case of a household-specific shock such as illness (prior to the introduction of government-provided health insurance). Local networks can offer limited support in the case of a covariate shock. When faced with negative shocks, households use a variety of coping mechanisms—working harder, relying on help from children who have left the home and are now working, borrowing money from informal sources, and selling or mortgaging assets.

Studies of collective action typically focus on nonfamilial groups. However, both the anthropological literature (see the review by Arce 2003) and the economic literature on the Philippines suggest that kinship affects participation in groups, notably risk-sharing networks (Fafchamps and Lund 2003; Fafchamps and Gubert 2007). The findings from our analysis of trust-based networks also suggest that "migration capital" and "local social capital" are substitutes. Given these findings, we examined the role of familial migrant networks in consumption smoothing. In our study sample, close to half—47 percent—of children 15 and older were migrants to rural, periurban, and urban areas in the Philippines, as well as overseas. Reflecting the national pattern, a higher proportion of migrants was female. Households with migrant children may invest less in local social capital because they can rely on transfers from their migrant children, particularly their daughters. We investigated this issue by examining the impact of migration and remittances, both endogenously determined, on various measures of the well-being of parent households (in this we drew from Quisumbing and McNiven 2010).

Table 4.8 presents estimates of the probability of having an adult migrant child (21 years of age and older), the number of migrants 21 years of age and older, the probability of receiving remittances from outside the *barangay,* and the amount received. Marginal effects are presented—that is, the change in the dependent variable resulting from a one-unit change in the regressor. We found that both household and community characteristics played an important role in the migration decision. Although the education of the household head had a weak negative impact on the number of adult migrants, greater educational attainment of the children themselves increased both the probability of their migrating and the stock of migrants, with daughters' completed schooling having a larger impact than sons'. Villages that had been connected to the main highway for a longer time tended to have fewer migrants, perhaps because workers could commute to the town center instead of having to relocate, but villages that had had electricity for longer periods tended to have more migrants. Finally, the percentage of migrants from other households in a *barangay* exerted a negative influence on both the probability of migration and the number of migrants. This result is somewhat counterintuitive, because other studies (see, for example, Winters, de Janvry, and Sadoulet 2000) have shown that potential migrants in communities with larger numbers of migrants are able to take advantage of information networks formed by former migrants. However, in communities where a large number of families are related and where migration rates are already high, there may be diminishing returns to additional migration.

Although parental wealth affects neither the probability of receipts from migrant children nor the amount received, remittances appear to perform a consumption-smoothing function. Cumulative shocks up to 2002 increased both the likelihood of receiving remittances and the amounts received. Schooling attainment of daughters, but not of sons, increased both the probability of receipt and the amounts received. This finding is consistent with those of previous studies (Lauby and Stark 1988; Quisumbing 1997) showing that females, particularly better-educated females, are more likely to make remittances to parents. Although positive shocks to migrant incomes increased both the probability of receipt and the amounts received, the marginal effects of shocks experienced by daughters were larger than those of sons. A 1 percent positive deviation from GDP in a region where a migrant son was located would increase remittance receipts by 1,420 pesos; if the 1 percent positive shock occurred in a region where a daughter lived, it would increase remittances by 1,988 pesos. These results support our earlier findings that parents invest less in local networks if they have more daughters living outside the village. Clearly, households' risk management strategies involve investing not only in local networks but also in migrant kin networks.

How do migration and remittances affect parent households? Table 4.9 presents the coefficient estimates for the number of migrants 21 years of age and older and the remittances for various outcomes of the parental household. Both migration and remittances were treated as endogenous in the IV regressions. Our estimates suggest that investment in migrant networks involves trade-

TABLE 4.8 Determinants of the probability of having a migrant child, number of migrant children, the probability of receiving remittances, and total remittances received in Bukidnon, Philippines, 2003

		Parents who were re-interviewed in 2003					
	Probability of having a migrant child over 21		Number of migrant children over 21		Probability of receiving remittances: Probit		Total remittances received: Tobit	
Variable	dF/dx	z-value	dy/dx	z-value	dF/dx	z-value	dy/dx	z-value
Age of household head, 2003	0.057	2.05**	0.190	1.57	-0.094	-2.00**	-1.407	-0.77
Age of head squared	0.000	-1.68*	-0.001	-0.79	0.001	2.02**	0.011	0.69
Education of household head	-0.001	-0.19	-0.054	-1.68*	0.005	0.43	0.556	1.14
Ln net worth in 1984/85	-0.009	-0.53	-0.105	-1.32	-0.032	-1.22	-0.418	-0.35
Area cultivated in 1984/85	-0.004	-0.68	0.016	0.53	-0.003	-0.31	0.386	0.86
Distance to town center	0.001	0.22	0.020	0.69	-0.009	-1.02	-0.693	-1.66*
Cumulative shocks, 1984–2002	0.018	1.10	0.085	1.13	0.090	3.44***	1.997	1.74*
Number of sons 21 years of age and older	0.006	0.44	-0.018	-0.32	-0.013	-0.69	-1.317	-1.57
Number of daughters 21 years of age and older	-0.010	-0.92	0.048	0.89	-0.014	-0.78	-0.030	-0.04
Mean education of sons 21 years of age and older	0.013	2.45***	0.077	3.06***	0.011	1.26	0.647	1.60
Mean education of daughters 21 years of age and older	0.021	4.65***	0.111	5.39***	0.013	1.80*	0.807	2.45**

	(1)		(2)		(3)		(4)	
	dF/dx	z	dy/dx	z	dF/dx	z	dy/dx	z
Length of time road had connected village to town	−0.004	−2.08**	−0.013	−1.87*	0.006	2.36**	0.327	2.87***
Length of time village had been electrified	0.009	2.18**	0.046	2.51**	−0.023	−3.50***	−1.088	−3.80***
Percentage of migrants from other households in village	−0.004	−2.68***	−0.029	−3.86***				
Percentage deviation from trend GDP in 2002, male migrants					0.042	2.13**	1.420	1.88*
Percentage deviation from trend GDP in 2002, female migrants					0.075	4.04***	1.988	2.91***
Observed probability	0.80				0.61			
Predicted probability	0.88				0.64			
Left-censored observations			59				111	
Uncensored observations			236				184	
Number of observations	295		295		295		295	
Likelihood ratio chi-squared	70.24		155.81		53.24		55.69	
Probability > chi-squared	0.00		0.00		0.00		0.00	
Pseudo R^2	0.31		0.13		0.17		0.01	

SOURCE: Authors' computations.

NOTES: Probit z-values computed using robust standard errors. dF/dx is the marginal effect: the change in the probability resulting from a one-unit change in the independent variable; dy/dx is the change in the number of migrant children over 21 resulting from a one-unit change in the independent variable. * means significant at the 10 percent level; ** means significant at the 5 percent level; *** means significant at the 1 percent level.

TABLE 4.9 Impact of migration and remittances on asset holdings and consumption expenditures of parent households in Bukidnon, Philippines, 2003

	Coefficient for number of migrants		Coefficient for remittances	
	Instrumental variable			
Outcome	Coefficient	z-value	Coefficient	z-value
Household assets, 2003				
Farm and business equipment	−0.219	−0.01	2.158	1.43
Livestock	−0.865	−0.80	0.127	1.40
Housing and consumer durables	−46.555	−2.01**	5.127	2.14**
Total nonland assets	−184.311	−1.67*	12.677	1.81*
Value of land	−136.673	−1.52	5.266	1.17
Value of land and assets	−320.984	−1.62	17.943	1.59
Expenditures per adult equivalent, 2003				
Total expenditure	−136.786	−2.74***	8.855	1.97**
Food	−21.113	−1.53	1.136	1.27
Clothing and footwear	−5.366	−1.97**	0.636	3.06***
Health	−13.058	−1.79*	0.625	1.44
Education	−13.636	−1.16	2.276	2.60***
Family events	−23.821	−2.10**	1.313	1.53
Alcohol and tobacco	−4.467	−3.37***	0.255	2.11**
Partial R^2 of excluded instruments	0.243		0.0647	
F-test of excluded instruments	20.31		2.200	
p-value	0.00		0.05	
Cragg–Donald weak identification statistic	2.090			
Anderson canonical correlation likelihood ratio statistic	19.56			
p-value	0.01			

SOURCE: Authors' computations.

NOTES: Instrumental variable regressions were estimated with attrition weights; standard errors are robust to clustering within villages. Regressors in outcome equation are as follows: age of household head, age squared, average years of schooling completed by household head, net worth in round 1 of 1984/85, area cultivated in round 1 of 1984, distance to town center, number of males older than 15 in household, number of females older than 15 in household, number of household members 15 years of age and younger, cumulative shocks up to 2002. Instruments are as follows: number of sons 21 years of age and older, number of daughters 21 years of age and older, length of time village had been connected to main road, length of time village had been electrified, average years of schooling completed by sons and daughters 21 years of age and over, percentage GDP deviation of migrant sons, percentage GDP deviation of migrant daughters, proportion of migrants from other households in village. * means significant at the 10 percent level; ** means significant at the 5 percent level; *** means significant at the 1 percent level.

offs. The number of migrants had significant negative impacts on expenditures on clothing and footwear, family events, alcohol, and tobacco and a weak negative impact on health expenditures (all per adult equivalent). Remittances, on the other hand, had significant positive impacts on housing and consumer durables and on the total value of nonland assets and total expenditure per adult equivalent. Similarly, expenditures on clothing and footwear, education, and alcohol and tobacco increased significantly with remittances. Clearly, financing the educational expenditures of family members is an important use of remittances. These positive impacts on productive assets and schooling mirror the findings of Yang (2004), who reported that favorable exchange rate shocks for overseas Filipino migrants led to more child schooling, reduced child labor, and increased educational expenditures in origin households.

Conclusions and Policy Implications

Using longitudinal data from Bukidnon, followed up with focused qualitative work in the survey villages, we have attempted to understand the roles of groups and networks in determining how the poor manage their exposure to risks and cope with shocks to their livelihoods. Shocks do not affect Filipino households in the same way. Although drought has a negative impact on all households, it has a stronger negative impact on households with less land and fewer assets. The death of a household head or his spouse has a stronger negative impact on per capita consumption in households that have more land and assets—probably because these households are more heavily engaged in agriculture.

The poor do not easily build up social capital. Disparities in ethnicity, assets, and education at the village level are also likely to discourage the formation of groups, although they do not affect the formation of trust-based networks. Thus, local heterogeneity is not necessarily "good" for social capital formation—which may partially explain the difficulty of some collective action efforts in the Philippines, which has a highly unequal income distribution. In contrast, networks composed of spatially diversified children may more effectively ensure against covariate shocks than do local networks. However, problems of asymmetric information, enforcement, and compliance are greater in spatially diversified networks. It is therefore no surprise that in the Philippines migrant networks are composed primarily of family members (children), because norms are easier to enforce within a family. Children, especially daughters, are socialized to have *utang na loob,* a debt of gratitude in the form of reciprocity for favors granted (Lopez 1991). As part of *utang na loob* children must obey and respect their parents and fulfill their obligations long after their parents have reared them to maturity. Indeed, children are expected to be everlastingly grateful to their parents not only for raising them but, more fundamentally, for giving them life itself (Racelis Hollnsteiner 1973). Failure to live up to these obligations is severely sanctioned, even with threats of divine retribution.[8] Thus, children, even those who live far away, continue to contribute to their parents.

Because shocks can have adverse consequences for both the short and the long term, understanding the appropriate role of public policy is important for sustainable poverty reduction. Policies to help poor households cope with shocks must take into account Filipino social and organizational culture, because policies that are not mindful of the social context may backfire by eroding indigenous social support mechanisms. Our results suggest a number of policy implications. First, development practitioners and policymakers need to be more realistic about the possibility of using collective action to deliver services directly to the poor or about encouraging those who are asset poor to accumulate social capital. Identifying the barriers that prevent the poor from participating in collective action is an important task for development practitioners. Poorer folk often express feelings of *hiya* (in Tagalog) or *kaulaw* (in Cebuano-Visayan, the language spoken by our respondents)—literally translated as "shame" but actually meaning the uncomfortable feeling of one in a socially unacceptable position (Lynch 1973)—in approaching wealthier individuals for help in times of need. Fear of being unable to reciprocate may also prevent poorer households from approaching richer households for help, because reciprocity is at the core of Filipino social transactions (Racelis Hollnsteiner 1973). Such feelings of discomfort may interfere with efforts to include a more heterogeneous mix of households in groups—and to achieve consumption smoothing within formal groups. Such shame may be tempered if the richer individual is a relative, even a distant one. Thus, it is not uncommon for kinship networks to perform consumption-smoothing functions.

Second, because local networks and other forms of collective action have limited effectiveness when there are covariate shocks, this is an appropriate arena for public policy. Here, public action can play an enabling role, for example, by reducing barriers to migration and by facilitating interventions (such as improvements in information and communications technology or reducing transaction costs in making remittances) that reduce the costs associated with developing and maintaining family networks. For example, the Philippine Overseas Employment Administration, created in 1982, not only regulates overseas employment but also provides basic assistance to overseas Filipino workers and their families, including the use of information technology to facilitate dissemination of labor market information and to help potential overseas workers arrive at informed decisions. Keeping in touch with relatives—

---

8. Among various Visayan-speaking groups, such as those at our study sites, failure to look after aging parents is sanctioned by *gaba,* or divine retribution. However, few persons attribute illness to *gaba,* or to *gaba* from that cause, which can be interpreted to mean that children actually live up to their obligations (Lopez 1991).

and making remittances—in the Philippines is convenient: one can now make bank payments and remittances via text messages using a cell phone.

Third, although certain types of networks do provide insurance against some types of idiosyncratic shocks (such as illness), the poor may be less able to invest in such networks and may be left unprotected. This presents another opportunity for public policy to preferentially offer the poor social protection such as subsidized health insurance. Interestingly, the province of Bukidnon was one of two provinces to pilot test a provincial health insurance program, the Bukidnon Health Insurance Project, which was acknowledged during its lifetime as an archetypal local government-initiated social health insurance scheme (Lorenzo et al. 2003). When the program was scaled up, the pilot program was terminated and was replaced by the Indigency Program of the Philippine Health Insurance Corporation.

Finally, policymakers need to be aware of indigenous networks that already exist and ensure that government action does not displace already functioning local networks.

The most interesting finding of this study in terms of the relationships among various aspects of the conceptual framework presented in Chapter 2 is that although the poor rely on social capital and institutions of collective action to protect themselves against shocks, their social capital endowments (in addition to other assets) may be lower than those of their counterparts, leaving them more exposed to the negative effects of different shocks. In addition, this chapter uniquely identifies migrant familial networks (intrafamilial social capital) as an important collective action institution that enables members of these networks to effectively deal with informational asymmetries in order to achieve certain poverty outcomes (income, provision of basic needs, security). Moreover, we have shown that the structure of collective action institutions is related to the scope of risks that they enable households to mitigate. As in Chapters 3 and 5, here asset heterogeneity is seen to affect the structure of and incentives for collective action as well as patterns of interaction (cooperation), leading to the exclusion of the poor from certain groups in some cases and to the sustainability of their networks in others.

References

Ahuja, V. 1998. Land degradation, agricultural productivity, and common property: Evidence from Côte d'Ivoire. *Environment and Development Economics* 3 (1): 7–34.

Alesina, A., and E. La Ferrara. 2000. Participation in heterogeneous communities. *Quarterly Journal of Economics* 115 (3): 847–904.

Arce, W. 2003. Values, organizational culture and organizations. *Loyola Schools Review School of Social Sciences Online.* Quezon City, Philippines: Ateneo de Manila University. Available online at <http://www.ateneo.edu/ateneo/www/SiteFiles/File/LS%20Review%20School%20of%20Social%20Sciences%20Online/08_Arce.pdf.> Accessed April 12, 2011.

Bardhan, P. 2000. Irrigation and cooperation: An empirical analysis of 48 irrigation communities in South India. *Economic Development and Cultural Change* 48 (4): 847–865.

Bouis, H. E., and L. Haddad, eds. 1990. *Agricultural commercialization, nutrition, and the rural poor: A study of Philippine farm households.* Boulder, Colo., U.S.A.: Lynne Rienner.

Constantino, R. 1975. *The Philippines: A past revisited.* Quezon City, Philippines: Renato Constantino.

Fafchamps, M., and F. Gubert. 2007. The formation of risk sharing networks. *Journal of Development Economics* 83 (2): 326–350.

Fafchamps, M., and S. Lund. 2003. Risk sharing networks in rural Philippines. *Journal of Development Economics* 71 (2): 261–287.

Foster, A., and M. Rosenzweig. 2000. Financial intermediation, transfers, and commitment: Do banks crowd out private insurance arrangements in low-income rural areas? In *Sharing the wealth: Demographic changes and economic transfers between generations,* ed. A. Mason and G. Tapinos. Oxford, U.K.: Oxford University Press.

Godquin, M., and A. R. Quisumbing. 2006. *Groups, networks, and social capital in rural Philippine communities.* CAPRi Working Paper 55. Washington, D.C.: International Food Policy Research Institute.

Godquin, M., and A. R. Quisumbing. 2008. Separate but equal? The gendered nature of social capital in rural Philippine communities. *Journal of International Development* 20 (1): 13–33.

Grootaert, C. 2001. *Does social capital help the poor? A synthesis of findings and recommendations from the social capital initiative.* Social Capital Initiative Working Paper 24. Washington, D.C.: Social Development Department, World Bank.

Haddad, L., and J. Maluccio. 2003. Trust, membership in groups, and household welfare: Evidence from KwaZulu-Natal, South Africa. *Economic Development and Cultural Change* 51 (3): 573–601.

Hoddinott, J., and A. R. Quisumbing. 2003. *Data sources for microeconometric risk and vulnerability assessments.* Social Protection Paper 0323. Washington, D.C.: World Bank.

Kariuki, G., and F. Place. 2005. Moving rural development through participation in collective action in the highlands of central Kenya. Paper presented at the 2005 CAPRi Workshop on Gender and Collective Action, October 17–21, 2005, in Chiang Mai, Thailand.

Lauby, J., and O. Stark. 1988. Individual migration as a family strategy: Young women in the Philippines. *Population Studies* 42 (3): 473–486.

Ligon, E., J. P. Thomas, and T. Worral. 2000. Mutual insurance, individual savings, and limited commitment. *Review of Economic Dynamics* 3 (2): 216–246.

Lopez, M. E. 1991. *The Filipino family as a home for the aged.* Comparative Study of the Elderly in Asia Research Report 91-7. Ann Arbor, Mich., U.S.A.: Population Studies Center, University of Michigan.

Lorenzo, F. M. E., R. N. Caragay, J. F. E. de la Rosa, E. P. Recon, and C. G. Pascual. 2003. Documenting the experiences and lessons learned from a local social health insurance scheme: The case of the Bukidnon Health Insurance Project (BHIP).

Institute of Health Policy and Development Studies, National Institutes of Health, University of the Philippines, Manila. Mimeo.

Lynch, F. 1973. Social acceptance reconsidered. In *Four readings on Philippine values,* ed. F. Lynch and A. de Guzman II. Quezon City, Philippines: Ateneo de Manila Institute of Philippine Culture.

McCarthy, N., and J. P. Vanderlinden. 2004. Resource management under climatic risk: A case study of Niger. *Journal of Development Studies* 40 (5): 120–142.

Munshi, K., and M. Rosenzweig. 2005. Why is mobility in India so low? Social insurance, inequality, and growth. Department of Economics, Brown University, Providence, R.I., U.S.A. Photocopy.

Narayan, D., and L. Pritchett. 1999. Cents and sociability: Household income and social capital in rural Tanzania. *Economic Development and Cultural Change* 47 (4): 871–897.

Place, F., G. Kariuki, J. Wangila, P. Kristjanson, A. Makauki, and J. Ndubi. 2004. Assessing the factors underlying differences in group performance: Methodological issues and empirical findings from the Highlands of Central Kenya. *Agricultural Systems* 82 (3): 257–272.

Quisumbing, A. R. 1997. Does parental gender preference pay off? Migration and child–parent transfers in rural Philippines. International Food Policy Research Institute, Washington, D.C. Photocopy.

Quisumbing, A. R., and S. McNiven. 2005. *Migration and the rural–urban continuum: Evidence from the Rural Philippines.* Food, Consumption and Nutrition Division Discussion Paper 197. Washington, D.C.: International Food Policy Research Institute.

Quisumbing, A. R., and S. McNiven. 2010. Moving forward, looking back: The impact of migration and remittances on assets, consumption, and credit constraints in the rural Philippines. *Journal of Development Studies* 46 (1): 91–113.

Quisumbing, A. R., S. McNiven, and M. Godquin. 2008. *Shocks, groups, and networks in Bukidnon, Philippines.* CAPRi Working Paper 84. Washington, D.C.: International Food Policy Research Institute.

Racelis Hollnsteiner, M. R. 1973. Reciprocity in the lowland Philippines. In *Four readings on Philippine values,* ed. Frank Lynch and Alfonso de Guzman II. Quezon City, Philippines: Ateneo de Manila University Press.

Rosenzweig, M. R. 2003. Pay-offs from panels in low-income countries: Economic development and economic mobility. *American Economic Review* 93 (2): 112–117.

Townsend, R. 1994. Risk and insurance in village India. *Econometrica* 62 (3): 171–184.

Winters, P., A. de Janvry, and E. Sadoulet. 2000. Family and community network in Mexico–U.S. Migration. *Journal of Human Resources* 36 (1): 159–184.

Yang, D. 2004. International migration, remittances, and household investment: Evidence from Philippine migrants' exchange rate shocks. Gerald R. Ford School of Public Policy and Department of Economics, University of Michigan, Ann Arbor, Michigan, U.S.A. Photocopy.

5 Rural Institutions and Imperfect Agricultural Markets in Africa: Experiences from Producer Marketing Groups in Kenya

BEKELE SHIFERAW, GEOFFREY MURICHO, MENALE KASSIE, AND GIDEON OBARE

Many Sub-Saharan African countries have liberalized their economies and developed poverty reduction strategies aimed at opening up new market-led opportunities for economic recovery and accelerated growth. The outcomes of these policy reforms have, however, been quite mixed (Winter-Nelson and Temu 2002; Dorward and Kydd 2004; Fafchamps 2004). Many smallholder farmers continue to engage in subsistence agriculture and are therefore unable to benefit from liberalized markets. Structural problems of poor infrastructure (Kydd and Dorward 2004; Dorward et al. 2005) and lack of market-enabling institutions (World Bank 2002, 2003) continue to characterize the subsector, contributing to high transaction costs, coordination failure, and pervasive market imperfections. Moreover, partial implementation of reforms and policy reversals in terms of increasing the use of discretionary trade policy instruments by the state or parastatal marketing boards have tended to mute the positive effects of liberalization (Jayne et al. 2002; Jayne, Chapoto, and Shiferaw 2009).

Although the opportunities afforded by liberalization have not been fully exploited, the expectation that removing or rationalizing state marketing boards would open opportunities for the private sector to take over these functions has not been fully realized in many areas. This is mainly because of underdeveloped infrastructure and missing institutions that support the proper functioning of markets. The private-sector traders are unlikely to offer input and output marketing services to smallholder producers in such less favored areas, where market infrastructure or enabling institutions are weak or missing. Lack of such infrastructure and institutions diminishes the incentives for the private sector to invest in agribusiness development and the provision of marketing functions, especially for food staples and other low-value grains produced in these areas. However, avenues exist in market institutions that make use of collective action to complement government and private-sector responses for enhanced coordination in rural commodity markets. This is because the individual marketing of produce may not make economic sense due to small quantities, large spatial distances from input and output markets, and the associated high transportation costs, all characteristics of small-scale production in Sub-Saharan Africa.

110

This chapter aims to analyze the role that institutional innovations can play in improving the performance of rural markets in less favored areas lacking market infrastructure. Presenting a case study of producer marketing groups (PMGs) in eastern Kenya, the chapter identifies potentials and constraints of rural institutions in providing market services for small-scale producers of food staples and grain legumes. Marketing outcomes and the potential sources of the differential success of marketing groups in relation to marketing and other collective action functions are highlighted. The rest of the chapter is organized as follows. First we review market institutions and their emerging roles in remedying market imperfections in rural areas. Next we outline the method-ological approach used in the case study. Then we present our main results, followed by a summary of the key findings and policy implications in the con-cluding section.

As for the conceptual framework in Chapter 2, this study illustrates how institutions of collective action can enable the poor to enhance their access to markets in order to increase their incomes while maintaining the sustainabil-ity of their marketing efforts. The study examines the role of assets (natural, human, and public) in creating incentives to join PMGs and also provides insight into how collective action can be leveraged to achieve certain poverty reduction outcomes for small-scale producers and how the legal frameworks can constrain the emergence and further development of such institutions. The central focus of the chapter is on food staple marketing in the semiarid areas of Kenya (the action arena). The actors discussed are mainly the internal ones (PMG members and nonmembers), and there is some mention of the state (and other nongovernmental agencies) as an external actor that creates certain contextual conditions for the emergence of new forms of cooperation around marketing activities (patterns of interaction). PMG bylaws (another pattern of interaction) are also discussed in detail to show their linkages with assets and their influence on outcomes (the economic viability of the market-ing groups). The inclusiveness of PMGs is mentioned in relation to the asset endowments as well.

This chapter, similar to Chapters 3 and 4, stands at the important inter-section between the natural resource management (NRM) literature and non-NRM poverty studies by focusing not only on the role of collective action institutions in overcoming certain structural constraints that the poor face (in this case, in marketing their agricultural products) but also on the structure and functioning of the groups themselves, which allow the farmers to achieve these outcomes. Collective action in marketing has been gaining attention in the lit-erature in recent years but has focused mostly on the operational rather than institutional side. This study contributes to the study of collective action institu-tions in non-NRM areas, for example, by examining the incentives to organize around marketing as well as the impact of rules and asset heterogeneity on group sustainability and inclusiveness.

Institutions in Imperfect Rural Markets

How Institutions Help Overcome Market Impediments

Institutions constitute formal constraints (that is, rules, laws, and constitutions) and informal constraints (that is, norms of behavior, conventions, and self-imposed codes of conduct) that structure human interactions and their enforcement characteristics (North 1990). Similarly, the World Bank defines *institutions* as the rules, including behavioral norms, by which agents interact and the organizations that implement rules and codes of conduct to achieve desired outcomes (World Bank 2002). The formal institutions include rules written into law by governments, as well as rules codified and adopted by the private sector and by public and private organizations operating under public law. Informal institutions, however, operate outside of the formal legal system and reflect the unwritten codes of social behavior. Both formal and informal institutions have their own external enforcement mechanisms, such as the judicial system and third-party arbitration. At initial stages of development, markets and trade rely more on the norm and on network-based informal institutions that reduce the transaction costs of collecting and processing information and the risks associated with market transactions. As the complexity of markets and trade increases, the number and range of partners involved in transactions expand significantly, and informal institutions fail to absorb costs and risks to allow efficient market transactions. The importance of formal institutions becomes more evident as the economies grow, the number of actors increases, and markets become more integrated. For example, interregional trade and participation in international markets require international rules and standards that facilitate market exchanges (World Bank 2002).

Market failures are often caused by underlying policy and institutional failures that lead to asymmetric information, high transaction costs, and imperfectly specified property rights (Shiferaw and Muricho 2009). They tend to be more pronounced in areas with underdeveloped public goods and market infrastructure (for instance, road and communication networks), which are typical of many rural areas in Sub-Saharan Africa (Shiferaw and Muricho 2009).[1] Without supporting market institutions, rural markets in these areas tend to be thin and imperfect, leading to high marketing and transaction costs. These costs undermine the exchange process (Kranton 1996; Gabre-Madhin 2001), leading to segmented and imperfect rural markets characterized by weak linkages among producers and different end users (Chowdhury, Negessa, and Torero 2005). Given such market arrangements, households respond by producing a

---

1. Market failure is a subjective concept associated with conditions when markets fail to facilitate mutually beneficial transactions due to certain constraints related to lack of information, exclusion, or inadequate provision of public goods. These underlying constraints often arise from policy failures or inadequate institutions.

limited range of goods and services for their own consumption, especially when they cannot rely on markets to ensure household food security (de Janvry, Faf-champs, and Sadoulet 1991). Further, missing complementary investments at one point in the supply chain undermine the incentives for important market players along the chain to undertake profitable investments, progressively lead-ing to coordination failures that hinder market performance (Dorward et al. 2005; Poulton, Kydd, and Dorward 2006). Associated shocks and vulnerabili-ties to production risks (that is, weather, pests, and sickness) and market risk also exacerbate market imperfections and lead to transaction failures (Dorward and Kydd 2004).

How, then, can institutions support market development? The important role of institutions is in reducing transaction costs related to inadequate infor-mation, infrastructure, incomplete definition and enforcement of property rights, and barriers to entry (World Bank 2002). This suggests that institutions (including the formal rules and informal norms of collective action and their enforcement mechanisms) perform multiple functions for markets:

- transmit information,
- mediate transactions,
- facilitate the transfer and enforcement of property rights and contracts, and
- manage the degree of competition.

They can therefore be used to help remedy market imperfections and impedi-ments in rural markets. This suggests that institutional innovations that reduce transaction costs and enhance market coordination—such as marketing groups and producer organizations that make use of collective action—can be instru-mental in overcoming some of these problems in imperfect markets.

Farmer Organizations for Improving Markets

The potential of producer organizations lies in their ability to convey market information, coordinate marketing functions, define and enforce property rights and contracts, and, more critically, enhance competitiveness and mobi-lize the membership to engage in markets (Shiferaw and Muricho 2009). Farmer organizations can be of several types, ranging from informal groups to formal cooperatives or collectively owned agro-enterprises. Depending on their anticipated functions and legal provisions in different countries, their organizational designs may take different forms—cooperatives, associations, and societies. A farmer association is a nonprofit organization that leverages collective action to access certain services (for example, agricultural exten-sion), enable the exchange of information, and provide members with repre-sentation and a voice. On the other hand, farmer cooperatives can engage in commercial activities, including the collective marketing of produce and the buying of commercial inputs.

Farmer cooperatives continue to play an important role in organizing the production and marketing functions of family farms in developed countries. There are more than 30,000 cooperatives representing over 9 million members within the E.U. alone, accounting for 50 percent of the market share for delivery of inputs and 60 percent for agricultural produce (World Bank 2008). Historically, farmer cooperatives were introduced in Sub-Saharan Africa during the colonial period for the purpose of promoting the production of cash crops by peasant farmers (Hussi et al. 1993). After the countries of the area achieved independence, many governments as well as donors promoted cooperatives and other rural organizations as potential sources of decentralized grassroots participation in agricultural credit, input, and commodity markets (Lele and Christiansen 1989; Hussi et al. 1993). However, despite the important contributions they made to the integration of producers into markets in the initial phase, the performance of cooperatives gradually declined over time. In Kenya, for example, semiautonomous agencies—such as the Kenya Tea Development Authority, and the coffee and dairy cooperatives—were important to the growth of smallholder production, while some parastatals and cooperatives showed mediocre results. Unsatisfactory performances are often attributed to technological problems, external interference, and poor management (Wolf 1986; Lele and Christiansen 1989).

Hence, the track record of farmer cooperatives in Africa during the preadjustment era in relation to the provision of essential services to members and poverty reduction has not been exemplary (Lele 1981; Hussi et al. 1993; Akwabi-Ameyaw 1997). Supported by governments, they functioned primarily as social service cooperatives rather than as business enterprises owned and governed by the members. They were not allowed sufficient marketing margins to cover their operational expenses and could not evolve into commercially viable enterprises. This deficiency gradually discouraged member participation and eroded the confidence of the stakeholders in the cooperative leadership (Lele 1981; Shiferaw and Muricho 2009). With structural adjustment and economic reforms, many of the service cooperatives lost their special protection from the state, which further reduced their viability in the ensuing competitive environment. In addition to the unsuccessful past efforts, which continue to overshadow future directions, today's farmer organizations face several internal and external challenges that could undermine their ability to compete more effectively or provide desired services to members at low costs.

Given these unsuccessful experiences of farmer cooperatives, African farmers are highly suspicious of and anxious about collective action in marketing. The new generation of farmer organizations must go through a slow process of confidence building to overcome persistent suspicion and fear on the part of their members, potential members, and business partners. This confidence can be nurtured only through greater participatory and democratic governance, openness and transparency in financial management that enhances the organizations' accountability to members, good business ethics, and finally, the rewards that they bring to their constituency. It is in this regard that PMGs as member-controlled and -governed farmer organizations can be useful in enhancing access to markets and in facilitating the transition from the discredited cooperatives of the past to the new generation of market-led and economically viable farmer cooperatives. The lessons from the past cooperative movement indicate that farmer organizations can succeed if farmers are allowed to manage them autonomously with minimal government interference and participate actively in decisionmaking at every stage of the process and if collective action reduces transaction costs and improves competitiveness. All this implies that new policies and institutional reforms would be needed to facilitate the evolution of these organizations as private-sector enterprises with clear business plans.

Although what we have just written shows that PMGs have the potential to enhance market opportunities for small producers through facilitated access to better markets, reduced marketing costs, and buying and selling practices synchronized to seasonal price conditions, collective action is a critical factor in realizing this potential. Participation in groups will depend on the magnitude of the expected benefits and their associated costs. Collective action is likely to materialize if the gains in terms of reduced transaction costs, better input or product prices, empowerment, and capacity enhancement outweigh the associated costs of complying with collective rules and norms.

Data and Context

Two sets of data that were obtained from a baseline survey in 2003 and a follow-up survey in 2005 are used in this study. We conducted the surveys in Mbeere and Makueni districts of semiarid eastern Kenya, where poverty is pervasive and smallholders frequently face drought-induced shocks. These districts were targeted by the International Crops Research Institute for the Semiarid Tropics (ICRISAT) as areas where dryland legumes such as pigeon peas and chickpeas could potentially be exploited to reduce poverty and vulnerability. The two districts are located in the part of the larger semiarid lands characterized by a low density of paved roads and limited access to major marketing centers. Farmers there produce limited marketable surplus. Despite climatic variability and recurrent droughts, smallholder agriculture is almost entirely dependent on rains.

The baseline survey of 400 households (240 in Mbeere and 160 in Makueni) was undertaken in 2003 before the PMGs were formed as part of an ICRISAT-led research project that aimed to pilot alternative institutional innovations for improving market access for smallholders. The households were randomly sampled from a list of all households in the target villages. Farmers were sensitized to PMG participation and assisted in forming PMGs.[2] Interested farmers

---

2. The form of assistance provided included mobilizing farmers to discuss production and marketing strategies for dryland legumes, training them on quality seed production and marketing, and providing information on organizing marketing groups. No direct subsidies or incentives were provided to farmers to join groups.

voluntarily established five PMGs in each district. The groups were formally registered, and each was provided a certificate of its legal constitution as a welfare society (self-help group) issued by the Ministry of Gender, Sports, Culture, and Social Services. Some of the households that had initially expressed interest in joining a group subsequently decided not to join. From the initial sample of 400 households, the distribution of members and nonmembers was decided after the PMGs were established based on the number of committed and paid-up members. Information on poverty indicators, agricultural production, market participation, and adoption of agricultural technologies was collected from the respondents.

During a follow-up survey conducted in 2005 in the same districts, data were collected at several levels: the community or village, the PMG, and the farm household. At the community or village level, 20 communities (two from each PMG) were purposely selected for the survey on the basis of which villages had the highest number of registered members in their respective PMGs. A group of about nine gender-balanced key informants was selected from each village based on peer perception and the village chief's advice regarding their ability to provide quality information that could be used to form socioeconomic profiles of the village economy. At the PMG level, all the 10 PMGs were surveyed separately. The key informants on the PMG activities included five to seven respondents selected from the PMG management and the ordinary membership. The data obtained included information on the objectives and aspirations of the groups, group characteristics, asset ownership, credit access, grading and quality control, bulking and marketing, governance, and major constraints to collective marketing. Finally, at the household level data were collected from 400 randomly selected households (210 from Mbeere and 190 from Makueni districts) in the PMG villages, including 250 PMG members and 150 nonmembers. This subsample consisted of 150 households resampled from 235 baseline households that had remained PMG members and 100 households resampled from 165 households that had remained non-PMG members. The information obtained included data on socioeconomic characteristics, assets, credit and savings, production, buying and selling, and participation in collective marketing.

Table 5.1 presents descriptive statistics for selected variables for all households, by participation or nonparticipation in PMGs (selling grain to a PMG). About 4.3 percent of the sample households sold grain to a PMG.

Econometric Specification

Do farmers participating in collective action (PMG membership) or selling grain to PMGs systematically receive higher grain prices for their produce? To answer these questions, we need a proper counterfactual that allows statistical comparisons between groups of households that are alike in all ways except

TABLE 5.1 Descriptive statistics for households surveyed in Mbeere and Makueni districts of Kenya (grouped by participation or nonparticipation in producer marketing groups), 2005

Description	Participant (n = 27)	Nonparticipant (n = 597)	All (n = 624)
Distance to the nearest village market (km)	2.389 (1.188)	2.052 (1.221)	2.067 (1.221)
Distance to the nearest main market (km)	4.389 (2.946)	7.934 (6.395)	7.780 (6.325)
Age of household head (years)	52.889 (12.738)	51.873 (14.217)	51.917 (14.149)
Gender of household head (1 = male; 0 = female)	0.889 (0.320)	0.834 (0.372)	0.837 (0.370)
Total household workforce	3.213 (1.962)	2.447 (1.408)	2.480 (1.443)
Dependency ratio	1.795 (1.492)	1.577 (1.509)	1.586 (1.508)
Whether household owns an oxcart (1 = yes; 0 = otherwise)	0.296 (0.465)	0.260 (0.439)	0.261 (0.440)
Whether household is located in a wet area (1 = yes; 0 = otherwise)[a]	0.148 (0.362)	0.075 (0.264)	0.079 (0.269)
Whether household is located in a dry area (1 = yes; 0 = otherwise)[a]	0.593 (0.501)	0.250 (0.433)	0.264 (0.441)
Per capita livestock assets (1,000 Ksh)	3.055 (2.773)	5.040 (6.518)	4.954 (6.413)
Per capita physical assets (1,000 Ksh)	0.805 (0.721)	2.970 (19.019)	2.877 (18.608)
Per capita total cultivated land (acres)	1.986 (2.253)	2.482 (2.185)	2.460 (2.188)
Land and livestock interaction (1,000)[b]	44.513 (5.846)	9.132 (19.467)	8.932 (19.101)
Per capita total number of oxen owned	0.100 (0.173)	0.253 (0.322)	0.247 (0.319)
Per capita household education stock (years)	6.479 (2.236)	5.653 (2.117)	5.689 (2.127)
Main occupation of household head (1 = farming; 0 = otherwise)	0.741 (0.447)	0.796 (0.404)	0.793 (0.405)
Whether household owns ICT assets (1 = yes; 0 = otherwise)[c]	0.815 (0.396)	0.824 (0.381)	0.824 (0.381)
Whether household has contact with NGOs (1 = yes; 0 = otherwise)	0.519 (0.509)	0.400 (0.790)	0.405 (0.491)

SOURCE: Authors' calculations.

NOTES: Figures in parentheses are standard deviations. Ksh means Kenyan shilling; NGO means nongovernmental organization; n = number of observations.

[a] Dryness or wetness is relative in the semiarid areas. The reference is households located in high-rainfall areas.

[b] This is an interaction variable that was created after multiplying the land holding (hectares) with total livestock value (KSh); thus it is not possible to state the units.

[c] Information and communication technology (ICT) assets include radios, televisions, and mobile phones.

participation in or selling grain to PMGs. We use the propensity score matching (PSM) method to address the potential selection bias resulting from PMG participation. Our main purpose in using the PSM method is to match "treatment" (PMG participation) and "control" (PMG nonparticipation) households that are similar in terms of observable characteristics that are expected to jointly affect their PMG participation status and the outcome variable (market price of the grain).[3] The seminal explanation of the PSM method is available in Rosenbaum and Rubin (1983), and its strengths and weaknesses were elaborated in subsequent literature, including Heckman et al. (1998), Dehejia and Wahba (2002), Smith and Todd (2005), and Caliendo and Kopeinig (2008).

Estimation of the propensity score per se is not sufficient to estimate the average participation effect (average treatment effect on the treated, or ATT). Because the propensity score is a continuous variable, the probability of observing two individuals with exactly the same propensity score is, in principle, zero. Various matching algorithms have been proposed in the literature to overcome this problem. Asymptotically, all matching algorithms should yield the same results. However, in practice, trade-offs in terms of bias and efficiency are associated with each algorithm (Caliendo and Kopeinig 2008). We therefore implemented three matching algorithms: (1) one-to-one nearest neighbor matching with replacement, (2) radius matching, and (3) kernel-based matching using the Epanechnikov kernel. Basically, these methods numerically search for "neighbors" that have propensity scores for nontreated individuals that are very close to the propensity scores of treated individuals.

Matching deals only with selection based on observables; if there are unobserved variables that simultaneously affect the participation decision and the outcome variable, a selection or hidden bias problem due to unobserved variables might arise, to which matching estimators are not robust. We checked the sensitivity of the estimated average participation effect to unobserved variables using the Rosenbaum bounds sensitivity approach (Rosenbaum 2002). The purpose of the sensitivity analysis was to investigate whether inferences about the participation effect could be changed by unobserved variables. It is not possible to estimate the magnitude of such selection bias using observational data. Instead, the sensitivity analysis involves calculating upper and lower bounds using the Wilcoxon sign rank test to test the null hypothesis that there is no participation effect for different hypothesized values of unobserved selection bias.

---

3. The outcome variable (price index, *PI*) is defined as a ratio of the price received by the farmer to the average price of the crop in the sample:

$$PI_i = \frac{p_{ij}}{\bar{p}_j}(100),$$

where PI_i is the price index for household i, p_{ij} is the unit price received by household i for crop j, and $\bar{p}_j$ is the average unit price of crop j in the sample.

Finally, in order to determine whether resource-poor smallholder farmers are excluded from PMGs, we used a bivariate probit model by analyzing the effect of household assets and wealth indicators on PMG membership. The bivariate specification was selected mainly because PMG membership is likely to be jointly determined with membership in other networks prevalent in rural areas. The bivariate probit specification is useful if the error terms for membership to different groups are correlated. This is a natural extension of Zellner's (1962) seemingly unrelated regression model for binary choice variables.

Results

Grain Markets and Marketing Channels

The key characteristics of rural grain markets in Africa are segmentation, the dominance of few traders, asymmetric information, high transaction costs, and high marketing risks. Analysis of the market structure in terms of transactions (number and volume of sales) by distance and market participation during 2003/04 in the study area shows that rural wholesalers accounted for 45 percent of the sales transactions and 49 percent of the volume traded, while brokers or assemblers accounted for 38 percent of the transactions and the traded volume (Table 5.2). Hence, rural wholesalers and assemblers jointly control more than 80 percent of the transactions and traded volumes. This is because they are well organized and agile and have the necessary capital and mobility to buy directly from dispersed farmers. PMGs accounted for 4 percent of the sales transactions and 2 percent of the volume, and rural consumers (that is, deficit producers) accounted for less than 10 percent of the sales and the volume purchased from farmers. Further, 45 percent of the traded volume was sold and 36 percent of the transactions were conducted at the farmgate.

A review of the relation between spatial distances and market engagement reveals that about 34 percent of the transactions (accounting for 25 percent of the traded volume) were conducted within 3 kilometers of the farmgate. Generally, with increasing distance from the farmgate the number of transactions and the volumes traded by market participant declined. These effects can be attributed to increasing transportation and transaction costs for the small quantities marketed as distances increase. They are consistent with the findings by Fafchamps and Hill (2005) for coffee marketing in Uganda. The prices also varied significantly over time, increasing gradually as local supplies declined and declining again as local produce reached local markets after harvest. About 79 percent of the selling occurred immediately after harvest, about 19 percent within two to three months after harvest, and only 11 percent more than four to five months after harvest. This finding illustrates potential business opportunities for PMGs through bulk marketing and spatial and temporal arbitrage.

TABLE 5.2 Total number of sales and volumes (tons) for all crops in Kenyan grain markets, 2004/05

| Buyer | Total | | Share (percent) | | Distance of sales from farmgate | | | | | | | |
| | | | | | Farmgate | | <3 km | | 3–5 km | | >5 km | |
	Sales	Volume	Sales	Volume	Sales	Volume	Sales	Volume	Sales	Volume	Sales	Volume
Consumer	33	6.5	5	3	21	4.7	6	0.7	3	0.5	3	0.7
Producer marketing group	27	3.7	4	2	4	0.8	10	0.7	12	2.2	1	0.1
Rural wholesaler	283	101.8	45	49	25	27.5	167	43.3	82	29.9	9	1.0
Broker or assembler	237	77.7	38	38	175	60.0	24	5.2	16	2.9	22	9.7
Urban wholesaler	13	6.4	2	3	1	0.0	3	0.2	3	0.2	6	6.1
Cotton ginnery	12	4.7	2	2	—	—	2	0.4	9	4.1	1	0.2
School	19	4.9	3	2	—	—	2	0.7	10	2.1	7	2.0
Total	624	205.7	100	100	226	93.0	214	51.1	135	41.9	49	19.7
Share (percent)	n.a.	n.a.	n.a.	n.a.	36	45	34	25	22	20	8	10

SOURCE: Authors' calculations.

NOTES: — means that the buyer did not buy at that particular distance from the farmgate; n.a. means not applicable.

However, the drought situation that prevailed during the 2004/05 production season significantly depressed the marketed surplus and the number of
transactions in 2005. The effect of the drought-induced shock on pigeon pea
marketing and on both the market shares and the prices paid by different buyers
are shown in Table 5.3. As a result of the drought, the number of transactions
completed by the surveyed households declined from 243 in 2003 to just 50 in
2005 as the traded volume plummeted from about 41.0 tons to 4.7 tons. The
total volume (of all crops) purchased by the PMGs declined from over 60.0 tons
in 2004 to about 15.0 tons the following year. Such a drastic change in market
participation is significant given that pigeon peas are one of the most drought-
tolerant crops grown in these areas. The results also show that the farmgate
prices paid by the PMGs, 27 Kenyan shillings (Ksh) per kilogram, were generally higher than those paid by other participants, who offered Ksh 23–25 per
kilogram. However, it is important to emphasize that this difference may not
have been the result of selling to the PMGs but instead may have been due to
differences in observed and unobserved household characteristics. Therefore,
we test this further using propensity score matching methods.

Collective Marketing and Its Outcomes

In this section we present and discuss the empirical results from the PSM method,
starting with the results from probit estimates of the decision to participate in a
PMG (an estimation of propensity scores) and following with the results from
the PSM estimation of the average participation effects.

ESTIMATION OF PROPENSITY SCORE.   Table 5.4 reports the results from the
probit analysis of PMG participation decision and the variables used in the
matching procedures. The participation regression results show that distance to
the nearest village market, a household's location in a drier village, the total
household female workforce, household education, and contacts with NGOs
have a positive and significant influence on the household's decision to sell
grain through a PMG. The fact that farmers located far from the nearest markets
are likely to sell their grain through PMGs ($p > 0.01$) underscores the importance of collective action in mitigating constraints on market access for smallholder farmers located in remote areas. Similarly, the fact that households
located in drier areas are more likely to sell through PMGs ($p < 0.05$) could
point to the conclusion that farmers in these areas have limited market opportunities, and collective action through PMGs offers a viable alternative. These
farmers probably find it beneficial to bulk their individually produced small
marketable surpluses into economical quantities, thereby increasing their bargaining power or enabling them to access niche markets that they would be
unable to access if they acted individually. In addition, the interaction of land
and livestock has a small but very significant positive effect on a household's
propensity to sell grain through the PMGs ($p < 0.05$). The positive effect of a
larger family workforce seems to be related to the ability to generate marketable

TABLE 5.3 Pigeon pea marketed volumes, sales, and channel use in semi-arid eastern Kenya, by participant and distance to market, 2003 and 2005

Buyer	Traded volume (tons)		Volume share (percent)		Number of transactions		Total sales, by distance of sales from farmgate								Mean price (Ksh/kg)	
							Farmgate		<3 km		3–5 km		>5 km			
	2003	2005	2003	2005	2003	2005	2003	2005	2003	2005	2003	2005	2003	2005	2003	2005
Consumer	2.0	0.36	5	8	23	3	20	0	2	1	1	2	0	0	22	25
Producer marketing group	—	0.35	—	7	—	7	—	1	—	3	—	3	—	0	—	27
Rural wholesaler	11.9	1.65	25	35	93	22	9	2	56	12	22	6	6	2	15.3	23
Broker or assembler	24.6	2.06	60	44	110	15	76	10	14	1	5	1	15	3	18.6	25
Urban grain trader	2.8	0.29	7	6	17	3	3	0	3	1	0	1	11	1	24.8	24
Total	41.3	4.68	100	100	243	50	108	13	75	18	28	13	32	6	18.1	25
Share (percent)	n.a.	n.a.	n.a.	n.a.	n.a.	n.a.	44	26	31	36	12	26	13	12	n.a.	n.a.

SOURCE: Authors' calculations.

NOTES: Ksh means Kenyan shilling; — means buyer did not buy pigeon pea grain in that survey year; n.a. means not applicable.

TABLE 5.4 Probit estimates of Kenyan households' propensity to sell grain to producer marketing groups, 2005

Variable	Coefficient	Robust standard error
Distance to nearest village market (km)	0.305***	0.104
Distance to nearest main market (km)	−0.046*	0.026
Age of household head (years)	0.002	0.011
Gender of household head (1 = male)	0.440	0.298
Total household female workforce	0.293**	0.114
Total household male workforce	0.083	0.118
Dependency ratio	0.103	0.071
Whether household owns an oxcart (1 = yes)	0.146	0.256
Whether household is located in a medium-rainfall area (1 = yes)[a]	0.319	0.356
Whether household is located in a dry area (1 = yes)[a]	0.618**	0.258
Per capita livestock assets (Ksh)	−0.097*	0.054
Per capita physical assets (Ksh)	−0.069**	0.029
Per capita total cultivated land	−0.035	0.053
Whether there is land and livestock interaction	0.000**	0.000
Per capita total number of oxen owned	−0.998	0.704
Per capita household education stock (years)	0.187***	0.072
Main occupation of household head (1 = farming)	−0.122	0.287
Whether household owns ICT assets (1 = yes)[b]	−0.340	0.301
Average contacts with NGOs	0.487*	0.284
Whether household has contact with NGOs (1 = yes; 0 = otherwise)[c]	n.a.	
Constant	−4.167***	1.005
Summary statistics		
Pseudo R^2	0.229	
Model chi-squared	55.054***	
Log likelihood	−84.512	
Number of observations	588	

SOURCE: Authors' estimation.

NOTES: Ksh means Kenyan shilling; n.a. means not applicable; NGO means nongovernmental organization; blank cells indicate no data. * means significant at the 10 percent level; ** means significant at the 5 percent level; *** means significant at the 1 percent level.

[a]Dryness or wetness is relative in the semiarid areas. The reference is households located in high-rainfall areas.

[b]Information and communication technology (ICT) assets include radios, televisions, and mobile phones.

[c]This variable was dropped because no contact with NGO = 0 predicts failure perfectly.

surplus and contribute to collective action. On the other hand, household education seems to enhance the ability of the household to more accurately analyze the gains to be realized by using the PMG channel ($p < 0.01$).

The results also show that the per capita value of livestock, land, and physical assets owned by household ($p < 0.001$) and the distance to the main market ($p < 0.1$) had negative effects on the household's propensity to use PMG channels for selling grain. It seems that greater asset wealth opens other alternative marketing opportunities for farmers. For example, farmers with bicycles or other forms of motorized transport are more likely to sell their grain directly to traders located in towns. This also indicates that the PMGs have the potential to be pro-poor marketing outlets for selling grain. The weak negative effect of distance to the main market seems to capture some spatial interaction effect, indicating that in some remote villages where access to the main market is limited, brokers and assemblers may be more efficient than small marketing groups in collecting and moving grain to the main marketing centers.

PROPENSITY SCORE MATCHING ESTIMATION OF THE AVERAGE PARTICIPATION EFFECTS. The impact of PMG participation (in this use of collective action to sell produce) on grain prices was estimated using three PSM techniques (Table 5.5). The analysis was done by implementing the common support and caliper; hence, the distributions of PMG participant and nonparticipant households were located in the same domain.[4] As suggested by Rosenbaum and Rubin (1985), we used a caliper size of one-fourth of the standard deviation of the propensity scores. Bootstrap standard errors based on 200 replications are reported. The outcome variable (as defined earlier) was the ratio of crop price received to the average price of the same crop in the sample. The matching estimates show that those households that sold their grain to PMGs received between 21 percent and 29 percent higher prices for their products than those using other channels. For completeness, we show the participation effects with and without matching, but the participation effect is higher when one takes into account matching on observables. This average participation effect is statistically significant and robust across the three matching algorithms.

Another potential source of selection problems results from the potential hidden bias resulting from observable characteristics that are expected to jointly affect PMG membership status and the outcome variable (the market price of the grain). The key issue here is whether PMG membership as such has any systematic effect on prices received by farmers. In order to test this effect, we followed the same procedure as outlined earlier for participation by selling through the PMGs and estimated the ATT of PMG membership on producer

---

4. Following Rosenbaum and Rubin (1985), Sianesi (2004), and Caliendo and Kopeinig (2008), we have checked the matching quality and balancing property of covariates. After matching, the balancing property is satisfied where there is no significant difference in means of covariates between participants and nonparticipants and the mean standardized difference is reduced significantly.

TABLE 5.5 Estimation of the average participation effect (ATT) of selling through producer marketing groups on prices received by Kenyan farmers, 2005

Matching method	Sample	Treated	Controls	Difference	Standard error	t-statistic
Nearest neighbor	Unmatched	120.03	99.09	20.93	5.49	3.80***
matching	ATT	120.03	97.56	22.47	9.57	2.35***
Kernel-based	Unmatched	120.03	99.09	20.93	5.49	3.81***
matching	ATT	120.03	97.17	22.86	7.94	2.88***
Radius matching	Unmatched	120.03	99.09	20.93	5.49	3.81***
	ATT	120.03	96.29	23.18	8.21	2.82***

SOURCE: Authors' estimation.

NOTES: The dependent variable is an index of the price ratio. Number of observations (n) = 588. *** means significant at the 1 percent level.

prices. The probit model used for estimating the propensity score was similar to the univariate model shown later in Table 5.10. The results from this analysis using different matching methods are presented in Table 5.6. The findings indicate that PMG membership on its own does not lead to differential producer price patterns. This indicates that, unlike when selling through PMGs, which ensures higher prices for producers (shown earlier), members of the PMGs do not necessarily receive higher prices if they do not use collective marketing channels.

What about the potential effect of unobservable factors on producer prices? Would this change these conclusions? The results of the Rosenbaum bounds sensitivity analysis to test this potential hidden bias are presented in Table 5.7. As noted by Hujer, Caliendo, and Thomsen (2004), sensitivity analysis for estimation of insignificant average participation effects of PMG membership (Table 5.6) is not meaningful, and thus we omit it here. For the statistically significant participation effect of selling through PMGs (Table 5.5), we increased the level of hidden bias, gamma, Γ (see Rosenbaum 2002) until the inference about the participation effect was changed. The p values represent the upper bound from the Wilcoxon signed rank test for estimation of the average participation effect for each level of unobserved selection bias (Γ). Given that the estimated participation effect (of selling through PMGs) is positive, the lower bounds under the assumption that the true participation effect has been underestimated were less interesting (Becker and Caliendo 2007) and hence not reported. For the assumption that the participation effects are overestimated, the results show that the estimated effect is not sensitive to unobserved selection bias (Table 5.7). The participation effect remains significantly positive even if we allow participants and nonparticipants to differ by a factor of 2.85 in terms of unobserved characteristics. The critical value of Γ, at which point we would have to question our conclusion that there is a positive effect of participation,

TABLE 5.6 Estimation of the average participation effect (ATT) of producer marketing group membership on prices received by Kenyan farmers, 2005

Matching method	Sample	Treated	Controls	Difference	Standard error	*t*-statistic
Nearest neighbor matching	Unmatched	101.28	97.80	3.48	2.34	1.49
	ATT	101.20	99.72	1.48	5.07	0.29
Kernel-based matching	Unmatched	101.28	97.80	3.48	2.34	1.49
	ATT	101.20	98.07	3.12	3.04	1.02
Radius matching	Unmatched	101.28	97.80	3.48	2.34	1.49
	ATT	101.20	97.67	3.54	3.11	1.14

SOURCE: Authors' estimation.

NOTES: The dependent variable is an index of the price ratio. Number of observations (n) = 616.

TABLE 5.7 Rosenbaum bounds sensitivity tests to check the influence of unobservable factors on the effect of selling through producer marketing groups on producer prices, 2005

Level of hidden bias (Γ)	*p*-critical
1.00	0.001
1.25	0.003
1.50	0.008
1.75	0.017
2.00	0.030
2.25	0.046
2.50	0.066
2.75	0.087
2.80	0.092
2.85	0.097
2.90	0.101

SOURCE: Authors' estimation.

starts from $\Gamma = 2.90$, indicating that the unobserved covariate would have to increase the odds of participation by 190 percent or more to change the sig-nifiicant participation effect. This is a large value because we included impor-tant variables that affect both the participation decision and the outcome vari-able. Based on this result, we can conclude that the average participation effect estimates in Table 5.5 are a pure effect of PMG participation.

We also conducted a simulation analysis to test the price advantage of PMGs over that offered by middlemen (brokers or assemblers). The simulation results showed that the prices paid by the PMGs to the member farmers—after covering operational costs—were about 22–24 percent higher than the prices paid by middlemen, the major competitors in rural areas (Table 5.8). However,

TABLE 5.8 The effect of collective marketing on pigeon pea prices in eastern Kenya, 2005

Buyer	Season	Point of sale	Price (Ksh/kg)	Producer marketing group (PMG) price advantage (percent)
PMG	Immediately after harvest	Farmgate	29.81	24.00
Broker or assembler	Immediately after harvest	Farmgate	24.04	
PMG	Immediately after harvest	5 km away	29.93	23.88
Broker or assembler	Immediately after harvest	5 km away	24.16	
PMG	4–5 months after harvest	Farmgate	31.16	22.72
Broker or assembler	4–5 months after harvest	Farmgate	25.39	
PMG	4–5 months after harvest	5 km away	31.29	22.62
Broker or assembler	4–5 months after harvest	5 km away	25.52	

SOURCE: Authors' calculations.

NOTE: Ksh means Kenyan shilling.

this gain came at the cost of delayed payments (on average, five weeks) to grain sellers. In contrast, other competing buyers paid on delivery or shortly thereafter. This explains why cash-constrained farmers opt to sell through other channels, even at the cost of lower prices. As we discuss later, capital constrains and lack of access to credit are major constraints on the growth and expansion of PMGs in Kenya.

The key question is whether the observed price differential is sufficient to provide economic incentives for smallholders to join marketing groups. This depends on the additional income that farmers gain from group membership after having paid the associated fees and indirect costs. A simple net benefit analyses of grain marketing using alternative prices—those offered by brokers and PMGs at the farmgate—can show these gains. Using the 24 percent farmgate price differentials for selling immediately after harvest (Table 5.8), Table 5.9 (first half) presents the estimated gains of members from selling through PMGs compared to using the broker channel. The associated average costs of membership (annualized joining fee and annual contributions) and the opportunity cost of capital for delayed payments were included as costs of collective action. The average income gain was about Ksh 678 per household but varied across household groups depending on the amount marketed. Although the income gain per unit sold was constant, farmers with larger amounts of marketed surplus obtained higher benefits. In our case, these varied from Ksh 152 for the bottom third of farms in terms of sizes to Ksh 1,133 for the upper third. These income gains were modest for two reasons: (1) the average amount marketed was severely reduced because of the drought that prevailed during the 2004/05 production season, and (2) about 60 percent of the member farmers

TABLE 5.9 Income effects associated with selling through marketing groups compared to the broker channel in Kenya, 2005

| | Value of grain sold (Ksh) | | | | | | | |
| | Income gain from using groups, by farm size class (n = 23)[a] | | | | Member lost income by not using groups by farm size class (n = 150) | | | |
Variable	Small	Medium	Large	Total	Small	Medium	Large	Total
Using producer marketing group price	2,303	5,387	7,418	5,155	14,381	19,284	22,452	18,705
Using broker price	1,872	4,413	5,988	4,188	10,518	14,407	16,743	13,889
Difference	431	974	1,429	967	3,862	4,877	5,708	4,816
Cost of collective action[b]	279	290	296	289	314	330	339	328
Net income gain or loss	152	684	1133	678	3,548	4,547	5,369	4,488

SOURCE: Authors' calculations.

NOTE: Ksh means Kenyan shilling; n stands for number of observations.

[a]The farm size classes represent the lower, middle, and upper thirds of household groups.

[b]The cost of collective action includes the annualized costs of the joining fee, the annual subscription fee, and the opportunity cost of delayed payments (calculated using the annual interest rate of 4.3 percent on savings by the commercial banks in Kenya).

chose to sell through non-PMG channels, partly because: (1) these buyers paid promptly, meeting the immediate cash needs of resource-poor farmers, and (2) some larger farmers faced lower transaction costs and opted to market their grain individually outside the village.

Because the main alternative marketing outlet at the farmgate is the broker or assembler channel, we used the amount marketed by the members outside the PMG channel to assess the income loss they sustained by not using the collective marketing channel. This is shown in the second half of Table 5.9. The average income lost by selling through the broker channel (instead of the PMG) was about Ksh 4,488 per year. This was about 7.4 percent of the poverty line income in these areas. The average annual household income from all sources for the sample was about Ksh 139,280. The income loss increased with the amount marketed through the broker channel. Nevertheless, the actual losses may have been slightly lower than indicated, because some larger farmers often sell outside of their village at prices slightly higher than the broker price. As indicated earlier, some farmers may also be compelled to use the non-PMG channels to settle loans provided by the grain traders or to meet immediate cash needs for various commitments. In many cases, grain markets represent the only option for resource-poor farmers to acquire cash in situations in which local credit markets are either missing or highly imperfect.

PMG Membership

The preceding analysis confirms that producer organizations exploiting the power of collective marketing could help increase the prices paid to farmers. However, this does not answer the question on the extent of participation and exclusion in group marketing functions. Could resource-poor and smallholder farmers benefit from such collective action? Here we analyze the determinants of farmers' participation in such groups and assess whether the poor are included or excluded due to various entry barriers. It is important to highlight that the performance and economic viability of farmer marketing groups require that they set certain restrictions on membership, including fees.[5] These fees are generally determined by groups in such a way as to make them affordable and to keep them from becoming significant barriers to joining, but so they are high enough to signify a member's commitment to the principles of collective action. Although economies of scale increase with group size, increasing size may escalate the transaction costs to mobilize dispersed farmers and may increase heterogeneity, undermining group cohesion. Similarly, inclusiveness and interest in tackling poverty may suggest wider and open membership, but the resource-poor may lack the ability to gener-

---

5. This includes a joining fee of about US$1 and an annual subscription fee that varies from none to about US$25 per member. Membership may also require good social standing in the community to win the trust and confidence of the other group members. These may lead to exclusion of some households.

ate marketable surplus or assets that foster trust and creditworthiness. This shows the balance that producer organizations have to maintain to minimize the potential trade-offs between economic viability and inclusiveness to facilitate poverty reduction (Bernard and Spielman 2009).

In order to shed some light on these questions, we investigated whether the PMGs in the districts we studied—voluntarily formed by farmers—were biased toward the wealthier households and excluded resource-poor and marginal farmers. This required careful analyses of the determinants of PMG membership and particularly tests of the effects of household assets and wealth indicators. Because households often belong to more than one group, we used a bivariate probit model to identify the determinants of PMG membership.[6] The bivariate specification was particularly used to test whether PMG membership is jointly determined with membership in other closely related groups, agricultural production networks (APNs). Membership in APNs thus constituted the second equation in the bivariate specification. The explanatory variables included village fixed effects (location, market access, infrastructure), household asset endowments, household characteristics, human capital, and access to information. Household characteristics were captured by dependency ratios, age and gender of household heads, male and female family workforces, per capita family human capital (education stock) in years, and the main occupation of the household head. Six variables were included to capture the effects of wealth and asset endowment: farm size, value of livestock, interaction between livestock and farm size, value of physical assets, ownership of means of transport (an oxcart), and oxen numbers (all in per capita terms). Access to information was captured through ownership of information and communication technology (ICT) (radios, mobile phones, and televisions) and contact with NGO extension personnel. In the absence of effective public extension services, NGOs continue to play a vital role in the economic development process in semiarid areas. In this case, the Catholic Relief Services was instrumental in farmer mobilization and sensitization for establishing PMGs, while ICRISAT facilitated access to improved germplasm and crop cultivars. Location effects were captured through distance to local and main markets and the average rainfall of the PMG villages. For comparison, we also report the univariate probit model results (see Table 5.10).

The results from the bivariate model show that the residuals of the two network membership equations are not independent ($p > 0.034$). The ancillary parameter ρ which measures the correlation of the residuals, shows that the two equations were strongly associated ($p = 0.034$), indicating the superiority of the bivariate specification. The results from the univariate specification, however, are compa-

---

6. About 11 percent of the non-PMG and 20 percent of the PMG member farmers belonged to agricultural production networks (APNs). These are informal groups involved mainly in agricultural production through the sharing of labor and information. The membership of the sample farmers in other local groups included 54 percent in resource conservation groups, 75 percent in saving groups (merry-go-rounds), and 50 percent in other social networks.

rable to those from the bivariate model (in both magnitude and sign). The high Wald chi-squared (χ^2) statistic indicates the statistical validity of both models, but the bivariate model is significant at less than the 99 percent level. Therefore, the discussion hereafter focuses on the results from the bivariate model.

The variables with significant effects on membership included the size of the female workforce in the household ($p = 0.018$), the ownership of ICT ($p = 0.067$), the log of per capita farm size ($p = 0.072$), the asset interaction term (log of per capita farm size $\times$ log per capita livestock) ($p = 0.042$), the stock of household education ($p = 0.014$), household occupation ($p = 0.078$), and access to information ($p = 0.095$). The distance and location effects were not significant. The size of the family workforce generally had a positive effect, but only the female workforce had a significant effect on PMG membership, indicating that PMGs could potentially enhance the participation and integration of the female workforce in markets. The other household characteristics were not significant.

The other important variables for the purpose of this study were household assets (wealth indicators). These showed that membership is likely to increase with livestock wealth but to decrease with the size of farmland per capita. This indicates that households with larger farm sizes alone are less likely to participate in collective marketing. For a given amount of livestock wealth, households with lower per capita farmland have a higher probability of participation. However, households with more land and livestock assets together are more likely to become members. Although the effect of livestock wealth alone was not significant, this potentially opposing effect may result when greater livestock wealth is associated with smaller areas of cropland, which reduces the marketed surplus and increases the gains from collective marketing. The results indicate that it is primarily those farmers with small landholdings (but not necessarily the resource poor) who participate in collective marketing. These are households that produce small surpluses and probably face higher transaction costs in marketing their produce. This finding is consistent with a similar middle-class effect on participation in farmer cooperatives found in Ethiopia (Bernard and Spielman 2009). We also found that education and farm orientation increase the likelihood of PMG membership. Farm size and the asset interaction terms had similar effects on the probability of participation in APNs. Participation in agricultural networks generally decreases with land and draught animal (oxen) assets, indicating that large farmers are less likely to engage in such exchanges. These findings are also consistent with those of Mude (2006) on coffee marketing in Kenya, although coffee is a high-value cash crop, unlike the food staples, the focus of our study.

We also found that households with limited contact with extension services (proxied by frequency of contact with NGOs) are less likely to join PMGs, showing the benefits of sensitization and education, but interestingly participation in indigenous APNs seems to be greater among households that have less contact with NGOs (common providers of agricultural extension in the area).

TABLE 5.10 Univariate and seemingly unrelated bivariate probit determinants of producer marketing group membership in Kenya, 2005

| | Bivariate probit | | | | Univariate probit | |
| | Producer marketing group (PMG) | | Agricultural production network | | PMG membership | |
Variable	Coefficient	p > |z|	Coefficient	p > |z|	Coefficient	p > |z|
Distance to village market (km)	−0.083	0.174	−0.090	0.202	−0.082	0.176
	(0.061)		(0.070)		(0.061)	
Distance to nearest main market (km)	0.006	0.661	−0.023	0.192	0.006	0.679
	(0.014)		(0.018)		(0.013)	
Age of household head (years)	−0.006	0.282	0.003	0.683	−0.006	0.285
	(0.006)		(0.007)		(0.006)	
Gender of household head (1 = male; 0 = female)	0.182	0.306	−0.111	0.593	0.179	0.316
	(0.178)		(0.207)		(0.179)	
Total household male workforce	0.024	0.771	−0.104	0.251	0.026	0.754
	(0.082)		(0.091)		(0.083)	
Total household female workforce	0.206	0.018	0.056	0.590	0.204	0.018
	(0.087)		(0.103)		(0.087)	
Dependency ratio	0.029	0.508	0.094	0.044	0.028	0.526
	(0.044)		(0.047)		(0.044)	
Whether household owns an oxcart (1 = yes; 0 = otherwise)	0.138	0.438	0.094	0.636	0.131	0.461
	(0.178)		(0.198)		(0.177)	
Whether household is located in a rainy area (1 = yes; 0 = otherwise)[a]	−0.120	0.550	0.041	0.851	−0.127	0.526
	(0.200)		(0.219)		(0.200)	
Whether household is located in a dry area (1 = yes; 0 = otherwise)[a]	−0.155	0.370	0.396	0.047	−0.158	0.361
	(0.173)		(0.200)		(0.173)	
Log of per capita livestock assets (Ksh)	0.842	0.114	−0.507	0.433	0.837	0.115
	(0.533)		(0.647)		(0.531)	

	Coef. (SE)	p	Coef. (SE)	p	Coef. (SE)	p
Log of per capita physical assets (Ksh)	0.916 (0.703)	0.193	−0.346 (0.854)	0.686	0.911 (0.699)	0.193
Log of per capita farm size (acres)	−2.093 (1.162)	0.072	−2.408 (1.330)	0.070	−2.114 (1.169)	0.071
Log of per capita livestock × log of per capita farm size	0.766 (0.376)	0.042	0.866 (0.397)	0.029	0.772 (0.381)	0.043
Per capita oxen numbers	−0.389 (0.316)	0.218	−0.922 (0.506)	0.068	−0.388 (0.321)	0.226
Per capita family education stock	0.097 (0.040)	0.014	0.069 (0.045)	0.126	0.099 (0.040)	0.013
Main occupation of household head (1 = farming; 0 = otherwise)	0.301 (0.171)	0.078	0.217 (0.202)	0.284	0.299 (0.171)	0.081
Whether household owns ICT assets (1 = yes; 0 = otherwise)[b]	−0.347 (0.190)	0.067	−0.102 (0.224)	0.647	−0.352 (0.192)	0.067
Whether household has average contact with NGOs (1 = yes; 0 = otherwise)	−0.179 (0.164)	0.273	0.243 (0.203)	0.231	−0.176 (0.164)	0.281
Whether household has no contact with NGOs (1 = yes; 0 = otherwise)	−0.351 (0.210)	0.095	0.490 (0.240)	0.041	−0.354 (0.210)	0.091
Constant	−2.744 (1.845)	0.137	−0.989 (2.236)	0.658	−2.726 (1.832)	0.137
Athrho	0.229 (0.108)	0.034				
p	0.225 (0.103)					
Wald chi-squared [df]	[46] 98.20: Probability > χ^2 = 0.000				[23] 39.44: $p > \chi^2$ = 0.0178	
Log pseudo-likelihood	−395.854				−243.069	
Wald test of $\rho = 0$	χ^2 [1] = 4.501: Probability > χ^2 = 0.034					

NOTES: Robust standard errors are in parentheses. Ksh means Kenyan shilling; df means degrees of freedom; NGO means nongovernmental organization.

[a]Dryness or wetness is relative in the semiarid areas. The reference is households located in high-rainfall areas.

[b]Information and communication technology (ICT) assets include radios, televisions, and mobile phones.

This shows that some NGOs may have better leverage in strengthening farmer organizations and facilitating formation of groups for collective marketing. Along with better education, NGO sensitization and information flow seem to be good instruments for facilitating participation in group marketing.

Governance of Marketing Groups

The governance of PMGs is inspired and defined by their constitution (bylaws), which lays out the norms of operations as well as the roles and responsibilities of various organs and members versus the management that oversees the running of the PMGs on behalf of members. All the PMGs we studied have written bylaws governing the running of their groups. The bylaws focus on the obligations of the members to the group but are relatively silent on the obligations of the group to members. For example, the bylaws require that members sell their grain through the PMG, make requisite payments or contributions, prioritize the farming of marketable crops (for instance, pigeon peas), and contribute actively to the development of the group. Successful governance can be inferred from the level of adherence to the bylaws. On average, 77 percent of active members abided by established bylaws. Members gave a number of reasons for violations of the bylaws, including ignorance of the bylaws, cash constraints that limited their ability to honor their payment obligations, lack of trust in the PMG leadership, and lack of commitment to the PMG cause (Table 5.11). Those members who violated the bylaws were either fined or expelled, especially if they were repeat offenders.

The PMGs had executive committees that were elected through a non-secret vote-counting process and given the responsibility of running the PMGs on behalf of the members.[7] The membership of these committees included a chairperson, vice chairperson, secretary, vice secretary, treasurer, vice treasurer, marketing representative, and a varying number of ordinary members. The mean number of annual executive meetings was 15, with a median of 12. The groups had convened 16 (in Mbeere) to 14 (in Makueni) general assembly meetings since their formation (Table 5.12). The percentage of members attending the general assembly meetings ranged from 65 percent in Makueni to 72 percent in Mbeere. The respondents also identified several factors that affect the governance and management of the PMGs. The quality of the chairperson (median = 2.0) was ranked as the most important factor, followed by the quality of the executive committee (median = 2.5), while other factors such as transparency in accounting, rules and norms for coordination, and rules and norms for conflict resolution (median = 3.0) were equally ranked (Table 5.13).

---

7. Nonsecret ballots could be vulnerable to manipulation and rent-seeking behavior, which might have a negative impact on group performance (for instance, see Mude 2006). Although most PMG leaders were elected through an open vote-counting process, some were "elected" through acclamation. There is a need to adopt proper democratic procedures for elections that also determine the period of service of elected leaders.

TABLE 5.11 Reasons stated by Kenyan producer marketing group (PMG) members for not following bylaws, 2005

Reason	Percentage of cases
Lack of awareness of bylaws	63
Lack of trust in group leadership and vision	63
Too busy with other commitments	38
Cash constraints (unable to pay PMG fees)	38
Lack of commitment to PMG goods	13

SOURCE: Authors' calculations.

TABLE 5.12 Producer marketing group (PMG) meetings and attendance levels in two districts of Kenya, 2004

Meetings and attendance	Mbeere ($n = 5$)	Makueni ($n = 5$)	Total ($n = 10$)
Executive meetings held since establishment	16 (12)	14 (12)	15 (12)
Executive meeting attendance (percent)	72	65	69
General assembly meetings since establishment	7 (5)	9 (6)	8 (6)
General assembly meetings in 2004	3 (3)	5 (3)	4 (3)
General assembly meeting attendance in 2004 (percent)	63	42	52

SOURCE: Authors' calculations.

NOTES: Figures in parentheses are medians; n refers to the number of PMGs.

TABLE 5.13 Mean and median rankings of factors important for producer marketing group (PMG) governance and management in two districts of Kenya, 2004

Attribute	Mbeere ($n = 5$)	Makueni ($n = 5$)	Total ($n = 10$)
Quality of the chairperson	2.6 (2.0)	2.2 (2.0)	2.4 (2.0)
Transparency in budget accounting	2.6 (3.0)	2.2 (2.0)	2.4 (2.5)
Quality of the executive committee	3.0 (3.0)	2.8 (3.0)	2.9 (3.0)
Rules and norms for coordination	2.8 (3.0)	3.0 (3.0)	2.9 (3.0)
Rules and norms for conflict resolution	3.0 (3.0)	3.0 (3.0)	3.0 (3.0)

SOURCE: Authors' calculations.

NOTES: Figures in parentheses are medians; 1.0 indicates most important; n refers to the number of PMGs.

The Performance of Collective Marketing Groups

One of the challenges in collective action studies is to measure the level of collective action and the lack of evidence of how such group action contributes to final performance outcomes. Generally, there are no standardized measures or indicators that can be used to assess the level, viability, and effectiveness (performance) of collective action (for example, see Place et al. 2002). However, depending on the situation, certain indicators may be identified as proxies for the differential level of collective action and the degree of effectiveness of such action in attaining stated group objectives. We used the PMG survey data to identify some indicators of the levels of cooperation and its effectiveness (performance) in attaining certain marketing outcomes.

The levels of collective action across groups can be inferred by attributes of the commitment of the individual members to the group activities and objectives. These include the extent to which individual members related to other members of the group within the confines of the existing institutional mechanisms and governance structures and their commitment to group ideals or the extent to which they shared a common vision. Accordingly, six indicators of collective action were identified: the number of elections since the group's formation, the share of members respecting the bylaws, attendance of meetings, annual member contributions to the group, cash capital, and agreed annual subscription fees. In order to facilitate comparison across groups, the indicators were standardized in per capita or percentage values. The agreed annual subscription fees varied from none (four PMGs) to Ksh 1,800 (about US$25) for Group E, which was significantly higher than all other groups with such agreed fees. The member contributions to the groups during 2004 also varied significantly across PMGs, ranging from zero to Ksh 247 for Group I and Ksh 264 for Group H. The liquidity of the groups in terms of per capita cash capital available for grain purchases in 2005 was also highest for these two PMGs, indicating high levels of collective action and ability to mobilize member resources.

An analysis of the standardized indicators reveals that the level of collective action varied across PMGs (Table 5.14). Based on the selected six indicators of the level of collective action, the PMGs were ranked according to the values of each indicator (1 = most successful) to identify those with a relatively higher level of collective action. A simple average rank was then computed across the six indicators. Although the assumption of equal weights for the six indicators is unlikely to hold for all groups, it was sufficient to show the relative ordering of the different groups on a scale of collective action indicators. The mean rankings show that groups with ranks less than the mean rank (5), namely Group I (3.0), Group E (3.2), and Group H (4.3), were more successful than the rest (Table 5.15). The identified PMGs have generally done well in terms of several of the indicators, and this finding is consistent with our field observations.

The correlations among the rankings of the six indicators were analyzed using a nonparametric test, Spearman's rank correlation. The ranks were not sig-

TABLE 5.14 Selected indicators of the level of collective action by Kenyan marketing groups, 2004 and 2005

Producer marketing group (PMG)[a]	Average annual elections since formation	Percentage of members respecting bylaws	Member attendance of general meetings in 2004 (percent)	Member contribution in 2004 (Ksh/member)	Per capita capital in 2005 (Ksh/ member)	Annual subscription fee (Ksh/member)
A	1.0	75	65	0	63	120
B	0.5	65	57	21	34	20
C	1.0	70	76	0	0	0
D	0.5	80	85	0	0	0
E	2.0	100	48	160	123	1,800
F	1.0	100	61	0	43	240
G	1.0	90	95	0	43	0
H	1.0	67	67	264	265	120
I	1.0	71	64	247	319	360
J	1.0	50	46	2	180	0

SOURCE: Authors' calculations.

NOTE: Ksh means Kenyan shilling.

[a]Without loss of generality, the identity of the PMGs is withheld, mainly to protect the respondents and to avoid unhealthy competition due to ranking their performances.

TABLE 5.15 Rankings of Kenyan marketing groups based on collective action indicators, 2004 and 2005

Producer marketing group (PMG)[a]	Average annual elections since formation	Percentage of members respecting bylaws	Member attendance of general meetings in 2004 (percent)	Member contributions in 2004	Per capita capital in 2005	Annual subscription fee	Mean rank
I	2	5	6	2	1	2	3.0
E	1	1	9	3	4	1	3.2
H	2	7	4	1	2	10	4.3
A	2	4	5	10	5	3	4.8
G	2	2	1	10	6	10	5.2
B	3	8	8	4	7	4	5.7
F	2	1	7	10	6	10	6.0
D	3	3	2	10	10	10	6.3
J	2	9	10	5	3	10	6.5
C	2	6	3	10	10	10	6.8

SOURCE: Authors' calculations.

NOTE: 1 indicates best.

[a]Without loss of generality, the identity of the PMGs is withheld, mainly to protect the respondents and to avoid unhealthy competition due to ranking their performances.

nificantly correlated ($p < 10$ percent) for any of the indicators except two—member contributions (2004) and per capita capital (2005). The rankings for member contributions closely parallel the rankings for per capita capital for the groups ($r = 0.735$), indicating the potential to use either of them as an indicator in situations in which data are not available on both variables. The lower rank correlations among the other variables means that these indicators were generally independent of one other and were measuring different aspects of collective action and that the potential for substitution among these indicators is quite limited. It may be argued, hence, that using a combination of different indicators was useful.

In order to see whether a good level of cooperation is associated with high performance in marketing functions, PMGs were compared on the basis of two outcome indicators: total assets built over time and total volume of grains traded (both standardized per member). The distribution of these indicators across PMGs is shown in Table 5.16. The aggregate rankings across the three indicators (that is, combining assets built over time and crop sales per capita) show that Group H (1.3), Group I (3.3), and Group E (3.5) performed much better than the others (Table 5.17). These are the three PMGs with higher levels of collective action, confirming that greater effectiveness and better perfor-

TABLE 5.16 Selected indicators of performance of Kenyan marketing groups, 2003–04

Producer marketing group (PMG)[a]	Per capita assets built over time (Ksh/member)	Per capita sales volume (kg/member)		Per capita total sales volume (kg/member)
		2003[b]	2004	2003–04
A	63	—	8	8
B	34	—	7	7
C	177	34	23	57
D	333	192	0	192
E	301	—	123	123
F	268	92	0	92
G	395	3	0	3
H	6,393	212	30	242
I	3,130	46	8	54
J	335	10	0	10

SOURCE: Authors' calculations.

NOTE: Ksh means Kenyan shilling.

[a]Without loss of generality, the identity of the PMGs is withheld mainly to protect the respondents and to avoid unhealthy competition due to ranking their performances.

[b]Dashes indicate missing data because PMGs were established later in 2003 and did not sell during that year.

TABLE 5.17 Rankings of Kenyan marketing groups based on performance indicators, 2003 and 2004

Producer marketing group (PMG)[a]	Per capita assets built over time	Per capita sales, 2003[b]	Per capita sales, 2004	Mean	
				Per capita crop sales	Aggregate crop sales
H	1	1	2	1.5	1.3
I	2	4	4	4.0	3.3
E	6	—	1	1.0	3.5
C	8	5	3	4.0	5.3
D	4	2	10	6.0	5.3
A	9	—	4	4.0	6.5
F	7	3	10	6.5	6.7
G	3	7	10	8.5	6.7
J	4	6	10	8.0	6.7
B	10	—	5	5.0	7.5

SOURCE: Authors' calculations.

[a]Without loss of generality, the identity of the PMGs is withheld, mainly to protect the respondents and to avoid unhealthy competition due to ranking their performances.

[b]Dashes indicate missing data because PMGs were established later in 2003 and did not sell during that year.

mance of groups is correlated with higher levels of collective action. Again, this finding is consistent with field observations on the level of group action and its effectiveness.

As in the case of collective action indicators, Spearman's rank correlation test was used to check the degree to which the groups were ranked similarly across the different performance indicators. The results show that the ranks of the performance indicators are closely related—that is, the ranks of cumulative assets owned were significantly correlated ($p < 0.01$) with cumulative sales (but not with annual sales values). The strong rank correlations between the cumulative assets and aggregate sales values mean that these two indicators are not necessarily independent. But the lower correlations between assets and annual sales values indicate that using a combination of these indictors was useful because they ranked groups differently—perhaps as a consequence of the high variability in production and marketed values in these drought-prone villages. However, the average rank of collective action indicators shown in Table 5.15 was strongly correlated ($r = 0.985$) with the average rank of the performance indicators given in Table 5.17. This reconfirms that groups that did well in terms of the different aspects of collective action were also the groups that performed better in terms of achieving their collective marketing functions.

Constraints on Collective Marketing

If the marketing groups offer new opportunities to improve the performance of imperfect rural grain markets, what are the policy-relevant factors of their growth and expansion? Our study identified several such constraints. The median ranks of the three most important constraints to collective marketing were given as lack of credit (1.0), price variability (3.0), and low volume of marketed surplus (3.0) (Table 5.18). Other less important operational constraints to group performance and effectiveness included weak linkages with buyers (poor demand) (4.0) and lack of business skills (6.0). In order to exploit the full potential of PMGs, future policies need to address these constraints.

The prominence of lack of credit as a major constraint is consistent with the pervasive financial market imperfections in rural areas (for instance, see Poulton, Dorward, and Kydd 1998; Kelly, Adesina, and Gordon 2003) and the wide recognition of the roll that this service can play in marketing and enterprise development (Kirkpatrick and Maimbo 2002; Bingen, Serrano, and Howard 2003). Credit constraints may be addressed through rural microcredit facilities, contract or outgrower schemes, and inventory credit arrangements.

The problem of price variability can be attributed to supply fluctuations and weak market linkages. With limited local demand, covariate risk leads to a negative correlation between local supply and prices. In rainfed systems, production and supply problems are often caused by changes in rainfall and its distribution. In some cases, farmers could turn such seasonal price changes to their advantage through temporal arbitrage. Nevertheless, the challenge of low volumes can be addressed only through increasing crop productivity or procuring

TABLE 5.18 Rankings of producer marketing group (PMG) collective marketing constraints in Kenya, 2005

Constraint	Mbeere ($n = 5$)	Makueni ($n = 5$)	Total ($n = 10$)
Lack of credit	1.4 (1.0)	1.2 (1.0)	1.3 (1.0)
Price variability	4.6 (5.0)	2.6 (2.0)	3.6 (3.0)
Low volumes	4.8 (3.0)	3.2 (3.0)	4.0 (3.0)
Lack of buyers	5.4 (4.0)	4.0 (4.0)	4.7 (4.0)
Lack of business skills	4.8 (6.0)	6.0 (6.0)	5.4 (6.0)
Low quality	7.2 (7.0)	6.2 (6.0)	6.7 (7.0)
Storage pests	7.6 (8.0)	7.6 (7.0)	7.6 (7.5)
Internal conflicts	8.0 (8.0)	8.2 (8.0)	8.1 (8.0)
Poor leadership	7.8 (9.0)	9.6 (10.0)	8.7 (9.0)
Lack of storage	11.3 (1.02)	8.2 (7.0)	9.4 (10.0)
Theft in storage	10.8 (11.0)	11.2 (12.0)	11.0 (11.0)

SOURCE: Authors' calculations.

NOTES: Figures in parentheses are medians; 1 indicates most important; *n* refers to the number of PMGs.

produce over a wider catchment area. The latter, however, implies coordination of marketing functions at a higher level of aggregation (for example, through a union of PMGs) to allow the spreading of some fixed costs.

Given the low level of market development and the lack of service providers in many rural areas, the PMGs are unlikely to prosper in a "business-as-usual" policy environment. There is a need for an enabling legal framework, improved access to market information, support to strengthen business skills, and access to essential finance and credit facilities. The PMGs were registered in Kenya as self-help groups; hence, they lack legal status as agribusiness enterprises. This restricts their access to essential credit from formal financial institutions—a major collective marketing constraint identified by the PMGs. Lack of legal status to operate as agro-enterprises also means that PMGs can neither be sued nor sue in case of any liability. This drastically diminishes the incentive for financial institutions to do business with PMGs in terms of providing essential financial services (credit, insurance, and so on). Hence, legal recognition as business entities is critical for their future development.

Another issue for the future of PMGs is the need to form a legal framework that facilitates their transition to cooperative societies. According to the Kenya Cooperative Societies amendment bill, Article 28, 2004, a cooperative society is required to have a committee of between five and nine members (Republic of Kenya 2004).[8] The committee is empowered to enter into contracts and carry out other business functions in accordance with the established bylaws. The act empowers the members to be responsible for their own registered cooperatives and stresses the need for elected committees to run their societies in accordance with accepted cooperative principles. The relationship between societies and the government is through the commissioner of cooperatives, who is responsible for the cooperatives' development and growth and provides organization, registration, operation, advancement, and dissolution services.

Although the amended act appears to provide for a stronger regulatory framework within which cooperative societies can operate (Manyara 2003; Argwings-Kodhek 2004), it fails to provide sufficient mechanisms for nascent farmer organizations, now registered as welfare groups, to develop fully and transit into cooperative societies. Without proper mechanisms for facilitating and supporting younger producer organizations, the strong regulatory framework stipulated in the act could also inhibit further development and competitiveness.[9] Moreover, agricultural marketing systems require grades and standards, as well as rules and regulations that facilitate trade and exchange through

---

8. The supplement includes amendments to the Cooperatives Act 12 of 1997, which was also a result of an amendment of the Cooperative Societies Chap. 490 of 1966. The latest amendments were motivated by the need to enable cooperative societies to operate as business entities.

9. Among other things, the framework requires that societies elect new office bearers annually and maintain financial statements that meet international standards. Failure to meet these requirements may lead to dissolution.

contract formation and enforcement. These may necessitate laws dealing with the adoption of quality grades and standards, good agricultural practices, and environmental and consumer protection issues to motivate acceptable norms of behavior for efficient market performance.

These findings contribute to poverty studies by highlighting the importance of the enabling legal and political environment for the effective functioning of local institutions, not just in NRM but in other poverty-related areas, such as smallholder marketing. Our study shows that unfavorable legal mechanisms (failure to give PMGs the status of agribusinesses) coupled with lower stocks of natural (land) and public (infrastructure, services) capitals pose constraints for smallholders in raising their incomes through market exchanges but at the same time create incentives for cooperation around these activities. The chapter also presents interesting findings on the impact of assets on the structure of collective action institutions by describing the "middle-class" effect that is seen around collective marketing. It shows the benefits of collective action in increasing incomes and overall welfare (that is, poverty reduction outcomes); at the same time, it describes how certain patterns of interaction (the creation of rules regarding such things as membership fees) can lead to exclusion of the less endowed households, echoing the findings from Chapter 3. The finding that higher levels of collective action result in a greater impact on poverty outcomes (that is, the higher marketing performance of groups) makes an important contribution to the study of collective action in the non-NRM poverty literature.

Conclusions

Many studies have emphasized that market liberalization is a necessary but not sufficient condition for increasing access to markets by smallholder farmers in many countries of Sub-Saharan Africa. Although full liberalization has not occurred and many countries have reinstated grain marketing boards with discretionary powers, the economic growth expected from the market reform policies has largely remained unrealized. With limited market infrastructure and institutions to support market development, the liberalization strategies were bound to fail in integrating smallholder farmers in less favored areas into the market system. Producer organizations and collective marketing groups provide alternative institutional innovations to enhance the adoption of productivity-enhancing technologies, to link farmers to markets, and to foster market participation and the commercialization of smallholder production, providing another illustration of the instrumental role of collective action in enabling development pathways for improving livelihoods.

The analysis and evidence presented here have shown that farmers selling to PMGs receive higher prices than otherwise, opening new opportunities for smallholder farmers to benefit from markets. Although the marketing channels in the study areas are characterized by long and complex chains and high transaction costs, which considerably lower the farmers' share of the consumer prices, PMGs improved market access for small producers by bulking, storage, grading, sorting, and selling the produce directly to buyers at the upper end of the value chain. The links to secondary and tertiary markets were enhanced through better coordination of production and marketing activities. There is no evidence that the PMGs benefited only the wealthier, resource-rich farmers. On the contrary, the incentive for joining collective marketing groups seems to be higher for those with smaller farmlands, but not necessarily for the poorest.

Nevertheless, only relatively successful PMGs were able to exploit this potential. The key challenges are related to mobilizing farmers in participatory governance and the provision of start-up capital to PMGs, coupled with training managers and members in marketing and agribusiness skills. In addition, the PMGs need to be supported in transitioning from their role as welfarelike societies, which restricts their ability to access essential financial and other services from the formal sector, to that of legal business entities. The economic viability of the PMGs was hampered by their lack of cash capital that would have allowed them to pay in time for produce deliveries by farmers. Many cash-constrained farmers are unable to delay cash payments, even when future prices would be significantly higher. These findings confirm the importance of the favorable legal and political environment for the effective functioning of local institutions, as highlighted in the conceptual framework (Chapter 2 of this volume). Provision of credit and access to financial capital are critical for the development of such groups. One strategy would be to test warehouse receipt systems in which crop inventory can be used as collateral for financial credit and to subsequently encourage financial institutions to extend credit services to organized farmer groups. The PMGs might also pay farmers a portion of the value of their grain on delivery to help them meet their immediate needs but defer full payments until the grain can be sold at better prices. Many farmers expressed interest in such a policy.

Establishment of second- and third-tier unions of PMGs would also help in expanding the horizontal and vertical coordination of production and marketing activities to address the problems of low volume and price variability and to make the groups economically attractive to service providers such as financial institutions. These strategies for enhancing institutions to improve the performance of imperfect markets should be pursued together with alternative options for smoothing and expanding supply through investments in drought-mitigating and water-harvesting techniques that would enable farmers in drought-prone areas to manage their production risks more effectively.

References

Akwabi-Ameyaw, K. 1997. Producer cooperatives resettlement projects in Zimbabwe: Lessons from a failed agricultural development strategy. *World Development* 25 (3): 437–456.

Argwings-Kodhek, G. 2004. *Feast and famine: Financial services for rural Kenya.* Tegemeo Rural Finance Paper. Nakuru, Kenya: Tegemeo Institute of Agricultural Policy and Development, Egerton University. <http://www.aec.msu.edu/fs2/kenya/wp12-ruralf.pdf>. Accessed November 26, 2009.

Becker, S. O., and M. Caliendo. 2007. Sensitivity analysis for average treatment effects. *Stata Journal* 7 (1): 71–83.

Bernard, T., and D. Spielman. 2009. Reaching rural poor through rural producer organizations? A study of the agricultural marketing cooperatives in Ethiopia. *Food Policy* 34 (1): 60–69.

Bingen, J., A. Serrano, and J. Howard. 2003. Linking farmers to markets: Different approaches to human capital development. *Food Policy* 28 (4): 405–419.

Caliendo, M., and S. Kopeinig. 2008. Some practical guidance for the implementation of propensity score matching. *Journal of Economic Surveys* 22 (1): 31–72.

Chowdhury, S., A. Negessa, and M. Torero. 2005. *Market institutions: Enhancing the value of rural–urban links.* FCND Discussion Paper 195/MTID Discussion Paper 89. Washington D.C.: International Food Policy Research Institute.

Dehejia, H. R., and S. Wahba. 2002. Propensity score matching methods for non-experimental causal studies. *Review of Economics and Statistics* 84 (1): 151–161.

de Janvry, A., M. Fafchamps, and E. Sadoulet. 1991. Peasant household behavior with missing markets: Some paradoxes explained. *Economic Journal* 101 (409): 1400–1417.

Dorward, A., and J. Kydd. 2004. The Malawi 2002 food crisis: The rural development challenge. *Journal of Modern African Studies* 42 (3): 343–361.

Dorward, A., J. Kydd, J. Morrison, and C. Poulton. 2005. Institutions, markets and economic development: Linking development policy to theory and praxis. *Development and Change* 36 (1): 1–25.

Fafchamps, M. 2004. *Market institutions in Sub-Saharan Africa.* Cambridge, Mass., U.S.A.: MIT Press.

Fafchamps, M., and R. V. Hill. 2005. Selling at the farmgate or traveling to the market. *American Journal of Agricultural Economics* 87 (3): 717–734.

Gabre-Madhin, E. Z. 2001. *Market institutions, transaction costs, and social capital in the Ethiopian grain market.* IFPRI Research Report 124. Washington, D.C.: International Food Policy Research Institute.

Heckman, J., H. Ichimura, J. Smith, and P. Todd. 1998. Characterizing selection bias using experimental data. *Econometrica* 66 (5): 1017–1098.

Hujer, R., M. Caliendo, and S. L. Thomsen. 2004. New evidence on the effects of job creation schemes in Germany—A matching approach with threefold heterogeneity. *Research in Economics* 58 (4): 257–302.

Hussi, P., J. Murphy, O. Lindberg, and L. Breneeman. 1993. *The development of cooperatives and other rural organizations.* Technical Paper 199. Washington D.C.: World Bank.

Jayne, T. S, A. Chapoto, and B. Shiferaw. 2009. Improving the performance of staple food markets to exploit the productive potential of smallholder agriculture. Paper presented at the Alliance for Green Revolution in Africa conference Toward Priority Actions for Market Development for African Farmers, May 13–15, 2009, in Nairobi, Kenya.

Jayne, T. S., J. Govereh, A. Mwavumo, J. K. Nyoro, and A. Chapoto. 2002. False promise or false premise? The experience of food and input market reform in Eastern and Southern Africa. *World Development* 30 (11): 1967–1985.

Kelly, V., A. A. Adesina, and A. Gordon. 2003. Expanding access to agricultural inputs in Africa: A review of recent market development experience. *Food Policy* 28 (4): 379–404.

Kirkpatrick, C., and S. M. Maimbo. 2002. The implications of the evolving microfinance agenda for regulatory and supervisory policy. *Development Policy Review* 20 (3): 293–304.

Kranton, R. E. 1996. Reciprocal exchange: A self-sustaining system. *American Economic Review* 86 (4): 830–851.

Kydd, J., and A. Dorward. 2004. Implications of market and coordination failures for rural development in least developed countries. *Journal of International Development* 16 (7): 951–970.

Lele, U. 1981. Cooperatives and the poor: A comparative perspective. *World Development* 9 (1): 55–72.

Lele, U., and R. E. Christiansen. 1989. *Markets, marketing boards, and cooperatives in Africa: Issues in adjustment policy.* Managing Agricultural Development in Africa (MADIA) Discussion Paper II. Washington D.C.: World Bank.

Manyara, M. K. 2003. *The development of cooperative law and policy in Kenya.* Nairobi: Oscan Print.

Mude, A. 2006. Weaknesses in institutional organization: Explaining the dismal performance of Kenya's coffee cooperatives. Paper presented at the 26th conference of the International Association of Agricultural Economists, August 12–18, 2006, in Brisbane, Australia.

North, D. C. 1990. *Institutions, institutional change and economic performance.* Cambridge, U.K.: Cambridge University Press.

Place, F., G. Kariuki, J. Wangila, P. Kristjanson, A. Makauki, and J. Ndubi. 2002. *Assessing the factors underlying differences in group performance: Methodological issues and empirical findings from the highlands of central Kenya.* CAPRi Working Paper 25. Washington, D.C.: International Food Policy Research Institute.

Poulton, C., A. Dorward, and J. Kydd. 1998. The revival of smallholder cash crops in Africa: Public and private roles in the provision of finance. *Journal of International Development* 10 (1): 85–103.

Poulton, C., J. Kydd, and A. Dorward. 2006. Overcoming market constraints on pro-poor agricultural growth in Sub-Saharan Africa. *Development Policy Review* 24 (3): 243–277.

Republic of Kenya. 2004. The Cooperative Societies (Amendment) Bill, 2004. *Kenya Gazette* supplement 17, Bill 5, vol. 106, no. 31. (Published as special issue on April 8.) Nairobi, Kenya: Government Printer.

Rosenbaum, P. R. 2002. *Observational studies.* New York: Springer.

Rosenbaum, P. R., and D. B. Rubin. 1983. The central role of the propensity score in observational studies for causal effects. *Biometrika* 70 (1): 41–55.

———. 1985. Constructing a control group using multivariate matched sampling methods that incorporate the propensity score. *American Statistician* 39 (1): 33–38.

Shiferaw, B., and G. Muricho. 2009. Farmer organizations and collective action institutions for improving market access and technology adoption: Lessons for African smallholder farmers. Paper presented at the Alliance for Green Revolution in Africa conference Toward Priority Actions for Market Development for African Farmers, May 13–15, 2009, in Nairobi, Kenya.

Sianesi, B. 2004. An evaluation of the Swedish system of active labor market programmes in the 1990s. *Review of Economics and Statistics* 86 (1): 133–155.

Smith, J., and P. Todd. 2005. Does matching overcome LaLonde's critique of non-experimental estimators? *Journal of Econometrics* 125 (1–2): 305–353.

Winter-Nelson, A., and A. Temu. 2002. Institutional adjustment and transaction costs: Product and input markets in the Tanzania coffee system. *World Development* 30 (4): 561–574.

Wolf, T. 1986. State intervention at the cabbage-roots: A case study from Kenya. *IDS Bulletin* 17 (1): 47–50.

World Bank. 2002. *World development report 2002: Building institutions for markets.* New York: Oxford University Press.

———. 2003. *World development report 2003: Sustainable development in a dynamic world.* New York: Oxford University Press

———. 2008. *World development report 2008: Agriculture for development.* New York: Oxford University Press.

Zellner, A. 1962. An efficient method of estimating seemingly unrelated regression equations and tests of aggregation bias. *Journal of the American Statistical Association* 57 (298): 500–509.

PART III

Natural Resource Management

This part of the book features six case studies of collective action and property rights in natural resource management (NRM). We begin with a study of watershed management in India, which is followed by two case studies on facilitating collective action, one for a range of NRM topics in the African highlands (Ethiopia and Uganda) and the other for securing property rights for forest communities in Indonesia. The next two case studies both deal with pastoralism in Ethiopia (Afar and Somali), but the issues that emerge as most salient differ: state sedentarization policies in Afar and enclosure of the commons with particular attention to water rights in Somali. The final case study, from Cambodia, deals with issues of NRM in a postconflict setting.

These case studies build on the rich literature highlighting the importance of collective action and property rights in managing natural resources. Like that literature, all of these chapters deal with issues related to the sustainability of the resource base. But sustainability is not the sole or even the primary emphasis. Rather, the focus of these chapters is on the effect on the poor. Thus, they examine the factors that affect collective action and property rights and the effectiveness of these institutions, but they also examine the inclusiveness of the institutions, how these affect access to resources by the poor, and consequences for their welfare.

The nature of "the poor" varies across the case studies. In India, it is the landless within the communities who are particularly vulnerable. In the African highlands, smallholder farmers and women face particular challenges; in the Indonesian case, it is people in forest-dwelling communities with insecure land rights who are the most vulnerable. In Ethiopia, pastoralists are marginalized communities but within these communities there are important wealth, power, and gender differences as well. At the Cambodian sites, most resource-dependent community members are poor, using a combination of private and common property. This variation highlights the need to look at intracommunity inequality and power relations as well as those between communities and outside forces.

The Indian case study provides fresh evidence of watershed programs that have received heavy investment from the state and NGOs. Although collective action does contribute to improved resource condition, it does not take root in the majority of cases, and the benefits to welfare take longer to be realized and may elude the landless poor. The African highlands and the Indonesian cases incorporate into their research strategy possible ways in which collective action failures can be addressed. The failure of external interventions for resource management to take into account pre-existing social structures and inequalities during implementation compounds the existing inequalities in access to resources and limits the effectiveness of interventions. The active facilitation of collective action by the Center for International Forestry Research and African Highlands Initiative (AHI) led to valuable insights into governance processes and arrangements for prompting collective resource management among communities, state agents, and resource practitioners where it previously did not exist. The Afar and Somali studies provide important insights into factors that motivate property rights transformation in dryland Ethiopia. This is an area of research that has great potential to inform policy given the recent wave of tenure reforms across much of the developing world. Although state policies (such as sedentarization and decentralization policies) can motivate resource privatization, drought shocks, relative prices, an influx of refugees, inequitable appropriation of collective resources, and failures in communal governance structures are also critical motivators. The rights of weaker groups in society, such as women and poorer herders, are further weakened or eliminated even as the elites capture the bulk of the benefits. The AHI and Indonesian cases also highlight the interrelationships between property rights and land use: changes in land use from extensive pastoralism to sedentary cultivation are associated with resource privatization.

The insights from these studies provide several suggestions for policy reform and implementation. Any resource reform or intervention process demands a careful analysis of existing social structures and incentives in order to build in implementation safeguards that protect against disenfranchising weaker members of society. Top-down authoritarian implementation processes are less likely than collaborative processes to achieve equitable resource governance and access. Such a paradigm shift toward collaborative governance requires a significant pooling of resources, knowledge, and skills to equip resource managers with the necessary attitudes and capabilities. Finally, land use and resource access regimes must be attuned to the nature of the resource. In the absence of the requisite technologies, the application of sedentarization and privatization policies in fragile settings that are characterized by low and variable productivity (as well as frequent drought) increases the vulnerability of already vulnerable populations.

Dynamism is a well-recognized feature of property rights and access to natural resources, whereas the exclusion of women and poorer individuals and groups is a common outcome of such processes. The case studies in this section show that collective action is also severely challenged by processes external to the group. More research is needed to identify the ways in which marginalized groups can increase their bargaining power and to identify factors that enable or constrain efforts to organize to resist external pressures and capture of resources, as in the Afar case. Strengthening internal group functioning might be a fruitful avenue for building resilience to external pressures; research can provide valuable insights into the conditions under which such group functioning might be strengthened.

6 Community Watershed Management in Semiarid India: The State of Collective Action and Its Effects on Natural Resources and Rural Livelihoods

BEKELE SHIFERAW, TEWODROS A. KEBEDE, AND V. RATNA REDDY

Watershed management is a landscape-based strategy that aims to implement improved natural resource management systems for improving livelihoods and promoting beneficial conservation, sustainable use, and management of natural resources. Integrated watershed management (IWM) has been promoted in many countries as a suitable strategy for improving productivity and the sustainable intensification of agriculture. The Government of India, in particular, accords high priority to watershed programs as a strategy for the integrated development of rural communities, especially in rainfed and drought-prone areas. It goes beyond conservation technologies and emphasizes the importance of the human dimension and the need to integrate technological tools with broad-ranging social, political, and economic changes. Instead of focusing exclusively on biophysical processes that improve resource conditions, IWM includes multiple crop- and livestock-based income strategies that support and diversify livelihood opportunities for the poor and creates synergies among targeted technologies, policies, and institutions to improve productivity, resource use sustainability, and market access (Kerr 2001; Reddy et al. 2004a; Shiferaw and Rao 2006).

Investment in IWM requires active cooperation among stakeholders at different levels. Much as in Chapter 2 of this volume, we define *collective action* broadly as action taken by a group (either directly or on its behalf through an organization) in pursuit of members' perceived shared interests (Marshall 1998). Effective collective action often requires formulating and enforcing rules that govern and condition the members' expectations to achieve their common goal. This indicates that several resource management and livelihood activities in rural areas manifest attributes of nonexclusion and require the coordination of resource users' efforts through collective action. The need for collective action depends on the resource type, the degree of spatial integration, and the time required to attain the desired outcomes.

Collective action tends to be more important in the context of many developing countries where formal institutions are missing or not functioning properly for the management of natural resources on which the livelihoods of many poor depend. Successful communities in terms of the sustainable management of common pool resources are usually characterized by exhibiting well-defined rules, the ability to monitor behavior and punish violators, and the existence of mechanisms for conflict resolution and a forum for negotiating future courses of action (Wade 1988; Ostrom 1990; Tang 1994; Baland and Platteau 1996; Lam 1998). As indicated by the conceptual framework presented in Chapter 2, the ability of communities to initiate, develop, and sustain collective action often depends on the internal socioeconomic characteristics of the communities and the biophysical and socioeconomic setting. There is evidence based on comparison of communities for collective action in natural resource management that the demographic characteristics and institutional and organizational structures of the community are related to cooperative and implementation capacity (McCarthy, Dutilly-Diané, and Drabo 2004). Heterogeneity along the lines of ethnicity, religion, and social class is found to have a negative effect on cooperation. The effect of inequality on wealth and community size is less clear-cut, although greater community size and inequality seem to reduce cooperation. Despite the increasing information on factors that deter or facilitate management of common property resources, there is a lack of knowledge and information on factors that influence the level and effectiveness of collective action in the context of community watershed programs. This is despite the increased policy support for decentralized management of natural resources and the significant amount of investment that both governments and communities undertake to enhance the poverty and environmental impacts of watershed programs.

In order to address some of these policy-relevant issues, the study reported in this chapter used socioeconomic data from 87 watershed villages in six districts of Andhra Pradesh, India; developed indicators of the degree of collective action; and examined its potential determinants. This was followed by analyses of key indicators of the effectiveness of collective action in attaining desired economic and environmental outcomes of watershed management. The study has provided useful insights on how community institutions determine the level of collective action in watershed management and how such collective action is related to the overall performance and effectiveness of watershed interventions. In terms of the conceptual framework presented in Chapter 2, the study focused on how assets and legal or political structures (especially watershed program bylaws and regulations) interact to affect collective action for watershed management. The key action arena is watershed management, in which farmers, government, and nongovernmental organizations are key actors. The extent of cooperation is the central pattern of interaction that we examine as emerging (or not) from the watershed programs. We then look at natural resource conditions (sustainability) as well as poverty reduction and inclusion of the landless as major outcomes, which then feed back to affect the asset base at the household and community levels. In addressing the overall theme of natural resource governance and access to resources, the study showed that collective action is strongly correlated with improvements in natural resource conditions, but there is limited evidence to link it with impacts on poverty. Thus, by examining the level of collective action, as well as its key determinants and natural resource and poverty outcomes in the context of watershed management in the dry areas, this study provides further insights into the links between the institutions of collective action and poverty, discussed in Chapter 2 of this volume.

The rest of the chapter is organized as follows. The next section outlines the theoretical issues that necessitate collective action in watershed management. The following section presents the data and empirical methods used in the analyses of the survey data. The next section discusses the major findings, and the final section concludes by highlighting the key findings and policy implications.

Collective Action in Watershed Management

A watershed is a catchment area from which all water drains into a common point, making it suitable for technical efforts to manage water and soil resources. It is a spatially defined unit that includes diverse natural resources that are unevenly distributed within a given geographic area. Due to this spatial aspect of watersheds, resources as well as resource users become interdependent over time and space. Watersheds connect different communities that are spatially separated, exploiting watershed resources depending on their specific position within the catchments. This creates interdependence in both the watershed resources and the user communities (for instance, among those on the upper, middle, and lower reaches), where the actions of one group will influence the production and investment decisions of others (Swallow, Garrity, and van Noordwijk 2002). The actual size of the watershed depends on topographic and agroclimatic conditions and may range from a few hundred to several thousand hectares. Thus, the effectiveness of watershed interventions depends on the ability to treat the entire hydrological landscape, not just a portion of it (Knox and Gupta 2000; Johnson et al. 2002).

Some of the investment activities of watershed management include construction of check dams for infiltrating surface water, terraces for soil and water conservation, and tree planting. The return to such investments is not often realized in a short period of time. The costs are incurred at the time of an investment, whereas economic returns are often delayed and accrue in small quantities over a long period of time. Hence, resource-improving watershed interventions require a relatively larger planning horizon compared to short-duration agricultural technologies such as the development of new seed varieties. Because of the problems of exclusion and the high initial costs, such projects that generate long-term positive externalities are less likely to be undertaken by individual households, indicating the need for collective action and decisions among potential beneficiaries.

Watershed management also potentially provides livelihood support for socially complex and diverse groups with differing entitlements and rights of access to and use of resources. Sustainable management of such resources requires institutional mechanisms for fostering cooperation in and coordination of the resource use and investment decisions among diverse stakeholders in the community. Effective collective management depends on the levels of existing community organizations and social capital to ensure equitable access to and use of watershed resources.

For the purposes of this study, we define *collective action* as decisions taken by a group to internalize negative externalities or to generate positive externalities in the use and management of watershed resources. Following McCarthy, Dutilly-Diané, and Drabo (2004), we identify two main components of collective action needed for the effectiveness of watershed management interventions:

- *Enabling institutions:* This component requires the development of rules and regulations for operation and management of the various common assets and structures, including grazing lands, check dams, agroforestry, and soil and water conservation practices. These rules will also include establishment of mechanisms for conflict resolution and regulation of behavior, as well as agreed norms for sharing costs and benefits.
- *Organizational performance:* This component involves the design and establishment of local mechanisms for the coordination and implementation of watershed activities. This often calls for the establishment of user groups, watershed committees, and watershed associations wherein the objectives and basic structure of authority and decisionmaking are determined.

These institutional and organizational structures of the community are critical for conceptualizing the need for collective behavior and facilitating the proper planning, design, and execution of specific actions to be taken by the community groups at various stages of implementing the watershed project, including mobilization and management of local and other resources, implementation of watershed activities, conflict resolution, and maintenance of such investments.

Making these arrangements is not without cost and may often require sensitizing and organizing widely dispersed resource users with diverging interests. However, these group activities can be used to capture the level of collective action in the community, whereas the specific watershed outcomes can be measured using objectively verifiable investments such as the number of check dams, tubewells, tanks, and the like built or jointly maintained by the watershed communities. These can be complemented by other qualitative measures to characterize nonquantifiable economic and environmental benefits to the community attributable to the watershed development activities.

The level of collective action, therefore, defines the ability of the community to create operational frameworks to achieve its goals. Our empirical analyses have focused on measuring the level of collective action in the community using multiple indicators consistent with the different facets of collective action in watershed management. The selected indicators of the degree of collective action have several dimensions spanning the two types of group actions described earlier. Hence, the different indicators are aggregated using statistical methods to develop indexes of the level of collective action. Our dataset enabled us to capture the critical elements of collective action in terms of the two categories: (1) enabling institutions and (2) participation and organizational performance. The selected indicators of each of the two categories representing the degree of collective action are discussed later.

Along with other factors hypothesized to influence the success of collective action, we investigated how the various facets of collective action determine the outcomes of such action. An important initial outcome of collective action in watershed management is improvement of the condition of the soil, water, and other natural resources on both private and common lands. This first-stage effect is captured by constructing an aggregate performance index for diverse outcomes defining changes in resource conditions and benefits derived from watershed management activities. In the second stage, collective action in watershed management is expected to improve the well-being of the community and the participants. This is the key driver of participation and of private and community investments in watershed activities. In order to measure this effect, we used information solicited from communities on various indicators of poverty and welfare changes within the watershed. These changes are those that respondents considered primarily attributable to or driven by the IWM interventions. We then tested whether the level of collective action was in fact associated with these positive welfare changes in the community. The different indicators and indexes are discussed in the next section.

Data and Empirical Methods

Data

Our study was based on a large survey carried out in 87 watershed villages from a stratified sample of six districts of Andhra Pradesh, India, in 2005. Meta-analysis of the impact of integrated watershed management in India identified water availability (using rainfall as a proxy) as a major determinant of the success of community watershed programs (Joshi et al. 2004a). In order to capture this effect, community watersheds were stratified into three categories on the basis of historical average rainfall: low-rainfall (less than 600 millimeters annually), medium-rainfall (600–900 millimeters), and high-rainfall (more than 900 millimeters) zones. Two districts were selected from each agroclimatic zone. A proportional random sample of 87 community watershed villages was selected from the six districts of the survey. In order to assess the degree of collective action and its effects on poverty and natural resource conditions, watersheds were sampled from a list of "mature" watersheds where major institutional arrangements for collective action and community development activities had been completed. This did not, however, preclude communities' continuing to maintain or upgrade the joint investments made during the project phase.

Data were collected from leaders, user groups, and key informants using standard data collection instruments at the community level. The number of respondents in each watershed representing group leaders and selected ordinary members of the community varied from five to eight local residents (including at least one woman) as key informants.[1] The group interviews were conducted in a transparent but informal setting that allowed all respondents to express their views as freely as possible and reach consensus on many debatable issues. The key informants often knew the troubled user groups and self-help groups, and this was further verified during discussions with user and self-help groups and their members. Because the survey was conducted after the projects had been completed, there was no cash at stake, making it easier for groups to be more open in expressing their governance and management problems. The data collected included information on a range of issues that characterized the village and the watershed groups, including data on demographics (number of households by ethnicity, land ownership), market access, commodity and resource prices, social services and investment in natural resource management, the process and evolution of collective action, and various indicators of the level and effectiveness of collective action, including the distribution of economic and environmental benefits from watershed management activities. The summary statistics for selected variables are given in Table 6.1.

Empirical Methods

Several variables have been identified to capture the degree and success of collective action in watershed management. However, the large number of indicators of the level and success of collective action can be reduced, using statistical data reduction methods, to a few indexes that capture most of the information on these variables. For this reason, the factor analysis approach has been used for measuring different aspects of collective action in natural resource management. This is commonly done by identifying a set of closely correlated variables that capture different dimensions of collective action (McCarthy, Dutilly-Diané,

---

1. The ordinary members of the community chosen as key informants were often suggested by a council of village elders based on their overall neutrality and knowledge of diverse local issues related to watershed management.

TABLE 6.1 Summary statistics for selected variables in sample watersheds in India, 2005

Variable	Mean	Standard deviation	Minimum	Maximum
Household and social characteristics				
Total number of households	380.89	270.18	76.00	1,280.00
Number of castes in village	10.41	5.01	1.00	22.00
Social (caste) diversity index	0.49	0.17	0.00	0.73
Share of forward caste	0.15	0.18	0.0	0.87
Share of backward caste	0.44	0.26	0.0	1.00
Share of scheduled caste	0.25	0.18	0.0	1.00
Share of scheduled tribe	0.16	0.28	0.0	1.00
Number of seasonal migrants before project	13.51	17.06	0.00	75.00
Number of permanent migrants before project	4.38	7.31	0.00	52.00
Share of marginal and landless households	0.32	0.20	0.00	0.97
Watershed project characteristics				
Age of watershed project	5.19	1.02	3.00	8.00
Area of watershed village (acres)	2,603.38	1,815.78	990.0	10,380.0
Project implementing agency (NGO = 1)	0.48	0.50	0.00	1.00
Assets				
Percentage of households owning open wells before project	22.16	27.66	0.00	170
Percentage of households owning open wells after project	20.05	25.75	0.00	170
Percentage of households owning tubewells before project	14.81	19.98	0.00	83.00
Percentage of households owning tubewells after project	21.72	22.88	0.00	95.00
Percentage of households owning cattle before project	55.00	18.01	20.00	100.00
Infrastructure and markets				
Distance to nearest market (km)	14.83	11.81	3.00	70.00
Distance to *mandal* (local administration) (km)	10.83	8.78	1.00	71.00
Distance to Hyderabad (km)	225.67	119.08	30.00	422.00
Quality of road to village (1 = poor; 4 = very good)	2.95	0.43	1.00	4.00
Highest school standard in village	6.62	2.23	0.00	10.00
Number of schools in village	1.49	0.93	1.00	5.00
Number of clinics	0.44	0.80	0.00	4.00
Number of phones per household before project	0.02	0.03	0.00	0.18
Number of phones per household after project	0.07	0.09	0.00	0.59

(continued)

TABLE 6.1 Continued

Variable	Mean	Standard deviation	Minimum	Maximum
Percentage of households with electricity before project	54.06	29.92	7.15	100.00
Percentage of households with electricity after project	65.86	35.54	8.16	100.00
Biophysical conditions				
Medium-rainfall zone (dummy)	0.36	0.48	0.00	1.00
High-rainfall zone (dummy)	0.32	0.47	0.00	1.00
Share of cultivated area rainfed	0.89	0.13	0.35	1.00
Share of total area degraded	0.01	0.01	0.00	0.06
Share of common property resources and forest area	0.10	0.14	0.00	0.67
Leadership and conflict management				
Whether leader is acceptable (yes = 1)	0.90	0.31	0.00	1.00
Popularity of leader (1 = low; 3 = high)	2.07	0.33	1.00	3.00
Leadership problems (1 = low level; 5 = high level)	1.91	0.39	1.00	3.00
Problems in transparency of using funds (1 = low level; 5 = high level)	2.44	0.60	1.00	4.00
Problems in conflict management (1 = low level; 5 = high level)	2.43	0.74	1.00	5.00
Whether minutes of previous meeting are read at each meeting (yes = 1)	0.61	0.49	0.00	1.00
Whether information is shared widely (yes = 1)	0.25	0.44	0.00	1.00
Whether employment is preferred for women (yes = 1)	0.03	0.18	0.00	1.00

SOURCE: Authors' estimation.

NOTES: n = 87 watersheds. NGO means nongovernmental organization.

and Drabo 2004; McCarthy et al. 2004). Similarly, we employed factor analysis to develop an aggregate index of the degree and success of collective action specific to each watershed community and to identify the relative importance of the selected indicators. Factor analysis allows clustering of variables on the basis of mutual correlations and a grouping of variables based on their similarities. The higher the loading of a variable, the more influence it has on the formation of the factor scores, and vice versa (Pett, Lackey, and Sullivan 2003). This was followed by regression analyses to identify the determinants of the level and success of collective action in watershed management. The advantages of using factor scores are that the new variables are not correlated and the problem of multicollinearity is avoided (Sharma 1996, 79–81). The resulting factor structure represents a distinct construct that can be meaningfully interpreted (Sharma 1996, 119). The ability to interpret and assign some meaning to the factors acts as an extremely important criterion in determining the final number of factors to extract (Frankfort-Nachmias and Nachmias 1996).

The Level of Collective Action

McCarthy et al. (2004) identified a set of variables that affect a group's capacity to cooperate—trust, network capacity, and organizational achievement. Trust reflects the degree of interdependence of and reliance among members on the behavior of individuals but is difficult to measure empirically. Network capacity is a function of variables that reflect the capacity to share information and facilitate the transformation of information into knowledge and action. Organizational achievement captures the implementation capacity of the group in terms of participation, number of rules devised, and contributions of individual members to collective efforts.

Along the same lines, we considered two sets of variables that capture the level of collective action in watershed management activities: (1) enabling institutions and (2) participation and organizational performance. In relation to the first factor, the development of institutions for defining and regulating individual behavior and shaping expectations is a critical first step and an enabling condition for community watershed management. This is an important indicator of collective action in terms of creating the initial enabling conditions for collective management. We used several proxy variables to capture the level of collective action in terms of establishing the ground rules for cooperation, including rules designed and adopted by the watershed community to address the different dimensions of collective natural resource management, the percentage of watershed association (WA) members respecting rules on cash contribution, and the percentage of WA members respecting the rules established on labor contribution. In relation to the second factor, participation of households in various joint community activities, including attendance of meetings and fund-raising events, is also decisive for the level of collective action. Community members show their commitment to collective principles through their labor and cash contributions, which can be considered key indicators of the degree of collective action in a given community. In this category we included the average amount of cash contributions per household, the community's share of cash contributions, labor contributions, and the number of households contributing to a maintenance fund. To indicate organizational performance, we used the proportion of smoothly running user groups, number of watershed committee (WC) meetings per year, and percentage of members attending WC meetings. These variables capture the broader dimensions of the level or degree of collective action in community watershed management.

As a first step in validating the choice of these selected variables, we checked for the existence of a positive and significant correlation among the selected variables that is required if these variables indeed provide information about the underlying capacity of the communities to cooperate (McCarthy, Dutilly-Diané, and Drabo 2004; McCarthy et al. 2004). We used a simple correlation analysis to check the level and overall significance of pairwise coefficients. The relatively strong correlation among the selected indicator variables was further captured in the factor analysis using the retained factors with eigenvalues greater than one (Pett, Lackey, and Sullivan 2003).

The Success of Collective Action

We used a mix of quantitative and qualitative indicators to measure the effectiveness or success of collective action in watershed management in terms of achieving various community objectives. In the first instance, we captured the outcomes of collective action in undertaking natural resource–improving investments. We identified three different variables as indicators of the community's achievements in improving the natural resource base in the watershed. These included the total number of improved or well-managed communal tubewells (drill wells), open wells, and check dams. In the second level of the analysis we identified certain indicators that measured the changes in the level of asset endowments or poverty profiles in the surveyed communities. To capture these changes we used six indicators, including increases in the number of households owning livestock, self-sufficiency in food staples, overall food security, and income growth to escape poverty as well as reduction in the number of households involved in seasonal and permanent out-migration.

Econometric Estimation

In both cases, we further investigated the indexes that were obtained from the factor analyses to identify their key determinants using regression analyses. The first set of equations estimated examines the likely determinants of the variation in the degree of collective action across the surveyed watershed communities. We then estimated the parameters for the determinants of the levels of collective action using ordinary least squares (OLS). The following general equation was estimated:

$$CA\ Index = \beta'X + \varepsilon, \tag{1}$$

where *CA Index* is a measure of the level of collective action, X is a vector of exogenous explanatory variables, β' is the parameter to be estimated, and ε is an error term that is normally distributed with zero mean and variance σ^2.

We used a second set of equations in an attempt to identify the variables that affect the performance or effectiveness of watershed activities. Along with several community characteristics and biophysical and socioeconomic factors, we particularly tested whether the indexes measuring the degree of collective action identified earlier would have any effect on the two indexes measuring the success or effectiveness of community watershed investments. This helped us to assess whether collective action expressed through joint watershed investments has generated joint public goods that offer benefits and create incentives for the conservation of community watersheds. We used the following generic equation to estimate the performance of collective action:

$$Perf\ Index = \beta_1' X_1 + \beta_2' X_2 + \varepsilon, \qquad (2)$$

where *Perf Index* is the dependent variable measuring the index of the performance of collective action, X_1 is a vector of exogenous regressors, X_2 is a vector of indexes of collective action used to capture the enabling institutions and organizational performance, β_1' and β_2' are estimated parameters, and ε is an error term that is normally distributed with zero mean and variance σ^2.

Using OLS for estimation of the performance of collective action may, however, lead to inconsistent estimates if unobserved variables affect both the level and the performance of collective action, leading to the endogeneity bias (Wooldridge 2002). In order to test this effect, we first estimated the full regression model for the performance equations and tested for the joint significance of selected variables. Those variables that were found to be jointly insignificant were then excluded from the performance regressions, and some of them were used as instruments for estimating the potentially endogenous variables (indexes of the level of collective action). We also tested for the validity of the instruments using standard tests for overidentifying restrictions (Baum, Schaffer, and Stillman 2003) and used the Hausman test (Hausman 1978) to evaluate the consistency of OLS compared to the two-stage instrumental variables approach. We undertook the analysis using the IVREG2 procedure in STATA Version 10 (Baum, Schaffer, and Stillman 2007).

Results and Discussion

Socioeconomic Characteristics of Communities

Socioeconomic characteristics of the 87 sample watershed communities are given in Table 6.1 to facilitate a better understanding of the context. As indicated earlier, the watershed communities were chosen to represent the three rainfall zones: low, medium, and high. The sample watersheds were chosen from these three zones and evenly distributed among the zones. About 48 percent of the watersheds were implemented by various nongovernmental organizations (NGOs) working with the communities. Although previous studies had indicated that projects implemented by NGOs were generally more successful (Kerr 2001), the second-generation watershed programs implemented by government agencies also pursued participatory approaches. Some NGOs also lack the capacity or the reputation to mobilize local communities and manage available project funds. The project implementing agency (PIA) is not therefore expected to have had any significant effect on the effectiveness of watershed projects included in this study. The important roles of the PIA were to facilitate community organization and training, motivate the formulation of local rules for collective action and resource mobilization, and design and facilitate the implementation of development plans for the watershed. The projects were funded by various governmental agencies—for example, the Drought Prone Area Program, the Desert Development Program, and Integrated Watershed Development Projects—facilitated through national and state governments and NGOs.

Because the survey included only completed watersheds, the average duration of watershed projects was about 5.16 years. The average size of the communities varied in terms of both the number of community members and the geographic areas covered. The average size of the groups was about 380 households, but the sizes varied between 76 and 1,280 households. The average size of the watershed villages was about 2,600 acres (1,054 hectares), but the sizes ranged between 400 and 4,200 hectares, showing wide disparities in the geographic areas covered by the projects. As is typical of rural India, the communities were composed of diverse social groups representing different castes. The number of social groups varied between 5 and 22 castes, with an average number of 10 castes. Using the conventional caste classification systems used in India, about 15 percent of the villagers belonged to the forward, 44 percent to the backward, and 25 percent to the scheduled castes, and the remaining 16 percent belonged to the scheduled tribes.[2]

The communities also varied in terms of infrastructure and market access variables. The distance to the nearest market varied between 3 and 70 kilometers, with an average of about 15 kilometers. The distance to the state capital, Hyderabad, varied from 30 to more than 420 kilometers, with an average of 119 kilometers. Similarly, the quality of the roads to the village varied significantly, from good to very bad condition. The proportion of households owning certain assets such as tubewells and livestock and with access to electricity and telephones also varied among the surveyed villages. On average, there were 1.5 schools and 0.44 clinics in these watershed communities. About 55 percent of the households owned cattle. Data were also collected on how asset ownership and access to social infrastructure varied before and after the project. For example, ownership of tubewells increased from about 15 percent before the project to about 22 percent after the project. Additionally, the number of phones per household changed from 0.02 to 0.07, and the share of households with access to electricity grew from 54 percent to about 66 percent. We took these factors into account in evaluating the likely determinants and impacts of collective action on watershed management.

---

2. The terms *forward caste* and *backward caste* are in common use in India. For clarity, and without any prejudice, we have adopted these classifications, which are in common use in the literature.

Indicators of Levels of Collective Action

In this section we discuss the results from analyses of indicators of collective action. As a preliminary validation step for the selected indicators, we conducted a simple pairwise test of the correlations among 10 indicators (Table 6.2). The pairwise correlations are positive and significant at the 10 percent level for most of the variables and hence validate the use of factor analysis to create the indexes of collective action (McCarthy, Dutilly-Diané, and Drabo 2004; McCarthy et al. 2004). The relatively strong correlation among the indicator variables is reflected in the factor analysis, which gives two useful factors with eigenvalues greater than one. The scoring coefficients for these factors are presented in Table 6.3.

The scoring coefficients for the first factor are relatively high for variables related to local institutions (rules and bylaws) defining the "rules of the game" and shaping the expectations of the participants. The scoring coefficients are particularly higher for the bylaws developed to strengthen local institutions of collective action and to address the specific uses and management of diverse resource types (community woodlots, check dams, grazing lands, and so on) in the watershed and the share of community members respecting the different rules, especially those related to cash and labor contributions. The first factor, therefore, is considered to capture the effect of "enabling institutions" on community collective action and participation. We call this the internal institutional capacity (IIC) of the community. The second factor receives most of its loadings from variables that show the degree of household participation in collective activities and their contributions to watershed activities. These include both cash and labor contributions for project activities and for the sustainability of project investments during the postproject period. The other variables have either low or negative but small factor loadings. Accordingly, we consider this factor as capturing mainly the effect of participation and organizational performance, which may be called internal mobilization capacity (IMC) of the community.[3]

The factor analysis therefore provides two indexes capturing internal institutional capacity and internal mobilization capacity. In order to see the degree of variation across watershed communities in terms of these two measures of collective action, we plot these indexes in Figures 6.1 and 6.2. These results show that watersheds vary significantly in terms of the degree of observed collective action, but the distributions for the two indexes are quite different. About 60 percent and 55 percent of the watershed communities have IIC and

---

3. McCarthy, Dutilly-Diané, and Drabo (2004) and McCarthy et al. (2004), following the same approach with a set of 10 largely positively correlated variables, identified two indexes of collective action—network capacity and implementation capacity. These are similar to IIC and IMC, respectively, in our analysis.

TABLE 6.2 Matrix of correlations among 10 indicators of the level of collective action in the 2005 Indian study

	1	2	3	4	5	6	7	8	9	10	
1											Community's share of total watershed development investment
2	+										Average household cash contribution to investment fund
3		+									Households contributing to maintenance fund
4		+	+								Labor contribution per household
5		+									Percentage of smoothly running user groups
6											Watershed committee (WC) meetings per year
7					+	+					Percentage of members attending WC meetings
8	–		+		+	+	+				Percentage of watershed association (WA) members respecting rules about cash contribution
9			+	+	+	+	+	+			Percentage of WA members respecting rules about labor contribution
10			+	+		+	+	+	+		The dimension of natural resource management covered by rules (bylaws)

SOURCE: Authors' estimation.

NOTES: + means positive correlation; – means negative correlation.

TABLE 6.3 Scoring coefficients for two retained factors for level of collective action in the 2005 Indian study

Variable	Institutional capacity	Mobilization capacity
Community's share of cash contribution	–0.0174	**0.1104**
Per capita cash contribution	0.0970	**0.4162**
Households contributing to investment maintenance fund	0.1256	**0.2945**
Labor contribution per household	0.0200	**0.2415**
Percentage of smoothly running user groups	0.1581	–0.0866
Watershed committee (WC) meetings per year	0.0361	–0.0419
Percentage of members attending WC meetings	**0.1143**	–0.1250
Percentage of watershed association (WA) members respecting rules about cash contribution	**0.2344**	–0.1298
Percentage of WA members respecting rules for labor contribution	**0.2248**	–0.0750
Dimension of institutions and natural resource management covered by bylaws	**0.3329**	–0.0097

SOURCE: Authors' estimation.

NOTES: The boldfaced values in the "Institutional capacity" column indicate those variables that are strongly correlated with internal institutional capacity. The boldfaced values in the "Mobilization capacity" column indicate those variables that are strongly correlated with internal mobilization capacity.

IMC values, respectively, above zero (skewed to the right).[4] Although the individual scores are difficult to interpret on their own, their relative values can shed light on the relative position of any given watershed community on the scale of the degree of collective action. Both indexes show that there were relatively fewer watersheds with significantly higher scores (for instance, greater than 1.0). The majority of the watersheds (about 60 percent) had values close to zero or slightly higher (± 0.5). About 8–10 percent of the sample watersheds had higher scores on both indexes (greater than 1.0). This clearly indicates that the level of collective action in terms of establishing and enforcing collective rules and mobilizing community resources for joint investments was generally low in many of the watersheds. This is consistent with similar findings of low levels of effective community participation in watershed programs across India (Joshi et al. 2004b; Reddy et al. 2004a).

---

4. The negative values for the IIC and IMC indexes are related to the negative scoring coefficients for some of the indicators used in creating the two indexes. Because the selected indicator variables capture different aspects of collective action, they were correlated differently with the two retained factors, but the magnitude of the negative coefficients is small. Some indicators of collective action that were negatively correlated with both indexes were dropped.

FIGURE 6.1 Percentage distribution of index of institutional capacity in the 2005 Indian study

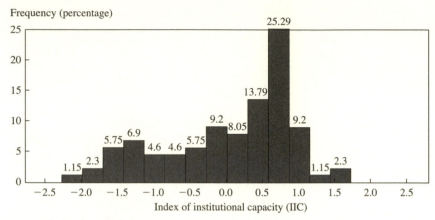

SOURCE: Authors' estimation.

FIGURE 6.2 Percentage distribution of index of mobilization capacity in the 2005 Indian study

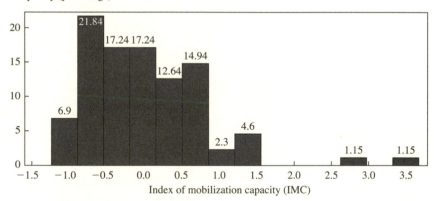

SOURCE: Authors' estimation.

Determinants of the Levels of Collective Action

In this section we discuss results from the analyses of the determinants of indexes of the degree of collective action. In order to identify the key variables associated with higher levels of community collective action, we included several variables that capture

- biophysical conditions (rainfall zone; village area; share of rainfed farmland; share of degraded land, community forest, and other commons; and so on),

- the socioeconomic profile of the village (distance to markets and local administration, number of schools, and ownership of selected assets such as phones and wells),
- type of implementing agency (NGO or government),
- socioeconomic characteristics of the groups (size, number of castes, and diversity of social groups), and
- leadership and organizational attributes of the groups (transparency in the management of finances, quality of leadership, role of women, and so on).

The regression results for the two indexes are presented in Tables 6.4 and 6.5. The major positive correlates with institutional capacity include high rainfall, distance to the nearest main market, number of castes, number of phones, acceptability of leadership, and agreed preferences for female employment in watershed works in the community. The negative correlates with institutional capacity include geographic size of the village, number of households, distance to the *mandal* (local administration), and proportion of households with electricity. The positive effect of distance to markets and the negative effect of access to electricity seem to indicate that the internal institutional capacity somehow decreases with market access and urbanization. Better market access seems to stimulate more integration with the economy outside the village, so people may be more focused on that and less interested in participating in village institutions. On the other hand, better water management and access to irrigation resulting from collective watershed management may also strengthen market orientation through the production of high-value irrigated crops such as vegetables. The exact influence of these factors on collective action is not immediately clear and may warrant more investigation in the future. The negative effects of the size of the village and the number of households indicate the transaction costs and coordination problems associated with large groups. However, the second term for group size was positive, indicating a relationship that differs from the common inverted U type of response for this variable. But these results are consistent with findings in the West African Sahel (McCarthy et al. 2004).

With regard to the determinants of the second index of the level of collective action, the positive correlates with the internal mobilization capacity include the size of the village, the proportion of degraded common lands in the village area, and the preference for female employment in watershed works. The negative correlates include the location of the village in the higher-rainfall zones of the semiarid region, the size of the group (number of households), the distance to the *mandal,* and the number of seasonal migrants from the village. Except for a few variables—rainfall, village area, and share of degraded land— the variables have similar effects for the two indexes of collective action. Although institutional capacity seemed to be higher in the high-rainfall areas, the mobilization capacity of the communities seems to have been lower in these

TABLE 6.4 Regression results for index of institutional capacity from the 2005 Indian study

Variable	Coefficient	Standard error	t-statistic	p-value
Project implementing agency (NGO = 1)	0.046	0.220	0.210	0.834
Age of watershed	−0.058	0.112	−0.520	0.605
Village area (acres)	−0.001	0.001	−1.700*	0.095
Medium-rainfall zone dummy	0.433	0.484	0.900	0.374
High-rainfall zone dummy	0.664	0.288	2.300**	0.025
Distance to Hyderabad	0.002	0.002	1.120	0.266
Distance to *mandal* (local administration)	−0.021	0.011	−1.870*	0.067
Distance to market	0.025	0.008	2.930***	0.005
Number of households	−0.005	0.002	−2.800***	0.007
Square of number of households	0.000	0.000	2.720***	0.009
Number of castes	0.091	0.033	2.720***	0.009
Caste heterogeneity index	−0.750	0.632	−1.190	0.240
Proportion of marginal and landless households[a]	−0.079	0.569	−0.140	0.890
Number of seasonally migrating households[a]	0.005	0.006	0.860	0.394
Number of permanently migrating households[a]	−0.016	0.013	−1.180	0.243
Highest school standard	−0.035	0.059	−0.590	0.557
Number of schools	−0.185	0.145	−1.280	0.206
Households with phones[a]	0.011	0.006	1.780*	0.081
Households with electricity[a]	−0.002	0.001	−2.110**	0.039
Transparency of funding	0.187	0.176	1.060	0.292
Leader's acceptability	0.680	0.380	1.790*	0.079
Information dissemination	0.207	0.259	0.800	0.428
Preference for female employment	0.823	0.469	1.750*	0.085
Proportion of degraded land	−33.597	21.661	−1.550	0.126
Proportion of rainfed land	−0.254	0.885	−0.290	0.775
Proportion of common property resources and forest	−0.595	0.763	−0.780	0.439
Constant	0.258	1.747	0.150	0.883
Number of observations	84			
R^2	0.58			

SOURCE: Authors' estimation.

NOTES: NGO means nongovernmental organization. * means significant at the 10 percent level; ** means significant at the 5 percent level; *** means significant at the 1 percent level.

[a]Refers to before-project conditions.

TABLE 6.5 Regression result for index of mobilization capacity for the 2005 Indian study

Variable	Coefficient	Standard error	t-statistic	p-value
Project implementing agency (NGO = 1)	0.287	0.146	1.970	0.054
Age of watershed	0.084	0.073	1.150	0.255
Village area (acres)	0.001	0.001	2.090**	0.041
Medium-rainfall zone dummy	−0.371	0.337	−1.100	0.275
High-rainfall zone dummy	−0.553	0.203	−2.720***	0.009
Distance to Hyderabad	−0.001	0.001	−0.870	0.387
Distance to *mandal* (local administration)	−0.025	0.008	−3.080***	0.003
Distance to market	0.005	0.006	0.800	0.426
Number of households	−0.007	0.001	−5.900***	0.000
Square of number of households	0.000	0.000	3.060***	0.003
Number of castes	0.004	0.024	0.170	0.867
Caste heterogeneity index	0.168	0.445	0.380	0.706
Proportion of marginal and landless households[a]	0.248	0.401	0.620	0.539
Number of seasonally migrating households[a]	−0.013	0.004	−3.010***	0.004
Number of permanently migrating households[a]	−0.002	0.009	−0.230	0.822
Highest school standard	0.017	0.042	0.410	0.684
Number of schools	0.050	0.100	0.500	0.619
Households with phones[a]	0.000	0.004	−0.110	0.915
Households with electricity[a]	0.001	0.001	1.460	0.151
Transparency of funding	−0.005	0.124	−0.040	0.969
Information dissemination	0.271	0.182	1.490	0.143
Preference for female employment	1.030	0.332	3.100***	0.003
Proportion of degraded land	36.621	14.623	2.500**	0.015
Proportion of rainfed land	−0.501	0.611	−0.820	0.415
Proportion of common property resources and forest	0.653	0.528	1.240	0.222
Constant	1.385	1.070	1.300	0.200
Number of observations	84			
R^2	0.72			

SOURCE: Authors' estimation.

NOTES: NGO means nongovernmental organization. ** means significant at the 5 percent level; *** means significant at the 1 percent level.

[a]Refers to before-project conditions.

same areas, indicating that the overall effect of rainfall may depend on the relative magnitude of these seemingly opposing effects. Similarly, the share of village degraded land seemed to have a positive effect on mobilization capacity, indicating that if communities are able to evolve the fundamental rules of the game (institutions), the capacity for mobilizing local resources for collective action is likely to be higher in villages where the perception of land degradation is great. The effect of these indexes on the selected poverty and natural resource outcomes of collective action will be investigated in the following sections.

Indicators of the Success of Collective Action

In this section we discuss the results from analyses of indicators of the effectiveness or success of collective action. We present findings for changes in natural resource conditions and various quantitative indicators of performance defining changes in the poverty and welfare conditions of a community. Using the rule of thumb of eigenvalues greater than one, only one factor is retained. The scoring coefficients for this factor for the three indicators capturing the outcomes related to improvements in natural resource conditions are presented in Table 6.6. The factor loadings are strongest for the community tubewells and open wells maintained in good condition through watershed investments. In the next stage we used factor analyses to develop an aggregate index for these indicators. The aggregate index (Perf Index I) of the improvements in the condition of natural resource assets of the community is depicted in Figure 6.3. The plot for the performance scores of the watershed communities shows that the level of success in terms of these indicators was generally low. The distribution is generally concentrated around zero (but skewed to the right), indicating that only few watersheds performed well on this index. About 5 percent had a score index greater than or equal to one. These were the ones that were the best-performing watersheds using this index.

In addition to improvements in community natural resources, we also identified six indicators measuring the changes in asset ownership and poverty conditions in the community. These were changes between conditions before and after the implementation of the watershed project that the key informants considered closely related to or attributable to the watershed project itself. As

TABLE 6.6 Scoring coefficients for indicators of improved management of natural resources in the 2005 Indian study

Variable	Scoring coefficient
Communal tubewells in good condition	0.4914
Communal open wells in good condition	0.4388
Communal check dams in good condition	0.0386

SOURCE: Authors' estimation.

FIGURE 6.3 Percentage distribution of Index I: Natural resource management indicators in the 2005 Indian study

Frequency (percentage)

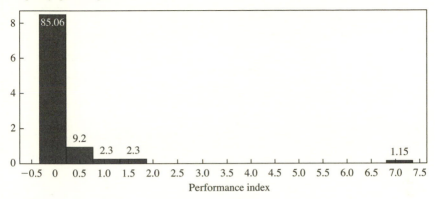

SOURCE: Authors' estimation.

in the previous case, only one factor had eigenvalues greater than one. The scoring coefficients for the selected indicators are presented in Table 6.7. Almost all the indicators have higher factor loadings toward an aggregate index (Perf Index II) measuring the potential impact of collective action in improving household asset endowments and welfare conditions in the community. The distribution of watershed villages using this index is presented in Figure 6.4. Unlike the previous performance index (Perf Index I), this index is centered on the middle scores, indicating that some watersheds did generally well in improving the welfare and poverty conditions in the villages. However, much as in Perf Index I, there are only very few communities with high levels of performance. About 4 percent of the watershed communities had performance scores greater than or equal to one.[5] This is also consistent with our findings (noted earlier) about the level of collective action. Our next task was to examine whether these changes in natural resource and livelihood conditions in the community are actually correlated with the levels of collective action assessed earlier.

Determinants of the Success of Collective Action

In this section we discuss the results from the analyses of the determinants of the effectiveness or success of collective action. One of the major tests conducted in this analysis was a test of the effect of the index of collective action

---

5. Two watersheds seemed to be outliers in their performance index. In Figure 6.3, the outlier in terms of improved natural resources was Kothapally, a successful watershed village in Rangareddy District. In Figure 6.4, this was Bandarlapally watershed in Ananthapur District, a much less successful watershed in terms of poverty impacts. However, the performance scores of these watersheds do not show unique patterns if one uses the collective action indexes (Figures 6.1 and 6.2).

TABLE 6.7 Scoring coefficients for index of changes in asset ownership and poverty in the 2005 Indian study

Variable	Scoring coefficient
Increase in livestock ownership	0.1889
Increase in staple food self-sufficiency	0.1397
Reduction in poverty	0.0633
Improvement in food security	0.1981
Reduction in seasonal migration	0.3333
Reduction in permanent out-migration	0.3122

SOURCE: Authors' estimation.

FIGURE 6.4 Percentage distribution of Index II: Poverty and asset indicators in the 2005 Indian study

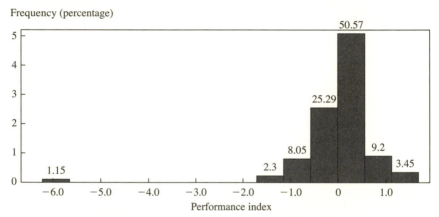

SOURCE: Authors' estimation.

on the measures of the effectiveness of community efforts. The analysis aimed to show the potential association between good levels of collective action and the outcomes measuring the effectiveness of community action in attaining its ultimate goals (in terms of improvements in poverty and environmental conditions in the watershed). Notwithstanding the measurement and valuation problems, if such relationships cannot be established empirically, there will be limited justification for individual households to participate in collective action in watershed programs. Along with the indexes measuring the degree of collective action in each community, we included variables that were hypothesized to capture observed differences within the watershed communities and influence the performance of community watershed activities. However, there was some concern whether unobserved factors that determine the index of institutional capacity and index of mobilization capacity also affect the measures of the success of collective action. This would imply that IMC and IIC variables will be correlated with the error terms in the performance regressions, making OLS parameter estimates inconsistent. In order to test this potential effect of endogeneity bias, we used an instrumental variables approach to see whether appropriate instruments can be identified. The validity of this approach, however, depends on whether suitable instrumental variables—exogenous variables that are good predictors of the IIC and IMC variables but that it is valid to exclude from the second-stage regressions for the success of collective action—can be identified. We started with a full OLS regression to isolate some variables that may be jointly insignificant in the separate performance regressions for both Perf Index I and Perf Index II. This allowed us to identify some instrumental variables that could be safely excluded from the performance regressions but could be used for predicting the potentially endogenous IMC and IIC variables. We also tested for overidentifying restrictions to examine the overall relevance of these instruments in the two-stage estimation process. The results are presented next.

Effects on Watershed Natural Resource Conditions

The determinants of the success of collective action measured in terms of improvements in the natural resource base estimated using both OLS and instrumental variables methods are presented in Table 6.8. First, it is important to note that the Hausman test indicates that the null hypothesis of consistent OLS parameters cannot be rejected (chi-squared (3) = 2.86; p-value = 0.4133). The identified instruments also passed the test for overidentifying restrictions (Sargan statistic: chi-squared (4) = 5.149; p-value = 0.2723), indicating that the instruments are valid and are not correlated with the model error term.[6] In order to further check why OLS remains consistent, we tested for the endogeneity of IMC and IIC variables. The Wu–Hausman endogeneity test (F (2, 56) = 0.73989; p-value = 0.48177) indicated that the null hypothesis that the two indexes are exogenous cannot be rejected. Based on these results, the OLS estimates are used in the subsequent discussion, while the instrumental variables results are also shown for completeness.

The significant (p-value smaller than 0.1) and positive correlates with this index include IMC, quality of the road to the village, number of permanently migrating households, highest school standard in the village, and preference for female employment. Other included variables that proxied the problems of leadership and conflict management in watersheds were not significant. Most notable in these results is the strong positive effect of collective action in terms of the IMC on this index (Perf Index I). There seems to be little doubt that com-

---

6. The selected instruments for this model include area of the village, distance to markets, distance to local council (*mandal*), number of castes, culture of sharing information, and share of the common lands in the total area of the watershed community.

TABLE 6.8 Determinants of the success of collective action in terms of improvements in the natural resource base in the 2005 Indian study

Variable	Ordinary least squares (OLS)			Instrumental variables method		
	Coefficient	Standard error	z-statistic	Coefficient	Standard error	z-statistic
Index of institutional capacity	0.098	0.092	1.070	-0.065	0.212	-0.310
Index of mobilization capacity	0.572	0.135	4.250***	0.762	0.250	3.040***
Project implementing agency	0.121	0.177	0.680	0.096	0.155	0.620
Age of watershed	0.040	0.091	0.440	0.055	0.081	0.680
Medium-rainfall zone dummy	0.313	0.249	1.260	0.326	0.216	1.510
High-rainfall zone dummy	0.014	0.268	0.050	0.186	0.272	0.680
Quality of road to village	0.324	0.166	1.950*	0.320	0.146	2.200**
Degree of conflict resolution problem	-0.179	0.155	-1.150	-0.191	0.142	-1.350
Degree of leadership problem	0.196	0.212	0.930	0.150	0.199	0.750
Leader's acceptability	0.251	0.292	0.860	0.551	0.305	1.810*
Degree of transparency in fund management	-0.095	0.141	-0.680	-0.051	0.129	-0.400
Reading of minutes in meetings	0.254	0.173	1.470	0.194	0.166	1.170
Share of backward caste	-0.162	0.333	-0.490	-0.240	0.325	-0.740
Share of forward caste	0.162	0.472	0.340	0.049	0.417	0.120
Share of marginal and landless households	-0.056	0.485	-0.110	-0.006	0.421	-0.020
Share of households owning cattle before project	-0.001	0.004	-0.340	-0.002	0.004	-0.620
Number of households	0.000	0.001	-0.010	0.000	0.001	0.430

Number of seasonally migrating households before project	−0.004	0.005	−0.740	−0.001	0.005	−0.170
Number of permanently migrating households before project	0.021	0.011	1.950*	0.022	0.009	2.360**
Highest school standard in village	0.106	0.044	2.410**	0.113	0.039	2.860***
Number of schools	0.011	0.109	0.100	−0.004	0.106	−0.040
Households with phones before project	−0.003	0.005	−0.720	−0.003	0.005	−0.590
Households with electricity before project	0.001	0.001	1.470	0.001	0.001	1.000
Preference for female employment	1.679	0.443	3.790***	1.570	0.486	3.230***
Proportion of degraded land	19.077	16.346	1.170	13.052	15.065	0.870
Proportion of rainfed land	0.418	0.718	0.580	0.631	0.630	1.000
Constant	−2.793	1.525	−1.830*	−3.350	1.365	−2.460**
R^2	0.69					
Adjusted R^2	0.55					
Hausman test (OLS is inconsistent under Ha, efficient under H0)	Chi-square (4) = 2.86; p-value = 0.4133					
Wu–Hausman endogeneity test (H0: Index I and Index II are exogenous)	$F (2, 56) = 0.73989$; p-value = 0.48177					

SOURCE: Authors' estimation.

NOTES: Ha means alternative hypothesis; H0 means null hypothesis. * means significant at the 10 percent level; ** means significant at the 5 percent level; *** means significant at the 1 percent level.

munities that are well organized in terms of coordinating joint watershed activities and investments have been better able to manage the joint natural resource assets (wells, ponds, check dams, forests, and grazing lands) of the community. Interestingly, better natural resource management is also positively correlated with the quality of the road and access to education. The importance of the permanent migration patterns before the project seems to capture the severity of land degradation and water scarcity problems in the village that may stimulate greater determination by the community to change these outcomes and reverse the downward spiral. Members of well-organized communities that perceive the threats to their current and future livelihoods are more likely to succeed in their collective efforts. A preference for female employment is also consistently significant in terms of both the level of collective action and performance regressions, indicating the importance of distributional mechanisms for the success of watershed programs.

Effects on Household Welfare and Poverty

This section presents the determinants of stated changes in the poverty levels and livelihood assets of households in the watershed communities. Before we present the results, we refer the reader to the conceptual framework presented in Chapter 2 to highlight the complexities involved in capturing the effect on poverty of collective natural resource investments through watershed management. Starting from initial conditions determined by the existing system of property rights, government policies, and household assets and by subsequent dynamic interactions, a variety of poverty outcomes are possible from changes in property rights and collective action institutions. The prevailing socioeconomic context represents the initial conditions that individuals face, which shape the opportunity set of possible actions in the action arena. In a dynamic social context, what happens in the action arena, in turn, affects the initial conditions and modifies the institutions and organizations that implement the actions.

We can deduce from this broader conceptual framework that the effect of collective action on natural resource conditions and poverty depends on the pre-existing policy and institutional setup, the asset conditions of the households, and the prevailing process of interaction in the action arena, which determines institutional capacity and organizational performance in the watershed development process. With the risk of oversimplifying the process and the potential impact of such institutional and organizational change on natural resource and welfare conditions, we present direct and indirect pathways of impact in Figure 6.5. This figure shows that for the benefit of econometric estimation the ultimate influence of collective action on household welfare and poverty can be transmitted through direct and indirect pathways. The joint investments in improved management of natural resources (for instance, wells, ponds, check dams, forests, and grazing lands) will initially influence the condition and availability of water, soils, and woodlots. The effect on natural resource

FIGURE 6.5 Direct and indirect effects of collective action in watershed management in the 2005 Indian study

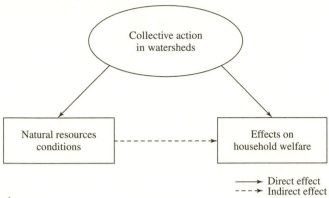

SOURCE: Authors.

conditions may, however, also take time to have a measurable impact on the condition of the resource. Depending on the distribution of natural resource assets and the resource gestation period, improved natural resource conditions may ultimately translate into economically useful ecosystem services that improve household welfare and reduce rural poverty. This is an indirect effect. However, watershed interventions may also have components that affect livelihoods relatively immediately and more directly. The effects may include increased employment opportunities for the poor that generate cash incomes and other associated watershed technologies (for example, new crop varieties, improved application of fertilizers, and better fodder for animals) that generate more immediate benefits to participating farmers. These can be considered direct effects on household welfare. The statistical analysis undertaken here aims to capture these direct and indirect effects.

As discussed earlier, the index for changes in the household asset ownership and poverty conditions (Perf Index II) measures the outcomes of both the direct and indirect effects of collective action. In order to capture the indirect effects of natural resource investments, we use the changes in the natural resource conditions directly affected by the community watershed project. Any direct effect of collective action on changes in poverty and household livelihood assets is captured by including the IIC and IMC indexes. In addition, other variables that were considered to influence the performance of watershed activities in terms of poverty and livelihood assets were also included. However, as in the case of Perf Index I, we cannot rule out the possibility that unobservable factors that affect performance will also affect the indexes of collective action (IMC and ICC). We used a similar instrumental variables approach to test this potential endogeneity bias based on a full regression and jointly insignificant variables excluded from the performance regressions but used to instrument the potentially endogenous variables. The model specification tests are presented later.

As in the case of Perf Index I, the Hausman test indicated that the OLS specification is consistent and there is much less to be gained from using the two-stage instrumental variables approach (Table 6.9). The consistency of OLS parameters cannot be rejected (chi-squared (4) = 4.31; p-value = 0.3652). However, the test for overidentifying restrictions showed that the hypothesis of correlation with the error term could not be rejected (Sargan statistic: chi-squared (5) = 12.405; p-value = 0.0296), indicating that we could not find more appropriate instruments for the potentially endogenous variables.[7] In order to further check why OLS remained consistent even when we lacked good instruments, we tested for the endogeneity of IMC, IIC, and the index of changes in the condition of natural resources variables. The Wu–Hausman endogeneity test (F (3, 55) = 0.4237; p-value = 0.73676) indicated that the null hypothesis that the collective action and natural resource indexes in this specification are exogenous cannot be rejected. Hence, we present mainly our discussions in relation to the consistent and efficient OLS results.

The variables with significant positive effects include quality of the road to the village, degree of information sharing and dissemination, level of access to telephones before the project, access to education in the villages, and preference for female employment. The significant and negative correlates include distance to Hyderabad and to the *mandal,* population share of the upper-caste households, number of households with access to electricity before the project, and the overall size of the group (number of households). Most important, none of the collective action variables had a significant effect on the changes in livelihood assets and poverty conditions in the community. Nor did we find any significant indirect effect of changes in natural resource conditions on the changes in poverty and livelihood assets in the community. However, this does not imply that the watershed projects did not generate any economic benefits to the community. It implies only that the effects of any such outcomes on the poor and landless members were limited. The evidence that preference for female employment has an effect on poverty and livelihood assets indicates that communities with better distributional arrangements for reaching out to the less privileged sections of the community will experience a positive effect on poverty. Age of the watershed had a positive and significant effect (in the instrumental variables model) on asset and poverty conditions, perhaps indicating that the anticipated impact is more likely to occur as institutions mature and natural resource conditions improve in the watershed.

---

7. The instruments used include village area, distance to markets, number of castes, level of permanent and seasonal out-migration before the project, number of schools, share of degraded lands, and share of common resources in the community.

The negative effects of some of the variables, such as access to electricity and the share of the forward caste in the community, require further research. Access to electricity is directly associated with better-off households and large farmers who own private tubewells for irrigation. In Andhra Pradesh, electricity is largely subsidized by the government, and the costs of pumping irrigation water to farmers who own tubewells are very minimal. The negative effect of well ownership (related to farm-level access to electricity) and the share of the forward caste in the community may therefore reflect the difficulties in designing meaningful institutions for collective action when access to and control of certain common watershed resources are not equitable (Deshpande and Reddy 1991). Large farmers owning tubewells and those who have the upper hand in benefiting from common resources are likely to have a greater interest in maintaining the status quo, hence reducing the poverty impacts of collective action (Reddy and Shiferaw 2007). Most of these effects seem to capture the effect of equity in sharing the benefits of collective action, indicating that the larger the proportion of the relatively better-off groups in the community, the lesser the chances for watershed collective action to improve conditions for poor and marginal households.

The insignificant direct and indirect effect of collective action on poverty and improvements in household welfare may be attributable to many factors. First, it may take many years for collective action to have any visible impact on poverty. This is a major attribute of natural resource investments, which often require a longer gestation period than many other types of investments to generate income gains to the resource users. Second, as described in the conceptual framework presented in Chapter 2, the poorest households often lack property rights that determine their access to and control of some of the most important productive assets (irrigation water, pastures, and so on) and may not directly benefit from investments that use land and water as the main entry points. In one of the districts covered in this study, Reddy et al. (2004b) found that more than 80 percent of the tubewells and open wells for irrigation were owned and controlled by the large farmers (farm size greater than 10 acres). Second, the translation of effects from improved natural resource conditions to productivity increases may involve a significant time lag and may not be realized within a period of four to five years (the common time span for completion of the watershed projects studied here). In the watersheds covered by this study, limited benefits seem to have trickled down to the landless. Only 11.5 percent of the watersheds have any special provisions for increasing the welfare of poor and landless households. A very limited number of the watersheds (2.3 percent) have reported that the landless benefited from using check dams in the watersheds (Table 6.10). However, most of the watersheds (92 percent) indicated that poor and landless farmers had benefited from the increased availability of temporary employment opportunities made available through the watershed devel-

TABLE 6.9 Determinants of success of collective action in terms of changes in asset endowments and poverty indicators in the 2005 Indian study

Variable	Ordinary least squares (OLS)			Instrumental variables method		
	Coefficient	Standard error	z-statistic	Coefficient	Standard error	z-statistic
Index of institutional capacity	-0.128	0.090	-1.420	-0.202	0.202	-1.000
Index of mobilization capacity	-0.067	0.145	-0.460	-0.372	0.274	-1.360
Index of changes in natural resources	-0.166	0.116	-1.440	-0.005	0.212	-0.020
Project implementing agency	-0.126	0.164	-0.770	-0.196	0.146	-1.350
Age of watershed	0.111	0.086	1.290	0.155	0.077	2.010**
Medium-rainfall zone dummy	-0.008	0.389	-0.020	-0.139	0.370	-0.370
High-rainfall zone dummy	0.036	0.257	0.140	-0.031	0.245	-0.120
Quality of road to village	0.461	0.171	2.700***	0.438	0.157	2.800***
Distance to *mandal* (local administration) (km)	-0.018	0.009	-2.000*	-0.022	0.009	-2.580**
Distance to Hyderabad (km)	-0.003	0.001	-1.950*	-0.003	0.001	-2.240**
Degree of conflict resolution problem	0.173	0.153	1.130	0.159	0.155	1.030
Degree of leadership problem	-0.310	0.220	-1.410	-0.506	0.222	-2.280**
Leader's acceptability	0.353	0.291	1.210	0.369	0.305	1.210
Degree of transparency in fund management	0.093	0.133	0.700	0.166	0.120	1.390
Reading of minutes in meetings	-0.028	0.163	-0.170	0.010	0.149	0.070
Information dissemination	0.555	0.230	2.420**	0.600	0.219	2.740***

Preference for female employment	1.292	0.477	2.710***	1.290	0.598	2.160**
Share of backward caste	−0.132	0.307	−0.430	−0.038	0.277	−0.140
Share of forward caste	−1.351	0.459	−2.950***	−1.416	0.407	−3.480***
Share of marginal and landless households	0.404	0.441	0.920	0.517	0.385	1.340
Number of households	−0.002	0.001	−3.280***	−0.003	0.001	−3.410***
Number of schools	0.219	0.107	2.050**	0.297	0.101	2.950***
Households with phones before project	0.011	0.003	3.350***	0.014	0.004	3.260***
Households with electricity before project	−0.002	0.001	−3.060***	−0.002	0.001	−3.080***
Households owning cattle before project	−0.007	0.004	−1.610	−0.008	0.004	−2.170**
Constant	−0.499	1.159	−0.430	−0.168	1.097	−0.150
Number of observations	85					
R^2	0.68					
R^2 adjusted	0.54					
Hausman test (OLS is inconsistent under Ha, efficient under H0)	Chi-square (4) = 4.31; p-value = 0.3652					
Wu–Hausman endogeneity test (H0: Index I and Index II are exogenous)	$F(3, 55) = 0.4237$; p-value = 0.73676					

SOURCE: Authors' estimation.

NOTES: Ha means alternative hypothesis; H0 means null hypothesis. * means significant at the 10 percent level; ** means significant at the 5 percent level; *** means significant at the 1 percent level.

TABLE 6.10 Percentage of watershed communities reporting benefits for the landless in the 2005 Indian study

Variable	Percent	Standard error
Benefits from check dams	2.3	0.151
Benefits from common woodland	58.6	0.495
Benefits from common grazing land	64.4	0.482
Employment during the project	92.0	0.274
Special provisions to the landless	11.5	0.321

SOURCE: Authors' estimation.

NOTE: n = 87 watersheds.

opment programs. Although the lack of direct or indirect evidence of the effect of collective action on changes in poverty levels shows that the impacts on the poorest groups is minimal, it does not imply that income levels have not increased. Rather, the distribution of income growth does not seem to favor the poor. More analysis of this issue will be carried out in the future using the household data collected from these villages.

Conclusions

Rainfed areas in the semiarid tropics are characterized by low and erratic rainfall, poor soils, high levels of agroecosystem degradation, and pervasive poverty. India is one of the countries in South Asia that has adopted microwatershed development as a strategy for poverty reduction and sustainable rural development in dryland areas. Some studies have shown that integrated watershed management interventions that also include improved access to markets and agricultural innovations are useful strategies for reducing poverty and improving livelihood resilience and sustainability in these less favored areas (Joshi et al. 2004a, 2004b; Reddy et al. 2004b). However, results from our analysis show that this approach cannot succeed without collective action and coordination of resource use decisions by several actors and communities at the landscape level. The real benefits of watershed programs in terms of improving livelihoods, reducing poverty, and enhancing sustainable intensification of agroecosystems will critically depend on the participation of resource users in community collective action. Whereas individual farmers often lack the capability and the incentive to improve local public goods, local institutions for collective action can help internalize externalities and reduce transaction costs for the management of local commons. These actions contribute to the empowerment of communities and facilitate joint investments for improving productivity and the sustainability of resource use at the landscape level.

Using empirical data from 87 watershed communities in semiarid India, our study has shown that collective action in watershed management can be captured through a set of variables that indicate the capacity of communities to design and enforce certain common institutional arrangements and their ability to mobilize local financial and labor resources for watershed investments. The level of collective action in terms of internal institutional capacity was affected negatively by the size of the groups (number of households and area of the village), while distance from markets and high rainfall seemed to increase it. On the other hand, collective action in terms of internal mobilization capacity decreased with rainfall, size of group, number of seasonal migrants, and distance from the seat of the local administration but increased with area of the village, flow of information within the village, and the share of land under village commons. The mobilization capacity also seems to have increased with equitable distribution of benefits and preference for employment of the rural poor and female workers. However, the results clearly show that in most watershed communities the level of collective action is very limited, indicating that only few communities have achieved higher levels of active participation of resource users in watershed programs.

At the same time, we also found only a few (10–15 percent) watersheds that were able to significantly harness the potential of collective action to achieve desired economic and environmental objectives. There is a strong correlation between higher levels of collective action and higher performance of communities in facilitating resource-improving investments, especially water-harvesting structures and good management of these resources. The effectiveness of watershed groups in terms of their performance on this index depended on other variables such as rainfall, access to education and other social services, governance structures in terms of conduct of meetings and proper archiving of information, resource degradation or scarcity problems (captured through the degree of out-migration), and the quality of the road to the village. On the other hand, the correlation between higher levels of collective action and changes in the index of poverty parameters was not statistically significant. The analyses also showed that changes in watershed natural resource stocks did not have a significant effect on changes in household welfare, indicating that the indirect effects of collective action on the poorest segments of the community are still limited. This offers evidence that the links between collective action and poverty are not always straightforward, because distribution of rights and other factors will condition how effectively the poor will be able to benefit from improved natural resource conditions in the watershed. These findings also highlight that the effectiveness of collective action in achieving poverty outcomes is dependent on the asset base of the communities and the overall enabling institutional environment, as indicated in the conceptual framework presented in Chapter 2 of this volume.

Overall, the results indicate that collective action has made a significant contribution in terms of improving the investment and management of critical jointly held natural resource assets (wells, check dams, community forests, grazing land, and so on), but there is a lack of evidence of its effects in improving the asset endowments of the resource poor and reducing poverty levels within the semiarid watershed villages included in this study. In order to improve the active participation of the resource users and the poverty impacts of watershed programs, there is a need to promote pro-poor policies and institutional arrangements that enhance the equitable sharing of both costs and benefits. Interventions that create incentives and benefits for the poor in the watershed context may include the production and marketing of biopesticides and organic fertilizers, small-scale poultry raising, increasing the rights of women and the landless to access communal resources (for instance, grazing land and fuelwood), preferring female and local employment, and promoting marketing groups to enhance the bargaining power of small-scale producers. These policies can be integrated into the watershed development guidelines to benefit future programs. Much less is known about the emergence of effective local institutions for watershed collective action and how such institutions adapt during the postproject phase and influence the propensity for the sustainable community management of local investments. Without effective and adaptable local institutions, the long-term sustainability of watershed investments will remain one of the key lingering questions. Future studies would need to investigate these factors and offer new insights on how a pre-existing proclivity to collective action, differences in biophysical and market conditions, and national and provincial policies may shape the process and determine the outcomes and impacts of watershed programs.

References

Baland, J., and J. P. Platteau. 1996. *Halting degradation of natural resources: Is there a role for rural communities?* Oxford, U.K.: Food and Agriculture Organization of the United Nations and Clarendon Press.

Baum, C. F., M. E. Schaffer, and S. Stillman. 2003. Instrumental variables and GMM: Estimation and testing. *Stata Journal* 3 (1): 1–31.

———. 2007. Enhanced routines for instrumental variables / GMM estimation and testing. Department of Economics Working Paper 667. Boston, Mass., U.S.A.: Boston College. <http://ideas.repec.org/p/boc/bocoec/667.html>. Accessed October 15, 2009.

Deshpande, R. S., and V. Ratna Reddy. 1991. Differential impact of watershed based technology: Some analytical issues. *Indian Journal of Agricultural Economics* 46 (3): 261–269.

Frankfort-Nachmias, C., and D. Nachmias. 1996. *Research methods in the social sciences.* 5th ed. London: Edward Arnold.

Hausman, J. 1978. Specification tests in econometrics. *Econometrica* 46 (3): 1251–1271.

Johnson, N., H. M. Ravnborg, O. Westermann, and K. Probst. 2002. User participation in watershed management and research. *Water Policy* 3 (6): 507.

Joshi, P. K., A. K. Jha, S. P. Wani, L. Joshi, and R. L. Shiyani. 2004a. *Meta-analysis to assess impact of watershed program and people's participation.* Comprehensive Assessment Research Report 8. Colombo, Sri Lanka: Comprehensive Assessment Secretariat.

Joshi, P. K., V. Pangare, B. Shiferaw, S. P. Wani, J. Bouma, and C. Scott. 2004b. Watershed development in India: Synthesis of past experiences and needs for future research. *Indian Journal of Agricultural Economics* 59 (3): 303–320.

Kerr, J. 2001. Watershed project performance in India: Conservation, productivity, and equity. *American Journal of Agricultural Economics* 83 (5): 1223–1230.

Knox, A., and S. Gupta. 2000. *CAPRi technical workshop on watershed management institutions: A summary paper.* CAPRi Working Paper 8. Washington, D.C.: International Food Policy Research Institute.

Lam, W. F. 1998. *Governing irrigation systems in Nepal: Institutions, infrastructure, and collective action.* Oakland, Calif., U.S.A.: ICS Press.

Marshall, G. 1998. *A dictionary of sociology.* New York: Oxford University Press.

McCarthy, N., C. Dutilly-Diané, and B. Drabo. 2004. Cooperation, collective action and natural resources management in Burkina Faso. *Agricultural Systems* 82 (3): 233–255.

McCarthy, N., C. Dutilly-Diané, B. Drabo, A. Kamara, and J. P. Vanderlinden. 2004. *Managing resources in erratic environments: An analysis of pastoralist systems in Ethiopia, Niger, and Burkina Faso.* Research Report 135. Washington, D.C.: International Food Policy Research Institute.

Ostrom, E. 1990. *Governing the commons: The evolution of institutions for collective action.* New York: Cambridge University Press.

Pett, M. A., N. R. Lackey, and J. J. Sullivan. 2003. *Making sense of factor analysis: The use of factor analysis for instrument development in health care research.* Thousand Oaks, Calif., U.S.A.: Sage.

Reddy, V. R., and B. Shiferaw. 2007. Collective action and property rights for poverty alleviation: A conceptual framework based on the experience of watershed management in semiarid India. Center for Economic and Social Studies, Hyderabad, India. Mimeo.

Reddy, V. R., M. G. Reddy, S. Galab, J. Soussan, and O. S. Baganski. 2004a. Participatory watershed development in India: Can it sustain rural livelihoods? *Development and Change* 35 (2): 297–326.

Reddy, V. R., M. Reddy, J. Soussan, and D. Frans. 2004b. Water and poverty: A case of watershed development in Andhra Pradesh. *Water Nepal* 11 (1): 51–73.

Sharma, S. 1996. *Applied multivariate techniques.* New York: John Wiley.

Shiferaw, B., and K. P. C. Rao, eds. 2006. *Integrated management of watersheds for agricultural diversification and sustainable livelihoods in Eastern and Central Africa: Lessons and experiences from semiarid South Asia.* Proceedings of the International Workshop held December 6–7, 2004, at ICRISAT in Nairobi, Kenya. International Crops Research Institute for the Semiarid Tropics (ICRISAT), Patancheru 502324, India.

Swallow, B. M., D. P. Garrity, and M. Van Noordwijk. 2002. The effects of scales, flows and filters on property rights and collective action in watershed management. *Water Policy* 3 (6): 457.

Tang, S. Y. 1994. Institutions and performance in irrigation systems. In *Rules, games, and common-pool resources,* ed. E. Ostrom, R. Gardner, and J. Walker. Ann Arbor, Mich., U.S.A.: University of Michigan Press.

Wade, R. 1988. *Village republics: Economic conditions for collective action in South India.* Cambridge, U.K.: Cambridge University Press.

Wooldridge, J. M. 2002. *Econometric analysis of cross section and panel data.* Cambridge, Mass., U.S.A.: MIT Press.

7 Enabling Equitable Collective Action and Policy Change for Poverty Reduction and Improved Natural Resource Management in the Eastern African Highlands

LAURA GERMAN, WAGA MAZENGIA,
WILBERFORCE TIRWOMWE, SHENKUT AYELE,
JOSEPH TANUI, SIMON NYANGAS,
LEULSEGED BEGASHAW, HAILEMICHAEL TAYE,
ZENEBE A. TEFERI, MESFIN T. GEBREMIKAEL,
SARAH CHARAMILA, FRANCIS ALINYO,
ASHENAFI MEKONNEN, KASSAHUN ABERRA,
AWADH CHEMANGENI, WILLIAM CHEPTEGEI,
TESSEMA TOLERA, ZEWDIE JOTTE,
AND KIFLU BEDANE

Spontaneously organized institutions of collective action and the institutional effects of exogenous development interventions are both known to have a profound effect on development outcomes.[1] Despite an in-depth academic understanding of the institutional foundations of development and natural resource management (NRM), development interventions continue to have a strong technological bias. Development and conservation interventions continue to be carried out with an uncritical view to equity and the possible negative repercussions of interventions on certain social groups and environmental sustainability, while local institutions (rules and structures) remain largely invisible to outside actors.[2] Yet the shortcomings lie not only with practitioners but also with research. Research on the institutional dimensions of development and NRM continues to emphasize the characteristics of existing institutions of collective action or institutional constraints on development rather than on ways to build stronger institutions where these are absent to address local development priorities.

---

1. *Collective action* may be defined as action taken by a group (either directly or on its behalf through an organization) in pursuit of members' perceived shared interests (Marshall 1998, cited by Meinzen-Dick, Di Gregorio, and McCarthy 2004).

2. Although the definition provided by North (1990, 3) has become prominent in academic scholarship ("institutions are rules of the game in a society, or more formally, are the humanly devised constraints that shape human interaction"), our emphasis on collective action makes the definition by Ostrom (1994), which equates institutions with "decision structures," equally appropriate. Thus, "institutions" are here taken to encompass both structural dimensions of collective organizing and collective choices that form the backbone of effective cooperation.

Background

The research reported in this chapter sought to address these shortcomings by integrating institutional analysis (for problem identification and targeting of interventions) with action research (for pilot testing of institutional innovations to address identified problems). The institutional analysis sought to understand forms and functions of existing institutions of collective action and patterns of benefit capture induced by local and external institutions and to identify the disconnects between local concerns and the institutions present to address these. Building on collective action theory, we then designed and tested institutional innovations in an action research mode to explore institutional arrangements for addressing the NRM concerns of local residents of four locations in the eastern African highlands (two in Ethiopia, two in Uganda).[3] Our findings suggest that by bringing theory into the realm of development practice, action research may provide fertile ground for research in support of practical development challenges.

With regard to the conceptual framework presented in Chapter 2, this study illustrates the complexity of feedback relationships between different elements of the conceptual framework. Contextual factors such as the initial endowments of financial and physical assets limit the extent to which local actors can leverage social assets (such as groups and networks) to improve their well-being. Similarly, low levels of collective action due to classical free-rider problems and failures of supporting organizations undermine the ability of resource users to access, manage, and draw benefits from natural assets such as forests, soils, and agricultural lands. NRM comprises the action arena. Negotiation support facilitated by external actors (the action arena) provides a platform for direct engagement among resource users and between resource users and government agencies. This results in the joint creation of new institutions such as bylaws and organizational practices (that is, patterns of interaction) that curb free riding, provide mechanisms for cross-scale coordination among groups of spatially distinct though interconnected resource users, allow equitable access to benefits, strengthen access to natural resources, and foster political commitment for the enforcement of agreements sanctioned through bylaws. These patterns of interaction have favorable implications for the welfare of local resource users at the study sites.

This chapter highlights the institutional dimensions of natural resource governance. It also focuses on how asymmetric power relations undermine equitable outcomes in NRM. Resource governance and power relations are key themes identified in Chapter 1. By implementing actions and processes that lead to the emergence of new institutions and structures that enhance collective action and equitable resource access and management, our study makes an important contribution to the broad literature of collective action, which continues to

---

3. Davis and North (1971, 6–7) define *institutional arrangement* as "an arrangement between economic units that governs the ways in which these units can co-operate and/or compete."

grapple with the problem of exclusion, especially that of marginal individuals and groups with low status and wealth.

Literature Review

Collective Action in Natural Resource Management

The role of collective action in agricultural development and NRM is by now well documented. Scholars have looked at the role of collective action in enhancing farmer participation and human capital (Coleman 1988; Heinrich 1993; Uphoff and Mijayaratna 2000; Woolock and Narayan 2000); determinants and operational principles of collective action (Ostrom 1990; Pandey and Yadama 1990; Wittayapak and Dearden 1999); and the conditions under which collective action can be a vehicle for enhancing equity in natural resource management (Kelly and Breinlinger 1995; Leach, Mearns, and Scoones 1999; Molyneux 2002). Yet the bulk of research on collective action has been in the context of common property resources (Ostrom 1990; Munk Ravnborg and Ashby 1996; Scott and Silva-Ochoa 2001; Gebremedhin, Pender, and Tesfay 2002).

Collective action is also a fundamental pillar of landscape- or watershed-level natural resource management. In addition to regulating rights and responsibilities to common property resources and public goods (Ostrom 1990; Gaspart et al. 1998), collective action has a role to play in managing biophysical processes that cut across farm boundaries (Munk Ravnborg et al. 2000). Collective action can also play a role in negotiating joint investments and technological innovations for enhanced productivity, regulating the distribution of exogenous resources within local communities (Meinzen-Dick et al. 2002), and negotiating solutions that optimize returns to diverse local interest groups (German, Charamila, and Tolera 2006; German et al. 2006a, 2006b). Given the sheer number of users in watersheds, the transaction costs of organizing, and the tendency for outside interventions to structure positions of privilege vis-à-vis any given resource (Schroeder 1993; Munk Ravnborg and Ashby 1996), representative structures and mechanisms for organizing the interface of outside actors with local communities are needed (German et al. 2006b). This is in recognition of the inherently political nature of NRM (Schroeder 1993; Rocheleau and Edmunds 1997), which requires that the outcomes and distribution of benefits of watershed management and related project interventions be transparently negotiated and monitored.

In addition to understanding what collective action can achieve, research has highlighted some of the conditions under which institutions of collective action for NRM emerge. These include the presence of clearly defined rules for resource management and access (including sanctions), clearly defined user groups and resource boundaries, adaptive management mechanisms (monitoring systems, the ability to modify rules as the need arises), conflict resolution mechanisms, and a user group and resource of manageable size (Ostrom 1990;

Pandey and Yadama 1990; Wittayapak and Dearden 1999). Each of these factors plays an important role in influencing levels of mutual trust as well as expectations of what may be gained through cooperation (Blau 1964; Burns, Baumgartner, and DeVille 1985). Yet there remain key gaps in our understanding of how to facilitate the evolution of institutions of collective action where these are absent. More research is needed to understand how equitable, meaningful (well-designed and enforceable), yet flexible rules can be generated and how to mobilize existing or new capacities for the participatory governance of natural resources (Carney 1998; Scoones and Thompson 2003).

Collective Action, Institutions, and Equity

Through their role in structuring access to other forms of capital (natural, financial, physical, human), local and external institutions alike play important roles in structuring opportunities and in benefits capture. Research has shown that collective action can contribute to asset accumulation or protect households from loss of assets through their ability to mitigate risks. These functions may play out directly, by improving people's ability to work together to overcome limitations of wealth, farm size, and bargaining power (di Gregorio et al. 2008) and to access and control assets that could be difficult to access individually (de Haan 2001; Knox, Meinzen-Dick, and Hazell 2002). For example, joint input or output marketing can enhance market access or improve profits by minimizing transaction costs (Place and Swallow 2002). Collective action also plays an indirect role by facilitating access to credit and microfinancing, information, and technologies (Grootaert 2001; Grootaert and van Bastelear 2002; Knox, Meinzen-Dick, and Hazell 2002). Each of these functions has implications for asset creation. On the other hand, collective action can help to minimize loss of assets during times of hardship by distributing risk among households—for example, by mobilizing resources during times of illness or death (see the *iddir* and Philippines case studies in this volume), helping individuals to better cope with risk (de Haan 2001; Place et al. 2002).

In addition to contributing to financial capital, collective action has been shown to underpin service delivery for infrastructure and social services (Nitti and Jahiya 2004). Action research findings also point to the role of collective action and diverse forms of social capital in enhancing human capital and spreading the transaction costs of improved NRM (Coleman 1988; Heinrich 1993; Wallis 1998; Uphoff and Mijayaratna 2000; Woolock and Narayan 2000; Meinzen-Dick et al. 2002). Yet despite the potential of collective action for enhancing access to other important development resources, group composition, dynamics, and governance are fundamental for these potentials to be realized (Davis et al. 2004). This is especially true for managing the distribution of benefits from such interventions (Jassey 2000; Grootaert 2001; Molyneux 2002). Therefore, the relationship between collective action and equity depends in large part on the functions and capacities associated with these forms of social capital.

External institutions also have a fundamental role to play in agricultural development and sustainable NRM. Yet uncritical development interventions by government and nongovernmental organizations (NGOs) have led to a host of unanticipated negative outcomes due to failure to understand existing institutions. Failure to recognize self-organizing local institutions in the management of common property resources and the imposition of overly rigid property rights regimes on traditional systems have proven to constrain rather than enable equitable, adaptive, and sustainable management of natural resources (Davison 1988; McDonald 1991; Bloch 1993; Munk Ravnborg and Ashby 1996; Lastarria-Cornhiel 1997; Kevane and Gray 1999; Ostrom 1999; Nemarundwe and Kozanayi 2003). Other authors document how outside interventions can increase risk due to more delimited resource access (Turner 1999; Ngaido and Kirk 2001). Finally, some interventions have proven to further entrench existing inequities by creating the conditions for elite capture of program benefits or natural resources (Schroeder 1993; Rocheleau and Edmunds 1997).

Despite these deficiencies, if outside interventions can influence the distribution of power and voice, there is potential for realigning the distribution of technologies, resources, and benefits (Knox, Meinzen-Dick, and Hazell 2002). Such efforts could help to counter the tendency of extension benefits to go to wealthier farmers (Grabowski 1990; Knox, Meinzen-Dick, and Hazell 2002) or the causal role played by wealth in structuring resource access (Meinzen-Dick et al. 2002). Given the context of decentralization and the devolution of policy structures in Ethiopia, Uganda, and elsewhere (Raussen, Ebong, and Musiime 2001) and the evidence of "elite capture" from similar experiences at the local level (Bachrach and Baratz 1970; Munk Ravnborg and Ashby 1996; Olsen 2001), lessons on how to engage and empower more vulnerable groups are sorely needed. This is particularly true given the many, often discrete, ways in which elite dominance can be asserted (Bachrach and Baratz 1970). These cases point to the need for a better understanding of the ways in which external institutions facilitate wealth acquisition by different social groups and of strategies to foster more equitable outcomes from external interventions.

Program Context

Our research was conducted under the rubric of the African Highlands Initiative (AHI), an ecoregional program of the Consultative Group for International Agricultural Research and the Association for Strengthening Agricultural Research in East and Central Africa convened by the World Agroforestry Centre. Since 2002, AHI has worked to develop a participatory, integrated approach to NRM at the landscape or watershed scale. Different from many other watershed management programs focusing primarily on soil and water conservation, AHI is developing an approach to integrate all components of the production system (crop, livestock, tree, soil) and the landscape (encompassing resources such as water, communal grazing lands, and forests). This chapter reports on findings from the institutional research associated with integrated social, bio-physical, and institutional interventions. The primary objective of this research was to develop and document successful approaches to facilitating equitable collective action processes and negotiated NRM solutions.

Research Questions and Hypotheses

Research Questions

Research questions are inherently distinct for empirical and action research,[4] and therefore they are presented independently.

Empirical research questions include the following:

- What is the role of existing institutions (groups, rules and norms, property rights, decentralization systems) in leveraging or constraining decision-making and resource access by diverse groups?
- What contextual factors (institutional, policy, historical, epistemological) hinder collective action and exacerbate poverty through inequitable decision-making and access to natural resources at each site?
- What are the impacts of action research interventions on participation in decisionmaking processes, identified watershed problems, policies, and the resulting livelihoods or assets of diverse groups?

Action research questions are as follows:

- What conditions (social, technological, policy, economic) and facilitation processes are required to enhance socially optimal voices (decisionmaking), choices (technological, social, and income options), and benefits (poverty alleviation, improved management and access to natural resources)?
- What policies, bylaws, and support from local governments are required to bolster community actions and collective action toward more effective and equitable NRM and income generation? What are the most effective approaches for engaging communities with local government and service providers to achieve these policy reforms?

---

4. Empirical research questions emphasize understanding of the current situation, whereas action research questions focus on the conditions for or elements of an effective change process. In many action research cases, this change process does not yet exist in reality but will be created through research. In action research, the research questions and hypotheses are necessarily broad, given the difficulty of holding both the context and approach constant. Although a generic approach to facilitating change was developed based on a review of collective action theory, the participatory nature of action research means that both the participants and the circumstances (for example, the specific problem to be addressed or resources available to address it) shape how it is applied.

Hypotheses

Research hypotheses were explicitly developed for the action research and focus on conditions for effective change:

- Strategies to improve NRM at the farm and landscape levels will be more effective if decisionmaking on technologies and natural resource governance is equitable, given the broad social support required to sustain collective action.
- Increased capacity to develop better-designed and more equitable bylaws will improve livelihoods by enabling technology adoption, enhancing collective action in NRM, and reducing the need for bylaw enforcement.

Methodology

Site Selection

Four sites were chosen for this research, two in Ethiopia and two in Uganda. All sites are highland microwatersheds characterized by smallholder farming systems, high population density, and evidence of natural resource degradation. For 5–10 years each of these sites has served as a benchmark site for AHI, where new approaches to integrated NRM are first developed and tested and from which regional lessons are drawn from comparative research. Each site is home to one or more ethnic groups with a long history of occupation of the area and limited in-migration from other groups or areas. Despite some similarities, each site has unique characteristics that merit attention in the context of collective action and NRM. Details on each site are available in German et al. (2008); however, all four sites face a broad range of NRM needs such as:

- enhancing the productivity and returns from crop, livestock, and tree components without further exacerbating system nutrient decline;
- reversing water resource degradation by fostering positive synergies among trees, soil conservation structures, and water in microcatchments;
- integrating technological innovation with improved natural resource governance to minimize the incidence of conflict emanating from small landholdings, limited economic opportunities, gender inequalities, and a tendency for land users to pursue individual over collective interests;
- enhancing equitable resource access, given the inhabitants' histories of ethnic conflict (cattle raiding);
- managing resources sustainably in the buffer zone of national parks, given histories of displacement and conflict; and
- increasing the quality of and access to support services.

The methodology consisted of four primary steps.

Situation Analysis

The situation analysis used an empirical research approach to understand (1) how resources are distributed within communities and (2) the role of internal and external institutions in enhancing or constraining resource access and decision-making by diverse groups. The situation analysis consisted of two primary methods. Focus group discussions were first used to identify local and external institutions and the participants, beneficiaries, and nature of benefits derived from each. The second step consisted of household interviews to quantify levels of and variation in household assets (the five "capitals," described later) by gender and wealth, as well as participation in local and external institutions (assessed as one component of social capital). At each site, at least 60 household interviews were conducted. Households were purposely sampled by gender (men, women from female-headed households, and women from male-headed households) and wealth (based on local indicators and thresholds). The primary local criteria for wealth ranking at all sites included landholdings, livestock holdings, and the quality of housing.

Stakeholder Workshops

Following the situation analysis, site and national stakeholder workshops were conducted to share findings and agree on action research priorities. Site-level workshops consisted of (1) sharing of findings from the situation analysis; (2) identification of NRM issues requiring collective action, changes in institutional practice, or bylaw reform; (3) prioritization of these issues based on a set of "minimal criteria"; and (4) development of preliminary action plans for prioritized topics. The screening criteria for action research themes included

- themes that involved change at multiple levels (local and outside institutions, policies);
- themes that involved current inequities or required close attention to diverse local priorities; and
- themes that could bring some change within one and a half years.

Action Research

Following stakeholder prioritization of action research themes, site teams developed action research protocols to clarify the research questions and strategies to be tested in facilitating local stakeholders' efforts to address identified problems. Each theme involved two levels of action research:

- local-level action research on how to foster collective action in NRM through explicit consideration of diverse views when negotiating access to benefits, NRM strategies, and policy proposals and

- higher-level (subcounty/peasant association or district/*woreda*) action research on how to support equitable collective action processes at the local level through changes in institutional practice, policies that reflect local priorities, and negotiation support.[5]

A common strategy was tested to foster negotiated solutions to identified NRM problems. This consisted of the following steps for each action research theme:

- identifying stakeholders, with an emphasis on local interest groups;
- meeting with the individual stakeholder groups (individuals who share a common position in relation to the issue) to raise awareness and elicit their views on the problem and solutions and their preferred approach to engagement;
- conducting multistakeholder negotiations, including
  1. providing feedback on the identified NRM issue and on earlier meetings with individual stakeholder groups;
  2. engaging in open dialogue (for validation and clarification of issues and interests);
  3. negotiating socially optimal solutions that do not bring harm to any given group and emphasize concessions on both sides, including agreed rules for resource management (often formally endorsed bylaws) and technologies that provide alternatives to practices restricted in bylaws; and
  4. development of action plans; and
- periodically conducting participatory monitoring and evaluation to evaluate progress, troubleshoot, and restrategize.

Participatory Assessment of Outcomes

The final step of the action research was to evaluate outcomes and impacts from the action research intervention. Site teams conducted focus group discussions to elicit individuals' perceptions of the types of impacts and then asked farmers to quantify the degree of change or the relative merits of different approaches using matrix ranking exercises. Although the findings are somewhat subjective and provisional, they nevertheless provide a sense of what variables matter to farmers and whether any changes in these variables have been observed. In such cases, caution should be used in deriving any quantitative conclusions from these data. In the few cases in which field measurements were taken by farmers

---

5. Under Ethiopia's system of ethnic federalism, there are three levels of local government: zone, *woreda,* and *kebele* administration (Ayele 2009). The lowest administrative structure, the *kebele*—often translated into English as "peasant association" (PA)—is a carryover from the Derg period and generally includes ten thousand or more people. The *woreda,* roughly equivalent to a district, is the second-lowest level of government and is the most important administrative unit in the Ethiopian local government structure.

or researchers (case studies 1 and 2, described later in this chapter), quantitative measurements are more reliable. Nevertheless, in the absence of a control group, the observed changes cannot be attributed with certainty solely to the interventions, because there may have been other contributing factors.

The findings presented in the next section are grouped according to the three phases of research: situation analysis, stakeholder workshops, and action research.

Situation Analysis Findings

Household Assets and Investment Potential

The surveys measured households' current levels of assets using the "five capitals": human capital (age and education level of household members), social capital (access to social networks, participation in local forms of collective action), natural capital (water, forest, land, and so on), financial capital (off-farm income, savings), and physical capital (roads, structures, transport, communications). The idea behind these was (1) to determine whether current assets determined households' ability to acquire new assets and (2) to understand the role of both local forms of collective action and outside institutions in asset accumulation.

Table 7.1 shows a two- to fifty-three-fold difference in land and livestock holdings between lower- and higher-income households. To determine the extent to which "wealth begets wealth," we analyzed the annual level of investment in productive activities by wealth category (Tables 7.2 and 7.3). This was used as an indicator of the extent to which wealth determines the ability to acquire additional wealth through investment. The data suggest a strong correlation between households' current wealth status and their ability to invest in productive activities.

The Influence of Local and External Institutions on Assets and Livelihoods

Local collective action institutions were abundant at all research sites. They included local savings and loan groups, merry-go-rounds (rotational savings plans), religious associations, funeral associations and stretcher groups, labor-sharing arrangements for private and communal works, traditional conflict resolution mechanisms, arrangements for saving or pooling resources for celebra-

TABLE 7.1 Land and livestock assets by wealth category in four sites in the eastern African highlands, 2005

| Type of asset | Areka | | Ginchi | | Kabale | | Kapchorwa | |
	High	Low	High	Low	High	Low	High	Low
Landholdings (hectares)	0.74	0.26	3.4	1.2	2.91	0.81	2.10	0.04
Head of cattle	3.7	0.6	6.4	3.2	0.13	0.06	8.22	0.49

SOURCE: Authors.

TABLE 7.2 Annual agricultural investments (in birr) by wealth category at the two Ethiopian sites, 2006

	Ginchi			Areka		
Investment	Low	Medium	High	Low	Medium	High
Seed	336.1	510.9	273.9	72.1	106.8	165.7
Pesticide	28.3	69.0	48.3	0.6	0.4	0.9
Fertilizer	133.2	210.7	407.6	46.5	84.9	173.2
Feed	65.8	170.9	232.5	10.8	20.6	55.0
Veterinary	23.3	55.1	72.9	9.8	10.5	15.0
Total	586.7	1,016.6	1,035.2	139.8	223.2	409.8

SOURCE: German et al. (2008).

NOTE: Exchange rate is 8.65 birr/US$1.00.

TABLE 7.3 Annual agricultural investments (in Ugandan shillings) by wealth category at the two Ugandan sites, 2005

Annual investment	Kabale			Kapchorwa		
	Low	Medium	High	Low	Medium	High
Seed	23,640	31,844	72,129	19,980	29,464	42,388
Pesticide	3,269	7,074	35,059	13,000	20,000	80,714
Fertilizer	119	279	19,823	1,035	10,963	18,000
Feed	2,144	11,820	20,882	2,000	76,683	100,000
Veterinary	226	3,270	7,177	4,666	20,000	86,000
Total	29,398	54,287	155,070	40,681	157,110	327,102

SOURCE: Authors.

NOTE: The exchange rate varied from 1,780 to 1,845 Ugandan shillings per US$1 during the data collection period.

tions, commercial labor groups (in Kabale District), and land- and livestock-sharing arrangements (at the Ethiopian sites) (German et al. 2008). The benefits of these institutions are both social and economic. Social benefits include strengthened social ties and networks and support during periods of hardship, while the economic benefits include access to resources for agricultural and domestic functions (labor, utensils, food, seed, and cash) and "safety-net" functions (for example, avoiding impoverishment following times of hardship). Due to their voluntary nature, nearly all local institutions of collective action were seen by focus group participants as benefiting all those who participate (see German et al. 2008 for a detailed discussion of the Ethiopian sites). One exception was found in Ethiopia, where contracting out land to others was seen as enriching some households (landowners) at the expense of others. Yet households continue to practice this activity when they have no alternative, generally due to the shortage of inputs (primarily labor).

Although all participants in collective action benefit in most institutions of collective action, certain participants benefit more than others in some of these institutions (German et al. 2008). For example, land- and livestock-sharing arrangements in Ethiopia confer unequal benefits to participants. Landowners benefit most in sharecropping because they receive the benefits from their land with limited investment, but they benefit least in contracting because they are paid poorly for the use of their land. Livestock-sharing arrangements are similarly imbalanced. In Areka, a livestock-sharing arrangement called *hara* benefits cattle owners most because they acquire offspring with limited investment, while the individuals rearing the cattle receive only livestock products. In Ginchi, on the other hand, a livestock-sharing arrangement called *ribi* most benefits the poor, who acquire offspring as well as livestock products from cattle owned by others.

Although local forms of collective action benefit all who participate, some social groups cannot gain access to certain forms of collective action. Resource-poor households, for example, generally cannot participate in savings and loan groups, while commercial labor groups are male dominated. The sick, elderly, and disabled seldom participate in local forms of collective action but often receive some form of assistance from others. In Kabale, women are more active in local forms of collective action, particularly those involving agricultural production.

Despite the caveats, communities generally agree that local institutions of collective action play a strong positive role in livelihoods. This function is achieved by enabling households to access resources and acquire assets that otherwise would have been unachievable, buffering households during shocks and crises, and expanding social networks for intrahousehold sharing and support.

Collective Action in NRM

With the exception of labor-sharing arrangements, there was a notorious absence of collective action for addressing shared NRM concerns (see German et al. 2008). Many NRM problems requiring collective action, therefore, remain unsolved. Through a detailed participatory diagnosis of landscape-level NRM concerns and several years of action research to explore means to address these concerns, reasons for the persistence of NRM problems requiring collective action despite these problems' negative effect on livelihoods were identified.

Two predominant scenarios may help to explain this disconnect. First, NRM problems affecting agricultural productivity and requiring collective solutions are treated as individual problems by the community and by external organizations. Extension organizations continue to work with individual households when promoting soil and water conservation technologies, despite the need to foster common drainage ways. No household wishes to have common drainage ways pass through their farms because they take up agricultural land and excess water can damage crops. The costs and benefits of soil and water conservation for farmers residing in upper and lower parts of the landscape also differ. Those residing in lower parts of the landscape may benefit from the deposition of fertile soil from the upper slopes or be negatively affected by excess runoff or deposition of infertile soil. Those residing on upper slopes have less incentive to invest because their farms are less affected by upslope cultivation activities. Soil and water conservation activities clearly require the negotiation of solutions to such problems to ensure that solutions are not overly harmful to any given land user and to enable the investments of any given household to align with the perceived benefits.

Another example of a situation that can be improved through collective action is the control of pests, disease, weeds, and wild animals. Although traditional forms of collective action for pest and disease control were found in Ethiopia, most contemporary approaches to pest and disease control emphasize control by individual households. Yet the effort that one household must expend to control these problems grossly exceeds the benefits of such effort, given the tendency of farm plots and livestock to be contaminated by adjacent farms and livestock.

A second reason for the disconnect between the need for collective action and the failure to engage in it is that land users emphasize individual economic returns over collective goods or collective impacts. One example is the cultivation of fast-growing tree species on farm boundaries. This practice benefits landowners economically but adversely affects the livelihoods of adjacent households given the competition of these trees with crops for light, nutrients, and water, as well as the allelopathic affects associated with some tree species.

Similarly, some land management practices—such as the pollution of springs and waterways with detergents, human waste, and pesticides; the cultivation of "thirsty" trees; and the consumption of high levels of irrigation water—achieve livelihood improvements for some land users at the expense of others. Such scenarios clearly require a governance solution in which harmful land-use practices are regulated according to collective choice arrangements.

Institutional Practice

Contrary to local institutions, which were generally seen as equitable and supportive to most households, a number of external institutions were seen by participants in focus groups as highly biased in terms of the groups benefiting. Institutional practice at times unknowingly favors some groups at the expense of others (Schroeder 1993; Rocheleau and Edmunds 1997; German et al. 2010), whereas local institutions have not stepped in to fill the gap and to govern development interventions and resources more equitably. At times this has led to increased social differentiation and loss of social cohesion in rural communities (Schroeder 1993; Thébaud and Batterbury 2001). Some government agencies are also seen as corrupt, undermining policies that they themselves are supposed to enforce—and the commitment of stakeholders at all levels to these policies (see, for example, the literature on decentralization: Bigombé Logo 2003; Colfer and Capistrano 2005; Oyono, Ribot, and Larson 2006). Table 7.4

TABLE 7.4 Perceived unequal benefits of formal institutions to local residents at four sites in Ethiopia and Uganda, 2005

Type of collective action	Site 1 (Ethiopia)	Site 2 (Ethiopia)	Site 3 (Uganda)	Site 4 (Uganda)
Agricultural research	Agricultural research favors farmers with previous exposure to technologies and information who live near roads and have some education.	Agricultural research benefits the few farmers who have enough land and labor.	On-farm experiments are conducted with few farmers, and the results or varieties are not shared with the community. There is little follow-through on experiments or technical follow-up.	Only those who can afford or access inputs value the research initiatives.
Agricultural extension	Educated farmers benefit most; extension has poor coverage of the area.	Farmers with a lot of land and labor benefit, especially male farmers.	The continuity of National Agricultural Advisory Services (NAADS) is affected by funding availability; support goes only to farmer groups that pay the annual fee of 10,000 Ugandan shillings. More support is available to the elite farmers who easily adopt technologies.	NAADS allegedly favors the relatively well off (who can co-fund), kinsfolk of leaders, and prominent members of society.

Local administration	Those living near the seat of the district government benefit most; some exhibit a bias toward their friends and relatives.	Local administration was not mentioned by farmers.	Local administration is biased toward the "politically correct."	Those related to or favored by staff of the local administration are given special attention.
Cooperatives	All members benefit equally from inputs; those who cannot make down payments do not benefit.	The poorest farmers benefit least.	Involved in marketing barley, coffee, and maize to the World Food Programme and serve mainly large-scale farmers or farmer associations.	This is seen as a more exclusionary savings and loan mechanism that mainly serves the more resource-endowed farmers, who are able to save.
National conservation authority	National conservation authority was not mentioned by farmers.	National conservation authority was not mentioned by farmers.	Local employees of the national conservation authority (park rangers) favor community members who engage in illegal extraction that is condoned by and benefits these officials.	The National Environmental Management Authority tends to pamper some communities, paying farmers to ferry planting materials and dig water trenches on their own land.

SOURCE: Authors.

summarizes local institutions seen to confer unequal benefits on local residents at the four sites. Clearly, institutional biases—mostly unintentional—are widespread, and urgent action is needed to avoid the elite capture of benefits from these interventions.

Stakeholder Workshop Outcomes

Site-level stakeholder workshops were the most instrumental in generating concrete strategies for addressing identified problems and are the focus of this section. Following feedback of findings from the situation analysis, participants were asked to identify NRM issues requiring collective action at their respective sites. A long list was derived and subjected to a prioritization process. At some sites where participant farmers were few in number, this involved reflecting on findings from household surveys in which individuals had prioritized those issues around which they would readily engage in collective action. At other sites where large numbers of farmers were present, workshop participants engaged in the prioritization process themselves. At each site, two to four issues given priority rankings were selected for intervention and joint learning through action research. These are summarized in Table 7.5.

Participants were asked to highlight forms of institutional intervention required for each of the prioritized action research themes. These are grouped into three categories: (1) negotiation support, (2) bylaw reforms, and (3) changes in institutional practice (Table 7.6).

Problems stemming from limited stakeholder collaboration at the local level (horizontal stakeholder engagement), as well as from poorly structured linkages with external organizations (vertical stakeholder engagement), were prioritized in action research. Table 7.7 summarizes how the case studies presented in the next section relate to these two levels of intervention. Although a few case studies may be clearly defined around horizontal or vertical stakeholder engagement, a few others clearly combine both strategies in the identification of solutions.

Action Research: Lessons from Implementation of Prioritized Actions

Although many of the interventions were at early stages of implementation at the time of writing, early successes suggested the promise of building on negotiation support in enhancing collective action in NRM at the local level and in improving institutional practice to enhance equitable benefits capture from development interventions. The results are presented in the form of case studies by action research theme. The first three of the four case studies illustrate horizontal stakeholder engagement processes, while all illustrate some degree of vertical stakeholder engagement involving outside institutions.

TABLE 7.5 Natural resource management (NRM) issues prioritized by stakeholders for action research at each benchmark site in the eastern African highlands, 2005

Areka	Ginchi	Kabale	Kapchorwa
Spring development (appropriate tree species and spring maintenance)	Spring management (appropriate trees, ensuring long-term water supply, maintenance of structures)	Harmonization of bylaws between conservation zones and adjacent areas (with an emphasis on free grazing)	Collective action in enterprise development and making land investments
Equitable approaches to technology dissemination	Soil and water conservation (gulley stabilization, common drainage, collective action for labor-intensive activities)	Soil erosion control, emphasizing steep slopes and impacts on valley-bottom plots	Co-management of resources of protected-area buffer zone and benefit sharing
Boundary tree management		Minimization of harmful agroforestry practices, especially on land boundaries	Collective action to mitigate conflicts in NRM accruing from diverse or unclear property regimes (land, trees, water, grazing rights) and sharing of benefit streams
Collective action for the control of pests, diseases, and wild animals			

SOURCE: Authors.

TABLE 7.6 Interventions proposed during national stakeholder meeting held in 2005 to enhance collective action in national resource management (NRM) for the four benchmark sites in the eastern African highlands

Intervention	Areka	Ginchi	Kabale	Kapchorwa
Negotiation support	Negotiating access to technologies by groups facing barriers (women, the poor) Mobilizing widespread support for porcupine control with the involvement of elders and local authorities and research on different "treatments" in different villages Involving peasant association and religious leaders to facilitate negotiations for farm boundary management by gender, wealth, and divergent interests (cultivating farmers versus neighboring farmers negatively affected by boundary trees) to identify appropriate niches	Negotiating regulations on livestock movement in outfields to facilitate soil conservation and agro-forestry investments Negotiating trees compatible with springs (among spring owners and users) and farm boundaries (among farm owners and affected farmers) Negotiating equitable contributions to spring maintenance Negotiating soil and water conservation structures (common drainage channels and balanced investments by upslope and downslope farmers) Negotiating the sharing of benefits of introduced technologies	Supporting local negotiations for increased cooperation within and among villages Lobbying for the political and technical leadership at the subcounty level to support ongoing project initiatives	Negotiating access to water points for all community members (in particular for livestock) Negotiating access to and control of communal grazing lands Negotiating access to or custodianship of natural resources in Mount Elgon National Park by indigenous people Negotiating compatible technologies Mobilizing for the adoption of eco-friendly practices for landscape conservation Negotiating equitable benefits from eco-enterprises

	for eucalyptus and appropriate substitute species		
	Fostering negotiations on spring management by gender, wealth, and divergent interests (land owners and spring users), involving government and religious leaders, to minimize the effect of eucalyptus on water and ensure equitable contributions to spring maintenance		
	Negotiating soil conservation activities among adjacent farms and administrative units, adapting technologies to land size and farming systems		
Bylaw reforms	Boundary trees: Writing a bylaw to replace eucalyptus with a profitable tree species that does not have	Springs: Writing a bylaw specifying which trees may be planted within a specific distance of springs (100 meters	Reviewing existing NRM bylaws or writing new bylaws to limit free grazing, establishing soil erosion control	Forming agreements between the Uganda Wildlife Authority and the Benet on use rights and responsibilities of

(continued)

TABLE 7.6 Continued

Intervention	Areka	Ginchi	Kabale	Kapchorwa
	negative impacts on cropland (such as *gravelia*) Springs and waterways: Writing a bylaw to replace eucalyptus with a profitable tree species that does not have negative impacts on springs (such as *gravelia*) Soil and water conservation: Writing a bylaw to ensure 100 percent participation (one nonconserving farmer jeopardizes all) Porcupine control: Considering the need for bylaws to ensure widespread collective action in porcupine control	upslope, 25 meters downslope) Farm boundaries: Writing bylaws on (1) a minimum (10-meter) barrier between eucalyptus and cultivated land; (2) payment of reparations if policy is ignored; (3) acceptable locations for eucalyptus Outfield management: To be determined following further negotiations Soil conservation: Writing bylaws (1) specifying that nonconserving farmers will compensate for losses to downslope farmers and (2) governing drainage and gulley management	structures (individually and collectively), and controlling bush burning and the planting of trees on farm boundaries Trees and grass: Merging or harmonizing community bylaws and later scaling them up to the subcounty level Sensitizing the community and wider subcounty residents on the harmonized bylaws and lobbying for the subcounty leadership to endorse and support implementation and enforcement of NRM bylaws	the Benet with regard to co-management Writing bylaws for resolving conflicts in watershed areas

Changes in institutional practice	Technology dissemination: Writing bylaws to regulate how technologies should be governed at the peasant association level (for example, through which social units and with which rules for access) Encouraging agricultural researchers and the Ministry of Agriculture to work together to research the institutional practices, negotiations, and bylaw reforms required to enhance equitable access Fostering negotiations among different support organizations at the *woreda* level (research, extension, development) to manage the "dependency syndrome"	Spring maintenance: Writing bylaws to balance benefits with contributions to maintenance Countering the "road bias" in agricultural research Mobilizing for improved extension coverage Fostering linkages between the peasant association and traditional law enforcement mechanisms	Encouraging local government and subcounty technical staff to work with project staff to sensitize the community and foster the implementation of NRM bylaws Enhancing support to the negotiation process, especially at community and watershed levels	Encouraging multi-stakeholder commitment to addressing prioritized issues Community visioning and priority setting involving community-based organizations Encouraging the Uganda Wildlife Authority to give greater attention to the Benet on co-management

SOURCE: Authors.

TABLE 7.7 Forms of stakeholder engagement promoted through different action research themes at various sites in the eastern African highlands following stakeholder planning meetings in 2005

Form of stakeholder engagement	Subjects of case studies
Horizontal	Porcupine control in Areka, Ethiopia
	Enabling outfield conservation investments in the Galessa highlands (Ginchi site), Ethiopia
Horizontal and vertical	Participatory governance of natural resources in Kabale District, Uganda
	Facilitation of equitable technology dissemination in Areka, Ethiopia
Vertical	Facilitation of co-management of the Mount Elgon National Park in Kapchorwa District, Uganda

SOURCE: Authors.

Case Study 1: Porcupine Control in Areka, Southern Ethiopia

BACKGROUND.   The crested porcupine is the most important vertebrate pest in Gununo watershed, as identified by farmers during a stakeholder workshop held in Soddo in 2004. Application of known control methods on an individual basis was ineffective in controlling the pest, given that porcupines travel more than 14 km in a single night and infestation rates from neighboring farms and villages were high. Collective action was therefore seen as essential to control this problem.

APPROACH.   The approach used to foster collective action in porcupine control consisted of the following main steps:

- identification of indigenous and chemical pest control methods and the landscape niches in which each is best applied through interviews with key informants, and design of "treatments" to test different control methods;
- discussion facilitated by scientists from Areka Agricultural Research Center (AARC) of the most appropriate forms of collective action for coordinating the porcupine control campaign and bylaw reforms;
- stakeholder identification through consultations with randomly selected households;
- AARC-facilitated negotiation among different local stakeholder groups to generate solutions acceptable to all;
- the conduct of village-level meetings by AHI-CAPRi community facilitators to formulate bylaws on porcupine control with the full participation of each village, based on agreements reached in the previous step;
- the delivery of short training sessions for farmers by expert farmers and AARC scientists on the application of indigenous and chemical methods

of porcupine control, emphasizing strategies previously unknown to participant farmers (namely, the wire trap method), and for local leaders on the collection of data on numbers of porcupines killed or caught, the methods used, and so on, using prepared data collection forms;

- mass mobilization by community members for application of the agreed "treatments"; and
- data collection, monitoring, and evaluation by local leaders and farmers.

OUTCOMES. Farmers presented many traditional methods for the control of porcupines but prioritized three methods considered most effective: the use of deeply dug pits at the outlets of porcupine caves, circular ditches around graveyards, and a wire trap system. A fourth treatment, use of the chemical zinc phosphide, was also combined with the first two methods as two additional treatments. In this fourth treatment, farmers modified the first method, deep digging to 3–4 meters' depth, to create shallower pits (1–1.5 meters deep) that were used in combination with zinc phosphide (RATOL®). Methods were selected based on their suitability to different landscape niches. These would be applied during the season when porcupines were most harmful to crops.

The large size of the *kebele* or peasant association (PA) meant that collective action had to be mobilized at a lower level. The de facto institutional structure for organizing community development actions in the study area is the sub-PA, or "developmental unit" (DU). Farmers selected DUs to coordinate collective action because they have the ability to enforce local bylaws and, with only 25–30 households, may easily mobilize collective action and monitor activities during implementation. During the campaign, each DU designated one to two "development days" per week to carry out collective efforts for porcupine control. It was further decided that the PA-level magistrate court and local leaders would follow up on bylaw enforcement during the collective action period.

Negotiations were then supported between farmers whose crops were frequently affected and the least affected households, as well as between farmers participating and not participating in the Safety-Net Program.[6] Bylaws were then formulated with the participation of each group of farmers and distributed to all PA and sub-PA leaders. Negotiations with farmers found to be particularly knowledgeable about certain porcupine control methods were also needed to enable agreements to be reached on knowledge sharing. This highly specialized

---

6. The Safety-Net Program is a government program designed to help low-income farmers by paying them to carry out development activities (construction of schools, offices, and health centers; road maintenance; and so on) for the PA. Some nonparticipating farmers are uncooperative in collective activities, arguing that Safety-Net farmers alone have the responsibility because they are paid for these activities by the government. However, negotiations led to the joint conclusion that porcupines are a problem to both parties and affect each group equally, requiring joint efforts by both groups.

knowledge had been coveted by these knowledgeable individuals because it could provide them with periodic income from other farmers, who hired them to control porcupines in their fields.

Once the control methods, administrative units, and bylaws for operationalizing collective action were established and the relevant individuals trained on control methods and data collection procedures, the campaign was launched. Farmers went out on foot and in vehicles with megaphones and local music to publicize the campaign across all DUs, villages, and PAs. Following the campaign, records were made by DU leaders on the number of porcupines caught or killed by different farmers and villages in various niches and using each control method.

The final numbers indicated that close to 1,000 porcupines were killed or caught through collective action in the watershed in a single growing season. In Gununo watershed, Offa village ranked first in the control of porcupines. This may be attributed to the high levels of collective action sustained by all households and to the higher levels of porcupine infestation in this village than in other villages in the watershed, as evidenced by the high number of porcupine niches known in the village (more than 100). The use of rodenticide in combination with the modified deep digging technique (digging to 1.5 meters depth) at the outlets of porcupine holes proved to be the most effective control method (Table 7.8). However, farmers were generally reluctant to use chemical control methods due to their cost and found deep digging and the use of wire traps reasonably effective.

Most important to households, however, were the livelihood impacts of porcupine control, as evaluated through the monitoring of local indicators (Fig-

TABLE 7.8 Methods to control porcupines in Areka, southern Ethiopia, by niche, and their effectiveness

Method of control	Niche where applied	Numbers of porcupines killed or trapped
Method 1: Rodenticide alone	Graveyards	197
Method 2: Circular ditch + rodenticide	Porcupine caves located near graveyards	126
Method 3: 3-meter hole at the outlet of a porcupine cave	All porcupine caves located away from graveyards	88
Method 4: 1.5-meter hole at the outlet of a porcupine cave + rodenticide	All porcupine caves located away from graveyards	455
Method 5: Wire body trap at the outlet of a porcupine cave	All porcupine caves	92

SOURCE: Begashaw et al. (2007).

FIGURE 7.1 Observed impacts of collective action in porcupine control at the Offa village, Areka benchmark site, Ethiopia, 2007

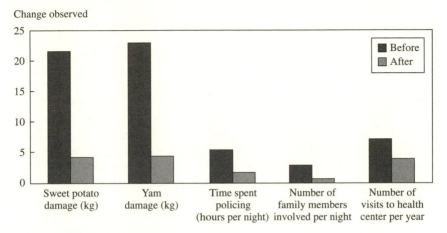

Change observed

SOURCE: Begashaw, Mazengia, and German (2007).

ure 7.1). Households reported a sharp reduction in crop damage, a reduction in the amount of time spent or the number of household members policing fields at night, and a reduction in visits to the health center because of weather-induced illness. Interestingly, the latter two were felt to have contributed the most to improving local livelihoods relative to the reduced crop loss.

LESSONS LEARNED. A number of important lessons may be distilled from this case study. The first is that collective approaches to pest control can yield much higher returns per effort expended than can individualized approaches, provided that the free-rider problem can be controlled through governance innovations. Here the challenge was to ensure that porcupine controls were applied on all farms irrespective of the level of damage, lest these farms harbor pests that would later attack neighboring farms. This raises the challenge of effectively balancing the costs and benefits of collective action for the most and least affected households, a well-known collective action principle (Ostrom 1990). Facilitating explicit negotiations between households that stand to gain more and less from the activity, with agreements backed up by locally negotiated (and thus socially legitimate) rules or bylaws, can help to substantially advance collective action by addressing the free-rider problem (defined, in this case, as household nonparticipation, which can easily undermine the returns from collective action initiatives). The second lesson is that the integration of local knowledge, introduced technologies, and collective action within a single strategy allowed for synergies in problem solving that would have been unattainable using piecemeal approaches.

*Case Study 2: Participatory Governance of Natural Resources
in Kabale District, Uganda*

BACKGROUND.   In Rubaya Subcounty, as in many other areas in the Kigezi highlands of southwestern Uganda, land degradation is a critical challenge. Soil conservation has mainly taken the form of scattered individualized efforts. Yet much of the damage caused by unconserved farmland comes from excess run-off from upslope farms—a more immediate concern of most farmers than the medium-term costs of soil loss. This creates a disconnect between the benefits and costs of soil conservation activities, with upslope farmers bearing the costs and those farther downslope reaping the benefits. Furthermore, most NGOs working in NRM in the region tend to emphasize the technological dimensions of NRM, often neglecting community perceptions and interests and the social and psychological dynamics underlying human behavior. Government organizations such as the National Environmental Management Authority had, for example, paid farmers to adopt soil conservation technologies (for example, digging water trenches on their own land), thereby undermining sustainability. Because development agencies supporting NRM through farmer groups often end up supporting few households and emphasize individualized decisions on land management, many problems that are collective in nature remain unaddressed. Examples of NRM challenges requiring collective action at the Rubaya site include land conflicts, the planting of incompatible trees on farm boundaries, destruction of crops from free grazing and bush burning, and acute land degradation (that is, from the formation of gullies and landslides).

Finally, poor leadership and nonenforcement of NRM bylaws had led to a situation in which rules were left unenforced. Local environmental committees (LECs) were established by local governments to coordinate and oversee environmental concerns at the parish and subcounty levels. These committees were perceived by farmers as dysfunctional due to financial and capacity constraints and lack of downward accountability. Other local institutional structures for NRM had also been established through research and development interventions. An earlier project by AHI and the International Center for Tropical Agriculture had established policy task forces (PTFs) in four pilot villages to address NRM conflicts through participatory bylaw reforms. Although collective action in NRM has been much stronger in these villages, the effectiveness of the bylaws in these villages is still undermined by inadequate enforcement, lack of political will, and inadequate support of technological options that would substitute for land-use practices curtailed through bylaws.

APPROACH.   AHI facilitated multistakeholder efforts to improve NRM in three subcounties of Kabale District. From the outset, AHI set out to build on existing institutional foundations—namely, LECs and PTFs. Earlier work on bylaws provided a strong foundation for early successes in Rubaya Subcounty. In each of the villages where these activities were carried out, AHI followed a series of eight steps to engage stakeholders to develop collective solutions to shared NRM problems. These included

- the holding of community forums by subcounty and village leadership representatives and volunteer community-based NRM facilitators and the sensitization of communities by leading them through an analysis of the role of collective action in NRM and livelihoods;
- the conduct of meetings facilitated by the AHI community facilitator (CF) at the subcounty level with representatives from pilot villages and local leaders (elected officials and opinion leaders) to identify or develop organizational structures for spearheading NRM at the subcounty and village levels;
- the capacity building of existing or new structures by the CF and local government on their roles and responsibilities in NRM;
- the provision of support to NRM structures to lead a participatory review of existing bylaws in the four villages with longstanding involvement in AHI and formulation of new bylaws in the two new villages to strengthen natural resource governance;
- cross-site visits organized by the CF to take members of villages new to participatory bylaw reforms and the subcounty leadership to communities that had successfully implemented model NRM bylaws and technologies;
- the conduct of a multistakeholder workshop to harmonize bylaws emanating from the six villages at the subcounty level with representatives of subcounty and village NRM structures, each village (representatives of the Local Council 1, the lowest tier of local government, and male and female farmer representatives), local government (the subcounty chief, subcounty chairperson, and secretary for production), and the National Agricultural Advisory Services coordinator;
- the provision of technical support by the CF to subcounty NRM structures to plan and facilitate parish and village meetings for the purpose of sensitizing community members and eliciting their feedback on newly revised or formulated bylaws at the subcounty, parish, and village levels; and
- the lobbying of the leadership to endorse bylaws that will apply at the subcounty level.

OUTCOMES. The subcounty leadership and community representatives resolved that new organizational structures be established to supersede both PTFs and LECs but incorporate their functions. Farmers and other stakeholders observed that some PTFs were not fully functional, and new pilot communities lacked these structures. LECs, on the other hand, were said to exist only in name. They were constituted via appointments by the subcounty leadership and were of limited effectiveness due to inadequate financial resources and ambiguity in their roles and responsibilities. Thus, natural resource protection committees (NRPCs) were constituted at the subcounty and village levels to spearhead NRM initiatives; they were comprised of subcounty and village leadership (ex-officio members) and elected committee members. NRPCs were seen as more representative than previous structures, extending to the village level through the involvement of LC1 leaders, farmer representatives, and community-based NRM facilitators. Furthermore, at the subcounty level they were composed of all representatives of LCs from pilot villages, village NRPCs, community-based facilitators, and ex-officio members at the subcounty level. PTFs included only two members at the parish level drawn from the pilot villages.

In villages where bylaw reforms were ongoing under AHI, participatory review of bylaws was carried out to address the deficiencies of existing bylaws. Some of the existing bylaws lacked punitive measures, such as fines. Other bylaws were too general in nature, failing to specify how they would be operationalized. In villages new to participatory governance, new bylaws were established. Most of these were adapted from the bylaws of other villages with previous experience in participatory bylaw reforms, taking into account the unique circumstances and land management challenges in a particular community or landscape or felt NRM needs. Following the formulation of bylaws on free grazing and soil and water conservation, technologies were seen as necessary for bylaw implementation. For example, prohibitions against free grazing require alternative sources of fodder, and soil and water conservation would require the planting of trees and grasses to stabilize conservation structures. Collective action emerged around communal tree nurseries for this purpose.

Cross-site visits proved instrumental in motivating additional interest in improved natural resource governance in villages new to the approach due to the concrete benefits observed. Community members were motivated by both the social cohesiveness for collective action and the effectiveness of technologies (check dams, water trenches). Cross-site visits catalyzed farmers' interest in immediately returning to their villages and implementing observed methods of controlling soil erosion. Pickaxes, spades, and forked hoes were provided on request as an incentive to farmers. Bylaws helped to mobilize collective action in constructing check dams across upper slopes to reduce runoff to farms below, while individually dug water trenches were used to capture excess water. Following the construction of soil erosion control structures, seedlings from previously established nurseries were transplanted to protect the conservation structures. This mobilization of collective action in four villages led to the establishment of 1,503 meters of check dams (where none had existed prior to the intervention), the establishment of 5,444 meters of water trenches (representing increases of between 47 and 2,080 percent for different villages), and a sharp reduction in soil erosion and flooding in some locations.

The meeting at the subcounty level to harmonize bylaws led to the development of one final set of bylaws for adoption at the wider subcounty level (Box 7.1). Several different criteria were used in this harmonization process. The

BOX 7.1 Reformulated and harmonized bylaws in Rubaya Subcounty

Soil and water conservation:

- Everyone shall dig water trenches (soil erosion structures), especially on hillsides, in their own land prior to any cultivation. Anyone who violates the above bylaw will be liable to a fine, which will be decided by the sub-county (LC 3) council, in collaboration with representatives of Policy Task Forces (PTFs).
- Napier/elephant grass and other grasses (and/or trees) shall be planted in landscapes where water trenches are not feasible, such as in very rocky or rugged terrain.
- Every farmer should consult neighboring land owners prior to breaking down the terrace or contour bund along common land demarcations or borders.
- No one shall cultivate their land without digging water trenches or planting trees and grasses to conserve soil and water in their own land.
- Prior to cultivating, everyone should excavate trenches, steps, and A frames.

Those who violate these bylaws shall be fined Sh. 5,000 or else they will be forwarded to the LC 3 council authorities for punishment.

Grazing:

- No one shall graze in the valley, whether or not the land in the valley is one's own.
- Everyone shall graze in their own land and if not, seek permission to graze in others' land. Any abandoned land—including hilltop land—should be utilized for growing agro-forestry species.
- No one is allowed to come from another country and graze in Uganda. [This bylaw is specifically in reference to neighboring Rwanda.]

Those who violate these bylaws will be fined Sh. 10,000.

Water:

- Everyone who draws water from a communal water source or well shall cooperate with others in its cleaning or maintenance.
- Anyone utilizing land near a communal well, road, footpath, or water trench should reserve a stretch of 1–2 meters of uncultivated land between their land and the said communal structures.
- No one is allowed to graze or cultivate land near, or wash clothes in, communal water sources.

Those who violate these bylaws will be fined Sh. 5,000.

Other:

- Burning of grasses, hillsides, weeds, and trees is strictly prohibited. (Those who violate this bylaw will be fined Sh. 10,000.)
- When cultivating, leave some reserve narrow strips of land along boundaries, the road side, livestock tracks, etc. (Those who violate this bylaw will be fined Sh. 5,000.)
- Whoever cuts down trees should plant more. (Those who violate this bylaw will be fined Sh. 5,000.)
- Every household should cultivate fruits, such as avocados. (Those who violate this bylaw will be fined Sh. 5,000.)
- Anyone who owns or rents land in another village should abide by the natural resource management bylaws obtaining in that village.
- Village PTFs should have representatives at the LC 3 (subcounty) level.

SOURCE: Meetings between authors and residents of Rubaya Subcounty
NOTE: Sh. means Ugandan shilling.

subcounty chief assumed veto power to ensure that locally formulated bylaws adhere to the national laws on maximum fines and are feasible under existing financial and land-use scenarios. Although fines were conflicting but not considered too high by the chief, participants selected a single figure through consensus-based decisionmaking. The levels of fines selected by participants depended on their determination of the balance between feasibility and fairness; they wanted fines that were not so harsh as to be unfair but at the same time high enough to ensure that the bylaws are followed. This supports the observation by Ostrom (1990) on the need for sanctions to be "graduated" or matched to the level of the offense. Farmers also strongly felt that local leaders should be exemplary in NRM. If they do not follow the bylaws, everyone else will feel that they too have no reason to respect the law. Elected leaders were often reluctant to support the enforcement of NRM bylaws for fear of alienating the electorate, in effect jeopardizing their source of votes. Accordingly, one of the key roles of NRPCs was to lobby the leadership structures to buy into the concept of supporting the establishment and enforcement of NRM bylaws.

Following this harmonization process, the NRPC assumed responsibility for calling NRM bylaw stakeholder meetings at the parish and village levels to increase the awareness of the harmonized bylaws and elicit feedback from farmers. Each bylaw was discussed in a plenary session. After this process was finished, amendments were made to the harmonized bylaws. The bylaw on bush burning, for example, was amended to include damage to property caused by wildfires in addition to the imposition of a fine of 10,000 shillings for those starting such fires. Farmers similarly requested an additional bylaw amendment on free grazing, requiring the culprits to compensate households for the value of crops lost, soil conservation structures damaged, and other damages incurred.

The NRPCs at the village and subcounty levels lobbied the subcounty leadership for bylaw endorsement. As a result of persistent lobbying, the bylaws were finally endorsed by the Rubaya Subcounty Local Council on January 17, 2007. Copies of the endorsed bylaws were distributed to local leaders in each village and to the village information centers. To bolster political support of bylaw enforcement, a publicity campaign at the village, parish, and subcounty levels and district endorsement of the bylaws were scheduled.

LESSONS LEARNED.   Several lessons may be learned from this case study. First, sustainable land management, often treated as the responsibility of individual households by farmers and development agencies alike, requires collective effort in the form of collective rules, regulations, and implementation of agreements. This experience also puts into question the way in which soil erosion has been perceived by development agents worldwide: namely, that the key challenge is loss of soil from one's plot. Yet for farmers, the more immediate concern is the economic damage caused by excess water from upslope runoff washing away seed, fertilizer, and property. Understanding this dynamic is essential to mobilize collective action, given the need to understand that the primary benefits of soil conservation activities flow to downslope rather than upslope farmers (which is commonly misperceived given the greater degree of erosion on upper slopes).

Second, the sensitization of farmers to the potential benefits of the intervention through the cross-site visit was essential in catalyzing interest in and commitment to collective action. Political commitment also plays a vital role in mobilization, sensitization, and ensuring commitment to collective choice rules (in the form of formal endorsement of local bylaws). The failure of local leaders to be exemplary in abiding by the bylaws on their own farms as well as to respect the bylaws through their enforcement is an important disincentive to others.

Effective collective action and natural resource governance also takes time, as illustrated by the greater responsiveness of farmers in the subcounty where bylaw reforms had a longer history. A final lesson is derived from the apparent synergy of bylaws (rules), technologies (the new knowledge acquired on check dams and on vegetation to protect newly formed soil conservation structures), and capital (in the form of tools) in addressing local NRM challenges.

Case Study 3: Equitable Technology Dissemination in Areka

BACKGROUND.   Gununo watershed is located in the highlands of southern Ethiopia, where land is scarce due to intense population pressure. The productivity of crops is very low due to several factors, one of which is poor genetic potential. Food shortage is common for at least three months per year, even in years of good rainfall. The government has tried to disseminate improved seeds to farmers on credit. However, repayment rates were very low, and the government has shifted to disseminating seeds in exchange for cash payments. Because most farmers in the watershed are resource poor, especially women, it has become difficult for them to access improved seeds through this system. During preliminary focus group discussions, women complained of an extreme gender bias in agricultural extension. Farmers in some villages stated that no female-headed households in their villages had ever accessed improved seeds through the formal extension system. Participatory action research was conducted to explore ways to enhance equitable technology access in the watershed.

APPROACH.   Following identification of gender inequities in agricultural extension during gender-disaggregated focus group discussions (situation analysis), community meetings were called by AARC scientists and AHI community facilitators to discuss the way forward. The meetings were held at the village level (in five villages of Gununo watershed) to identify and prioritize local problems and possible solutions. These solutions, involving bylaw formulation and technology multiplication and dissemination following the specifications laid out in the bylaws, were then reviewed and approved at a watershed-wide forum facilitated by the AARC site team. Innovative farmers were selected by the watershed community, and five farmer research groups (FRGs) were formed (one per village) in two PAs to evaluate crop varieties and identify those with high levels of acceptance by farmers. As varieties were being evaluated, draft bylaws specifying rules and procedures for equitable technology multiplication and dissemination were developed at the village level through gender-disaggregated focus group discussions with farmers. Following PA-level harmonization of collective choice rules emanating from different social groups, draft bylaws were authenticated by local PA leaders for subsequent enforcement. Seeds of tested crop varieties (Boloso-I for taro, Simba for wheat) were given to farmers according to rules established in the bylaws, through a system of in-kind credit and following training on management practices. These farmers agreed, in turn, to multiply the seed and transfer the same amount of seed they had been given to other selected farmers according to agreed bylaws. Follow-up monitoring to ensure compliance with agreed bylaws was done by FRG leaders, FRG members, and other male and female watershed residents at various stages of the process. FRG leaders were charged with the responsibility of reporting offenders to members of the local administration, who would, in turn, take action through the PA courts. Data were collected on the repayment process and farmers' perceptions of the effectiveness of the approach.

OUTCOMES.   The outcomes were as follows.

FRG establishment.   To implement the proposed community plan of participatory seed technology evaluation, multiplication, and dissemination, FRGs were established to enable a greater number of farmers to participate in research and extension activities in the watershed. FRG members were selected by the community and included farmers from different social categories (women and men, poorer and wealthier farmers). A total of five FRGs were established in the five zones of the watershed. Each was established according to location (village) rather than technology. This was done to reduce the difficulty in management and thus facilitate greater coverage.

Bylaw formulation.   To enhance crop production and address challenges of technology access, farmers felt it necessary to identify local seed multiplication and dissemination channels that would give equal consideration to different categories of farmers, independent of gender or wealth. Thus, local bylaws were established. A number of meetings were held with key informants and focus groups to develop draft bylaws. Finally, agreement was reached on one bylaw that it was believed would equally benefit all social categories throughout the watershed. This bylaw was authorized by two PA leaders and by social court judges. The bylaw required that women farmers be included among beneficiaries and outlined mechanisms of seed transfer and sanctions for offenders (Box 7.2).

Seed multiplication and dissemination.   Planting material for selected varieties of taro and wheat was distributed to farmers as starter seed through FRG leaders. Farmers were given planting material on credit so that they would pay back an equal amount of planting material to be transferred to other selected farmers until all farmers in the watershed gained access. Five kilograms of improved wheat seed (varieties Wabe and Abola) were given to each of 160

BOX 7.2 Articles in the bylaw for equitable technology dissemination, Areka, Ethiopia

- One-third of the beneficiaries must be women when selecting beneficiary farmers.
- A farmer has to manage the new starter seed given to him/her better than or equivalent to his/her own private seed. He/she has to transfer amounts of improved seed equal to what he/she was given initially to another farmer selected by farmer research group (FRG) leaders immediately after harvest.
- If he/she needs to sell the surplus product, he/she has to sell it to farmers within the watershed at a free market price until all the watershed community gets access to the improved seed. If there is no one who wants to buy the seed within the watershed, the seed owner can sell his/her product outside the watershed after informing FRG leaders.
- If a farmer disobeys the bylaw, he/she will be reported by FRG leaders to the peasant association (PA) court. The PA court will make the judgment, and the PA leaders will take action based on the ruling of the judge.
- If a farmer partially loses his/her seed through natural disasters, he/she will repay a smaller amount determined by the FRG leaders.

SOURCE: Meetings between authors and residents of Gununo watershed, Areka, Ethiopia.

farmers from five villages. Similarly, corms of an improved taro variety called Boloso-I were distributed as planting material to more than 120 farmers. The FRG leaders monitored seed multiplication from sowing to harvest. The yield of the new variety of taro was higher than that of the local cultivars. The high yield was attributed to the high number of tillers (up to 40) and corms per hill, coupled with the new variety's relative tolerance to low-moisture stress.

Credit repayment and bylaw implementation.   The available evidence suggests that the bylaws contributed to a substantial improvement in credit repayment rates, with 100.0 percent of farmers successfully repaying taro and from 43.3 to 97.0 percent of farmers repaying wheat (Figure 7.2). Yet even in the villages with the lowest repayment rates, rates of default still fell dramatically relative to those seen under previous credit systems (shown in the first two columns), indicating the improved effectiveness of the new credit system supported by bylaws. Farmers who did not repay their loans were taken to local courts by FRG leaders. Although most of them admitted to being aware of the bylaw, they had expected exemption from repayment, in line with their previous experience. Following moral persuasion by their colleagues, the farmers in most villages paid voluntarily. In Gegecho and Ofa, where the lowest repayment rates were recorded, this informal follow-up led 25 percent of participants to repay their loans. However, a few households said that their wheat yield was poor and they were unable to repay.

Livelihood benefits.   Farmers said that the new taro variety had enhanced food security in the watershed due to its high productivity, short growing season, and resistance to decay when stored in the fields for long periods. These features have extended the season in which food is readily available in farmers' fields to three to four months per year. The variety is also becoming a cash crop. Some farmers said that they had never received so much income from any other crop, even coffee (Ethiopia's primary cash crop). Some farmers declared a 225 percent increase in income relative to the local variety on the same amount of land. One farmer received more than 2,000 birr (US$230) from taro in 2006, and several households are expanding their area under taro cultivation. As a result of these successes, the new taro variety is being disseminated very quickly —primarily through purchase. Farmers also claimed that the new variety saved on fuelwood and that they had gone from three bundles of fuelwood to one to cook a pot of taro. The Ministry of Agriculture at the district level is now trying to use this variety of taro as part of its food security program. The performance of new wheat varieties was similar to that of the local variety and variable across farms and villages due to differences in fertilizer application and weeding, and therefore of less interest to farmers.

The benefits of the approach used go beyond the technologies. According to focus group–based evaluations of the approach, it has brought more equitable benefits to women and poor farmers relative to the formal extension service (Table 7.9). In-kind credit was also seen as more favorable to farmers than loans

FIGURE 7.2 Credit repayment rates associated with bylaws, by village, compared to earlier credit systems at the African Highlands Initiative–Areka benchmark site, Ethiopia, as evaluated in 2006

Repayment rate (percent)

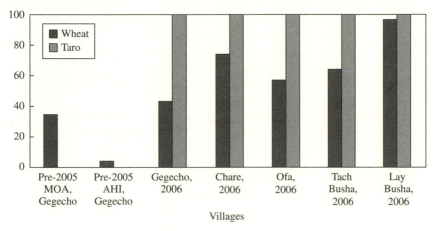

SOURCE: Mazengia (2006).

TABLE 7.9 Farmers' perceptions of the equitability and benefits of the African Highlands Initiative (AHI)/Areka Agricultural Research Center (AARC) approach as an alternative to the approach used by the extension service, Gununo watershed, southern Ethiopia, 2006

Indicator	Formal extension service (average rank)	AHI/AARC (average rank)
Equitable access by women farmers	13.4	86.6
Equitable access by poor farmers	26.6	73.4
Form of credit (repayment in kind, as opposed to cash)	17.6	82.4
Awareness of technology prior to wider dissemination	14.4	85.6
Quality and frequency of technical support	23.6	76.4

SOURCE: Mazengia (2006).

NOTE: Results were derived from group-based matrix ranking of the two approaches, with 100 seeds divided among the two approaches for each indicator (and more seeds representing better performance) and the results averaged across the five villages.

to be repaid in cash, as was the ability of farmers to learn about new technologies prior to adoption through prior testing of technologies within FRGs. Unlike under the previous credit system, in which farmers consumed or sold all of their produce to escape repayment, most farmers have maintained improved seed for the next planting season. Surprisingly, some farmers claimed to prefer the new approach over the then-current Safety-Net Program, which gave seed to resource-poor farmers at no cost. That approach, which required them to submit to on-farm screening prior to taking loans, was also instrumental in improving varietal performance and farmers' ability to repay at harvest, although the benefit was attributable to the variety. Farmers outside of the pilot site have begun requesting that local government agencies adopt a similar system of in-kind loans.

Given their previous experience, farmers were reluctant to work with researchers at the beginning. The relationship between researchers and farmers has improved due to the active participation of farmers and greater consideration of their interests by researchers.

LESSONS LEARNED.   A number of lessons may be learned from this case study about collective action in general and about approaches to enhance equitable technology access in particular. First, farmers were found to respect collective-choice rules much more than government-imposed rules for credit repayment, suggesting that locally negotiated bylaws have great promise for enhancing collective action and local governance. Second, a higher number of farmers who had failed to pay their loans on time were found to pay following informal persuasion as opposed to formal prosecution, which tends to breed resentment and resistance. The effectiveness of informal persuasion was strongly grounded in the group decisionmaking process during which the bylaws were negotiated, because all farmers present had agreed to the terms. Because social pressure often makes it difficult for local leaders to enforce bylaws with harmful consequences for others (such as fines), informal enforcement efforts such as moral persuasion may be an important tool that complements formal bylaw endorsement and enforcement. In this case, however, restricting offenders from taking new loans remained a crucial complement to moral persuasion in enhancing credibility in the system and also in controlling free riders. Third, loan repayment rates were higher when FRG leaders performed their roles and responsibilities as agreed, pointing to the crucial importance of good leadership and bylaw enforcement in enhancing collective action. In this case, the absence of an article in the local bylaws to hold FRG members and local administrative leaders accountable to agreements undermined repayment rates. The lesson is that the roles and responsibilities of all parties, including leaders and enforcement agents, must be clearly articulated.

Case Study 4: Co-Management of Mount Elgon National Park

BACKGROUND.   In the 1930s, the British colonial government declared the Mount Elgon area a Crown forest and gazetted it as a forest reserve, officially excluding people from the area. Up until the 1970s, cultivation in the forest was forbidden, and the forest was largely intact. Through an informal understanding, the Benet (Ndorobo) were allowed to continue hunting and gathering in the forest and cultivating in the moorlands. At that time the forest was overseen jointly by the Forest Department and community leaders. The Benet continued to occupy the area until 1983, when the Government of Uganda changed the official designation of the area to Mount Elgon Forest Park, forcing all people still residing within the park's boundaries to leave the protected area. This, in effect, cut the Benet off from their traditional resource base and livelihood system. Prolonged pressure from the Benet community (a group of elders) and district leaders caused part of the forest reserve to be degazetted for use by the Benet. However, some of the Benet were not resettled and remained landless. Livelihood changes induced by resettlement and growth in the human and livestock populations have increased the pressure on park resources, compromising both livelihood and conservation objectives.

In 1993, the Government of Uganda again changed the designation of the protected area to Mount Elgon National Park, shifting management from the Forest Department to the Uganda Wildlife Authority. This led to tighter restrictions on protected-area access by local people, further souring relations between communities and park staff and intensifying the illegal harvesting of park resources by local residents—a practice tacitly accepted by park rangers. Harsh enforcement of exclusionary policies resulted in rapid deterioration of the relations between the Benet and the government. Livestock grazing and cultivation of Irish potatoes in the moorlands were prohibited, and any Benet homes found inside the protected area were burned. Benet elders, with the support of Action Aid and Land Alliance, formed a legal entity called the Benet Lobby Group. The Benet Lobby Group and Benet Settlers Association worked at the local and national levels to increase the awareness of immediate risks to their livelihoods. They initiated and sustained a court case against the Government of Uganda until its resolution in favor of the Benet in 2005. Exclusionary policies had a number of other negative spin-offs; for instance, protected-area officials encouraged bribes from local elites (mostly non-Benet) for access to forest resources. Also, women and children who entered the park to collect forest products without paying bribes were physically abused. Communication between local communities and the Uganda Wildlife Authority (UWA) had largely broken down.

In 1995 a new co-management policy was implemented for all protected areas in Uganda. This policy was designed to improve relations with local people through the sharing of the benefits of and responsibilities for park management and conservation. Participatory action research was conducted in two communities neighboring the national park to explore approaches to reducing conflict and enhancing the benefits flowing to customary rights holders.

APPROACH. The Kapchorwa District Landcare Chapter (KADLACC), with support from AHI, has worked to end this impasse between the Benet and UWA. The intervention strategy included the following steps:

- Participatory stakeholder mapping with district stakeholders to identify relevant stakeholders for co-management and benefit sharing.
- Focus group discussions facilitated by KADLACC with each of the identified stakeholder groups: four Benet villages located in the degazetted zone, UWA (community rangers with their sector head), and the Benet living outside the resettlement zone.
- Stakeholder meeting facilitated by district champions to initiate dialogue on co-management among relevant government departments, community-based organizations, farmer groups, and NGOs. A consensus was reached on key issues from the community's point of view, and community members presented requests for technologies that could address their livelihood and conservation needs.
- A visit by KADLACC to the UWA sector warden's office to communicate the Benet's interest in acquiring technologies found at the UWA field office. UWA obliged by providing tree and fodder planting materials.
- A district-level meeting facilitated by KADLACC involving community representatives, subcounty council members, the UWA sector head, district leaders, and local government departments. The following were discussed: (1) the livelihood consequences of conservation and (2) possibilities for co-management of the park despite an ongoing court case between the Benet and UWA. The dialogue resulted in the development of an action plan, including specified days when the Benet can collect honey and bamboo shoots, in exchange for community contributions to the control of illegal activities within park boundaries.[7]
- Informal discussions between community members and KADLACC on the types of activities that could be negotiated to further build the relationship with UWA while posing no significant threat to the conservation objectives of the protected area.
- Multistakeholder meetings facilitated by KADLACC at the parish level with community representatives, an UWA official, and representatives of subcounty government to elicit community views on protected-area management and negotiate rights and responsibilities in co-management.

OUTCOMES.   The reconciliation process was jump-started by UWA efforts to share technologies with the Benet and to initiate collaboration around mutual interests. Representatives were identified for each stakeholder group, and a trust-building process was initiated at different levels of organization. Through informal lobbying, the parties were sensitized to each other's points of view, and agreements were reached on how to facilitate the development of a shared understanding among the stakeholders. During the negotiation process, UWA

---

7. Such activities include nonpermitted activities for the involved villages, as well as all activities by others (those without customary rights or negotiated access agreements).

representatives and the Benet were encouraged to consider the interests of the other party, with the conservation of biodiversity forming an agreed "bottom line" objective based on conditions set by UWA for engagement in dialogue. This enabled them to move beyond the former positioning around particular outcomes (for instance, total exclusion versus restoration of the Benet's historical tenure and use rights) to dialogue around resource use options that would not compromise the bottom line while ensuring that the needs of both parties would be better met. This led the Benet to expand their expectations beyond land rights to include access to resources within park boundaries. The two parties were then able to reach a mutual agreement on shared custodianship of the park. This was associated with strengthened access rights for customary users of resources within park boundaries (Figure 7.3) in exchange for their assistance in regulating access by outsiders and led to a reduction in the number of arrests per week. Only time will tell whether this innovation can be sustained and whether it will produce any improvements in the resource base.

LESSONS LEARNED. A number of lessons may be derived from this early stage of co-management. First, the role of a neutral facilitator cannot be overemphasized. KADLACC provided a forum for both parties to engage positively despite their history of conflict and an ongoing court case that had kept enmities strong. Given the negative social and economic costs of conflict, in the most serious conflicts there may be opportunities for reconciliation with appropriate mediation. A first gesture of reconciliation (in this case, UWA's sharing the

FIGURE 7.3 Changes observed in local indicators in 2006 following methodological innovations for co-management in Kapchorwa District, Uganda

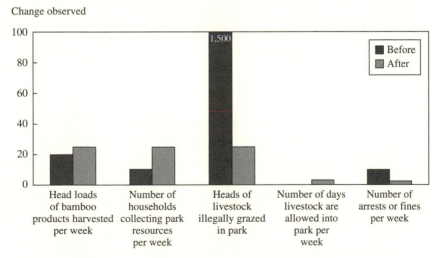

Change observed

SOURCE: Tanui (2006).

requested technologies with farmers) can also go a long way toward thawing tense relations. A second lesson for engaging in negotiations involving prior conflict is the need to respect stakeholders' "bottom lines" (in this case, bio-diversity conservation for UWA) while fostering shared sacrifices (here, the granting of increased access rights to neighboring communities in exchange for their assistance in policing against the entry of those without customary rights). If only one party is seen to compromise for an outcome beneficial to the other party, the party bearing most of the costs with the least benefit will quickly withdraw from dialogue. This supports the observation in the collective action literature that the perceived benefits of collective action must be equal to or greater than the costs (Ostrom 1990). Finally, parallel multistakeholder dia-logues at diverse levels may help to bridge the gap between policy intent (in this case, co-management of protected areas) and action on the ground. In this case, UWA representatives at higher levels within the administrative hierarchy were found to have more favorable attitudes toward co-management than park guards, attitudes which could be leveraged to support behavioral changes among park guards and increase the chances of a more equitable solution.

Discussion and Conclusions

Local communities were found to have a rich array of collective action institu-tions, which in turn provide a variety of economic and social support functions. Although some of these were seen to support some groups more than others, most forms of collective action were found to have a positive effect on local liveli-hoods. The practices of several external agencies were found to be biased by wealth, gender, or levels of political influence, and greater attention must be given to methods for fostering more equitable forms of development assistance.

Despite the apparent benefits derived from local forms of collective action, they were seldom found to foster solutions to priority NRM problems other than the provision of inputs (land, labor, capital). Action research findings illustrate the potential for improving livelihoods and fostering more sustainable use of natural resources by catalyzing collective action on NRM where it is absent. Effective collective action seems to require the use of both informal negotiation support processes and formal bylaw reform and enforcement. Participatory bylaw reform creates stakeholder buy-in, which reduces ambiguity and makes people feel more accountable to other parties for their actions. A combination of formal and informal mechanisms is needed to revitalize natural resource governance and related livelihood and environmental service outcomes. NGOs, community-based organizations, or local governments can play an important role in reducing the transaction costs of organizing through information provision, community mobi-lization, facilitation, advocacy, monitoring, and negotiation support.

Our findings support the two research hypotheses. Strategies to improve NRM at the farm and landscape levels were more effective when more equitable decisionmaking processes were used that explicitly acknowledged diverse "stakes." Bylaws helped in holding each party accountable for following the resolutions reached through negotiations. Adapting bylaws to local conditions and to stakeholder priorities also induced livelihood improvements by enabling collective action and technology adoption. But bylaws need enforcement. Our study suggests that participation in bylaw formulation increases the likelihood of rule compliance and of offenders' adherence to sanctions, provided that these rules are backed by formal or informal means of enforcement. Improved governance of natural resources is a process that involves overcoming past expectations and behaviors, such as individualized solutions, nonpayment of loans, and nonenforcement of bylaws, and gradually learning the value of collective solutions built on trust.

Implications for Practitioners and Policymakers

There are three particular implications of our findings for NRM practitioners and policymakers. First, collective action serves critical development and social support functions in local communities. Development organizations should seek ways to build on local institutions that are highly valued or seen to contribute most to local livelihood goals, in particular for women and poorer households.

Second, by failing to serve the needs of disadvantaged groups, any development intervention can result in winners and losers or simply exacerbate existing socioeconomic inequalities. Extension and development organizations must make greater efforts to understand their clientele and their diverse circumstances prior to development interventions and to identify different political or economic interests within a community that could be fostered or undermined through a particular intervention (as well as socially optimal solutions[8]). They must then learn to work explicitly with these diverse groups and divergent political interests to foster more equitable solutions to development and NRM challenges through stakeholder identification and negotiation support. More effort must also be given to monitoring the outcomes for different social groups.

Third, fostering equitable collective action where it is absent requires an understanding of local interest groups, informal negotiation of solutions among these groups, and a means to formally endorse collective-choice rules (whether through local government, customary leaders, or another moral authority seen as legitimate by all parties). A well-facilitated process of participatory bylaw reform may create stakeholder buy-in, thereby reducing the cost of enforcement and ambiguity. However, bylaw enforcement by communities themselves is a challenge, because it involves sanctioning friends and relatives. In many cases, there may be complementary roles for moral persuasion (as a first option) and

---

8. These may be defined by their ability to benefit all social actors and to ensure that no harm is done to any given group or individual.

for local government or another form of authority to assist in the enforcement of collective-choice rules (as a second option). In many situations, neither formal nor informal mechanisms for rule formulation and enforcement would be fully effective without the other.

Local forms of collective action emphasize enhancing incomes and "safety-net" functions, leaving many common NRM problems unaddressed. Many individualized efforts at NRM are undermined by the effort that must be expended relative to the returns, as seen in the case studies on controlling excess run-off and pests. External support for "horizontal" negotiations among local resource users combined with technological inputs can go a long way in supporting collective solutions to NRM problems. There is also an urgent need for NGOs, local governments, and other development actors to facilitate the evolution of democratic governance through the development of collective-choice rules at the local level as a means to address environmental concerns while operationalizing (largely ignored) national environmental policies.

Mechanisms and incentives for institutional cooperation toward more equitable and negotiated solutions to NRM are sorely needed. The partitioning of mandates among research, extension, and law enforcement agencies causes these issues to be treated separately and important synergies to be lost. Rural development and law enforcement agencies need to forge partnerships and synergies to revitalize natural resource governance at the local level. Managers of research and development organizations must also seek ways to bridge the gap between knowledge generation and development practice. This may include providing increased support to action research (with appropriate support from social theory) or enhanced efforts by those engaged in research to go further downstream in supporting development practitioners—building knowledge on social theory and increasing their efforts to integrate this understanding into everyday extension and facilitation practices.

References

Ayele, Z. 2009. Decentralization and local governance in Ethiopia. Cape Town, South Africa: Community Law Center. <http://www.communitylawcentre.org.za/clc-projects/local-government/10th-anniversary-of-the-local-government-bulletin/Zemelak%20Ayele.pdf/?searchterm=None>. Accessed February 18, 2011.

Bachrach, P., and M. S. Baratz. 1970. *Power and poverty: Theory and practice.* New York: Oxford University Press.

Begashaw, L., W. Mazengia, and L. German. 2007. *Mobilizing collective action for vertebrate pest control: The case of porcupine in Areka.* AHI Brief E3. Kampala, Uganda: African Highlands Initiative.

Bigombé Logo, P. 2003. *The decentralized forestry taxation system in Cameroon: Local management and state logic.* Environmental Governance in Africa Working Paper 10. Washington, D.C.: World Resources Institute.

Blau, P. M. 1964. *Exchange and power in social life.* New York: John Wiley and Sons.

Bloch, P. 1993. An egalitarian development project in a stratified society: Who ends up with the land? In *Land in African Agrarian Systems,* ed. T. Bassett and D. Crummey. Madison, Wisc., U.S.A.: University of Wisconsin Press.

Burns, R., T. Baumgartner, and P. DeVille. 1985. *Man, decisions, society.* London: Gordon and Breach.

Carney, D. 1998. *Sustainable rural livelihoods: What contribution can we make?* London: Department for International Development.

Coleman, J. S. 1988. Social capital in the creation of human capital. *American Journal of Sociology* 94 (supplement): S95–S120.

Colfer, C. J. P., and D. Capistrano. 2005. *The politics of decentralization: Forests, power and people.* London: Earthscan.

Davis, K., S. Franzel, P. Hildebrand, and N. Place. 2004. Extending technologies among small-scale farmers in Meru: Ingredients for success in farmer groups. Paper presented at the annual conference of the Association for International Agricultural and Extension Education, May 23–29, in Dublin, Ireland.

Davis, L. E., and D. C. North. 1971. *Institutional change and American economic growth.* Cambridge, U.K.: Cambridge University Press.

Davison, Jean. 1988. Who owns what? Land registration and tensions in gender relations of production in Kenya. In *Agriculture, women and land: The African experience,* ed. J. Davison. Boulder, Colo., U.S.A.: Westview Press.

de Haan, N. 2001. Of goats and groups: A study on social capital in development projects. *Agriculture and Human Values* 18 (1): 71–84.

di Gregorio, M., K. Hagedorn, M. Kirk, B. Korf, N. McCarthy, R. Meinzen-Dick, and B. Swallow. 2008. *Property rights, collective action, and poverty: The role of institutions for poverty reduction.* CAPRi Working Paper 81. Washington, D.C.: International Food Policy Research Institute.

Gaspart, F., M. Jabbar, C. Melard, and J. P. Platteau. 1998. Participation in the construction of a local public good with indivisibilities: An application to watershed development in Ethiopia. *Journal of African Economies* 7 (2): 157–184.

Gebremedhin, B., J. Pender, and G. Tesfay. 2002. *Collective action for grazing land management in mixed crop–livestock systems in the highlands of northern Ethiopia.* ILRI Socioeconomics and Policy Research Working Paper 42. Addis Ababa, Ethiopia: International Livestock Research Institute.

German, L., S. Charamila, and T. Tolera. 2006. *Managing trade-offs in agroforestry: From conflict to collaboration in natural resource management.* AHI Working Paper 10. Kampala, Uganda: African Highlands Initiative.

German, L., K. Masuki, Y. Gojjam, J. Odenya, and E. Geta. 2006a. *Beyond the farm: A new look at livelihood constraints in the eastern African highlands.* AHI Working Paper 12. Kampala, Uganda: African Highlands Initiative.

German, L., H. Taye, S. Charamila, T. Tolera, and J. Tanui. 2006b. *The many meanings of collective action: Lessons on enhancing gender inclusion and equity in watershed management.* CAPRi Working Paper 52. Washington, D.C.: International Food Policy Research Institute.

German, L., H. Taye, S. Ayele, W. Mazengia, T. Tolera, M. Tsegaye, K. Abere, K. Bedane, and E. Geta. 2008. Institutional foundations of agricultural development in Ethiopia: Drawing lessons from current practice for agricultural R&D. *Quarterly Journal of International Agriculture* 47 (3): 191–216.

German, L. A., A. Ruhweza, and R. Mwesigwa, with C. Kalanzi. 2010. Social and environmental footprints of carbon payments: A case study from Uganda. *In Livelihoods in the REDD? Payments for environmental services, forest conservation and climate change,* ed. L. Tacconi, S. Mahanty, and H. Suich. Cheltenham, U.K.: Edward Elgar.

Grabowski, R. 1990. Agriculture, mechanization and land tenure. *Journal of Development Studies* 7 (1): 43–53.

Grootaert, C. 2001. *Does social capital help the poor? A synthesis of findings from local level institutions studies in Bolivia, Burkina Faso, and Indonesia.* Local Level Institutions Working Paper 10. Washington, D.C.: World Bank.

Grootaert, C., and T. van Bastelear. 2002. *The role of social capital in development: An empirical assessment.* Cambridge, U.K.: Cambridge University Press.

Heinrich, G. 1993. *Strengthening farmer participation through groups: Experiences and lessons from Botswana.* OFCOR Discussion Paper 3. The Hague, the Netherlands: International Service for National Agricultural Research.

Jassey, K. 2000. Farmer research group: Who benefits? In *Farmer Participatory Approaches,* ed. G. M. Heinrich. Proceedings of the Regional Workshop on Farmer Participatory Approaches in Bulawayo, Zimbabwe. Hyderabad, India: International Crops Research Institute for the Semi-Arid-Tropics.

Kelly, C., and S. Breinlinger. 1995. Identity and injustice: Exploring women's participation in collective action. *Journal of Community and Applied Social Psychology* 5 (1): 41–57.

Kevane, M., and L. Gray. 1999. Diminished access, diverted exclusion: Women and land tenure in Sub-Saharan Africa. *African Studies Review* 42 (2): 15–39.

Knox, A., R. Meinzen-Dick, and P. Hazell. 2002. Property rights, collective action and technologies for natural resource management: A conceptual framework. In *Innovation in natural resource management: The role of property rights and collective action in developing countries,* ed. R. Meinzen-Dick, A. Knox, F. Place, and B. Swallow. Baltimore: Johns Hopkins University Press.

Lastarria-Cornhiel, S. 1997. Impact of privatization on gender and property rights in Africa. *World Development* 25 (8): 1317–1333.

Leach, M., R. Mearns, and I. Scoones. 1999. Environmental entitlements: Dynamics and institutions in community-based NRM. *World Development* 27 (2): 225–247.

Marshall, G. 1998. *A dictionary of sociology.* New York: Oxford University Press.

Mazengia, W. 2006. Enhancing improved seed dissemination through local bylaws in Gununo Watershed, southern Ethiopia. Paper presented at the Africa-Wide Research Workshop on Bylaws, November 27–29, in Nairobi, Kenya.

McDonald, J. H. 1991. Small-scale irrigation and the emergence of inequality among farmers in Central Mexico. *Research in Economic Anthropology* 13: 161–189.

Meinzen-Dick, R., M. Di Gregorio, and N. McCarthy. 2004. *Methods for studying collective action.* CAPRi Working Paper 33. Washington, D.C.: International Food Policy Research Institute.

Meinzen-Dick, R., A. Knox, F. Place, and B. Swallow, eds. 2002. *Innovation in natural resource management: The role of property rights and collective action in developing countries.* Washington, D.C.: International Food Policy Research Institute.

Molyneux, M. 2002. Gender and the silences of social capital: Lessons from Latin America. *Development and Change* 33 (2): 167–188.

Munk Ravnborg, H., and J. A. Ashby. 1996. *Organizing for local-level watershed management: Lessons from Rio Cabuyal Watershed.* AgREN Network Paper 65. London: Overseas Development Institute.

Munk Ravnborg, H., A. M. de la Cruz, M. del Pilar Guerrero, and O. Westermann. 2000. *Collective action in ant control.* CAPRi Working Paper 7. Washington, D.C.: International Food Policy Research Institute.

Nemarundwe, N., and W. Kozanayi. 2003. Institutional arrangements for water resource use: A case study from southern Zimbabwe. *Journal of Southern African Studies* 29 (1): 193–206.

Ngaido, T., and M. Kirk. 2001. Collective action, property rights and devolution of rangeland management: Selected examples from Africa and Asia. In *Collective action, property rights and devolution of natural resource management: Exchange of knowledge and implications for policy,* ed. R. Meinzen-Dick, A. Knox, and M. DiGregorio. Feldafing, Germany: Zentralstelle für Ernährung und Landwirtschaft.

Nitti, R., and B. Jahiya. 2004. Community-driven development in urban upgrading. *Social Development Notes* 85: 1–6.

North, D. C. 1990. *Institutions, institutional change, and economic performance.* Cambridge, U.K.: Cambridge University Press.

Olson, M. D. 2001. Development discourse and the politics of environmental ideologies in Samoa. *Society and Natural Resources* 14 (5): 399–410.

Ostrom, E. 1990. *Governing the commons: The evolution of institutions for collective action.* Cambridge, U.K.: Cambridge University Press.

———. 1999. *Self-governance and forest resources.* CIFOR Occasional Paper 20. Bogor, Indonesia: Center for International Forestry Research.

Ostrom, V. 1994. *The meaning of American federalism: Constituting a self-governing society.* San Francisco, Calif., U.S.A.: Institute for Contemporary Studies.

Oyono, P. R., J. C. Ribot, and A. M. Larson. 2006. *Green and black gold in rural Cameroon: Natural resources for local governance, justice and sustainability.* Environmental Governance in Africa Working Paper 22. Washington, D.C. and Bogor, Indonesia: World Resources Institute and Center for International Forestry Research.

Pandey, S., and G. N. Yadama. 1990. Conditions for local level community forestry action: A theoretical explanation. *Mountain Research and Development* 10 (1): 88–95.

Place, F., and B. Swallow. 2002. Assessing the relationships between property rights and technology adoption in smallholder agriculture: Issues and empirical methods. In *Innovation in natural resource management: The role of property rights and collective action in developing countries,* ed. R. Meinzen-Dick, A. Knox, F. Place and B. Swallow. Baltimore: Johns Hopkins University Press.

Raussen, T., G. Ebong, and J. Musiime. 2001. More effective natural resource management through democratically-elected, decentralized government structures in Uganda. *Development in Practice* 11 (4): 460–470.

Rocheleau, D., and D. Edmunds. 1997. Women, men and trees: Gender, power and property in forest and agrarian landscapes. *World Development* 25 (8): 1351–1371.

Schroeder, R. A. 1993. Shady practice: Gender and the political ecology of resource stabilization in Gambian garden/orchards. *Economic Geography* 69 (4): 349–365.

Scoones, I., and J. Thompson. 2003. *Participatory processes for policy change.* PLA Notes 46. London: International Institute for Environment and Development.

Scott, C. A., and P. Silva-Ochoa. 2001. Collective action for water harvesting irrigation in the Lerma-Chapala Basin, Mexico. *Water Policy* 3 (6): 555–572.

Tanui, J. 2006. Enabling negotiation and conflict resolution for area wide planning: The case of collective action for watershed management. Paper presented at the Africa-Wide Research Workshop on Bylaws, November 27–29, in Nairobi, Kenya.

Thébaud, B., and S. Batterbury. 2001. Sahel pastoralists: Opportunism, struggle, conflict and negotiation. *Global Environmental Change* 11 (1): 69–78.

Turner, M. D. 1999. Conflict, environmental change, and social institutions in dryland Africa: Limitations of the community resource management approach. *Society and Natural Resources* 12 (7): 643–657.

Uphoff, N., and C. M. Mijayaratna. 2000. Demonstrated benefits of social capital: The productivity of farmers' organizations in Gal Oya, Sri Lanka. *World Development* 28 (11): 1875–1890.

Valdivia, C., and J. L. Gilles. 2001. Gender and resource management: Households and groups, strategies and transitions. *Agriculture and Human Values* 18 (1): 5–9.

Wallis, A. 1998. Social capital and community building: Part 2. *National Civic Review* 4 (87): 317–336.

Wittayapak, C., and P. Dearden. 1999. Decision-making arrangements in community-based watershed management in northern Thailand. *Society and Natural Resources* 12 (7): 673–691.

Woolock, M., and D. Narayan. 2000. Social capital: Implications for development theory, research and policy. *World Bank Observer* 15 (2): 225–249.

8 The Role of Collective Action in Securing Property Rights for the Poor: A Case Study in Jambi Province, Indonesia

HERU KOMARUDIN, YULIANA L. SIAGIAN, AND
CAROL J. PIERCE COLFER WITH NELDYSAVRINO,
YENTIRIZAL, SYAMSUDDIN, AND DEDDY IRAWAN

Like many countries around the world (Colfer and Capistrano 2005), Indonesia has initiated a process of decentralization, particularly since the fall of Suharto in 1998. This process has included devolving extensive authority for day-to-day governance to the districts (*kabupaten*). In the forestry sector, district heads immediately began making use of forest resources as the main source of district income. Concerns over increased uncertainty and adverse impacts on the sustainability of resources, community livelihoods, and stakeholder relations led the central government to reduce the district heads' authority in 2002 (Barr et al. 2006; Dermawan, Komarudin, and McGrath 2006; Yasmi et al. 2006).

A revised law on decentralization was issued in 2004, aiming to clarify the 1999 law on the roles and responsibilities shared among the government units and open opportunities for central and regional governments to improve their relationship while providing the regional governments with continued freedom to develop their regions. The new arrangements allow local communities to articulate their development needs and participate in policymaking processes. However, despite legal and institutional reforms, challenges remain. Longstanding conflicting laws on natural resources also complicate finding legal solutions to problems, and property rights remain unclear. Decisionmaking processes for land use planning and local communities' access to resources are also unclear. There are limited mechanisms for meaningful input from communities, particularly from women.

Unclear property rights over forestlands in Indonesia are one of the contentious issues. The country's forest communities typically have traditional systems of land tenure that bear little resemblance to the land classifications recognized by the government. Although the country's forestlands are strongly controlled by the central government, much of the official forestland is actually inhabited by indigenous or in-migrating communities, leading to disputes not only between local communities and private companies but also between district and central governments. The district governments' demand for forest conversion in order to meet development needs also poses challenges. These challenges are put in sharper focus by the increasing national and global attention

235

to the potential of forests to mitigate climate change and particularly to the ability of forest communities to benefit through reduced emissions from deforestation and degradation (REDD) mechanisms. The objectives of our study have been to (1) understand the current policies and issues relating to forestlands in a decentralized context and to local people's access to property rights and decisionmaking processes and (2) learn how collective action among community groups and interaction among stakeholders can enhance local people's rights over lands, resources, and policy processes for development. The study has involved facilitating stakeholder interactions within the forestry decentralization setting and catalyzing collective action among villages and district governments. This chapter presents an approach to supporting a process of self-empowerment so that poor and marginalized communities can act collectively to secure their assets and property rights in order to achieve better livelihoods and maintain their environments.

With regard to the conceptual framework presented in Chapter 2, this chapter emphasizes the context, the action arena, and patterns of interactions. Specifically, the security of property rights to forest resources (natural assets) for forest-dependent communities remains unresolved even with the implementation of decentralization reforms (the legal and political structure of the context). Elite capture and conflict portray this insecurity. Facilitated negotiation (the action arena) through multistakeholder consultations brought together conflicting actors with varied forms of power and action resources (see Appendix 8A), built trust among them, increased the bargaining power of communities, and created a mechanism for coordinated action. These facilitated negotiations positively influenced official and private-company decisionmaking practices, supported clarification and strengthening of local rights, opened up development planning processes to resource users, and identified and supported income-generating opportunities for them. In short, facilitated negotiation resulted in patterns of interactions among actors (that is, cooperation) that have favorable implications for the well-being of resource users.

Beyond spotlighting how collective action by the poor (and related actors) can help to strengthen their rights and access to resources critical to their well-being, this chapter also showcases two thematic areas identified in Chapter 1: natural resource governance processes and the challenge presented by elite capture of benefits due to power imbalances during reform processes. Through its contribution to these two thematic areas the chapter speaks to broader concerns in the decentralization literature and suggests that elite capture during the implementation of decentralization reforms can be effectively countered by a structured, transparent negotiation process (see Section 5 below) that is brokered by a trusted third party.

The first section of the chapter describes the physical, technical, and socioeconomic as well as policy governance conditions. The following section describes our research approach and methods, and the next section describes our findings, exploring the action arena, where we identify stakeholder interaction and action resources and outline the processes of facilitating and catalyzing collective action among district and community stakeholders. Then we analyze these findings and describe research outcomes, concluding in the final section with policy implications and recommendations.

The Context

Jambi, Indonesia

Jambi Province, located in the middle of Sumatra, covers 5.1 million hectares of land, 43 percent of which is categorized as state-owned forestlands (*kawasan hutan;* Office of the Jambi Governor 1999). The forestlands represent different forest functions, and two categories are of particular interest: nature reserves or protection forests (870,250 hectares) and production forests (1,309,190 hectares). We use the term *forestland* to refer to *kawasan hutan,* the formal governmental designation for a type of land tenure. When discussing other forms of tenure, we use other terms, such as *forest, land, fields, plots,* and so on. Between 1990 and 2000, Jambi forest cover decreased from 2.40 million to 1.40 million hectares (Taher 2005). In 2002, Jambi forests were estimated to cover 1.38 million hectares, or 27 percent of the total province. Jambi's growing population is highly dependent on natural resources, and an estimated 75 percent of its rural people live below the official poverty line.

Forest cover in Bungo District has also experienced drastic change, declining from 43 percent of the total district area to 31 percent between 1990 and 2002. Unclear, "open-access" status, among other factors (Hadi, Komarudin, and Schangen 2007), contributes to this ongoing degradation. Tanjabbar District's forest resources have been logged and its forestland converted, and the district's forest cover has also declined by almost 40 percent in the past 20 years (Sudirman and Herlina 2005; internal data from the Center for International Forestry Research). About half of the remaining forest is within protected areas. Some 22 percent of the district's population (242,355) lived beneath the poverty line in 2005, compared to 13 percent (234,813) in 2004.

Our two study sites, Sungai Telang in Bungo and Lubuk Kambing in Tanjabbar, have relatively strong kinship ties, medium levels of conflict between villagers and outside actors, and high levels of poverty and are located close to national parks and forestlands (2–10 kilometers). Their differences are presented in Table 8.1 (for greater detail, see Komarudin, Siagian, and Colfer 2007).

Forest Management Policies and Communities' Access to Resources

Under the New Order government, before 1998, the central government firmly controlled the management of natural resources, including forests. The 2001 decentralization law gave the districts greater autonomy to formulate their own

TABLE 8.1 Community characteristics of the village research sites, 2005

Criteria	Sungai Telang (Bungo District)	Lubuk Kambing (Tanjabbar District)
Conflict level	Latent conflict between the indigenous community and transmigrants	Relatively good relations between the indigenous community and migrants
Institutional setting	Village government, village representatives, customary institutions, youth groups, men's groups, women's groups	Village government, village representatives, customary institutions, men's groups, loggers' groups, women's groups
Population	1,256	~4,000

SOURCES: Lubuk Kambing Village Government (2005) and Sungai Telang Village Government (2005).

policies and exert control over their resources. In Bungo and Tanjabbar districts, as in many other forest-rich regions, the district heads issued small-scale timber concessions (forest product utilization permits). Between 2001 and 2003, for instance, the Tanjabbar District Government issued 85 permits for timber extraction for different types or statuses of forests (Sudirman and Herlina 2005) to cooperatives, farmer groups, or foundations.

Due to concerns about environmental degradation, failure to provide benefits to local people, and the creation of an uncertain business climate, the central government withdrew the district heads' authority to issue small-scale concession permits through a 2002 governmental regulation.[1] When our research started in 2005, the two local governments of our study sites were no longer issuing the permits.

Three forestry programs (described by Hadi, Komarudin, and Schangen 2007) were considered to affect property rights and collective action. These included Bantuan Usaha Produktif in Bungo, a program providing community groups with revolving funds to stimulate their productive efforts; Rekonstruksi Tata Batas, a forest gazettement program to clarify forestland–village boundaries; and Rehabilitasi Hutan dan Lahan, a program to replant and reforest critical lands. The last two were implemented in both districts.

In October 2004, the Ministry of Forestry issued a policy on *ijin pemanfaatan kayu* (timber use permits), again granting authority to district heads to issue these permits to cooperatives, individuals, and state-owned and private companies. Although most district governments were enthusiastic about issuing small-scale concessions during the early stages of decentralization, the two

---

1. Government Regulation 34/2002, on the forest and the formulation of forest management plans, forest use, and the use of the forest estate (*tata hutan dan penyusunan rencana pengelolaan hutan, pemanfaatan hutan dan penggunaan kawasan hutan*). This regulation has now been replaced by Government Regulation 6/2007 (issued January 8, 2007).

research districts responded differently. Tanjabbar issued a number of licenses, Bungo none.

In short, the two communities and districts have seen a dynamic see-saw of forest-related policies, with formal, legal authority shifting back and forth between the central and the district governments over the period of our research and immediately preceding it. This has presented a very uncertain policy context to decisionmakers at all levels. The longstanding lack of congruity among the perceptions of local people, district governments, and the central government on land tenure and use rights has further fueled the uncertainty. These factors, combined with the presence of powerful outsiders (such as conservation projects and timber and oil palm companies, as discussed in the next section), have created serious pressure on both the local people and the environment. The lack of certainty about rights to resources has created an open-access situation, with serious adverse consequences for the resources upon which local people have traditionally depended.

Research Approach and Methods

One catalyst for our research was the perceived need for mechanisms, in particular at the community level, to deal with potential rewards (such as payments for environmental services or, more recently, REDD payments) in an equitable and efficient way that would maintain or improve the environment and human well-being. We believed that accomplishing this goal would require both collective action and local empowerment vis-à-vis local government and other powerful actors. We therefore applied participatory action research (PAR) at both the community and the district levels, with the intention to strengthen potential interests (and resulting links) between the two levels, as a pathway to local empowerment and benign governmental effectiveness. The PAR approach combines action and research to inform action and enables participants to learn through critical reflection about what happens when they act (see Greenwood and Levin 1998 for details on action research methods). We facilitated bottom-up identification of priorities through the phases of needs assessment, planning, action, monitoring, reflecting, and designing further steps and collecting necessary information.

We employed open-ended, semistructured interviews and focus group discussions to collect information, triangulate, and observe people's stances on specific issues as the research developed. We also facilitated shared learning workshops to enable participants to interact with each other, share their knowledge and experiences, and disseminate lessons to a wider audience. A detailed outline of our study methods is available in Komarudin, Siagian, and Colfer (2007).

Our two study districts in Jambi, Bungo, and West Tanjung Jabung (or Tanjabbar) are shown in Figure 8.1. The villages of Sungai Telang (Bungo District)

FIGURE 8.1 Research sites in Bungo and Tanjabbar Districts, Jambi Province

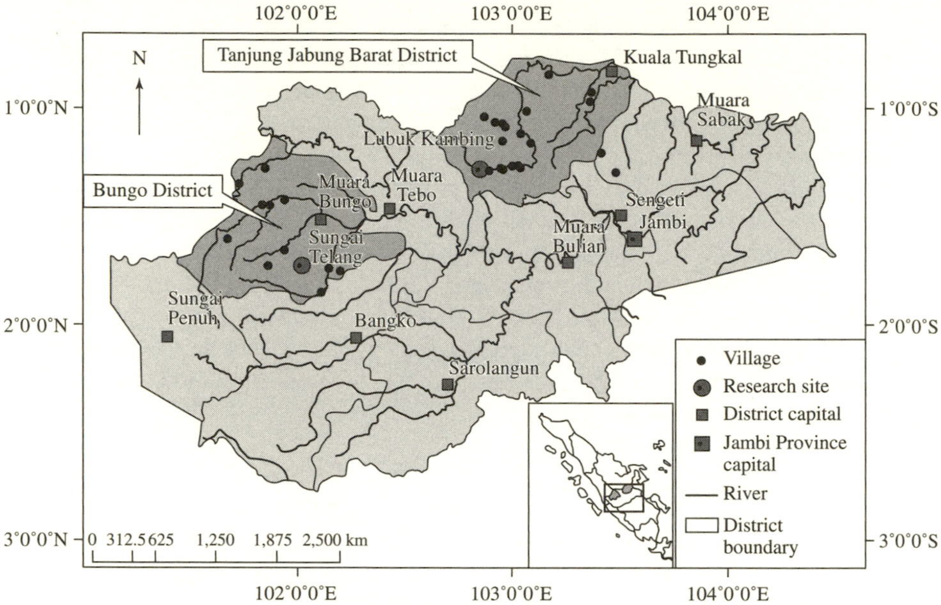

SOURCE: Komarudin, Siagian, and Colfer (2007).
NOTE: Tanjabbar is an acronym standing for Tanjung Jabung Barat or West Tanjung Jabung.

and Lubuk Kambing (Tanjabbar District)—both located in the poorest sub-districts of their districts—were selected based on the following criteria and what we hoped to gain from each:

- Representation of matrilineal, patrilineal, or bilateral inheritance systems —to examine the gender-based differences related to inheritance systems.
- Relatively high dependence on forest products and access to forest resources —to gain insights into tenure issues within forestlands.
- Pressures from outsiders on the community and potential conflicts or threats to community and forest sustainability—to understand how conflicts among stakeholders are handled and how they could be dealt with more effectively.
- Opportunities for overlap of interests between the community and existing (or planned) district government development programs—to strengthen the links between communities and government actors.
- Existing research activities or other development agencies or institutions (government, university, or international organizations) working in the village area to gain access to secondary literature and develop links between communities and other outside actors.

Group Selection

At the district level, we worked with six government officials (three from each of the two districts) from the district agency for development planning (Bappeda) and district forestry services. The officials had been appointed by their superiors or proposed by the Center for International Forestry Research (CIFOR) or had come forward on their own initiative. Three had been trained in PAR. These individuals were recognized champions of community empowerment. Some had been involved in cooperative projects with organizations outside the government.

At the village level, pre-existing community groups were selected. Individuals in such groups worked together in their day-to-day activities and already had good personal connections. We could thus build on and acknowledge existing communication patterns, which reinforced their self-confidence, another important factor in bringing about effective collective action (Colfer 2007).

The groups selected also represented ethnic diversity (especially Minang, Malay, Javanese), local versus transmigrant populations, gender differences, and the interests presented in Table 8.2. We worked primarily at the hamlet (*dusun*) level in order to reduce transportation and communication costs and to build on previous experience (for example, see Kusumanto et al. 2005).

Key Research Issues

Given the goal of local empowerment, the research questions had to be "owned" by local actors. We therefore began with a multistakeholder "inception" workshop in Jambi, at which important local issues were meshed with our own plans. When fieldwork was initiated, we used these broad topics to further "drill down" to more specific levels where actual community- and district-level actions would be taken. Figure 8.2 provides a schema illustrating the two levels of our analysis, the key research issues at each level identified during the inception workshop, and the mediating role of collective action and property rights. It builds on and adapts the schema presented in Chapter 2 of this volume by Di Gregorio et al.

Findings

This section describes the process of working with district government and the communities, outlining examples of topics addressed and actions taken at both levels. This makes up the "action arena" part of the Institutional Analysis and Development framework while exploring the responsibilities, interests or concerns, and action resources of relevant actors as listed in the appendix.

Indonesia's forestlands are under the strong control of the central government. The Forestry Law granted the Ministry of Forestry power to designate the status, boundaries, and functions of the forests. This power remains despite

TABLE 8.2 Group characteristics at the village research sites, 2006

Group	Characteristics and functioning	Motivation	Action plan
Sungai Telang			
1. Gotong Royong (women's group)	Has 17 members, all women. Was formed in 2001. Members are of mixed ethnicity (Minang, Malay, and Javanese). Includes women of all ages, married and unmarried.	Members share labor in agriculture. Members not participating in group work when requested pay a fine of Rp.10,000–15,000 per day of absence. Payment schedule is flexible. Members must settle debts before the fasting month (Ramadan[a]). Cooking oil and sugar are bought with group earnings for each member.	Sells rattan and bamboo weavings to supplement their income.
2. Kelompok Tani Sinar Tani (men's group)	Has 17 members, all male. Is an association of individuals with land in one area. Includes Minang locals and Javanese in-migrants. Aims to help small farmers. Receives support from an agricultural extension agent. Draws members from all Sungai Telang hamlets.	Was formed in 1998 when the government provided funds to improve water canals for irrigated rice. Continued even after government funding ended. In 2001 received government aid (rice seedlings), but few members were interested.	Pursues land certification and income-generating activities through propagation of the nontimber forest product *jernang* (*Daemonorops draco*).

3. Pelhin (women's group)	Is a women's group (gender is a longstanding, traditional grouping mechanism).	There is a reciprocal sharing of work among members.
	Is ethnically homogenous, with Minang women working together in farming activities.	There is a long history of Pelhin groups.
	Includes all women within a family and their friends.	Serves as a control, continuing to participate in their customary activities, mostly related to agriculture.
	There is no designated leader; members are considered equal.	
	The number of members is flexible, depending on women's needs and willingness to join.	
4. Bukit Lestari Makmur (men's group)	Is all male, designed to aid small farmers.	Was initially formed by four members of Sinar Tani who were disappointed with the corruption of elites.
	Was formed in 2006.	Members are enthusiastic about establishing an alternative source of income (wild *jernang* seedlings).
	Includes 10 young farmer members.	Propagates and markets *jernang*.
	Includes Minang and Malay locals and Javanese in-migrants interested in propagating non-timber forest products.	
	Holds meetings frequently to monitor progress.	
	Applies strict group rules and sanctions.	

(*continued*)

TABLE 8.2 Continued

Group	Characteristics and functioning	Motivation	Action plan
Lubuk Kambing			
1. Dasawisma (women's group)	Was formed in 2005. There are 20 Malay women in each group, formed at the lowest administrative level of each village. Is automatically led by village head's wife.	Was formed as part of a formal government program, the Family Welfare Movement, started in 1967 and focusing primarily on women in rural areas.	Generates alternative income opportunities (for example, selling cakes and raising ducks) using the program budget.
2. Kelompok Tani Tunas Harapan (men's group)	Had 34 members, all male. Was formed in 1997. Included in-migrants of mixed ethnicity (Javanese, Malay, Batak, and Palembang) focusing on agricultural crops. Initially focused on individual agricultural activities. Conducted meetings rarely, though members shared work (*gotong royong*) with the hamlet community.	Initially formed by people with influential positions in the community. Focused only on daily agricultural labor. Includes members with great enthusiasm for working together.	Found alternative income-generating activities. Found ways to increase agricultural productivity.

SOURCE: Data were generated through authors' semistructured interviews and group discussions with the respective groups' leaders and members.

NOTE: Rp. means Indonesian rupiah.

aRamadan ends with the most significant holiday for Muslims, one in which much money is needed to buy new clothes, sacrifice a goat, and so on.

FIGURE 8.2 The key research issues addressed in the case study at the village and district levels, with relevant elements such as gender and the approach to research, and their relations to collective action and property rights institutions

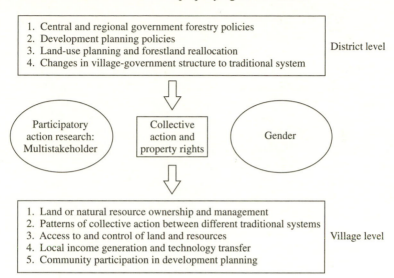

1. Central and regional government forestry policies
2. Development planning policies
3. Land-use planning and forestland reallocation
4. Changes in village-government structure to traditional system

District level

Participatory action research: Multistakeholder

Collective action and property rights

Gender

1. Land or natural resource ownership and management
2. Patterns of collective action between different traditional systems
3. Access to and control of land and resources
4. Local income generation and technology transfer
5. Community participation in development planning

Village level

SOURCE: Komarudin, Siagian, and Colfer (2007).

the issuance of Law 22/1999, later revised by Law 32/2004 concerning de-centralization, which gave a greater mandate to the regional governments to tackle all affairs, including forestry. Due to an increased need for development, which also occurred across the other regions of the country, Jambi's district and provincial governments have contested the sole authority of the Ministry of Forestry and proposed forest conversion in a number of areas. Conflicts over lands between local people and private companies are numerous. Attempts have been made to revise the Tata Guna Hutan Kesepakatan (TGHK), or the Forest Land Use by Consensus zoning plans, which categorize different forest functions, including those intended for nonforestry development. The TGHK was issued by the Ministry of Forestry in the 1980s, and some have tried to synchronize it with the Rencana Tata Ruang Wilayah Provinsi (RTRWP), or Provincial-Level Land Use Plan; the result has been the RTRWP/TGHK *paduserasi* (integrated land use scheme). However, demands by regional governments for forest conversion continue, combined with local people's struggles to clarify their rights over forest resources and lands relative to the district, provincial, and central governments or private companies. It is in this context that the research took place and the facilitation began.

District-Level Facilitation: Can Property Rights over Land Resources Be Strengthened through Regional Land Use Planning?

The regional land use plans—RTRWP, and Rencana Tata Ruang Wilayah Kabupaten (RTRWK), or District-Level Land Use Plan—indicate how the uses of land and forestland have been allocated. Land use planning can serve as a key to tenurial reform even when it is considered to have no direct linkage with land status (Contreras-Hermosilla and Fay 2006). Forestland status and function can affect local communities' access to resources. The plans are dynamic and can change over time. In Bungo, the district government revised its district land use plan twice between 2000 and 2005. The first revision took place following the division of Bungo Tebo District into two new districts, Bungo and Tebo. The second was carried out to anticipate regional development dynamics, including large-scale land use by businesses and investors for plantations and coal mining. In Tanjabbar, the district government developed its land use plan in 2001 and is currently revising it.

The two districts share challenges in preparing sound, all-inclusive plans. Lack of resources and personnel with either skills or educational backgrounds in planning caused the RTRWK plans for one district to be prepared by inexperienced personnel and those for the other district to be prepared by external consultants. Budgetary and time constraints made it difficult to accommodate stakeholders' input.

Each district has a committee, the Tim Tata Ruang Daerah (District Land Use Planning Committee), that is responsible for preparing or subcontracting the plan, overseeing its implementation, and monitoring the use of allocated lands. This committee, comprised of representatives from Bappeda, the district-level national land agency, the district forest office, and the district secretariat, also served to mediate land conflicts between local communities and private companies.

Law 24/1992 and Government Regulation 69/1996 provide ample opportunities for public participation in land use planning.[2] In addition, Law 41/1999 stipulates that local people have the right to know the fate of lands surrounding their villages and provide input to the government, including raising objections to proposed plans.[3] Because of its formal authority, the district government played the dominant role in determining the direction of spatial planning policy in both districts. The district land use planning committees argued that the proposed RTRWK land use plans in the two districts had been

---

2. Law 24/1992, regarding land use planning, has now been revised by Law 26/2007. Government Regulation 69/1996, on the rights, obligations, forms, and procedures related to public participation in land use planning (Pelaksanaan Hak dan Kewajiban serta Bentuk dan Tata Cara Peran Serta Masyarakat dalam Penataan Ruang). This regulation is an implementing rule for Law 24/1992, on land use planning.

3. Law 41/1999 is the Forestry Law.

developed in a participatory way: technical discussions had been held at the district and subdistrict levels and with nongovernmental organizations (NGOs). Stakeholders had also been invited to a seminar at which their input comprised corrections to data included in the RTRWK. The term "people's participation" was interpreted differently by different stakeholders. To some government officials, sending a proposal to the district house of representatives and deliberations within the house on the draft are indications of people's "participation."

Although Law 24/1992 on land use planning requires plans to be developed according to the hierarchy of governance levels, accommodating inputs from the lower levels of governance (subdistrict and village spatial plans traditionally developed by local people) is a challenge.[4] Although soliciting inputs from the villagers represents a useful strategy to reduce future conflicts over land, some stakeholders objected, citing the need to consider broader ecosystems and to avoid fragmentation, as well as the difficulty of harmonizing the different standards and categories used. Some officials also had difficulties deciding which *masyarakat* (community) should be involved.

To further meet development needs, the two district governments proposed that the status of forestlands be changed into "areas for other uses," or *areal penggunaan lain* (APL), normally allocated for the development of large-scale plantations. Growing populations in need of land, increased investment opportunities potentially important for district revenues, and greater district responsibilities in governance plague district governments throughout the country. Once the status of the lands changes, it is the district governments that will control the lands. The districts argued that forestland with no forest cover would be more productive if managed for agriculture. Much of the national forestlands is land the communities claim as part of their traditional territories.

Tanjabbar and Bungo districts proposed changing the status of 46,185 hectares and 12,880 hectares of state forestlands, respectively, mostly from production forest to APL.[5] If the proposals are approved, there will be a decrease in the total area of forestlands from 257,344 hectares to 211,259 hectares and an increase in agricultural and nonagricultural areas from 241,081 hectares to

---

4. Law 24/1992 recognized three different types of spatial plans: national, provincial, and district. Subdistrict and village spatial plans are not recognized in the law.

5. In total, around 98,577 hectares of forestland in seven districts of Jambi were to be proposed for conversion. During a shared learning workshop titled Spatial Planning and Forestland Allocation toward Strengthening Property Rights and Promoting Good Governance, organized by CIFOR in January 2007, a Jambi provincial Bappeda official presented this figure and shared the provincial government's arguments for conversion with participants, including those from the Ministry of Forestry's Agency for Forestry Planning (Baplan). The initial extent of the changes to state forests proposed by the Tanjabbar District Government was only 11,312 hectares, but then— as revealed during another workshop—it grew to 46,185 hectares. The Jambi provincial Bappeda responsible for handling proposals from all districts throughout Jambi used only the initial figure of 11,312 hectares in its formal proposal.

287,266 hectares. The Tanjabbar government argued that the state forestlands in these proposed locations are already community lands, with rubber, oil palms, and other crops as well as settlements, logged acacias, and shrub.

In Bungo District, the expansion of community farming into production and protection forests has led to conflicts between indigenous communities and new-comers and between villagers in Sungai Telang and the transmigration office, which has allocated a transmigration site on state forestland also claimed by the community. In other places there are land conflicts between communities and plan-tation companies. The Bungo government proposed to convert a total of 12,880 hectares of forestland to farmlands, oil and rubber plantations, and cooperatives. Additionally, the Bungo government proposed to convert around 14,000 hect-ares from APL to protection forests and has already allocated around 2,000 hectares for *hutan adat* (customary forests) to be managed by communities.

The series of facilitated workshops and focus group discussions, some of which were primarily for Ministry of Forestry and district government stake-holders, resulted in insight into why the district proposals had been ignored and into the stands of the respective parties. While emphasizing that proposals must be in accordance with relevant laws and regulations, the Ministry argued that the forestland map used by the two districts was established through a harmo-nization process between TGHK and the RTRWP of 1999. Because there had been consultations between the Ministry and provincial and district govern-ments, the Ministry thought the process had been adequately participatory. The Ministry stressed the need to have a shared understanding of what the "review of spatial plans" meant. Instead of fundamentally changing land allocations—which were seen to lead to an "uncertain business and investment climate"—the "review" should merely update changes in field conditions in the past five years.[6] Despite its firm stance on retaining forestlands, the Ministry was fully aware of the increasing need for land for regional development and had issued a decree that tolerated conversions of forestlands for strategic purposes if such conver-sions did not adversely affect ecosystem services and functions.[7]

Land use planning is often seen as one of the avenues for local people to secure their rights.[8] To reinforce their proposals for forest conversion, the dis-trict governments often made use of arguments that the lands were no longer

---

6. One of the Ministry's officials stated this clearly in a shared learning workshop, Spatial Planning and Forestland Allocation towards Strengthening Property Rights and Promoting Good Governance, organized by CIFOR on January 29–30, 2007, in Bogor, Indonesia.

7. Minister of Forestry Decree 70/2001, which was amended by Minister of Forestry Decree 48/2004, on the designation of forestlands and includes changes in the status and functions of forestlands.

8. Most community groups interviewed considered secure property rights over lands, either ownership or use, important, as exemplified in Komarudin, Siagian, and Colfer (2007). This cor-roborates the findings of other studies (Colchester and MacKay 2004; Colchester et al. 2006; Adnan et al. 2008).

covered with forests and had been occupied by local people to improve their livelihoods. Yet interestingly, in many cases the entire process ended up in lands allocated for large-scale estate crop plantations, giving less benefit to local people who had previously used the lands. When approving forest conversion, the Ministry of Forestry pays little attention to how the converted lands will benefit local people. Instead, in its regulations it specifies the maximum areas in hectares allocated for large-scale plantations (that is, oil palms).[9]

Land Conflicts and Collective Efforts to Resolve Them

Part of the impetus for the previously described workshop was a conflict between a large-scale industrial forest plantation and local people in Tanjabbar. The central government had allocated the land to the company, but local people, resident in the area long before the company's arrival, had cleared some of the land for crops. The company wanted a clear and clean working area so they could do business smoothly. To do this, they had to help clarify property rights for the local people. A clear working area would mean that they would pay taxes to the government according to the actual lands they were entitled to manage. To resolve the issue, the provincial and district forest services commissioned a team to conduct an inventory of disputed forestlands already occupied by local people, including the villagers of Suka Maju, a Lubuk Kambing hamlet.[10]

Three types of land issues faced the company, termed "overlaps," "overlapping claims," and "occupation." Overlaps, which are fairly easy to resolve with government help, refer to boundary disputes between a company's working areas and the adjacent areas of other companies. Overlapping claims are cases in which local communities claim rights to a company's working areas still in secondary forest, evidence that the land had been cleared (the main traditional means of establishing ownership). The community's claims are based on people's having inherited the land from their ancestors. This is the issue most difficult to resolve, because people's claims to land are often uncertain in terms of size and location, and different groups within a community (and outside) may have claims to the same land. Occupation, about which a company can do nothing, refers to land where there were already settlements and construction when the company entered the area.

When the inventory team went to the disputed area to meet the residents of Suka Maju, the members of the community were antagonistic, partly because they had heard from the village head that the company would flatten their houses and usurp their lands. They also knew of prior experience with PT Inhutani (a state-owned concessionaire), which had evicted other communities (the evic-

---

9. For example, Ministry of Forestry Regulation 31/2005, amended by Regulation 22/2009, concerning forest conversion intended for the establishment of estate crops plantations.

10. It is estimated that of 290,000 hectares of the company's working area in five districts in Jambi, around 50,000 hectares were already occupied by local people.

tions and women's dramatic leadership in resisting eviction are elaborated in Komarudin, Siagian, and Colfer 2007). The members of our research team, with whom the community was familiar, mediated the disagreement, making clear to the community the genuine purpose of the team's visit. The community finally agreed to discussions with them.

The inventory team asked the community to tell the history of the lands they cultivated at the time and fill out a detailed form describing themselves, their group, and their livelihoods. The inventory team also presented options for resolving various cases. For areas where trees and crops had been grown for more than five years and which were well maintained, community groups might continue working in the area. A plan is under way to seek legal rights for these residents to continue managing the area. For areas where trees and crops had not been planted but the soil was well managed, a similar option was offered. A partnership with the company through, for example, product sharing was also a possibility. Harsh action would be taken against anyone who cleared forests but left the land untouched. One general condition for villagers choosing any of the options was that they not expand their agricultural lands further into the area managed by the company.

The inventory team recognized that the community groups living in Suka Maju were highly committed to managing land resources and would likely be good candidates for the district program on social forestry (small-scale forest plantations). Building on this idea, the research team facilitated a focus group discussion on the possibilities for implementing the Ministry of Forestry's Hutan Kemasyarakatan (HKm), the community forestry program, designed for people's empowerment. Through this strategy, community groups or cooperatives are granted the right to manage forestlands. Local stakeholders considered it timely for the districts to implement the centrally designed HKm program as a kind of compromise or quid pro quo in their struggle to gain the forestland conversion described earlier. They also proposed that around 10,000 hectares of forestlands with significant ecological value in other Tanjabbar and Bungo subdistricts be considered as HKm projects.

The facilitated engagement through the workshop, focus group discussions, and field facilitation had not produced concrete results as of 2007. Although the stakeholders met and repeatedly discussed the issue of forest conversion, no firm approvals of the proposals were forthcoming from the Ministry of Forestry. However, participants learned about each other's views, interests, and expectations. The Ministry and provincial and district governments agreed on strategies to deal with the district proposals and resolve conflicts over lands. These included, among others, forming a communication forum, public consultation and participatory assessment of the proposed forestlands, inventory of already occupied lands and the socioeconomic conditions of surrounding communities, and seeking forestry strategies for people's empowerment through social forestry programs. Local people involved in the dispute gained knowledge of the need for more formal recognition of their traditional land claims. Those who had obtained their lands by inheritance or purchase tended to fight for ownership rights, whereas those whose lands had been obtained by occupation were typically satisfied with secure use rights.

Community-Level Facilitation

To convey the process of facilitation and collective action, in the following sections we discuss the specific actions that community groups undertook, focusing on group formation and activation, social learning, tenure issues, and voice.

PROVIDING A SPARK FOR COMMUNITY COLLECTIVE ACTION.   Table 8.2 describes the characteristics, motivation, and activities of the groups in which we catalyzed collective action in the two villages. Central issues included income-generating activities (selling cakes, raising ducks) and addressing property rights issues through land certification and government-sponsored rubber sapling programs.

In Sungai Telang, we identified two different types of women's (farmer) groups, Gotong Royong and Pelhin. Gotong Royong, selected and facilitated as our primary group, provides paid labor to help members in their agricultural work. Pelhin, observed without our facilitation, operates on a reciprocal work basis, exchanging work on a days-worked basis. When a woman takes part in a Pelhin work day, she is then owed a day of work by the owner of the farm. This can be paid off when the woman calls a Pelhin day herself. The Pelhin group represents a kind of control, a good example of longstanding collective action among the members of a matrilineal group (described further later). In Lubuk Kambing, we identified and facilitated the Dasawisma group, a women's group interested in income generation.

Once sufficient rapport had been developed within the communities, we began to lead the groups through the PAR steps of planning, action, monitoring, and reflection. Throughout this process we worked with the group to ensure that the relevant villagers were present at group planning discussions to ensure that all stakeholders would have a share in the action processes. Action, which often meant going to officials at the subdistrict (*kecamatan*) or district (*kabupaten*) level for information, involved rotating the members of the groups meeting with government officials.

Members of the Minang Gotong Royong group expressed their interest in producing a product with good market potential to supplement their cash income. Most of these women were already weaving mats and baskets for home use as a regular part of their activities (Yentirizal 2007). They wanted to market their weavings but were not sure how to do so. They decided that the best course of action would be to invite representatives of a women's group from the village of Baru Pelepat (Kusumanto et al. 2005), who had been successful in marketing their own weavings, to give them advice. Three women from Baru Pelepat came to Sungai Telang at the end of July 2005 to help members of the Gotong Royong group. Members of the other two Gotong Royong groups in the village also attended.

The members of Sinar Tani, the Minang men's group in Sungai Telang, expressed their interest in pursuing land certification. They were concerned about possible land conflicts, wanting to clarify their land boundaries and ensure a legal way for their children to inherit their land. Having reflected on the need for information on the certification process, the group invited government officials from Bappeda, the forest service, and the district-level national land agency (BPN) to attend a meeting and answer their questions. At the meeting they learned about Program Nasional Agraria (PRONA), a national agrarian program that provides mass land certification for poor people at low cost. Sinar Tani started to collectively work on proposals and interact with district officials.

The Dasawisma group was formed as a result of Pemberdayaan Kesejahteraan Keluarga, a top-down government program for empowerment of family welfare, of which the village head's wife is the mandated leader. She selected members from various neighborhoods, appointing two vocal women as leaders, ignoring the considerable distances between their homes and the resulting difficulties in meeting. The members were dissatisfied with the way the group had been formed and the members selected. Two Dasawisma groups were interested in supplementing their cash income from agriculture using their existing skills. Each Dasawisma group comprises 20 Malay women. The Dasawisma Semangka group decided to sell cakes, while the Dasawisma Pisang Lilin planned to raise ducks and market the eggs. These ideas derived from women in the group who had prior experience in these fields.

A male farmers' group, Tunas Harapan in Lubuk Kambing's Suka Maju hamlet, was initially formed when the government offered relevant programs to help the farmers. The group was primarily made up of members new to the area and of mixed ethnicity, coming from Java, North Sumatra, Aceh, and Palembang. Some village elites persuaded the new group to clear land in preparation for oil palm investors who never materialized. The group later decided to work together to improve their annual crop yields, such as soybeans raised on land previously used for irrigated rice fields. They estimated that each member could afford to cultivate at least 1 hectare, hoping that this would become their main source of income. Tree crops planted by Suka Maju farmers had not yet come into production, leaving the community dependent on upland rice fields and other foodcrops as their main source of income. Having reflected and learned about the lack of information and skills for cultivating soybeans, the Tunas Harapan members realized that they would need someone to provide them with information on good agricultural practices. The group's first step was to approach the district agriculture service and persuade an agricultural extension agent to provide the group with information on agricultural technology and possibilities for funding support, expanding the network, and creating a better relationship with district and subdistrict authorities.

BUILDING A STRONGER GROUP THROUGH A LEARNING PROCESS. In addition to pursuing land certification and improving agricultural products, the men's group Sinar Tani in Sungai Telang was also interested in generating additional income. Initially the group wanted to develop rubber but was limited by its financial resources.

Through our facilitation some group members began to interact with officials from the district agriculture services and forestry office, sharing their concerns and learning new information, including about funding possibilities. They learned about the District Forestry Office's Bantuan Usaha Produktif, a program to help local groups with the necessary skills to develop small enterprises. Through this program the office allocated US$1,080, in a revolving fund, to each selected community group throughout the district once its proposal for funding was accepted.

Although the farmer groups were theoretically allowed to choose their activities, the district forestry service had a program to encourage duck-raising, and the group changed its focus in response to this opportunity. However, the onset of the avian flu epidemic hit Indonesia, altering government priorities and rendering their plan unworkable. They then developed another plan.

The group learned about the high value of the abundant rattan fruit *jernang* (*Daemonorops draco*), internationally known as dragon's blood. They also learned that the Forest Service was proposing Sungai Telang as a center for *jernang* seedlings. Stimulated by the potential market value of the fruit and the district's endorsement, the group members prepared and submitted a successful proposal on *jernang* cultivation (Komarudin, Siagian, and Oka 2007). They were granted US$1,087 to be used to purchase polybags and seedlings or for the capacity-building of their members.

Once the first advance of US$760 was received, three group leaders misused the money, and a forestry extension agent was also reportedly involved. The District Forestry Office postponed disbursement of the second payment.

On reflection, the group members agreed that a lack of transparency in spending, lack of internal sanctions against abuses in the use of funds, shortcomings in group decisionmaking, and lack of guidance and monitoring from the District Forestry Office had contributed to their failure. They formed a new group of ten people, with only four members coming from the previous group. None were elite.

The men called their new group Bukit Lestari Makmur and formed a set of rules (see Box 8.1) reflecting their commitment not to repeat past mistakes. Even though by 2007 the District Forest Service had not decided whether the rest of the funds will be allocated to this new group, the group developed a weekly schedule for collecting wild seedlings, finally raising more than 200 seedlings. Each member has also started to pay the group US$0.30 each month, which has been used to buy nails, polybags, and a lock for a small nursery.

SEARCHING FOR PROOF OF TENURE SECURITY AND RECOGNITION. In Sungai Telang, land inheritances are transmitted verbally to men and women by *ninik*

**BOX 8.1 Ten rules developed by the
Bukit Lestari Makmur group**

1. If the members or the board fail to join group activities three successive times, they will be excluded from the group.
2. If the members and the board are found to break the rules, a warning will be issued.
3. The board is not allowed to use the funds without consultation with the group's members.
4. A commonly agreed decision cannot be contested.
5. Members should be responsible for the nursery.
6. Those wishing to join the group should obey the group's rules.
7. All members have rights to express their opinion for the interest of the group.
8. The group's cash funds are not for loan.
9. The chair, secretary, and treasurer should be fully committed to fulfilling their duties.
10. Each group member is obliged to adhere to the agreed rules.

SOURCE: Group discussion with members of Bukit Lestari Makmur group and other Sungai Telang villagers.

---

mamak (community elders). Unclear land rules and boundaries, including lack of clarity between the local and formal government systems, have resulted in considerable legal uncertainty about land. Most villagers emphasized their desire for guaranteed access to the land and natural resources they had always managed. Ownership was actually not an issue when the Sinar Tani group was initially formed in response to a previous 1998 government program that required communities to organize into a formal group in order to receive assistance from the government. The issue of uncertain rights over natural resources became more pronounced when the group realized that the owners of neighboring fields had moved boundary markers to expand their fields and that they were unable to provide legal proof of the boundaries.[11] As in the case of inheritance, when land is bought or sold in the village, there is no proof of ownership or transaction letters, and the size and borders of the land remain unclear.[12]

Village women's desire for a new high school building sparked collective action among the group to seek secure lands. A government extension agent

---

11. Hereditary Minang customs are still employed when dividing inherited land in Sungai Telang, with *ninik mamak* elders sharing out inheritances verbally to women (rice paddy fields) and men (rubber farms and upland rice fields), witnessed by community leaders but with no proof of ownership or inheritance letters conferred.

12. Recognition of land ownership has been based only on trust. The arrival of newcomers (transmigrants) complicates this issue.

had told them about a program offering government support to build a school but only on certified land. The follow-up action taken by the men's group was to plan for the new school buildings and to seek support from the District Education Office.

The group members also became interested in certifying their own land when they heard about the land conflicts that had resulted from improperly allocated transmigration sites (see Adnan and Yentirizal 2007). In addition, the village land available for the next generation is diminishing. Despite their strong desires, the group members realized that there was lack of knowledge regarding land certificates among the villagers and between village men and women.

In search of more information, the group members then interacted with Bappeda and BPN officials, who then gave a talk at a village meeting on land certification. These officials responded positively to the group's concerns and to a proposal that they have their lands certified collectively. Through a facilitated workshop, the village people discussed such issues as the nature of certification, relevant land regulations, and the procedures, tax fees, and cost of land certification.

Group members agreed to jointly seek land certification as proof of their land ownership and decided to get their land certified through PRONA. The group submitted the request to BPN. Unfortunately, although BPN received the request, the district's PRONA quota of 250 certificates for 2005 had been used up, and the Sinar Tani members had to wait for land certification the following year.

Attempts to seek recognition of property rights over resources were also made by the Tunas Harapan group of Suka Maju hamlet, Lubuk Kambing. As mentioned earlier, the residents of this hamlet were migrants. Some had purchased land from local inhabitants, while some had opened new lands in 1996. Tunas Harapan members sought government recognition of their claims by trying to secure government agricultural support. They developed a proposal through a program called Development of Estate Crops in Specific Areas. However, the village head refused to sign the proposal letter, claiming that the villagers submitting the proposal were not registered as inhabitants of Lubuk Kambing. After numerous attempts to persuade the man to sign the letter, eventually the group bypassed him and communicated with Merlung Subdistrict, which then forwarded the proposal to the relevant district authorities (Siagian and Neldysavrino 2007)—a clear case of successful coping with an attempt at elite capture.

Meanwhile, several threats (plans to establish large-scale forest and palm oil plantations) encouraged villagers to work together to seek letters of land status notification and to apply for letters of land recognition (*sporadik*) for their land to strengthen their claims.[13]

---

13. Sporadic registration of land is part of land registration or land titling where lands are registered on a case-by-case basis, usually as the result of a specific trigger such as the sale of the

Compared to the villagers in Sungai Telang, those in Lubuk Kambing are less optimistic about securing land rights through PRONA. They have continued to seek government development aid in the belief that development aid provided by the government would be a clear sign of acknowledgment of their existence and ownership.[14]

MAKING PEOPLE'S VOICES HEARD THROUGH COLLECTIVE ACTION. The bottom-up and participatory planning approach of Law 25/2004 took the form of Musyawarah Perencanaan Pembangunan (*musrenbang;* development planning consultations or DPCs), which were conducted in stages from the village level through the subdistrict and district levels.[15] The process is designed to plan annual development programs and budgets and to provide communities with opportunities to voice their aspirations and participate in producing development programs that suit their needs. Through these DPCs we catalyzed collective action among the community groups, particularly in Lubuk Kambing, and encouraged the village head to ensure the participation of all parties.

Throughout the facilitation process, the villagers learned to identify problems, prepare activity plans, and understand the reasons some groups succeed and others fail to achieve their objectives. Although the villagers were uncertain whether they should participate in the DPCs, the facilitation process and the interaction with district government officials boosted their self-confidence and encouraged them to act collectively and express their hopes. Through group activities, villagers have played a major role in pushing the village head into mobilizing the village authorities and BPD to prepare a village DPC. The village head also became more active in passing on information to the community. He finally opened the door to participation in the village DPCs not only to the village authorities, village consultative board, and farmer groups but also to the women's group.

The women's group also showed positive developments: they had rarely or never been involved in DPC or similar meetings. Three women who attended the village DPC meetings were appointed to the subdistrict DPC, partly due to their courage to speak in mixed public forums after practicing in small women-only groups. The words of the village head's wife—"I wanted to take part in subdistrict meetings but the village head wouldn't allow me to; he never invites

---

property, and proposed by concerned individuals or groups of people. Another type of registration is more systematic and more costly but takes less time to achieve complete coverage of all titles within the jurisdiction. There is a third, even more systematic version of land titling that is more costly and takes more time.

14. A man from Sukamaju said, "The district head gave us a corrugated tin roof for the primary school building in our hamlet. That showed he already acknowledged the community in this hamlet." Another man said, "If the government has opened the road, it means our hamlet is recognized as a part of West Tanjung Jabung District."

15. Law 25/2004 had to do with the Sistem Perencanaan Pembangunan Nasional, the National Development Planning System. DPC procedures and mechanisms are further described by Syamsuddin, Komarudin, and Siagian (2007).

me to meetings in the subdistrict"—reflect how women's wishes to express their hopes and access information may be obstructed by those closest to them. In addition, although most male community members suggested development priorities related to physical infrastructure development, women's representatives prioritized capacity-building, skill enhancement, and education.

Analysis and Outcomes

Here we look again at what happened in the districts and communities and analyze what factors contributed to success. We are particularly interested in the issues of rights to land, local men's and women's participation in forest-related decisionmaking, improvements in collective action, reduction of elite capture, and income generation efforts. We conclude this section with a discussion of the outcomes of our efforts and the problems we had to address.

Decentralized Forest Policies, Property Rights, and Collective Action

There have been no marked differences between the two districts in their response to the Ministry of Forestry's policies and how they have dealt with property rights and collective action. Officials from the two District Forestry Offices, for example, recognized their lack of power vis-à-vis the central government to make significant decisions on forests, such as granting use rights to local communities. The two districts shared concerns over growing needs for more land for development and clarifying property rights for local people, factors that encouraged them to propose forestland conversions to the Ministry.

Local forest people feel a strong need to secure their traditional farmlands and rubber gardens, whether outside or inside forestlands. There are various options (such as HKm) that could potentially provide them with more security regarding their lands, but there remain significant fears within the central government about local people's ability to sustainably manage and derive benefits from the forest.

The insecurity of local people's tenure over lands and forest products is due to governmental frameworks that ignore the needs of forest-dependent people. Some regulations and ministerial decrees, for example, favor large-scale investment and continuing to issue licenses to current or expired large-scale concessions. Although some regulations gave local groups or cooperatives the right to manage or use forests, their implementation has been riddled with problems. There are conflicting sectoral rules or priorities and values, a chronic tug-of-war over forest authority between different levels of governments, and a lack of checks and balances in policy implementation. In certain cases, districts misinterpreted the "right to manage" community forests, and higher levels of government failed to support local efforts.

However, other parties that have continually monitored and engaged government partners in discourse on forest and natural resource issues have contributed to shaping local policies. In Bungo, longstanding interaction among

NGOs, research institutes, community groups, and government agencies has contributed to local stakeholders' beginning to internalize principles of transparency, openness, and participation in government circles. An improved district land use plan and the District Forestry Office's initiative to implement revolving fund projects for local groups were also linked to this network. Through collective action civil society can apply healthy pressure to government to improve its performance.

Factors Driving Collaboration

Two of the most important factors leading to effective collaboration among groups managing natural resources (in particular, among district officials from different agencies and between the district and central governments) are trust and clearly delineated authority. In the groups we studied, trust developed through the creation of a mechanism whereby people could share their concerns and desires openly and regularly. Such trust-building resulted in improved understanding of local problems and willingness to work toward resolving land use and forest management issues.

Government officials also became more likely to abide by what was written in laws when a clear division of authority was laid out in the legislation. Such legal clarity encouraged government people to work together more effectively. However, centrally designed legislation was effective only when developed and agreed to by the various levels together. Legislation that came to districts as surprises caused resistance in many cases.

More collaboration was deemed important from the beginning of this research, and it became clear that involving a broader array of nongovernmental stakeholders would require greater trust. Research institutions and NGOs have played an important role in developing and maintaining trust among stakeholders, in particular with government officials. Among district officials we observed increasing appreciation of external actors' inputs and suggestions. Changes in NGOs' approaches to governments—from very obvious attacks to a more appreciative attitude—have also helped to build effective collaboration with government institutions (Yuliani et al. 2006).

At one of our workshops governmental and nongovernmental participants agreed that for effective collaboration there should be a clear platform (in terms of medium, rules, and sanctions) for interaction and clarity of roles among the parties. Nongovernmental members argued that there should be equality among the stakeholders or at least attempts to empower the disadvantaged. Government members, fearing the rigidity of their system, proposed that there be flexibility in the collaborative process in terms of time and resources.

Factors Motivating Groups' Collective Action

Through semistructured interviews and group discussions we asked 112 people from Sungai Telang and Lubuk Kambing to list the factors they considered most critical to their own collective action. One hundred respondents (54 women and 46 men) were members of the groups listed in Table 8.2; 12 others were migrants. For the results, see Table 8.3. Analysis of the results follows.

As indicated in Table 8.3, most participants agreed that individual members of a group should have strong motivation to work together as a base for collective action. Some thought that group members should be trustworthy and honest as well as respectful of others' opinions when working together. The women's groups considered trust and honesty crucial for group effectiveness, for building effective leadership, and for sustaining group cohesion. Several members of the female Gotong Royong group felt that friendship and familial ties have enhanced group effectiveness, building a sense of trust and making members more optimistic about reaching their common goals.

Leadership received the lowest ranking in terms of importance in collective action. The Minang Pelhin women tend to believe that every individual has a sense of leadership and that honesty, trustworthiness, and respect are requisites for a good leader. The men's groups from both villages argued that to be a good leader one should be able to speak freely, be powerful, and have courage to deal with government officials. This explains why Sinar Tani and Tunas Harapan elected a village head and a hamlet head—formal leaders—as their group leaders.

However, most men and women emphasized the drawbacks of a formal leader, among others the way he or she is selected and established. Some government programs, for example, allow officials to create groups and select community leaders and require groups to follow an inflexible, predetermined organizational structure. The village head's bad behavior reinforced people's

TABLE 8.3 Local people's perceptions of the important factors in effective collective action (CA) in Sungai Telang and Lubuk Kambing, 2005–06

Important factors in making CA effective	Women $n = 54 + (4)$	Men $n = 46 + (8)$	Total $n = 100 + (12) = 112$
Motivation	11	15	26
Trustworthiness, honesty	10	5 + (3)	18
Being respectful of others' opinions	7	8 + (1)	16
Willingness to share opinions	7	6 + (1)	14
Being hardworking and responsible	10	3 + (2)	15
Being clear or transparent	2	7	9
Holding frequent meetings	3 + (4)	1 + (1)	9
Confidence	3	1	4
Being a good leader	1	—	1
Total	58	54	112

SOURCE: Data were generated through authors' semistructured interviews and group discussions with 112 people from Sungai Telang and Lubuk Kambing villages.

NOTES: Numbers in parentheses refer to Javanese migrants; — means no respondents provided answers.

perceptions of the problems with formal leadership. In our research groups, the group leaders who were also formal heads or had ties to holders of formal positions misused their power.

One of the leaders, for instance, used his power to misappropriate the group's money. Another leader, of the Malay women's group, who is also the wife of the local village head, misused her power to mobilize women for her own interest. In another case the village head exploited group members by making them pay a land fee and made unwarranted unilateral decisions. These cases reinforced the group's distrust of and disrespect for formal leaders.

The traditional Pelhin groups rotate their leaders, and each member has the opportunity to lead the group. The group members make decisions democratically. Each member can speak freely and is equally respected and committed to the group's rules and sanctions. These factors have all contributed to the longstanding institutional nature of Pelhin.

The Gotong Royong group also elected its leader in a democratic (though not rotating) way. This group also appears likely to continue after facilitation ends. Similarly, the members of the Bukit Lestari Makmur men's group, though still at an early stage of its development, tended to show group cohesion, as indicated by its success in establishing *jernang* seedlings without external help. A democratically elected leader and group decisionmaking, along with clear rules and sanctions, are factors that have sustained this group.

Different levels of power among group members affected group dynamics in decisionmaking. Groups that included elites, such as Sinar Tani, tended to let people with power, confidence, and the ability to speak publicly dominate the group's discussion, which discouraged others from participating. Other groups—Pelhin, Gotong Royong, and Bukit Lestari Makmur, with members who had equal positions and leaders without ties to formal position holders—tended to perform collective efforts well. In these groups, members had equal opportunities to participate in decisionmaking.

Self-initiated groups such as the Minang women's group Pelhin and the men's group Bukit Lestari Makmur tended to be characterized by informality in their setting, whereas government-initiated groups such as the men's group Sinar Tani, of mixed ethnicity, and the in-migrant men's group Tunas Harapan applied more hierarchical roles and responsibilities.

The repetitive steps of planning, action, monitoring, and reflection were key to the learning process for these facilitated groups. Those involved have gained more opportunities and have benefited from wider networks of resources than have nonparticipants. By building stronger relations with government officials, research institutions, and NGOs, the group members increased their confidence and bargaining power. The Minang women's groups overcame their shyness and began to participate actively in training and meetings and to gain self-confidence. Eight of 17 members of Gotong Royong acknowledged feeling more confident about their collective action. This was particularly evident from their proposal for government aid; attendance at workshops on spatial plans, gender issues, and village–forest borders; and dealing with government officials in Bungo. In Lubuk Kambing, the women were eager to voice their aspirations through *musrenbang.*

Elite Capture: Can Collective Action Contribute to Avoiding It?

There were several examples of elite capture in this study. At higher levels of governance, for example, some agencies applied pressure in the district development planning process to prioritize their own programs, to the exclusion of more urgent needs. Some village development projects ignored suggestions from the DPCs and instead implemented proposals from district parliamentarians who prioritized development in their home areas. At the village level, elite capture was demonstrated by village heads who took advantage of their positions to extort fees from villagers, misuse public funds, or even block villagers' access to government grants.

At the district level, an effective strategy for avoiding elite capture has been the convening of facilitated forums wherein all concerned parties come together to disclose and discuss the implications of policies for resources and livelihoods, as well as the potential winners and losers from policy implementation. Although the forums initially involved only "government champions" and their non-governmental partners, these forums gained influence with time. Stakeholders increasingly involved in policy- and decisionmaking processes have helped government actors to be more transparent and accountable. For example, the amount of leftover development funds, which are often misused, was reduced.

Village groups avoided elite capture in three ways. First, group members united, agreed on shared desires and risks, and stuck to their commitment not to sell land to the oil palm company individually, and they also collectively refused to pay fees to the village head. Second, with regard to the village head who attempted to block access to a government grant, the group simply nagged him, then complained to the subdistrict, and one of the selected members eventually met directly with the district head. By building relations with outsiders and drawing attention to misconduct, villagers forced the elites concerned to stop their actions. Third, the members of this same group built a new group that excluded the elites who misused funds and also imposed stricter rules to constrain their own behavior.

But collective action alone as described earlier may not be enough. A higher level of collective action and support may be needed to avoid elite capture more effectively.

Is Collective Action a Viable Route to Property Rights?

In our planning for this case study, we took the position that improvements in both people's and forests' well-being will depend on (1) clarification of land ownership and use rights for both men and women, (2) clearly defined authority shared among national and local governments equipped with clear mechanisms for accountability, and (3) a stronger civil society to contribute to the development of locally appropriate policies and legislation and to monitor government. We have hypothesized in this research that collective action is a viable route to accomplishing these goals.

We have engaged with actors at the community, district, and, to a lesser extent, national levels to realize these hypothesized requirements. We have seen progress at the local and district levels toward clarifying land ownership and use rights as groups in both communities have sought such clarification and as district level officials have worked together with powerful industry actors and the central government to gain similar clarity on a broader scale. Progress has been made; we are not where we want to be yet, but at the district level we have worked with officials from several agencies to clarify areas of expertise and resource management options and to improve both transparency and accountability, especially in land use planning and participatory policy development. To a lesser extent, we have also worked with central government officials to clarify the shared division of authority and roles in land allocation and natural resource management. Whereas we have made significant progress in raising awareness, particularly at the district level, about the implications of the different perceptions of land tenure and management issues, the actual changes in policy are modest—primarily in the form of an increased willingness of central officials to work together with their district partners to resolve outstanding issues (for instance, forestlands' reallocation). New attitudes emerged among the district officials about involving more local people who are directly affected by land use changes in the deliberation of land allocation.

The efforts to strengthen civil society as a means to contribute to policy formulation and more seriously monitor government have also been an important avenue for identifying and strengthening mechanisms for accountability. Facilitated community groups have shown their capacity to participate in decisionmaking processes for development, build alliances and networks, and reduce elite capture locally, and their interest in doing so is likely to have affected the thinking of officials with whom they have interacted at the district level (cf. the willingness among district agencies to work across sectors through a multistakeholder forum and to adopt participatory approaches to preparing the district's mid-term development plans). Our study has policy implications as described in the appendix, which also lists the relevant actors and action resources.

Conclusion and Policy Implications

Collective action in the form of coordinated activities and information-sharing among stakeholders is necessary to make interaction more effective, triggering shared learning among stakeholders and offering opportunities to address contentious issues related to property rights, such as ensuring equitable access to land, preventing elite capture, increasing incomes, or improving women's status. Making collective action effective in dealing with property rights issues requires support from external agents in the form of facilitation, sound regulatory instruments, monitoring, and supervision. Collective action also helps local communities (including women's groups) to increase their self-confidence and capacity to interact with external parties and strengthen groups. Action research is an effective strategy for fostering collective action and maintaining the learning process that leads groups to be more organized and cohesive and district government officials to be more receptive to other stakeholders' inputs. Our conclusion is that collective action is necessary, if not sufficient. Effective collective action in this context requires both bonding and bridging social capital —as has been demonstrated quantitatively for India by Krishna (2002). The experience of trying to foster both kinds of social capital and collective action among officials has convinced us of both the importance and the difficulties of doing so, bearing in mind the hierarchical, inertial, and powerful nature of governmental institutions.

The findings of the study are relevant for Indonesia's forest policy, which attempts to get local people more involved in forest use and plantation schemes, HKm, and people's forest plantations, as well as the current mechanism for bottom-up consultation for development, *musrenbang.* The forest policies aim to provide opportunities for local people to gain access to forest resources and to improve local livelihoods. However, there is a tendency to put more emphasis on formal institutions such as farmer cooperatives and to create new groups of forest farmers, neglecting the presence of old and informal groups. Although this allows policies to be implemented in a relatively short time, there is a risk that such schemes will not endure and that policy goals will not be achieved. Unless more attention is paid to how groups are formed and how internal systems (that is, regarding the presence of elites and selection of group leaders) within the group are working, the benefits will not be fairly distributed. So governments should provide greater opportunities for existing groups, often unstructured but self-sustaining, to take part in policy implementation. There is also a need to ensure that elite capture is prevented by developing a monitoring system for performance, setting up an effective resolution mechanism for grievances (that is, a special office to hear complaints, radio programs that air complaints, and so on), and developing a system of incentives and disincentives favoring the groups that perform best, regardless of the formal structure.

Although it now has a better arrangement than during the New Order era, the DPCs should take a closer look at the diverse groups within the communities and adopt ways of gathering input that enables women's groups and other groups often disregarded to effectively and freely convey their messages. Our research shows that women's groups make concrete proposals for development, ones largely ignored by most men's groups. Providing opportunities for and building the capacity of those groups to increase their confidence (that is, when speaking in public forums) are key to ensuring that inputs to development discourse are inclusive. In addition, Bappeda, as a coordinating agency for planning and development at the provincial as well as the district level, needs to be strengthened in applying participatory and appreciative inquiry approaches when conducting programs to enable shared learning among the parties involved. Given the complexity of attempts to resolve outstanding issues concerning pressure to convert forestlands for development and local people's struggle to clarify their rights over lands, there is a need to employ (third-party) facilitation and support multistakeholder forums. As shown in the case study, these tools are instrumental in enhancing the communication among disputing parties and bringing about changes in perceptions and attitudes toward problem solving. Governments at different levels need to be open and flexible regarding the ways such initiatives can be integrated into their programs and systems. If necessary, they need to issue policies supporting such tools (that is, allocating funds for them in their state or regional budgets).

Appendix 8A: Supplementary Table

See table on pages 265–267.

TABLE 8A.1 Actors and action resources in two districts of Jambi Province, Indonesia, 2006

Actor/institution	Major mission	Concerns and interests relevant to this research	Action resources
The Ministry of Forestry's Agency for Forestry Planning (Baplan)	Prepare guidelines for use and management of forestry plans; designate and gazette forestlands; supervise and promote decentralized forestry policies	Sustainable forest use and management; retaining control of state-owned forestlands	Authority over forestlands; authority to provide recommendations to the Ministry of Forestry for forestland conversion and forest management; extensive information, knowledge, and political networks
The Ministry of Forestry's Land Rehabilitation and Social Forestry Directorate General	Reforest and regreen degraded forest; provide guidelines for watershed management; implement community-based forestry programs (CBFM)	Empowering communities and strengthening local institutions or farmer groups	Authority over forest rehabilitation, watershed management, and providing recommendations to the Ministry of Forestry for the issuance of CBFM permits or rights; extensive information, knowledge, and political networks
National Land Agency	Administer land and issue land certificates; provide guidelines for control, ownership, and use of lands outside forestlands	Securing property rights over land, particularly those outside forestlands	Authority to give licenses for ownership and use rights over lands outside forestlands

(continued)

TABLE 8A.1 Continued

Actor/institution	Major mission	Concerns and interests relevant to this research	Action resources
Provincial forestry services	Coordinate district and provincial forestry institutions and operations; provide recommendations for large-scale forestry concessions; issue small-scale timber use rights	Sustainable use of resources, community empowerment, and state revenues	Authority to coordinate the province's forest institutions and provide recommendations to the governor on forestry policies; information, knowledge, and political networks
District forest services	Implement delegated forest management tasks; develop forestry and estate crops programs involving local communities	Sustainable use of resources, community empowerment, and state revenues	Authority to recommend that the district head grant small-scale nontimber forest use licenses and develop district forestry programs: information, knowledge, and political networks
District and provincial Agency for Development Planning (Bappeda)	Coordinate provincial and district development programs; facilitate development planning consultations (*musrenbang*) and develop spatial planning and land allocation	Coordinating actions and programs among provincial and district institutions; encouraging the full participation of stakeholders in development planning	Authority to coordinate district sectorwide institutions and to decide on regional programs proposed by other provincial district institutions; information, knowledge, and political networks

Stakeholder	Role	Interests	Resources
Private companies	Run forestry and oil palm plantations; develop partnerships with local communities	Profits; continued operations	Capital and expertise or knowledge; power and sometimes political networks
Village head	Provide a link to district government; coordinate with the local community; implement delegated tasks	Social consciousness, prestige, power	Networks, contacts, power
Village consultative board	Articulate people's interests; maintain a power balance with the village head	Making leaders accountable; avoiding elite capture; strengthening civil society	Village-level networks (across/within), informal authority
Farmer (male) groups	Seek secure rights over land and resources; look for capacity building and development support	Secure and sustainable income; improvement of income	Land, labor, trust, confidence, traditional knowledge, and ability to work together
Local communities	Seek improved education facilities; seek legal ways to inherit land through certification	Clarity of ownership of lands and resources; improvement of skills in negotiation and conflict resolution	Land, labor, trust, confidence, local knowledge, and ability to work together
Women's groups (Pelhin)	Seek income-generating activities; provide services in land cultivation to other self-help groups in land cultivation	Improved livelihoods; stronger position in negotiations with other community members and outsiders	Land, labor, trust, confidence, and ability to work together

References

Adnan, H., and Yentirizal. 2007. *Blessing or misfortune? Adapting institutions and community collective action in accommodating the transmigration program.* Governance Brief 36. Bogor, Indonesia: Center for International Forestry Research.

Adnan, H., D. Tadjudin, E. L. Yuliani, H. Komarudin, D. Lopulalan, Y. L. Siagian, and D. W. Munggoro, eds. 2008. *Belajar dari Bungo: Mengelola sumberdaya alam di era desentralisasi.* Bogor, Indonesia: Center for International Forestry Research.

Barr, C., I. A. P. Resosudarmo, A. Dermawan, and J. McCarthy. 2006. *Decentralization of forest administration in Indonesia: Implications for sustainability, economic development and community livelihoods.* Bogor, Indonesia: Center for International Forestry Research.

Colchester, M., and F. MacKay. 2004. *In search of middle ground: Indigenous peoples, collective representation and the right to free, prior and informed consent.* Moreton-in-Marsh, U.K.: Forest Peoples Programme.

Colchester, M., N. Jiwan, M. Sirait, A.Y. Firdaus, A. Surambo, and H. Pane. 2006. *Promised land: Palm oil and land acquisition in Indonesia: Implications for local communities and indigenous Peoples.* Bogor, Indonesia: Forest Peoples Programme and Sawit Watch.

Colfer, C. J. P. 2007. *Simple rules for catalyzing collective action (especially in natural resource management contexts).* Bogor, Indonesia: Center for International Forestry Research.

Colfer, C. J. P., and D. Capistrano, eds. 2005. *The politics of decentralization: Forests, power and people.* London: Earthscan.

Contreras-Hermosilla, A., and C. Fay. 2006. *Memperkokoh pengelolaan hutan Indonesia melalui pembaruan penguasaan tanah: Permasalahan dan kerangka tindakan* (Strengthening forest management in Indonesia through land tenure reform: Issues and framework for action). Bogor, Indonesia: World Agroforestry Centre.

Dermawan, A., H. Komarudin, and M. McGrath. 2006. Decentralization in Indonesia's forestry sector—Is it over? What comes next? Paper presented at the Eleventh Biennial Global Conference of the International Association for the Study of Common Property, June 19–23, in Bali, Indonesia.

Greenwood, D. J., and M. Levin. 1998. *Introduction to action research: Social research for social change.* Thousand Oaks, Calif., U.S.A.: Sage.

Hadi, M., H. Komarudin, and M. Schangen. 2007. Kebijakan kehutanan, aksi kolektif dan hak properti: Sebuah pelajaran dari Bungo (Forestry policies, collective action and property rights: A lesson from Bungo). In *Belajar dari Bungo: Mengelola sumberdaya alam di era desentralisasi,* ed. H. Adnan, D. Tadjudin, E. L. Yuliani, H. Komarudin, D. Lopulalan, Y. L. Siagian, and D. W. Munggoro. Bogor, Indonesia: Center for International Forestry Research.

Komarudin, H., Y. L. Siagian, and C. J. P. Colfer. 2007. *Collective action to secure property rights for the poor: A case study in Jambi Province, Indonesia.* Bogor, Indonesia: Center for International Forestry Research for Collective Action and Property Rights.

Komarudin, H., Y. L. Siagian, and N. P. Oka. 2007. *Linking collective action to non-timber forest product market for improved local livelihoods: Challenges and opportunities.* CAPRi Working Paper 73. Washington, D.C.: International Food Policy Research Institute.

Krishna, A. 2002. *Active social capital: Tracing the roots of development and democracy.* New York: Columbia University Press.

Kusumanto, T., E. L. Yuliani, P. Macoun, Y. Indriatmoko, and H. Adnan. 2005. *Learning to adapt: Managing forests together in Indonesia.* Bogor, Indonesia: Center for International Forestry Research.

Lubuk Kambing Village Government. 2005. Data monografi desa: Desa Lubuk Kambing tahun 2005, Kecamatan Merlung (2005 village monograph of Lubuk Kambing, Merlung Subdistrict Government). Merlung, Jambi, Indonesia.

Office of the Jambi Governor. 1999. *The designation of forestlands in Jambi Province based on harmonized maps of land use by consensus and Jambi provincial land use plan.* Jambi Governor's Decree 108. Jambi, Indonesia: Government of Jambi Province.

Siagian, Y. L., and Neldysavrino. 2007. *Collective action to secure management rights for poor communities.* Governance Brief 35. Bogor, Indonesia: Center for International Forestry Research.

Sudirman, W. D., and H. Herlina. 2005. *Local policy-making mechanisms: Processes, implementation and impacts of the decentralized forest management system in Tanjung Jabung Barat District, Jambi.* Case Study 14. Bogor, Indonesia: Center for International Forestry Research.

Sungai Telang Village Government. 2005. Data monografi desa: Desa Sungai Telang tahun 2005, Kecamatan Bathin III Ulu (2005 Village Monograph of Sungai Telang, Bathin III Ulu Subdistrict Government). Muara Buat, Jambi, Indonesia.

Syamsuddin, N., H. Komarudin, and Y. L. Siagian. 2007. *Are community aspirations being accommodated in development plans? A lesson from collective action in Jambi.* Governance Brief 34. Bogor, Indonesia: Center for International Forestry Research

Taher, M. 2005. *Potret perubahan kondisi hutan Jambi 1990–2000: Dasawarsa hilangnya sejuta hektar hutan* (Portrait of Jambi forests from 1999 to 2000: A decade of losing one million hectares of forests). Jambi, Indonesia: Warta Warsi.

Yasmi, Y., G. Z. Anshari, H. Komarudin, and S. Alqadri. 2006. Stakeholder conflicts and forest decentralization policies in West Kalimantan: Their dynamics and implications for future forest management. *Forests, Trees and Livelihoods* 16: 167–180.

Yentirizal. 2007. Mencari alternatif di Sungai Telang (Looking for alternatives in Sungai Telang). In *Dari desa ke desa: Dinamika gender dan pengelolaan kekayaan alam,* ed. Y. Indriatmoko, E. L. Yuliani, Y. Tarigan, G. Gaban, F. Maulana, D. W. Munggoro, D. Lopulalan, and H. Adnan. Bogor, Indonesia: Center for International Forestry Research.

Yuliani, E. L., D. Tadjudin, Y. Indriatmoko, D. W. Munggoro, F. Gaban, F. Maulana, and H. Adnan. 2006. *Multistakeholder forestry: Steps leading to change.* Bogor, Indonesia: Center for International Forestry Research.

9 The Transformation of the Afar Commons in Ethiopia: State Coercion, Diversification, and Property Rights Change among Pastoralists

BEKELE HUNDIE AND MARTINA PADMANABHAN

Change in natural environmental conditions has constantly influenced pastoral livelihoods in the Afar Region of Ethiopia, though the uncertainty of ecological conditions and insecurity of property rights have increased only relatively recently (Scoones 1995; McCarthy et al. 1999). As a result of these changes, the reliable flow of life-sustaining goods and services previously wrought from the area's erratic rangeland ecosystems is diminishing, putting pastoral livelihoods at great risk (Gadamu 1994). The adaptation of these pastoralists is not confined to a simple human–land relationship in an isolated setting but is rather influenced by demographic change, agricultural expansion, attempts to incorporate them into the national economy, and insecurity arising from conflicts and border instability (Davies and Bennett 2007). Due to the widespread nature of droughts (Berkele 2002) and ethnic conflicts (Hagmann 2005) in several areas of Ethiopia, livestock mobility between alternative water and grazing areas has also been severely constrained (Padmanabhan 2008), weakening livestock and causing a significant increase in livestock mortality. The cumulative effect of these factors has led to the weakening of traditional authority, degradation of natural resources, and growing vulnerability of different pastoral groups to ecological and economic stress, often resulting in poverty (Unruh 2005; Rettberg 2006).

Historically, Ethiopian pastoralists have been the most marginalized groups in the policy arena (Helland 2002; Yemane 2003). During the Imperial regime (1930–74), pastoralists were considered aimless wanderers who led a primitive way of life (Getachew 2001; Abdulahi 2004); moreover, they were considered to have been using natural resources wastefully (Gebre 2001). Hence, during this time the main ambition of government officials, who were entirely from peasant or urban backgrounds, was to convert these "primitive" societies into sedentary farmers who would use resources more efficiently. Different government policies emphasized that efficient resource use was possible if the vast and "inefficiently used" resources in pastoral areas came under the control of the state, legitimizing government intervention (Gebre 2001).

This "modernist" discourse, viewing pastoralism as a stage in a gradual development toward agropastoralism and finally sedentary agriculture, had been

270

the basis for most policy formulation under the socialist regime (1974–91) and still causes great grievance and irritation in the public policy debates on pastoralists today (Hundie 2008). On the one hand, with its increasing involvement in land use politics since the 1960s, the state as a powerful external force has inflicted severe changes on the property rights regimes that govern pastoralist life. The influence of the state farms established in the Awash Valley on dry-season pastures has forced the institutional arrangements of the commons into diversification. On the other hand, the current endeavors of development interventions to promote farming are opening up other opportunities. Modernist thinking, characterized by a linear development path, has influenced the pastoral situation in the past through forced diversification, whereas today we observe voluntary farming activities.

In this chapter we discuss two cases of pastoralist involvement in agriculture and investigate the challenges and opportunities of this transition. We focus on the drivers of crop production from a dual perspective: first, as an outcome of state coercion and, second, as a voluntary response to natural calamities. Specifically, the chapter addresses the following questions: (1) Why was the Ethiopian government interested in transforming traditional communal rights at the beginning? (2) How smooth or how rough was the process of change? (3) What are the outcomes in terms of property rights arrangements and pastoral livelihoods? (4) What factors explain pastoralists' responses to drought-induced changes? The first case portrays the conflictive transformation of the traditional land use arrangements of Afar pastoralists, which resulted from coercive state intervention aimed at expanding commercial farming, while the second case shows a nonconflictive change induced by recurrent droughts in the presence of support from the state.

Property rights changes are at the center of this analysis of diversification. As we shall demonstrate, the state (through its functionaries) expropriated large tracts of the traditionally administered prime rangeland for mechanized farms, which resulted in deterioration of the livelihoods of pastoralists. With regard to responses to drought, there is considerable difference within pastoral communities in motivations for diversification, predominantly along the lines of factors such as per capita livestock assets, suitability of the land for farming in general, access to wage employment as an alternative income source, and external support for farming activities. The impact of these processes on property rights and collective action regarding poverty will also be discussed. In doing so, we shall show that the transformation of traditional property rights in Afar has involved two seemingly contradictory phenomena, conflicts and cooperation. Although the results of our study build on the existing information discussing the challenges of pastoralism in East Africa (for example, Rutten 1992; Markakis 2004; Lesorogol 2005; Mwangi 2005) and elsewhere in Africa (for instance, Galaty and Johnson 1990; Kirk 1999; Niamir-Fuller 1999; Blench 2001; Chatty 2007), it provides a unique insight into the situation in Afar, where information is relatively scarce.

With regard to the conceptual framework presented in Chapter 2, this chapter examines how natural assets (land) and rights to these assets, private and communal, shape the institutions of collective action. Political risks serve as a source of uncertainty, exacerbated by the sedentarization policies of the state (that is, legal and political structures). Increasing instances of drought or natural risks also lead to transformation in property rights institutions and the emergence of new collective action structures. These contextual factors result in the action situation of an interface between a pastoral lifestyle and collective farming (a sedentary lifestyle), where several types of internal actors (better-off and poorer pastoralists) interact with the state (external actor) by means of conflict and cooperation (patterns of interaction). The chapter carefully discusses these interactions to show their effects on the desired outcomes of fulfillment of basic needs, security, and social and political inclusion. The links between the institutions of collective action and property rights are also examined.

The chapter also provides further insight on some of the broader themes that are of interest to the authors represented in this volume. Situated in the natural resource management section, it shows that political risks are as important in shaping institutions of collective action and property rights as natural and economic risks, the two types that are most often mentioned in the literature, and how these institutions, in turn, are used by the poor to respond to these types of uncertainties. The interactions between the pastoralists and the Ethiopian state also touched on the theme of conflict and the fact that property rights lie at the heart of such conflicts and are changed as a result of it. The cross-cutting theme of power, including elite capture, is also spotlighted to show that it is an important factor to consider in poverty outcomes, especially when the powerful actors increase the vulnerability of their less powerful cohorts to natural and political risks.

The remainder of the chapter is structured as follows. The section that follows briefly discusses the theory of transformation of property rights, and the next section places the study at hand in the wider theoretical debate on property right changes. The following section describes the study sites and methods, and the one after that describes the current institutional arrangements of Afar pastoralists. The next two sections discuss the transformation of the traditional land use arrangements of Afar due to coercive state intervention and natural challenges, respectively. And the final section summarizes the main findings and provides policy suggestions.

Theoretical Perspectives of Property Rights Changes, Diversification, and Collective Action

The notion of property rights refers to a "bundle" of rights that individuals or groups have to a certain material or intellectual resource (Alchian and Demsetz 1973; Schlager and Ostrom 1992). Bromley (1991, 1998) defines these bundles of rights as including the right to derive benefits from the resource, the right to exclude others, the right to manage the resource, and the right to transfer the resource to others through various arrangements, backed up and enforced by the collective. Rights may be time bounded or intermittent. Rights holders are claimants to a resource—including individuals, communities, or legal entities —that may enjoy all the rights in a bundle or be limited to only some of them. In most cases, conflicts arise among different individuals or communities regarding who should have command over a resource, how to use it, when to use it, and so on (Mwangi 2005). There are a great number of cases in which different people or communities bear overlapping claims to resources (Meinzen-Dick and Pradhan 2002; Di Gregorio et al., this volume, Chapter 2). For example, grazing lands in pastoral areas are common-pool resources to which a great number of herders have de facto rights (Swallow and Bromley 1995; Kirk 1999). For a detailed discussion of the linkages between land rights and access to water, see Beyene and Korf, this volume, Chapter 10.

Although rights imply the access of right holders to benefit streams, they do not guarantee the realization of benefits. Ribot and Peluso sharpen this distinction by providing a broader framework in which they highlight separate definitions for access and property. Accordingly, they write that "access is about all possible means by which a person is able to benefit from things," while "property generally evokes some kind of socially acknowledged and supported claims or rights" (Ribot and Peluso 2003, 155). With this reconceptualization, they show how capability differences arising from access to different resources influence the quantity and quality of benefits that can be generated from them.

Studies in diversification strategies (for example, Kituyi 1990; Little 1992; Holtzman 1996; Zaal and Dietz 1999) show that diversification may have mixed effects on the livelihoods of pastoralists. On the one hand, in pastoral areas some consider cultivation a major avenue of diversification for pastoralists and hence a viable risk management strategy (Campbell 1984; Smith 1998). On the other hand, others consider it an unsustainable or even destructive option that accentuates the risks pastoralists face (Hogg 1988). Fratkin (1991) and Nathan, Fratkin, and Roth (1996) show the potentially negative ecological and social effects of pastoral sedentarization and diversification. Yet for Holtzman (1996) diversification is seen as a cyclical rather than a linear process whereby herders combine different income strategies at different points in their life cycles. Equally, income diversification strategies among pastoralists, such as farming, do not necessarily lead to a diminished interest in livestock investments and production (Little et al. 2001).

One driving factor of property rights changes is diversification through the adoption of nonpastoral livelihood strategies. Berhanu, Colman, and Fayissa (2007) show the importance of human capital investment and related support services for improving the capacity of Borana pastoralists in southern Ethiopia to manage risk through a diversified income portfolio. The increasing privatization of rangelands for crop production and private grazing along this diversification is explained by Kamara, Swallow, and Kirk (2004). They discuss how certain national policies have created an avenue for spontaneous enclosures, thereby resulting in conflicts between traditional and formal systems and in deterioration of human welfare. A study in Kenya also shows that households' gains from privatization depend on land tenure, patterns of diversification, and the way in which agriculture was integrated into the pastoral livelihood (Lesorogol 2005). In this case, local norms reinforced the value of land ownership for residents, thereby preserving the pastoral way of life.

Collective action is a central feature structuring the use of rangelands by herders. On the one hand, collective ownership and differentiated use patterns in herd management are the preconditions for pastoralists' existence in a marginal environment (Hundie 2008). On the other hand, pastoralists react to changes in property rights by venturing into crop production as a means of livelihood diversification (Ahmed et al. 2002). If collective action is the voluntary action taken by a group to achieve a common interest (Meinzen-Dick and di Gregorio 2004), herding as well as commonly adopted agriculture is aimed at improving the welfare of the group members.

Study Sites and Methods

The Afar Region extends from central to northeastern Ethiopia, following the East African Rift Valley. The study districts—namely, Amibara, Awash-Fentale, and Semu-Robi-Gele'alo—are found in the southern part of the Afar (Figure 9.1). Amibara and Awash-Fentale are located in the middle Awash Valley, within the Rift Valley, whereas Semu-Robi is found across the lowland–highland interface, toward the western border of the Rift Valley. All study areas are characterized by a semiarid climate, with average annual temperatures ranging from 21 to 38°C; the lowest temperatures occur between December and February and the highest between April and June. The average annual rainfall is about 697 millimeters, coming primarily in two rainy seasons, namely *karma* (July–September) and *gilel* (March–April).

The dominant source of livelihoods in the study areas is pastoralism, and there are limited levels of crop cultivation and other activities (Table 9.1). Afar pastoralists raise mixed species of primary livestock, including camels and cattle, and keep supplementary herds of goats and sheep, usually for commercial purposes. They manage their livestock under an extensive mobile system, with natural pasturage the main source of livestock feed.

To investigate both historical and recent changes in the traditional property rights of Afar pastoralists, we pursued both primary and secondary data sources and employed various procedures for data collection. "Coercive Means of Property Rights Change" is based mainly on secondary data, including several unpublished documents accessed from the Middle Awash Agricultural

FIGURE 9.1 Location of the Afar Region and the study districts

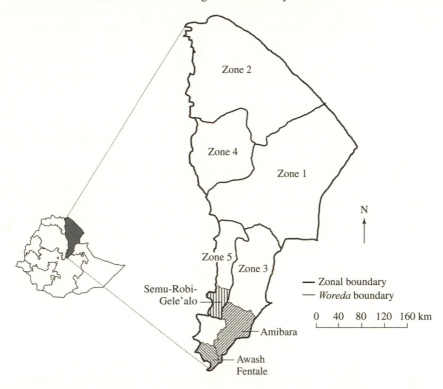

SOURCE: Authors.

NOTE: A *woreda* is the second-smallest formal administrative unit, equivalent to a district. Ethiopia has five levels of formal administrative units: they are, in descending order of size, the federal state, the regional state, the zone, the *woreda,* and the *kebele.*

Development Enterprise (MAADE), the Melka Werer Agricultural Research Center, and the Afar Region Administration. The information obtained from these and other documents was augmented with data generated through key informant interviews and discussions with groups of pastoralists.

"Noncoercive Means of Property Rights Change" is based mainly on the data collected from 180 pastoral households dwelling at six purposely selected sites: Ambash and Qurqura in Amibara District, Doho and Dudub in Awash-Fentale District, and Harihamo and Daleti in Semu-Robi District (see Table 9.1). Spatial variability in resource endowment was taken into account while selecting the study sites, based on the presupposition that resource endowment can influence both conflictive and cooperative interactions among actors as well as pastoralists' response to natural calamities. In this regard, each of the study sites can be placed in one of the following three categories: (1) areas with potential

TABLE 9.1 Backgrounds of the three study sites

Location	Amibara	Awash Fentale	Semu Robi
Household economy	Pastoralism, farming	Pastoralism, farming (recently begun)	Pastoralism, farming (recently begun)
Ethnic and clan groups	Afar clans: Sidhabura, Rakbadermella Non-Afars: Amhara, Oromo, and others	Afar clans: Rakbadermella, Mafay, Ayraso	Afar clan: Sidhabura
Kebeles[a] studied	Ambash, Qurqura	Doho, Dudub	Harihamo, Daleti
Number of households interviewed	60	60	60
Location	Southern part of Afar Region (in the middle of Awash Valley)	Southern part of Afar Region (in the middle of Awash Valley)	Southwest part of Afar Region (across the lowland–highland interface)

SOURCE: Authors.

[a]A *kebele* is the lowest formal administrative unit, also termed a peasant association.

for rainfed agriculture (constituting Harihamo and Daleti), (2) areas with potential for irrigated agriculture (constituting Ambash and Doho), and (3) areas without agricultural potential (constituting Qurqura and Dudub). It is also worthwhile to note that one of the sites, namely Ambash, was selected because of some historical events with respect to property rights changes.[1]

A two-stage procedure was used to select the sample households. First, using lists of household heads at each site (generated for the purposes of this study), with the help of the local elders pastoral households were stratified into three groups: poor, medium-income, and better-off. Thereafter, 10 households were selected from each stratum using systematic random sampling technique. In most cases, household heads (usually male) were interviewed, though in a few cases responses were taken from an adult family member who was not the household head. A group of trained enumerators conducted the interviews with individual sample households, guided by a structured questionnaire prepared for this purpose.

The overall data collection process encompassed two phases. The first phase (December 2004–May 2005) involved several tasks, including implementation of the household survey, collection of secondary data, and collection

---

1. Ambash was selected mainly because of the existence of historical state intervention to expand commercial farming.

of detailed qualitative data though group and key-informant interviews. The second phase (October 2006) was organized for a short period in order to strengthen the evidence gathered from the first phase by reviewing secondary sources and conducting expert interviews.

Traditional Institutional Arrangements

Clan is the lowest and de facto most important unit of traditional administration in Afar, although there are also smaller social units, such as the *dahla,* or sub-clan. As Getachew (2001, 54) notes, each clan comprises "a group of people related to each other by descent, living within shared territory and sharing common rituals and political leadership." Each clan has a well-established geron-tocracy, whereby decisionmaking power regarding land and other natural resources resides within the clan council, consisting of the clan leader, elders, the *feima,* and local wise men.[2]

Each clan manages its resources collectively based on customary princi-ples. Accordingly, herd management follows rotational grazing patterns. When rainfall is normal for successive seasons, clan members are instructed not to use reserved pasture areas. These areas are made accessible to the members only after other areas have been exhaustively used. Although each clan member has an inalienable use right to the resources, intraclan customary laws (or opera-tional rules) regulate these use rights.

The traditional institutions of the Afar allow two types of resource users. The first category includes clan members who use the rangeland permanently. They are primary rights holders (*waamo*) who have the right not only to use the resources on the rangeland but also to exclude others and to transfer the resources to their heirs. The second type of resource users comprises groups of neighboring pastoralists whose demands for pastoral resources go beyond their own endowments, particularly during drought years. These groups are second-ary rights holders. They can be classified as rights holders because they fre-quently have access to clan resources that is generally recognized and accepted by clan members and traditional leaders. However, secondary rights holders must fulfill certain obligations in order to obtain access to the resources. Ex ante negotiation is required with *waamo* rights holders, the success of which depends on the relationship between the two groups and resource conditions. If they are allowed access, secondary rights holders are required to honor the customary rules of the host group. For instance, they should refrain from actions such as cutting trees, allowing other herders to use the resources, and rushing their livestock into reserved areas.

---

2. A *feima* is a rule-enforcing authority in Afar traditional administration. It consists of a principal leader (*feima-abba*), a deputy leader (*erenna-abba*), and ordinary members.

Coercive Means of Property Rights Change:
The State Subverting the Commons

Triggers and Processes of Coercive Change

The intervention of the state in Afar was very limited prior to the 1960s. Farming was limited to the lower Awash flood-fed plains, where some pastoralists in the Asahimarra section of Afar had been practicing mixed crop–livestock farming for generations (Getachew 2001). However, since the 1960s state interventions in these areas have increased, mainly for two reasons. First, the Afar plains—specifically areas in the middle Awash Valley—were found to have great potential for wide-scale irrigated farming. The most attractive feature of these areas was their suitability for cotton production, which was critically important for expanding the country's textile industries, a primary focus of the first and the second five-year national development plans (IGE 1957, 1962). Second, pastoralism was not accepted as a livelihood strategy in the reigning national political mindset of the time. Rather, it was considered a primitive and nonviable way of life, to be avoided rather than preserved (Getachew 2001; Abdulahi 2004). Thus, the intention of the policymakers was to change this mobile mode of life to sedentary farming. However, the pastoralists neither participated in the decisionmaking process nor were convinced about the goal of change.

In 1962, the Awash Valley Authority (AVA) was established by decree as an agent of institutional change. AVA was responsible for undertaking several activities, such as the founding and management of state farms, coordination and financing of pastoral settlements and other schemes, and monitoring of the overall transformation process, for which some 70,000 hectares of dry-season rangeland was targeted (Getachew 2001). AVA had direct military and financial support from the government to implement the planned changes, using its military power, for example, to threaten the pastoralists. MAADE began operations on the expropriated rangeland with the main objective of satisfying the demand of domestic textile industries for cotton. Initially, it had an operating area of 300 hectares, which was increased to 13,116 hectares in 1985. In addition to MAADE, several pastoral development schemes were implemented with directives coming from AVA. These included collective settlement farms and irrigated pastures.[3] The costs to cultivate the settlement farms were covered by the state, while the pastoralists contributed nothing except their labor. The output of the settlement farms was distributed among registered households.

---

3. The irrigated pasture scheme was envisaged to plant a variety of improved grass seeds through the participation of the settler pastoralists so that the latter would appreciate the improved techniques and thereafter manage the irrigated pastured independently. However, this did not take place, and the irrigated pastureland served the dairy farm that had been established to fulfill the milk consumption needs of the staff of the state farms.

The implementation of the state-driven projects resulted in a mixture of property rights in the area. First, by using its coercive power the state became a de facto owner of part of the land over which the pastoralists had had inalienable rights for generations. Second, the introduction of collective settlement farms brought a new variant of common property, apart from the traditional communal ownership of the rangeland. Indeed, the nonriverine parts of the area remained under the control of the pastoralists and were allocated entirely to livestock grazing, whereas traditional rights at the riverine sites were nullified by order of the state. This implies that the intervention of the state created a "legal dualism": claims to the riverine sites were governed and protected by statutory laws, whereas the nonriverine sites remained outside direct state protection and legitimacy.

Because the state, by the power vested in it, redefined the land use rules without consulting the pastoralists, the process of change was not smooth, with the pastoralists resisting every action of the state. Indeed, throughout the 1980s and 1990s Afar pastoralists put great pressure on the administration of the state farms.[4] The pastoralists expressed their dissatisfaction with and opposition to the implementation of the commercial farm schemes, mainly by damaging mature crops in the field; a typical example was the recurrent damage caused by local people on banana plantations, which eventually forced the state farms to abandon banana production. Initially, the state farms allocated compensatory funds to be paid to clan leaders and elders in the form of employment benefits that would, it was hoped, placate the dissatisfied pastoralists. This reward system did not put an end to the grievances, however, because the power of the pastoralists emanated from their great number, which was increasing over time.

In the course of time, the relative power of the two actors has changed in favor of the pastoralists. At the beginning, AVA had the power to mobilize resources to constrain the choices of the pastoralists and was capable of controlling their actions. However, it could not maintain this power to continuously influence the choices and actions of its counterparts. This is partly attributable to a decline in the attention paid by the government to state farms after 1989. Especially after the economic reform of 1991, the stake of the state in business ventures dramatically declined. As a result, AVA did not receive enough financial, political, and other support from the government to maintain its power. In addition, the shift in the national political structure toward ethnic-based federalism and the concomitant establishment of the Afar National Regional State recalibrated the power balance in favor of the pastoralists.

---

4. The resistance was also supported by the Afar Liberation Front, which declared armed struggle against the government on June 3, 1975, following the dramatic expansion of the commercial farms by the military government. See http://www.arhotabba.com/alf.html, accessed June 23, 2005.

These changes had effects on the existing property rights and land use arrangements. With the efforts of the Afar regional government and in line with a decision of the Transitional Government of Ethiopia, MAADE handed over a significant part of its land, including irrigation infrastructure and facilities, to the Afar in 1993.[5] This, in turn, resulted in the existence of two distinct forms of property relations, increasing the number of actors involved. First, the pastoralists subdivided part of the returned farmland and started private farming in collaboration with highlanders, implying the individualization of the traditional communal rangeland. Second, the pastoralists leased out part of the returned land to local investors, who annually transfer cash payments to the pastoralists, implying the introduction of a lease contract regime into the area.[6]

In general, this subsection shows that the state is the major source of property rights changes in the middle Awash Valley of Afar. Empirical evidence from other areas of East Africa also confirms the significant role of the state with regard to property rights changes in pastoral areas. In some East African countries, such as Kenya and Uganda, the intervention of the state in forming modern ranches subverted traditional property rights arrangements and the existing ways of life (Helland 1977; Rutten 1992; Fratkin 1997; Muhereza 2001; Mwangi 2005). By the mid-1980s, Kenya was promoting and titling its extensive lowland plains for individual cultivators. Given the inadequacy of rain in the lowland areas for crop production, irrigation was considered a feasible solution to enable farming, as was clearly indicated in its national development plan of 1989–93 (Markakis 2004). As a result, significant numbers of pastoralists in some districts (such Kajiado and Samuburu) became crop cultivators (Rutten 1992; Lesorogol 2005). Sudan has been even more aggressive than Kenya in expanding agriculture in its rangelands. The central wetlands and the eastern clay plains of the country experienced expansion of large-scale commercial farms as early as the 1940s (Shazali and Ahmed 1999). Although the expansion of commercial farms was slow and did not trespass the grazing basins before the 1960s, it rapidly increased after this time (particularly after 1968) and covered substantial areas of dry-season rangelands. The same was true in Tanzania, which adopted a radical reform under the Ujamma movement (Kirk 1999).

Furthermore, the pro-conservation policies of many East African governments resulted in the transfer of large areas of rangelands from pastoralists to the state (Fratkin 1997; Lane 1998; Kisamba-Mugerwa 2001; Markakis 2004),

---

5. The state farms handed over about 6,547 hectares, with the entire irrigation infrastructure intact (MAADE 2005).

6. As we learned from group discussions, investors pay 30 percent of their annual profits to pastoralists in the form of rent. In addition to making financial payments to the pastoralists, the investors have promised to improve local infrastructure, including schools, watering trenches, and health stations. However, the pastoralists complain that none of the investors have honored their word regarding infrastructural development.

as did the pro-farming policies that facilitated the rapid expansion of large-scale commercial farms in pastoral areas of these countries (Rutten 1992; Fratkin 1997; Shazali and Ahmed 1999; Lesorogol 2005). None of these state-led transformations of traditional common property regimes were characterized by peaceful interaction between the state and the local people, and all took coercive lines.

Impacts of Coercive Change on the Livelihoods of Pastoralists

The direct intervention of the state has, step by step, changed the traditional property regime of the pastoralists and brought about new forms of land use arrangements that have direct implications for their livelihoods. Four distinct forms of land use arrangements have been realized since the initial interventions of the state: state farms, settlement farms, individual small farms, and private large-scale farms. These new variants of property rights have one main feature in common: they are all related to the production of crops. However, each of them is unique in terms of the types of actors interacting with pastoralists and the impacts on the rights and capabilities of pastoralists to secure livelihoods that they entail. The existence of state farms implies de facto state ownership as well as the nullification of customary rights that pastoralists had had to the land for generations. Indeed, the contemporary rights of pastoralists to this portion of the former commons have been limited to use rights to crop residues, and those can be exercised only with the consent of officials from the state farms. On the other hand, the expropriation of large tracts of dry-season rangeland without compensation has resulted in the reduction of the capability of pastoralists to secure their livelihoods through the traditional means of livestock production. In this respect, the present vulnerability of Afar pastoralists to recurrent droughts is at least partly associated with such expropriatory actions by the state (Sen 1981; Getachew 2001; Yemane 2003).

The settlement farms, established for compensatory reasons, reflect a kind of interaction between the state and the pastoralists. In this case, the new resources necessary to produce crops were entirely supplied by the state. The existing irrigation infrastructure and the road networks were built by the state through a large outlay. Similarly, farm machinery and facilities were purchased by the state. The technical personnel and the management staff had also been installed through the efforts of the state. Although these resources defined capabilities to exercise rights within the parameters of the new land use system, pastoralists already had well-recognized rights to the benefit streams from the land. In other words, they had the rights as well as the capabilities to generate benefits from the settlement farms.[7] However, the state was not "benevolent" forever but rather stopped its support in the mid-1980s. The termination of state

---

7. In fact, pastoralists were restricted to using the land consistent with formal regulations for the area. For instance, they could not use it as rangeland.

support and the concomitant transfer of all machinery and facilities to the state farms have debilitated the capability of the pastoralists to extract benefits from their land, although their rights to the land have remained intact. Lacking the knowledge and physical resources needed for farming, the pastoralists have not been able to continue crop production on the former settlement farms, despite their rights to do so. As a result, the entire settlement farm has been out of production and is covered, at present, by an inedible exotic weed (*Prosopis juli-flora*). In fact, this part of the former rangeland is neither cultivated nor efficiently used for livestock production, which has direct implications for the livelihoods of the pastoralists.

The return of the confiscated land in 1993 was an important action that reduced the influence of the state on the traditional lands of the pastoralists. Actually, the pastoralists were free to decide what to do with the returned land. Accordingly, the land was partly allocated to clan members and was partly leased to local investors. In regard to individual parcels of land, the Afar have established partnerships with agriculturalists from the highlands. Individual landowners have the right to choose their partners, define and redefine the land use contracts, and terminate contracts if required. In the lease arrangements, the new partners of the pastoralists are local investors. Under this form of contract, the pastoralists collectively earn 30 percent of the investors' profits in return for the use of their land, which they distribute among themselves based on pre-defined criteria. They have formed a standing committee, including an accountant, to monitor all transactions of the investors. The committee has been entrusted to defend the rights of its principals and, hence, to take action when errors or other problems arise.

Although the current situation shows the restoration of the rights of the pastoralists over their traditional land, capability limitations are apparent in terms of maximally exploiting the new venture. First, the pastoralists have poor knowledge of farming techniques and lack the resources (such as farm implements) necessary to cultivate crops. As a result, the highlanders are responsible for all farm operations in return for larger shares of the net farm proceeds (up to 70 percent), whereas the contributions and earnings of the pastoralists are minimal. Actually, the share of the highlanders reflects the costs to be paid by the pastoralists due to their limited capabilities to produce crops on their own. Second, the capacity of the committee to actually carry out its responsibilities concerning the lease arrangements is questionable. The members have no accounting knowledge, and some of them do not even read or write. Hence, everything is done based on trust, implying the possibility that the pastoralists could be cheated if the investors desire to do so. Again, this implies the weak position of the pastoralists under such arrangements.

It is also worthwhile to pinpoint the distributional effects of the changes in property rights. Traditional property rights allowed a multitude of users to share a resource system in accordance with certain predefined rules. Under the traditional arrangements, all clan members had equal rights to grazing resources and, hence, could extract benefits, provided that they had livestock. However, equality in rights to the communal heritage has not been ensured following the state-induced changes in property rights. During the initial period of the transformation, elites and their allies abandoned the customary rules and facilitated their own entitlement to the benefits from the settlement farms. Others used their physical fitness and connections with project leaders to secure their own benefits, while those households lacking such resources were denied access to them (Getachew 2001). The procedures following the subdivision of the newly returned land have also not been immune to discrimination. Contrary to the traditional land law, about 31 percent of the sample households were left out of consideration during the subdivision. A closer look at the assets of the sample pastoralists chosen for this study shows that those who have not been benefiting from the subdivided land are poorer (with an average 0.89 total livestock unit [TLU] of per capita livestock asset) than those who have been benefiting (2.91 TLU). This inequity and mistreatment are even more visible with regard to women. Female-headed households neither were considered when the returned land was distributed among clan members nor have they been beneficiaries of the leased-out land because of tradition-based criteria: women are de facto minors in Afar customary laws.[8]

The Afar pastoralists are not unique in being affected by antipastoralist policies. Other pastoral groups in Ethiopia and other East African countries are also victims of such policies. For instance, Gebre (2001) shows that Karrayyu, Somali, and many pastoral groups in southern parts of Ethiopia lost large tracts of their best rangeland for different irrigation projects and other development schemes initiated by the state (Tolera 2000; Gebre 2001; Yemane 2003). Similarly, pastoralists in other East African countries lost their traditional land to state-driven agricultural projects. In Sudan pastoralists lost large tracts of their land due to the expansion of large-scale farms in the central wetlands, the eastern clay plains, the west (Habila in Nuba Hills), the southeast (Agadi-Grabeen and Dali-Mazmoum complexes in Blue Nile), and the south (Renk in Upper Nile) under the auspices of the Mechanized Farming Corporation (Shazali and Ahmed 1999). In Tanzania, a large number of pastoralists were displaced when their prime grazing lands were given to modern companies such as the National Agricultural and Food Corporation, international seed companies, and breweries (Fratkin 1997; Markakis 2004).

---

8. Women have no ownership rights to land or other resources, including livestock. They hold conditional rights and thus are entitled to benefit streams only via their husbands. When a woman's husband dies, all jointly owned assets, including livestock, are transferred to her husband's family, and the widow loses the right to control "her" former resources. As a small form of compensation, she can, though, maintain control of the livestock given to her as presents by her husband during their marriage.

Noncoercive Means of Property Rights Change:
Voluntary Adoption of Farming

Triggers of Voluntary Change

Afar pastoralists in the study areas have been threatened not only by the coercive actions of the state but also by recurrent droughts. Two major droughts have hit these areas since the mid-1990s, and short dry spells are common as well. The prevalence of drought has adversely affected the pastoral economy in two ways. First, it has reduced the total livestock assets and productive capacities of the area, thereby increasing mortality and morbidity rates. Sanford and Habtu (2000, cited in Mesfin 2003) have estimated that a 5–15 percent reduction in livestock assets occurred in Afar due to the drought of 1999/2000. In fact, this estimation corresponds to the best-case scenario. Under the worst-case scenario, livestock loss has been estimated to range from 15 to 45 percent. The emergency assessment reports of various development organizations and relief agencies indicate that the prolonged drought of 2002/03 had even more serious consequences for the Afar pastoralists (FEWS NET 2002; UN-EUE 2002a, 2002b).

Second, the successive droughts have resulted in calibration of the terms of trade against the pastoralists. Although no systematic records have been found yet, the assessment reports of aid agencies indicate a sharp decline of livestock prices during the droughts. A United Nations (UN) assessment mission in the area indicated that pastoralists faced a reduction of more than 50 percent in livestock prices following the drought of 1999/2000 (UN-EUE 2000). Similarly, livestock prices fell by 50 to 60 percent due to the drought of 2002, while maize prices simultaneously rose by about 235 percent (Davies and Bennett 2007). The adverse effects of the droughts on the terms of trade were compounded by other factors, such as export restrictions imposed by Saudi Arabia in September 2000 following a Rift Valley fever outbreak and insecurity around the northern border of the Afar Region in the aftermath of the war between Eritrea and Ethiopia in 1998.

These livestock losses coupled with the deteriorating terms of trade against pastoralists worsened food insecurity in the study areas, with the degree of food insecurity reaching its climax in 2002/03 because of the intensified drought. A serious famine hit the area during which a large number of pastoralists lacked anything to eat. On July 12, 2002, the Disaster Prevention and Preparedness Commission issued a special alert that publicized the deterioration of food security in several parts of the country, particularly in the Afar Region and the neighboring East Shewa zone of Oromia. According to the special alert, 448,500 people in the Afar Region needed emergency aid, of whom 45.3 percent were located in Zone 3 (constituting Amibara and Awash-Fentale) and Zone 5 (constituting Semu-Robi).

The deterioration of food security in pastoral areas in general and Afar in particular necessitated an intensified intervention of external agents (governmental and nongovernmental organizations) in pastoral livelihoods. Although the most immediate external intervention was the provision of food aid to save human lives, a number of programs and projects—financed by the government and nongovernmental organizations (NGOs) such as the Food and Agriculture Organization of the UN (FAO), Farm–Africa, CARE–Ethiopia, and Oxfam GB —were designed to improve the livelihoods of pastoralists. One intervention was focused on designing projects and programs to facilitate the expansion of crop cultivation in these areas.

Both traditional authorities and external agents were important facilitators of collective action to begin farming operations. In this respect, external agents (local governments and NGOs) sponsored meetings at the *kebele* level.[9] Although there are no formal records on the number of local meetings at the study sites, the average number of meetings reported by the sample households ranged between 7.2 (for the Dudub site) and 18.6 (for the Daleti site) for the year preceding the survey. During the meetings, the external agents explained their visions of and commitment to improving the livelihoods of pastoralists, mainly through programs tailored to farming. The interventions of the external actors were even more direct at three of the study sites, namely Harihamo, Daleti, and Doho. In Harihamo and Daleti, the government directly supported collective activities in relation to farming through its food security program. Assistance included providing farm tools, covering the initial costs of farm operations (for example, the costs of a tractor for tillage), providing oxen, and offering other logistic and advisory support. At the Doho site, support was provided mainly by an FAO livestock recovery project office at Awash-Fentale that provided financial support for the initial development of irrigation infrastructure and farm inputs, mainly seeds. Moreover, district-level experts on agriculture were responsible for providing advisory support to the "agropastoralists."

Similarly, the role of traditional authorities was substantial. Specifically, activities such as mobilizing clan members for meetings; organizing and supervising all activities, such as bush clearing and land leveling; and imposing sanctions on free riders required the active participation of the *feima* members. Traditional sanctions were to be applied, including asset penalties, such as slaughtering the breeding cows of free riders, and corporal punishment, such as beating free riders in public to shame them.[10]

---

9. A *kebele* is the lowest formal administrative unit, also termed a peasant association.

10. Although all of the sample households were aware of the existence of these sanctioning mechanisms, none of them reported having faced any sort of punishment in relation to the collective preparations for farming.

Here *collective action* applies only to activities groups performed together prior to the allocation of the land to the participants. These activities included bush clearing and leveling the fields to facilitate tillage. Although individual pastoralists were free to decide whether to participate in collective action to start farming, involvement in those activities was a prerequisite to obtain farmland and associated support from external agents. Therefore, we can argue that in the case at hand the decision to engage in collective action cannot be distinguished from the initiative to start farming. The collective land clearing was the compulsory entry point to plant production. Only after this initial collective effort could the decision to continue or terminate agricultural enterprises be made in an individual fashion. Although there are strong reasons to assume that our analysis captures the factors influencing the decision to engage in collective action, we cannot completely dismiss the fact that the analysis also captures factors that favored a switch to crop farming, independent of whether this switch required collective action as a precondition. Individuals were supposed to continue their cultivation practices by their own efforts once they were given an initial impulse, but this long-term outcome is beyond the scope of this study. The preparatory activities were undertaken intermittently for about four months in Semu-Robi and for two months in Awash-Fentale. The exact duration in Amibara is not clear, but according to sample respondents it ranged between 30 and 180 days. The overall rate of participation in these cooperative activities across districts was 39.1 percent ($n = 70$), with 13.3 percent ($n = 8$) in Amibara, 23.3 percent ($n = 14$) in Awash-Fentale, and 81.4 percent ($n = 48$) in Semu-Robi.

Analytical Model and Variables

"Triggers of Voluntary Change" indicates that farming is an enterprise that has been induced because of natural shock to the area. Engaging in farming presupposes participation in collective action to gain access to the common land. Understanding the movement of pastoralists toward farming entails comparing the situations under farming and pastoralism. Thus, assuming that individuals make decisions by comparing the expected utilities associated with the two enterprises, this binary choice can be modeled following the utility function approach. Let U_{i1} and U_{i0} be the utilities of individual associated with farming and pastoralism, respectively. We expected that community members would be heterogeneous in terms of the level of utilities generated from farming. We also expected that community members would vary in terms of the level of utilities they would generate from pastoralism. Thus, U_{i1} and U_{i0} can be formulated as a function of other variables such that $U_{i1} = \alpha_{i1} + \beta_{i1}X_i + \varepsilon_{i1}$ and $U_{i0} = \alpha_{i0} + \beta_{i0}X_i + \varepsilon_{i0}$, where α and β are parameter estimates and X is a vector of exogenous variables that cause heterogeneity among community members. As a utility maximizer, individual i decides in favor of farming if $U_{i1} - U_{i0} > 0$ and otherwise if

$U_{i1} - U_{i0} < 0.$[11] Accordingly, participation in collective activities to start farming reveals that $\varepsilon_{i0} - \varepsilon_{i1} < (\alpha_{i1} - \alpha_{i0}) + (\beta_{i1} - \beta_{i0})X_i$. If we replace $\varepsilon_{i0} - \varepsilon_{i1}$ by ε_i, $\alpha_{i1} - \alpha_{i0}$ by α_i, and $(\beta_{i1} - \beta_{i0})X_i$ by $\beta_i X_i$ for brevity, the probability that individual i will participate in collective action to start farming can be specified as $P(C_i = 1) = P(\varepsilon_i < \alpha_i + \beta_i X_i)$. If a normal distribution function is assumed for ε_i, the model turns out to be a probit model (Amemiya 1981). Alternatively, if a logistic distribution is assumed, the model becomes the logit one (Amemiya 1981). The two alternative models produce similar outputs, except in rare cases when the data concentrate around the tails of the distributions (Amemya 1981; Greene 2000). Here the logit model is used because it lends itself to easier interpretation.

Table 9.2 describes the independent variables considered for logistic regression analysis and their hypothesized signs. The dependent variable takes on a value of one if a pastoralist participated in collective action to start farming and zero otherwise. The explanatory variables had been tested for their importance by using descriptive statistics before they were subjected to regression analysis. The results show that participants are significantly different from nonparticipants with respect to all but one variable.[12]

Regression Results and Discussion

The outputs of the regression are shown in Table 9.3. The signs of the coefficients in the regression are all in agreement with prior expectations. The chi-squared statistic is significant, implying that the explanatory variables (taken together) are important in explaining the variability in the dependent variable (cooperation to start farming). The model was able to correctly predict 86 percent of the cases vis-à-vis participation in collective activities. Because the standard coefficients in the logistic regression equation are not directly interpretable, the marginal effects of explanatory variables were computed by using an additional algorithm in the LIMDEP statistical software version 7.

Four variables are important for explaining cooperation of pastoralists in collective activities geared toward starting farming: suitability of the area for agriculture, per capita livestock holding of a household, access to wage employment, and external support. Each of them will be discussed in some detail as follows.

The proxy variable for suitability for farming (SUITAGR) is positively related to the level of cooperation for farming. This variable was supposed to capture the variability among the study sites with respect to their potential for crop cultivation. In this respect, the study areas were classified into two groups

---

11. There could be indecision if $U_{i1} - U_{i0} = 0$, but this happens with zero probability if $U_{i1} - U_{i0}$ is a continuous random variable.

12. The exception was EDUCATE.

TABLE 9.2 Description of variables and working hypotheses

Variable code (X_j)	Description	Mean of X_j (percent of $X_j = 1$)	Hypothesis
AGEHH	Age of household head in years	40.1	Older pastoralists were expected to be more conservative and therefore to resist the adoption of farming.
EDUCATE	A dummy variable that takes on the value of one if the household head is literate, zero otherwise	(25.7)	Education was expected to have an effect on pastoralists' decision to start farming, either negative or positive. The sign depends on the person's judgment whether he or she would make a better living from livestock or crops.
ACTIVLB	The number of household members within the age range 10–60 years[a]	4.9	A larger number of active family members to provide labor implies the potential of the household to engage in different activities. Hence, a larger active labor force was expected to enhance one's decision to engage in farming.
SUITAGR	A dummy variable that takes on the value of one if the area is either suitable for rainfed agriculture or can be irrigated given existing water resources and capacity to irrigate, zero otherwise	(66.5)	The suitability of the area for farming was expected to increase the likelihood of one's decision to adopt farming because it shows the potential to benefit from farming.
PERCPLS	Per capita livestock holding of household (total livestock unit)	3.1	Livestock holding was expected to relate negatively to the adoption of farming because a smaller livestock holding implies (within the context of pastoral areas) higher vulnerability to natural shocks and hence higher potential gains from a diversified livelihood.

EMPOPP	A dummy variable that takes on the value of one if the household generates income from wage employment, and zero otherwise	(10.6)	Wage employment was supposed to compete with farming in terms of labor and hence was supposed to reduce the probability of engaging in farming. Moreover, an opportunity for wage employment implies less vulnerability to natural shocks, which may reduce the probability of being engaged in farming as a strategy of postshock recovery.
SUPPORT	A dummy variable that takes on the value of one if external agents provided direct support[b] before and during collective activities, zero otherwise[b]	(49.7)	Support from external agents in relation to farming was expected to increase the probability that pastoralists would start farming.
LIVDIVRS	Index of heterogeneity among pastoralists as measured by the coefficient of variation (measured as the standard deviation of livestock holding at each site divided by the corresponding mean)	0.953	A higher level of heterogeneity was supposed to affect the level of collective action negatively because it implies a divergence of ideas among pastoralists and might reduce the degree of consensus among them.

SOURCE: Authors' survey data.

[a]Classification was made based on local information.

[b]External support includes financial, material, and advisory services. Moreover, the role of external agents in organizing local meetings has been taken into account to define the variable.

TABLE 9.3 Determinants of cooperation among pastoralists to start farming

Determinant	Coefficient	Standard error	Marginal effects
Constant	−3.0032*	1.3431	−0.5146
AGE	−0.0121	0.0153	−0.0020
EDUCATE	0.5912	0.5531	0.1013
ACTIVLAB	0.0721	0.0792	0.0101
SUITAGR	3.9420**	1.1715	0.6755
PERCPLS	−0.1623**	0.0610	−0.0279
EMPOPP	−2.0276*	0.8911	−0.3474
SUPPORT	1.7735**	0.6607	0.3039
LIVDIVRS	−0.3240	0.2693	−0.0555
Chi-squared	110.2745**		
Log likelihood function	−64.65321		
Percentage of correct prediction	86		
Number of cases	179		

SOURCE: Authors' survey data.

NOTES: For descriptions of the determinants, see Table 9.2. * means significant at the 5 percent level; ** means significant at the 1 percent level.

based on the perceptions of the pastoralists. Ambash, Doho, Harihamo, and Daleti were classified as potential sites for agriculture either because of the presence of irrigation infrastructure (Ambash and Doho) or because of better rainfall distribution (Harihamo and Daleti). On the other hand, Qurqura and Dudub were classified as nonpotential areas. The heterogeneity of the study sites with respect to their potential for agriculture implies the existence of spatial variation regarding the costs of running a new enterprise (that is, crop production). In areas where shifting to farming is easier, because of either better rainfall or the possibility of irrigation, mobilizing people for collective action is easier because people anticipate that they would incur relatively low costs in realizing benefits that would be reasonably higher than the alternative engagements. The regression result indicates that the probability of cooperation in collectively organized action to start farming increases by about 68 percent in areas where people perceive the possible benefits of farming. The perceptions of the pastoralists on the potential of their localities vis-à-vis farming influence their decisions because expectations about the benefits of cooperation in farming arise from individual perceptions. However, note that other location characteristics (such as roads) are not controlled for in this regression (for example, we have not included location fixed effects), and to the extent to which these are correlated to the suitability of the area for farming, the coefficient on SUITAGR will be biased.

The second influential factor is the level of wealth of pastoral households, as implied by per capita livestock ownership (PERCPLS). The expectation was that households with few livestock assets would have a relatively high incentive to go into cultivation compared to better-off households, for the simple reason that livestock are not dependable sources of livelihood. This expectation holds true, as confirmed by the regression analysis results. More specifically, the probability that a household will cooperate in farm-preparing activities increases by about 2.8 percent for each TLU reduction in per capita livestock holding, implying that households with few livestock assets are more likely to cooperate.[13] In this regard, the variation among the pastoral households can be explained from a number of different perspectives.

First, the possible differences in labor demands between those with fewer livestock assets (<4.5 TLU)—hereafter called "poor households"—and those with more livestock assets (>4.5 TLU)—hereafter considered "better-off households"—can be associated with differences in cooperative behavior between the two groups.[14] Actually, better-off households own significantly larger quantities of livestock (67.3 TLU) than do poor households (11.2 TLU), whereas, in terms of active labor-force potential, the better-off households are in a slightly lower position (4.4 persons) compared to the poor households (5.0 persons). Given the fact that those with more livestock assets require more labor to properly manage their animals, the output reveals that labor is scarcer among households with more livestock assets. Thus, it can be deduced from the results that the introduction of crop production into the existing system would lead to greater pressure on better-off households with regard to labor allocation. When competition occurs between crop cultivation and livestock husbandry, it is less likely that better-off pastoralists would prefer to shift their labor to the "imported" enterprise (that is, crop cultivation).

Second, the decisions of the pastoralists concerning farming activities reflect their ways of reacting to natural hazards, mainly droughts. Pastoralists have exercised several traditional portfolio management techniques to mitigate their risk. Livestock accumulation is one way to mitigate risk (Herren 1991; McPeak and Barrett 2001). McPeak (2005) shows that a larger precrisis herd size implies a larger postcrisis herd. Diversification of livestock ownership is another ex ante risk management strategy in which pastoralists adjust the composition of their livestock in a direction that could minimize asset loss due to disaster. Pastoral households also spread their livestock spatially throughout their personal networks to reduce risk.

---

13. For instance, 1 camel = 1 TLU; 1 head of cattle = 0.7 TLU; 1 donkey = 0.5 TLU; 1 sheep = 0.1 TLU (ILCA 1992).

14. In this region, 4.5 TLU per capita (or about 5 cows) is the minimum threshold level required to sustain family members without requiring additional income from other sources (McPeak and Barrett 2001).

Although these ex ante risk management strategies (though not exhaustive) may be used in many pastoral areas, the poor and better-off households do not have equal capability to exercise them. The poor appear to have less capability to exercise any of the indicated options simply because livestock are large investments for them. In this regard, the poor occupy lower positions not only in terms of total amount of livestock but also in terms of the diversity of these assets. A comparison made between the two groups vis-à-vis diversification (within pastoralism) shows that better-off households keep more livestock types (3.6 species) than poor ones do (3.3 species). Moreover, better-off households own more camels (about 30 head) than do poor households (about 3 head), which shows that the former are in a better position to withstand recurrent droughts.[15] Although keeping livestock at different locations across personal networks seems a rational way of mitigating risks, especially those arising from localized, not regionwide shocks, this strategy is also less likely to be feasible among poor households because they do not have enough livestock to distribute spatially.

Differences in ex ante risk management strategies and capabilities between the poor and the better off also affect their ex post risk management strategies and capabilities to cope. In this respect, better-off households possess better resources to meet basic needs without resorting to other occupations, whereas poor households need to find opportunities outside of pastoralism to sustain their families. Therefore, the differences in cooperative behavior observed between poor and better-off pastoralists with regard to farming are also attributable to their differences with respect to ex post risk management strategies.

Third, the difference observed between the two groups with regard to cooperative preparations to start farming can also be seen from the perspective of property rights. Common property regimes allow multitudes of users to share a resource system in accordance with certain predefined rules (Ostrom 1990, 1992). Nevertheless, this does not mean that all rights holders derive equal benefits from the resource system. Rather, benefits are a function of the rights and capabilities of individual actors to use a resource system (Ribot and Peluso 2003). A pastoralist who has limited financial ability to purchase additional stock obviously derives less benefit from the communal pasturage than his livestock-rich neighbor given that the rate of livestock ownership is below the optimum. In other words, the poorer pastoralist exploits only a small portion of his rights compared to the better off, although, in principle, he has the right to derive as much benefit as his neighbor. Indeed, not only rights but also capabilities determine the actual benefit structure among a group of people. This is

---

15. Camels are best suited to arid areas such as Afar. In times of water scarcity, they can endure without water for more than two weeks, whereas cattle need water at least once every three days. Moreover, camels feed on the foliage of trees and bushes, which fare better in resisting drought than do the grasses on which cattle are dependent.

particularly apparent with regard to common-pool resources, particularly in the case of rangelands, where there is de facto open access for all group members.

Capability differences among rights holders to realize benefits from a communal resource system may result in differences in their reactions to new challenges or opportunities that may affect benefit streams. For the nearly stockless Afar households, the incentive to cooperate in farming activities would be high because in this way they could better exercise their rights over the resource system. The current literature indicates that traditionally pastoral communities do provide opportunities for poor members with little or no livestock to make grazing contracts with better-off community members or outsiders so that they can build their own herds (Ngaido 1999). However, our evidence shows that, with regard to contractual arrangements, there is no special institutional treatment of poor households, implying that the only feasible option that is available to them for exercising their rights is to take up crop production, provided that entry is made possible for them.

Pastoral areas are generally marginal in terms of intensive crop production. Consequently, livestock production appears to be the best and, in some areas, the only option under the existing technologies (Ahmed et al. 2002). However, as a result of challenges (mainly drought) that have caused rapid deterioration of pastoral livelihoods, these days pastoralists usually seek out alternative means of survival, at least on a transitory basis. Because opportunities are lacking in most pastoral areas, resorting to agriculture is the main option that pastoralists pursue. Indeed, a growing trend toward crop cultivation is now observable in many pastoral areas of Ethiopia in general and Afar in particular (Yemane 2003). In areas where alternatives are available, it is expected that pastoralists will make choices from the "bundle" of nonpastoral activities to sustain themselves, at least until the conditions for their main occupation improve. In such situations, alternative activities compete for pastoralists' resources and, hence, the decision to cooperate in farming activities is a matter of evaluating the existing opportunities from the perspective of each pastoral household, differentiated as they are in terms of existing assets and capabilities. In this vein, our results indicate that wage employment opportunities (EMPOPP) tend to have a negative influence on the decision to cooperate in farming activities. The probability of opting for cooperation declines by about 35 percent if a household earns income from wage employment. Nevertheless, it is possible that the decision to take or give up wage employment is itself influenced by the decision to start farming (rather than vice versa), so there may be a problem of reverse causality with this variable, though the income opportunities differ largely in amounts and security.

Almost all (about 93 percent) of the sample pastoralists we surveyed indicated that their livestock ownership had shown a declining trend within a few years before the survey. The main reason for this was the devastating drought that occurred in 2002/03 rather than the demand for farming. Our data from secondary sources also indicate that the underlying trigger for farming in the area was the drought, which caused significant livestock losses among the pastoralists. Nevertheless, the question of reverse causality is reasonable, because it is plausible that the pastoralists dropped their employment because of their decision to start farming. However, the survey asked about the level of connectedness to organizations such as NGOs, local administrations, agriculture offices, state farms, Awash National Park, health stations, schools, and others over time in recent years, as well as whether the trend was improving, declining, or unchanged and for what reasons. Seventy-two percent of the respondents responded that their rapport with state farms—the monopolistic source of employment—showed no change, while 24 percent reported a slight improvement. Only 4 percent indicated that their connection has declined. Even those who indicated a declining relationship did not offer withdrawal from employment by state farms as a reason. Rather, a change of residence was responsible for the decline of the relationship with state farms.

State farms are the major sources of wage employment for pastoralists in the study areas, particularly in some locations of the middle Awash Valley. Although the Afar is recruited only for lower-level positions, those who are given the chance do not hesitate to join state farms. All in all, about 11 percent of the sample pastoralists were employed on commercial farms. There are reasons that pastoralists prefer employment on state farms to farming by themselves. First, they can generate a more stable (and perhaps higher) income by being wage laborers, whereas farming is a risky business. Second, in most cases pastoralists are employed as guards to protect crops (mainly cotton) from livestock, which is less tiresome than farmwork and is preferable to pastoralists, who are well versed in tending animals.

Gaining employment on state farms is one cause of conflict between the pastoralists and the state farms, because the pastoralists feel that it is their right to benefit from development opportunity on their land. As a result, the state farms have allocated large amounts of money to employing local people on the state farms. Information obtained from MAADE indicates that there is great pressure from the surrounding areas to feed livestock on cotton stocks. Although cotton harvesting normally comprises three rounds, pastoralists have been rushing their animals into the cotton fields immediately after first-round picking. In order to reduce this pressure from the local herders, guards are recruited from different clans. A large amount of money is allocated by MAADE to mitigate the problem by using the guards as social capital. For instance, a total of 294,335 birr (~US$34,000) was allocated in 2004/05 for this purpose (MAADE administrative officer, personal communication with author BK, February 2005). This supports the interpretation of econometric findings that farming is not superior to wage employment on state farms and, hence, that pastoralists are less likely to drop their wage employment in favor of farming.

Finally, support from external actors (SUPPORT) has been found to be positively and significantly related to participation in collective action to start farming. The probability that a household will participate in collective action increases at the mean level by 30.3 percent in the presence of external support. There are two possible explanations for this result. First, the participation of external actors in organizing meetings facilitates discussions and information exchange among pastoralists. Some pastoralists may not participate because they are completely unaware of the intervention. Others may be ambivalent because of incomplete information with regard to the intended activities. Thus, the existence of external support increases the likelihood of participation of those households that fail to cooperate, either unwittingly or due to ambivalence, thereby improving their awareness regarding what has been intended for their locality, the costs and benefits of cooperation and noncooperation, the commitment of external supporters, the reactions of other members of the community, and the "rules of the game."[16]

Second, financial and material support provided by external actors could increase the likelihood of participation. Such support, which augments the capacity of households to invest in the new venture, can particularly increase the participation of the poor, who may otherwise refrain from participation due to financial and material limitations. The positive effect of this variable is not, however, exclusively associated with poor households. Even the participation of better-off households can be enhanced in the presence of financial and material support as a result of possible reductions in costs of participation vis-à-vis the anticipated benefits. Moreover, better-off households may be persuaded to have their "share" of the resources externally injected into the system.

Summary and Policy Implications

Traditional communal landholding has been prevalent in Afar, accommodating the interests of different user groups for many generations. This is attributable to the ecological conditions of Afar, which entail the use of pastoral resources scattered over a wide area of land to produce livestock. However, this traditional land use system is changing because of pressures from both governmental policy and natural events (UN OCHA-PCI 2007). The study reported in this chapter has examined both political and natural forces that have induced the transformation of the traditional land use arrangements in selected areas of Afar. State intervention, which has been imposed mainly since the early 1960s, had detrimental effects on the livelihoods of pastoralists. First, through the employment of coercive means, the state expropriated large areas of dry-season

---

16. There is also a possibility that external agents may romanticize the outcomes of forthcoming cooperative efforts to persuade those who have not yet decided to join them.

rangeland, resulting in the exacerbation of feed scarcity in the area. Second, the state had been enforcing the transformation of pastoralism into sedentary farming without taking into account pastoral households' capacities to produce crops. More specifically, the development schemes initiated and financed by the state could not enhance the capabilities of pastoral households in a way that would enable them to derive full benefits from their land. Devoid of public participation, these schemes paradoxically fostered a dependency syndrome among pastoralists that remained even after their termination. Third, state intervention created a window of opportunity for some pastoralists, while others such as women and the poor were deprived of benefits from the new arrangements.

When faced with challenges, pastoral households employ coping strategies that may involve different ways of using the available resources, even looking beyond pastoralism. The situation of recurrent drought, which was intensified in 2002 and 2003, imposed difficulties on pastoral livelihoods in Afar. On the one hand, the emergence of this natural challenge triggered the intervention of external actors to facilitate cooperation among pastoralists, providing a catalyst for the motivation of the pastoralists to take up farming. On the other hand, this natural challenge increased the expectations of people that they would be able to generate greater levels of utility by participating in such collective efforts, given the existence of external assistance. These expectations, whether realized or not, produced cooperative decisions to engage in organized activities. However, individual households are heterogeneous in their capability to withstand the natural challenge. In the case studied, our results show that poor households are more interested in farming and, hence, promote the transformation process. Whether this demand on the part of the poor could lead to permanent individualization of the previously communal land remains to be seen.

Overall, the study indicates that communal land ownership, which forms the basis for pastoralism, is under pressure as a result of state intervention and natural challenges, as has also been depicted by several other studies in pastoral areas (Ensminger and Rutten 1991; Blench 2001; Helland 2002; Markakis 2004). Though the same collective property rights might be shared, the individual capability of the rights holder to use the resource varies to a great extent. This explains why diversification into agriculture with the help of external intervention is more attractive to poor households with less livestock. Nevertheless, the transformation of the property rights regime is an effect of coercive and voluntary collective action.

This chapter also provides insight into the relationships between certain parts of the conceptual framework from Chapter 2. First of all, it shows that political risks play an important role, similar to that of environmental risks, in shaping the institutions of the poor. Forced collectivization, land confiscations, and other antipastoralist actions of the Ethiopian government introduce new risks to the traditional pastoral livelihoods, creating incentives for collective activities around farming. Therefore, this type of uncertainty can be linked to the emergence of new collective action institutions, which in turn trigger the transformation of property rights arrangements, highlighting the inter-connectedness of these two types of institutions in pastoral areas. The involvement of external actors (the Ethiopian state, in this case) created additional incentives for the emergence of new forms of cooperation around farming, which is consistent with the findings on collective action institutions from the literature. These findings also show how action resources held by various actors, such as the decisionmaking and enforcement power of the state, shape the institutions of collective action and property rights and the outcomes of greater personal and livelihood security, on the one hand, and political exclusion, on the other. Interestingly, the patterns of interaction that emerge from the action arena in this case are both cooperation (around farming activities) and nonviolent conflict (damaging crops on the banana plantations). The transformation of property rights arrangements from communal ventures, with equal access to resources by all pastoralists, to state farms and subdivision into private plots also led to certain forms of elite capture, across both asset endowments and gender, as a pattern of interaction, leading to more social differentiation of assets in the future (feedback effects).

A remark is required with regard to the quantitative results. Our units of analysis are pastoralists who were randomly selected. This indicates that our results can be extrapolated to some extent to similar locations. However, due to the fact that the locations we studied were selected purposely, extrapolating the results requires some degree of care. Given that, the following two points are worthy of policy attention:

- *The importance of averting possible continuation of state coercion.* The coercive expropriation of pastoral land has been slowed down since 1991, and Afar pastoralists have regained some of the rights to the traditional land they lost. However, the current national policies are not immune from an antipastoral ethos. For instance, the 2005 national land use proclamation declared the possibility that communal rural landholdings will be converted to private holdings if the government finds such transformation necessary (Article 5, No. 3). There is also a clear plan to expand the existing irrigated land in the Awash Basin (about 66 percent in the Afar Region) from 68,800 hectares to 151,400 hectares (Flintan and Tamirat 2002). The implementation of such a plan would be impossible without evicting pastoralists, and the costs of eviction are usually underestimated.

  Moreover, it is usually assumed that simply providing financial compensation will be sufficient for those who lose their land. However, for pastoralists who do not have enough skills to engage in other occupations, providing financial compensation without further assistance is akin to facilitating their movement toward destitution. The failure of past "compensation" schemes in Afar (as discussed earlier in this chapter) indicates that investment expansion through compensation schemes may not lead to a situation in which all stakeholders benefit. Current experiences in non-pastoral areas of the country also show that critical problems are associated with the expansion of investments in rural areas of Ethiopia: undervaluation of land, a great variance between what investors pay and what evictees receive in compensation, and ultimate failure of evictees to start new livelihoods (Bekure et al. 2006). These problems are attributable to a lack of effective institutions and appropriate governance structures, including (1) a lack of clear guidelines on land valuation, (2) marginalization of landholders in the process of land transfers, and (3) a weak organizational setup to administer the transformation process. Indeed, such experiences provide good lessons that should be taken seriously in the national and regional policy arena before promoting investments in rural areas of Afar.

- *The need to harmonize policy emphasis with the potentials of pastoral areas.* The transformation of property rights due to natural challenges has had important implications for the livelihoods of pastoralists. In this regard, this chapter has shown that poor households (in terms of livestock assets) are more interested in farming compared to better-off households. The decisions of pastoralists to commence farming activities could reflect their reactions to recurring natural hazards; farming is considered a postshock source of livelihood by those households that cannot call upon their pastoral assets in seasons following a drought.

With regard to farming, two points can be noted. First, efforts to produce food crops under rainfed conditions may not provide any substantial remedy to the decline of food security that occurs with a drought; during a prolonged drought, it presumably will not. This is because crops are also biological products (like livestock) and, hence, can be negatively affected by drought. Livestock appear to be even somewhat more tolerant of drought conditions than crops, because they are mobile. The existence of mobile pastoralism in dry regions of the world implies the relative viability of livestock production compared to rainfed agriculture in these regions. Second, although crops can be produced using irrigation in some ecological niches (for instance, near major rivers), an irrigation-based production system is less appealing in many parts of Afar, given the scarcity of water. Consequently, livestock production appears to be the best and, in some areas, the only option under the existing technologies. The relatively low level of participation of better-off pastoralists in collective action to start farming also implies that crop production is not a substitute for livestock production in such dry areas but rather is subsidiary to the raising of livestock. Therefore, instead of overrating the sustainability of farming and its impact on poverty reduction, it would be worthwhile to focus on livestock production (that is, the core enterprise in pastoral areas). In this regard, improving key services such as the livestock-market information system as well as veterinary and financial services, investing in infrastructure (roads and other facilities), and enhancing feed management are key to turning the silent transformation of the commons into a viable development path for the Afar. Moreover, there is a need for policies to introduce some form of drought insurance system. In this regard, the current investigations and experiments into livestock insurance schemes, such as those in northern Kenya (Orindi, Nyong, and Herrero 2007), are a promising new institutional mechanism to enable pastoralists to restock after drought and to save the value represented by surplus male animals in pastoral systems.

References

Abdulahi, M. 2004. Pastoral development strategies/policies in Ethiopia: A critical analysis and evaluation. In *Proceedings of the Third National Conference on Pastoral Development in Ethiopia: Pastoralism and Sustainable Pastoral Development*. Addis Ababa, Ethiopia: Ethiopia Pastoralist Forum.

Ahmed, A. G. M, A. Azeze, M. Babiker, and D. Tsegaye. 2002. *Post-drought recovery strategies among pastoral households of the Horn of Africa: A review*. Development Research Report Series 3. Addis Ababa, Ethiopia: Organisation for Social Science Research in Eastern and Southern Africa.

Alchian, A., and H. Demsetz. 1973. Property right paradigm. *Journal of Economic History* 33 (1): 16–27.

Amemiya, T. 1981. Qualitative response models: A survey. *Journal of Economic Literature* 19: 481–536.

Bekure, S., A. Mulatu, G. Abebe, and M. Roth. 2006. Removing limitations of current Ethiopian rural land policy and land administration. Paper presented at the Workshop on Land Policies and Legal Empowerment of the Poor, November 2–3, 2006, at the World Bank, Washington, D.C.

Berhanu, W., D. Colman, and B. Fayissa. 2007. Diversification and livelihood sustainability in a semi-arid environment: A case study from southern Ethiopia. *Journal of Development Studies* 43 (5): 871–889.

Berkele, Y. 2002. Magnitude of famine for the pastoral areas: Past and present. In *Proceedings of the Roundtable on Drought and Famine in the Pastoral Regions of Ethiopia*. Addis Ababa, Ethiopia: Pastoralist Forum Ethiopia.

Blench, R. 2001. *You can't go home again: Pastoralism in the new millennium*. Overseas Development Institute. <http://www.odi.org.uk/resources/details.asp?id=5155&title=you-cant-go-home-again-pastoralism-new-millennium.> Accessed August 17, 2004.

Bromley, D. W. 1991. *Environment and economy: Property rights and public policy*. Oxford, U.K.: Blackwell.

———. 1998. Determinants of cooperation and management of local common property resources: Discussion. *American Journal of Agricultural Economics* 80 (3): 665–668.

Campbell, D. J. 1984. Responses to drought among farmers and herders in Southern Kajiado District, Kenya. *Human Ecology* 12 (1): 35–63.

Chatty, D. 2007. Mobile peoples: Pastoralists and herders at the beginning of the 21st century. *Reviews in Anthropology* 36 (1): 5–26.

Davies, J., and R. Bennett. 2007. Livelihood adaptation to risk: Constraints and opportunities for pastoral development in Ethiopia's Afar region. *Journal of Development Studies* 43 (3): 490–511.

Disaster Prevention and Preparedness Commission. 2002. *Special alert newsletter,* July 12.

Ensminger, J., and A. Rutten. 1991. The political economy of changing property rights: Dismantling a pastoral commons. *American Ethnologist* 18 (4): 683–699.

FEWS-NET (Famine Early Warning System Network–Ethiopia). 2002. Emerging food crisis in Afar region and east Shewa zone, Ethiopia. *Food Security Warning,* July 8. Addis Ababa, Ethiopia. Mimeo.

Flintan, F., and I. Tamirat. 2002. Spilling blood over water? The case of Ethiopia. In *Scarcity and surfeit: The ecology of Africa's conflicts,* ed. Jeremy Lind and Kathryn Sturman. Pretoria, South Africa: Institute for Security Studies.

Fratkin, E. 1991. *Surviving drought and development: Arial pastoralists of Northern Kenya.* Boulder, Colo., U.S.A.: Westview.

———. 1997. Pastoralism: Governance and development issues. *Annual Review of Anthropology* 26: 235–261.

Gadamu, F. 1994. The post-revolutionary rethinking of arid land policy in Ethiopia. Special issue (*The Pastoral Land Crisis: Tenure and Dispossession in Eastern Africa*), *Nomadic Peoples* 34–35: 69–79.

Galaty, J. G., and D. L. Johnson, eds. 1990. *The world of pastoralism: Herding systems in comparative perspective.* New York and London: Guilford.

Gebre, A. 2001. *Pastoralism under pressure: Land alienation and pastoral transformation among the Karrayu of eastern Ethiopia, 1941 to the present.* The Hague, Netherlands: Shaker.

Getachew, N. K. 2001. *Tradition, continuity and socioeconomic change among the pastoral Afar in Ethiopia.* Utrecht, Netherlands: International Books in Association with the Organisation for Social Science Research in Eastern and Southern Africa.

Greene, W. H. 2000. *Econometric analysis,* 4th ed. Upper Saddle River, N.J., U.S.A.: Prentice Hall International, Inc.

Hagmann, T. 2005. Beyond clannishness and colonialism: Understanding political disorder in Ethiopia's Somali Region, 1991–2004. *Journal of Modern African Studies* 43 (4): 509–536.

Helland, J. 1977. Group ranch development among the Maasai in Kenya. In East African pastoralism: Anthropological perspectives and development needs. Paper presented at a conference held August 22–26 in Nairobi, Kenya. Addis Ababa, Ethiopia: International Livestock Center for Africa.

———. 2002. Land alienation in Borana: Some land tenure issues in pastoral context in Ethiopia. In *Resource alienation, militarisation and development: Case studies from East African drylands,* ed. M. Babiker. Addis Ababa, Ethiopia: Organisation for Social Science Research in Eastern and Southern Africa.

Herren, V. 1991. Droughts have different tails: Response to crisis in Mukogodo Division, North Kenya. *Disasters* 15 (2): 93–107.

Hogg, R. 1988. Water, harvesting and agricultural production in semi-arid Kenya. *Development and Change* 19 (1): 69–87.

Holtzman, J. D. 1996. Transformations in Samburu domestic economy: The reconstitution of age- and gender-based processes of production and resource allocation among a Kenyan "pastoral" people. Ph.D. dissertation, Department of Anthropology, University of Michigan, Ann Arbor, Mich., U.S.A.

Hundie, B. 2008. *Pastoralism, institutions and social interaction: Explaining the coexistence of conflict and cooperation in pastoral afar, Ethiopia.* Aachen, Germany: Shaker.

IGE (Imperial Government of Ethiopia). 1957. *First five-year plan.* Addis Ababa.

———. 1962. *Second five-year plan.* Addis Ababa, Ethiopia.

ILCA (International Livestock Centre for Africa). 1992. *Livestock production system.* Addis Ababa, Ethiopia.

Kamara, A. B., B. Swallow, and M. Kirk. 2004. Policies, interventions and institutional change in pastoral resource management in Borana, Southern Ethiopia. *Development Policy Review* 22 (4): 381–403.

Kirk, M. 1999. The context of livestock and crop–livestock development in Africa: The evolving role of the state in influencing property rights over grazing resources in Sub-Saharan Africa. In *Property rights, risk and livestock development in Africa,* ed. N. McCarthy, B. Swallow, M. Kirk, and P. Hazell. Nairobi, Kenya, and Washington, D.C.: International Livestock Research Institute and International Food Policy Research Institute.

Kisamba-Mugerwa, W. 2001. Rangeland management policy in Uganda. A paper prepared for the International Conference on Policy and Institutional Options for the Management of Rangelands in Dry Areas, May 7–11, in Hammamet, Tunisia.

Kituyi, M. 1990. *Becoming Kenyans: Socio-economic transformation of the pastoral Maasai.* Nairobi, Kenya: African Centre for Technology Studies Press.

Lane, C. R. 1998. *Custodians of the commons: Pastoral land tenure in East and West Africa.* London: Earthscan.

Lesorogol, C. K. 2005. Privatizing pastoral lands: Economic and normative outcomes in Kenya. *World Development* 33 (11): 1959–1978.

Little, P. D. 1992. *The elusive granary: Herder, farmer, and state in Northern Kenya.* Cambridge, U.K.: Cambridge University Press.

Little, P. D., K. Smith, B. Cellarius, D. L. Coppock, and C. Barrett. 2001. Avoiding disaster: Diversification and risk management among East African herders. *Development and Change* 32: 401–433.

MAADE (Middle Awash Agricultural Development Enterprise). 2005. MAADE information document. Melka Werer, Ethiopia. Mimeo.

Markakis, J. 2004. Pastoralism on the margin. Report. Minority Rights Group International, London.

McCarthy, N., B. Swallow, M. Kirk, and P. Hazell, eds. 1999. *Property rights, risk and livestock development in Africa.* Washington, D.C.: International Food Policy Research Institute.

McPeak, J. 2005. Individual and collective rationality in pastoral production: Evidence from Northern Kenya. *Human Ecology* 33 (2): 171–197.

McPeak, J., and C. B. Barrett. 2001. Differential risk exposure and stochastic poverty traps among East African pastoralists. *American Journal of Agricultural Economics* 83 (3): 674–679.

Meinzen-Dick, R., and M. di Gregorio, eds. 2004. *Collective action and property rights for sustainable development.* Focus 11. Washington D.C.: International Food Policy Research Institute.

Meinzen-Dick, R. S., and R. Pradhan. 2002. *Legal pluralism and dynamic property rights.* CAPRi Working Paper 22. Washington, D.C.: International Food Policy Research Institute.

Mesfin, T. 2003. Immediate causes for the famine: The drought dimension. In *Proceedings of the Roundtable on Drought and Famine in the Pastoral Regions of Ethiopia.* Addis Ababa, Ethiopia: Pastoralist Forum Ethiopia.

Muhereza, F. E. 2001. Ranchers and pastoralists: The restructuring of government ranching, Uganda. In *African Pastoralism: Conflicts, institutions and government,* ed. M. A. M. Salih, T. Dietz, and A. G. M. Ahmed. Addis Ababa, Ethiopia: Organisation for Social Science Research in Eastern Africa.

Mwangi, E. 2005. *The transformation of property rights in Kenya's Maasai land: Triggers and motivations.* CAPRi Working Paper 35. Washington, D.C.: International Food Policy Research Institute.

Nathan, M. A., E. Fratkin, and E. A. Roth. 1996. Sedentism and child health among Rendille pastoralists of northern Kenya. *Social Science and Medicine* 43 (4): 503–515.

Ngaido, T. 1999. Can pastoral institutions perform without access options? In *Property rights, risk and livestock development in Africa,* ed. N. McCarthy, B. Swallow, M. Kirk, and P. Hazell. Nairobi, Kenya, and Washington, D.C.: International Livestock Research Institute and International Food Policy Research Institute.

Niamir-Fuller, M. 1999. Managing mobility in African rangelands. In *Property rights, risk and livestock development in Africa,* ed. N. McCarthy, B. Swallow, M. Kirk, and P. Hazell. Nairobi, Kenya, and Washington, D.C.: International Livestock Research Institute and International Food Policy Research Institute.

Orindi, V. A., A. Nyong, and M. Herrero. 2007. *Pastoral livelihood adaptation to drought and institutional interventions in Kenya.* Human Development Report 2007/2008, *Fighting climate change: Human solidarity in a divided world.* Human Development Report Office Occasional Paper 54. New York: United Nations Development Programme.

Ostrom, E. 1990. *Governing the commons: The evolution of institutions for collective action.* Cambridge, U.K.: Cambridge University Press.

———. 1992. The commons, property, and common-property regimes. In *Making the commons work: Theory, practice, and policy,* ed. D. W. Bromley. Richmond, Calif., U.S.A.: Institute for Contemporary Studies.

Padmanabhan, M. 2008. Pastoral women as strategic and tactical agents in conflicts: Negotiating access to resources and gender relations in Afar, Ethiopia. *Quarterly Journal of International Agriculture* 47 (3): 239–266.

Rettberg, S. 2006. Local risk discourses in Afar: Socio-ecological challenges to pastoral livelihood security. Presentation at the CAPRi workshop held October 2006 in Addis Ababa, Ethiopia.

Ribot, J. C., and N. L. Peluso. 2003. The theory of access. *Rural Sociology* 68 (2): 153–181.

Rutten, M. M. E. M. 1992. *Selling wealth to buy poverty: The process of individualization of land ownership among the Maasai pastoralists of Kajiado District, Kenya, 1890–1900.* Fort Lauderdale, Fla., U.S.A.: Verlag Breitenbach, Saarbrücken.

Sanford, S., and Y. Habtu. 2000. *Emergency response interventions in pastoral areas of Ethiopia.* London: Department for International Development.

Schlager, E., and E. Ostrom. 1992. Property rights regimes and natural resources: A conceptual analysis. *Land Economics* 68 (3): 249–262.

Scoones, I. 1995. New directions in pastoral development in Africa. In *Living with uncertainty,* ed. I. Scoones. London: International Institute for Environment and Development.

Sen, A. 1981. *Poverty and famines: An essay on entitlement and deprivation.* Oxford, U.K.: Clarendon.

Shazali, S., and A. G. M. Ahmed. 1999. Pastoral land tenure and agricultural expansion: Sudan and the Horn of Africa. Paper presented at the DFID workshop Land Rights and Sustainable Development in Sub-Saharan Africa, February 16–19, at Sunningdale Park Conference Centre, Berkshire, U.K.

Smith, K. 1998. Sedentarization and market integration: New opportunities for Rendille and Ariaal, women of Northern Kenya. *Human Organization* 57 (4): 459–468.

Swallow, B. M., and D. Bromley. 1995. Institutions, governance, and incentives in common property regimes for African rangelands. *Environmental and Resource Economics* 6: 99–118.

Tolera, Assefa. 2000. Problems of sustainable resource use among pastoralist societies: The influence of state interventions on the pastoral life of the Karrayyu. In *Pastoralists and environment: Experiences from the greater Horn of Africa,* ed. L. Manger and M. Abdel Ghaffar. Addis Ababa, Ethiopia: Organisation for Social Science Research in Eastern and Southern Africa.

UN-EUE (United Nations Emergencies Unit for Ethiopia). 2000. Afar pastoralists face consequences of poor rains. Report of a rapid assessment mission, April 19–24. Addis Ababa, Ethiopia.

———. 2002a. Afar: Insecurity and delayed rains threaten livestock and people. Report of an assessment mission, May 29–June 8. Addis Ababa, Ethiopia.

———. 2002b. Afar and Kereyu pastoralists in and around Awash National Park struggle with deteriorating livelihood conditions: A case study from Fentale (Oromia) and Awash-Fentale (Afar) *woredas.* Report of a UN-EUE-FAO joint assessment mission, July 2–4.

UN OCHA-PCI (United Nations Office for the Coordination of Humanitarian Affairs Pastoralist Communication Initiative). 2007. *The future of pastoralism in Ethiopia.* Addis Ababa, Ethiopia.

Unruh, J. D. 2005. Changing conflict resolution institutions in the Ethiopian pastoral commons: The role of armed confrontation in rule-making. *GeoJournal* 64: 225–237.

Yemane, B. 2003. Food security situation in the pastoral areas of Ethiopia. Oxfam GB, Ethiopia. Mimeo.

Zaal, F., and T. Dietz. 1999. Of markets, meat, maize, and milk: Pastoral commoditization in Kenya. In *The poor are not us: Poverty and pastoralism in East Africa,* ed. D. M. Anderson and V. Broch-Due. Oxford, U.K.: James Currey.

10 Unmaking the Commons: Collective Action, Property Rights, and Resource Appropriation among (Agro-)Pastoralists in Eastern Ethiopia

FEKADU BEYENE AND BENEDIKT KORF

In Ethiopian development policies, pastoralist areas have recently attracted more attention. Funding for (agro-)pastoralist development has increased significantly in the past decade. However, much debate and policy advice are still based on stereotypical representations of pastoralist areas as backward, prone to starvation and food insecurity, and hotbeds of violent conflict and contraband trade. Policy has also been based on modernist thinking among the ruling elite, which considers pastoralism an outdated mode of life that needs to be directed toward the path of modernity (that is, sedentary farming, urban life), and on technical interventions that focus on (partial) sedentarization of pastoralists (Hogg 1996; Moris 1999; Gadamu 2000; Yacob 2000; FDRE, Ministry of Federal Affairs 2002; FDRE, Ministry of Finance and Economic Development 2003; Hagmann 2006). A kind of highlander (sedentary farming) versus lowlander (pastoralist) dichotomy continues to prevail in public discourse and provides a discursive "clash of civilizations" between the ruling elite, which originated in the highlands, and the Somalis (and other pastoralist lowlanders), who consider themselves politically marginalized (Hogg 1997; Manger 2000; Gebre 2001; Abdulahi 2004).

This highland bias (Yacob 2000) in the state's policies and politics toward the pastoralist lowlands has resulted in land tenure policies that have largely ignored the specificities of the pastoralist lowlands (Gadamu 1994; Helland 2006; Abdulahi 2007). The highland bias considers sedentarization the precondition of progress in the pastoral rangelands (Moris 1999; FDRE, Ministry of Finance and Economic Development 2003). Typically, the state aided the expansion of agriculture into the lowlands but failed to regulate the tenure transformations that accompanied the diversification of rural resource use (Hagmann 2006). The arid and semiarid lowlands continue to be considered a reserve of "large tracts of unsettled land" to be developed through sedentarization and

We thank Tobias Hagmann, Esther Mwangi, and three anonymous referees for incisive suggestions on earlier drafts of this chapter and Ayalneh Bogale, Bekele Hundie, Konrad Hagedorn, and Martina Padmanabhan for continual exchange and collaboration.

agricultural resource use, which is thought to be best done through irrigated cultivation along the river banks (Moris 1999; FDRE, Ministry of Finance and Economic Development 2003, 31, cited in Hagmann 2006, 210; Halderman 2004).

At the same time, pastoralist livelihoods are undergoing considerable social change. In Somali and neighboring regional states, property rights to land are undergoing significant transformation that goes hand in hand with dynamic economic changes. Periurban places in pastoralist areas have become important market locations for cross-border exchange of livestock products and trading goods. New economic elites invest in periurban places and their surrounding spaces, where land tenure relations shift from communal and collective use to enclosed and individual use (rights). The influx of displaced people from neighboring Somalia encourages opportunistic exploitation of ecological resources, such as charcoal production for export to Somaliland and the Gulf states. At the same time, the (agro-)pastoralist livestock economies continue to struggle for survival at the resource margins, hampered by repeated droughts in past decades (Samatar 2004; Devereux 2006; Hagmann 2006).

These dynamic shifts that (agro-)pastoralist resource regimes are currently undergoing are not confined to Ethiopia but mirror broader trends in pastoralist livelihoods in the Greater Horn of Africa (Lane 1998; Little et al. 2001; Salih, Dietz, and Ahmal 2001; Watson 2003; Mwangi 2007; Hagmann and Mulugeta 2008; Homewood 2008; Hundie 2008). Pastoral commons are undergoing processes of enclosure and territorial subdivision with major ramifications for communally managed water resources and traditional practices of collective action within clans or kinship groups and cooperation between different clan and ethnic groups. It is arguable that this trend toward "unmaking the commons" has significant implications for poverty reduction and income distribution: First, trends toward enclosure exclude marginal households and individuals from access to pasture and water resources or confine them to a shrinking communal resource base. Second, trends toward privatization and individualization of resource tenure undermine incentives for collective action, especially among elite groups as their benefits from using communally managed resources are diminished.

This chapter explores these dynamics in the pastoralist commons of eastern Ethiopia. We study current practices of managing water and pasture resources of pastoralist and agropastoralist groups at three sites in Somali Region, Ethiopia. We investigate how changing property rights regimes affect incentives to participate in collective action. Our studies suggest that in the process of unmaking the commons, benefit streams to significant water and pasture resources are individualized, whereas social duties to manage communal resources through collective action are externalized. Such patterns disturb customary practices of reciprocal resource-sharing arrangements, which in the past have been instrumental in managing risk in pastoralist livelihoods and unraveling intraclan social obligations that have helped the poor. With regard to the conceptual framework presented in Chapter 2, this study illustrates how relationships between elements of the initial context and the action arena can lead to the emergence of patterns of interaction that have negative implications for the well-being of people, especially poorer, less powerful individuals in society. Specifically, kinship and the elaborate clan system (social assets) supply norms and rules that regulate communal access to water resources (natural assets) and allow flexible and reciprocal access, which helps communities to cope with frequent drought (environmental risk). However, water resource management (the action arena in this study) is challenged by difficulties in excluding nonmembers who do not participate in the regular maintenance of collective water facilities. This depresses overall incentive to invest in maintenance, because increased construction of private cisterns further depresses incentives to manage communal wells; wealthier herders in particular withdraw from communal management and focus on developing private water facilities. These interactions in the action arena result in patterns of interaction typified by reduced collective action for the maintenance of shared water resources and increases in the privatization and commercialization of water resources, including a monopolization of rents by wealthier herders. Poorer herders who cannot afford to pay for water are excluded from water access, an outcome that has unfavorable implications for their well-being.

This chapter highlights two thematic areas identified in Chapter 1. First, it provides a window into water access conflicts in dryland settings inhabited by pastoralists. And second, it illustrates how power dynamics (between the state and society and among community actors) can shape the trajectory of property regimes. The study further contributes to the broader literature on the interactions between collective action and property regimes. It demonstrates that robust systems of collective resource control can be destabilized by strong external pressures, resulting in more atomized and exclusive property arrangements that further undermine collective control.

Pastoralism, Property Rights, and Collective Action

Collective action can be understood as an action taken by a group of individuals to achieve common interests (Marshall 1998). These individuals sharing a common goal or interest are characterized by well-defined group membership or boundaries without necessarily encompassing the whole society. In pastoralist economies, collective action is essential for managing natural resources for livestock herding, in particular water and pastureland.[1] Property rights to natural resources do not necessarily imply sole authority to use and dispose of

---

1. As well as herding itself, though herding is not subject to the analysis in this chapter.

a resource (that is, full ownership), but these rights are often differentiated according to specific users and benefit streams. Property rights are relational in the sense that they define the rights and duties of an individual vis-à-vis a collective (Bromley 1991). In pastoralist societies, many resources are based on communal property rights, that is, resources are used by a group of users, normally the (sub-)clan that holds customary rights to a specified territory. Secondary user rights exist in territories held by other clans. Secondary access and user rights are subject to negotiation with the primary rights holders.

In the theoretical literature on collective action, a number of factors have been identified that induce cooperative behavior in natural resource management: asset ownership (Agarwal 2000; McCarthy, Dutilly-Diane, and Drabo 2004; Place et al. 2004), homogeneity of group members (Bardhan 2000; Dayton-Johnson 2000; Banerjee et al. 2001; Gächter, Herrmann, and Thoni 2004), mutual vulnerability of group members (Singleton and Taylor 1992), and dependence on the resources (Runge 1986; Wade 1987). In addition, Ostrom (1998) has emphasized the institutional arrangements that induce cooperative behavior. Elements of these arrangements include establishment of penalty systems and enforcement of rules (Gebremedhin, Pender, and Tesfay 2004), social norms (Cleaver 2000), and encouragement by peer groups (Kandel and Lazear 1992). Social norms and encouragement by peer groups are particularly important, because interaction among group members is not confined to activities in resource management but embedded in broader social networks. Samuel and Pender (2006), for example, demonstrate that even in the absence of monitoring, rule violations can be limited when rule obedience is based on mutual trust that others would do the same.

The mobile, transhumant mode of livestock keeping of (agro-)pastoralist livelihoods demands a flexible tenure regime based on nonexclusive use rights to pasture and water resources (Scoones and Graham 1994; Cousins 1996). Rules governing access to resources are flexible, based on multiple negotiations and rules (Thébaud and Batterby 2001). These flexible access regimes of property rights are practiced through social networks of kinship and economic exchange in which the settlement and mobility patterns of members of a group favor a spatially diversified risk-sharing arrangement to adapt to erratic climatic conditions (Vanderlinden 1999). These access regimes are based on the principle of reciprocity and balance the rights and duties of different groups (primary and secondary rights holders to specific resources). There is often an implicit assumption in the studies cited that livelihoods in those environments were static in their rules, norms, and practices (the so-called customary practices), although many pastoralist societies are undergoing dynamic processes of social and economic transformation. More recently, market-based, individualized arrangements have emerged in the form of contract grazing (Vedeld 1994; Ngaido 1999; Hagmann and Mulugeta 2008), whereby outsiders (secondary rights holder) pay grazing fees to insiders (primary rights holder), that is, to those holding customary property rights, or secondary rights holders share benefits with primary rights holders that they derive from using the communal resources of another group (Bogale and Korf 2007).

Case Study: Pastoral Water Management in Eastern Ethiopia

This chapter presents a case study on pastoral water management in eastern Ethiopia, where embedded customary practices in the management and use of the pastoral commons involve various forms of collective action that are governed by a set of rules. These practices have evolved in parallel to environmental stress (drought), political vulnerability (violent conflict, precarious statehood), and economic threats and opportunities (for example, contraband trade). These kinds of stress and instability are endemic to pastoral lives in Somali Region and the borderland of Oromiya Region with Somali Region. They are not of recent origin, as is often implicitly or explicitly assumed, but their dynamics and significance to the lives and vulnerabilities of pastoralists have changed (Sgule and Walker 1998; Watkins and Fleisher 2002; Kassa, Beyene, and Manig 2005; Devereux 2006; Hagmann 2006; Beyene 2008).

Two types of resources are essential in the (agro-)pastoralist livestock economy: (1) pasture and fodder and (2) water (for livestock, humans, and farming). Mobility patterns across seasons and across different years need to take account of both resource types. A herder's possibility of transforming pasture resources into economic value depends on the quality of the pasture as much as on the availability of water, because both are complementary inputs to livestock production. Management of water sources and water points has become even more important due to erratic rainfall patterns. Collective action around water sources is point or location specific, that is, water sources are spatially fixed (immobile), whereas collective action relating to herd management requires spatial mobility and therefore different organizational forms of collective action.

We study three different technologies that make water available for various uses: ponds, cisterns, and wells. Each of these three technologies is governed by different sets of rules for use and practices. These will be discussed in the subsequent sections. We will discuss (1) the physical attributes of the technologies, (2) the rights and duties associated with them, and (3) the political economy of practices of collective action and property rights changes. The case study focuses on three districts (*woreda*) in eastern Ethiopia: Mieso (Oromia Region, formerly jointly administered with Somali Region), Kebribeyah, and Harshin (both Somali Region). These three sites represent different (agro-) pastoralist household economies and political settings (Table 10.1) that demonstrate the complexity of (agro-)pastoralism in the semiarid parts of eastern Ethiopia, which have reasonable market access. In Mieso, we have studied agropastoralists belonging to the Oromo ethnic group, whereas in Kebribeyah,

TABLE 10.1 Backgrounds of the three study sites

Location	Mieso	Kebribeyah	Harshin
Household economy	Agropastoralist	Agropastoralist	Pastoralist
Ethnic and clan groups	Oromo, Ittu, Alan, and Nole	Somali, Abskul, and others (Akisho, Bartere, and Ogaden)	Somali, Isaaq, and others
Kebeles[a] studied	4	2	2
Number of households interviewed	80	40	39
Pastoralist water management issues studied	Communal ponds, communal wells	Communal ponds, communal wells, private and communal cisterns	Communal wells, private and communal cisterns
Location	Borderland of Somali and Oromiya regions, close to highway and rail-way to Addis Ababa road	55 kilometers east of the regional capital, Jijiga	Borderland with Somaliland (30 kilometers away), trading routes mainly to Hargesa, Somaliland

SOURCE: Authors.

[a]A *kebele* is the lowest formal administrative unit, also termed a peasant association.

agropastoralists are from the Somali ethnic group, as are the pastoralists from Harshin, although the two belong to different clans.[2]

To collect data we employed a mixed-methods approach consisting of (1) focus group discussions using rapid rural appraisal techniques to familiarize the research team and the local population, to gain a basic understanding of community perceptions, needs, and aspirations, and to collect basic information on demographic and socioeconomic characteristics of the communities; (2) a detailed household survey in which we gathered data on the assets, incentives, and opportunities of households for resource management with the support of enumerators and experienced translators; and (3) key informant interviews with government officials, staff of nongovernmental organizations, local elders, and

---

2. Although the term *agropastoralist* also has a political connotation in Ethiopian politics (because it implies a linear progressive advancement from pastoralism toward agropastoralism and on toward sedentary farming, and this kind of thinking is believed to drive the mindset of Ethiopian policymakers), we use the term here to differentiate the household economies. An agropastoralist household is one that derives a significant part of its income from farming activities, whereas a pastoralist household may also do some farming but to a lesser extent.

other key informants to generate information on institutions of resource governance. Data were collected in two phases: in the first field phase (2004–05), the focus group discussions, the household surveys, and selected key informant interviews were carried out. The second field phase (July–August 2006) focused on key informant interviews to complement the prior data collection. Our empirical study provides a one-shot collection of perceptions, assets, and rules, with retrospective information on the past. It cannot deliver an in-depth longer-term perspective of historical changes over past decades, a weakness shared by many similar studies on livelihoods.

Pasture Management, Water Technologies, and Collective Action

In this section, we analyze collective water management practices related to three technologies (wells, cisterns, ponds). Based on our field data, we first describe the physical attributes of the technology, outline the rights and duties concerning collective action in managing these technologies, and analyze everyday social practices in collective action and how changes in property rights affect these practices. In the section thereafter, we provide an explanation for these findings.

Wells

Hand-dug wells are an important communal water source for livestock and human consumption. Wells are traditionally established, managed, and used by a group. They are often located far away from settlements at strategic places on the routes used for livestock herding. Traditional wells have been a common feature of pastoralist livelihoods in recent decades and centuries, and some wells have existed for more than 100 years as indicated by the reports of early travelers to the region. Although wells are a well-established technology for providing water for human and livestock consumption, elders report declining levels of maintenance of communal wells. These observations raise the question of why customary rules governing the maintenance and use of traditional wells that have worked for a long time have become less effective or efficient.

PHYSICAL ATTRIBUTES.   Hand-dug wells vary in depth. A well's discharge depends on its depth and the users' ability to manage it. Digging deeper wells is costly and requires extensive labor, but maintenance of wells is easier than that of ponds. Elders from Mieso reported that in their locality, a properly managed well can serve its purpose for up to 60 years. This lifespan may differ at other sites. Wells, however, require high costs for extraction, which is mostly done by hand. Water extraction is highly labor intensive, in particular for watering animals. At our three study sites, Mieso and Harshen had shallower water tables compared to Kebribeyah, making well construction there less costly.

RIGHTS AND DUTIES.   User rules are quite differentiated, but there are some commonalities across different locations and ethnic groups. At all sites, the usual norm in defining watering priorities is "first come, first served," but users with a small number of livestock are usually given priority over large livestock owners because they require relatively little time to water their animals. Membership in a group using a well is usually defined based on a household's contribution of labor to the digging and maintenance of the well. Initial well diggers who do not contribute to maintenance in one season are expected to do so in the following season. Repeated noncooperation will lead to access restrictions. These internal rules are tailored to preventing continuous, rather than occasional, free riding. Internal informal sanctioning mechanisms are in place whereby members observe who has done maintenance, but this seems to be upheld as a principle rather than being practiced, because in real life it is difficult to distinguish users who have contributed to maintenance work from those who have not because the time of contribution is variable. Monitoring contributions is therefore virtually impossible. Therefore, only in principle is delineation of use rights based on the consideration of a group member's contribution to maintenance.

The norms of access to water are differentiated taking into consideration labor investment costs and (potential) reciprocal gains. In fact, the rules and norms governing access to and exclusion from wells are further differentiated beyond a cost–benefit logic that considers the contribution of users to well construction and maintenance. For instance, a household that contributes much to well maintenance may temporarily migrate away while other members are using the resource. In most cases, it appears that any contributing member from a village or subclan can use as much water as needed irrespective of the amount of labor contributed. Poor clan members often contribute significantly, although they use small amounts of well water. They do this to gain wider social recognition within the clan. The practices of granting access to well water further consider the livelihood interdependence among clan members and with outsiders.[3]

Although members reserve the right to exclude nonmembers from access to water, they do so in consideration of longer-term reciprocal relationships. Rights to access water are usually granted in expectation of future reciprocity. A good example of those reciprocal arrangements can be observed between the Ala and Ittu clans in Mieso, where the water tables are shallow and the labor contributions to well construction were not immense. These longer-term reciprocal relations are important because of the spatially differentiated rainfall patterns, which can cause water scarcity in one location but not necessarily in another location not too far away. In other locations where water tables are deep and well construction requires large labor inputs, access to water is usually restricted or denied for nonmembers. This indicates that reciprocal sharing is more common where initial investment costs have been low.

---

3. Outsiders (that is, nonmembers) are those neighbors or other (sub-)clan members who have not contributed.

SOCIAL PRACTICES.   Communal well management and maintenance have faced several challenges since the late 1980s, especially after the downfall of the Siad Barre regime in Somalia, when violent fighting in Somalia brought a large influx of refugees to the Somali Region in Ethiopia. At many sites, elders reported declining water tables, indicating overextraction of water resources. The second challenge derives from more severe droughts in recent years, which have increased the pressure on well-endowed wells. In times of crisis and feed stress, pastoralist households seek to use grazing resources and well water based on kinship relations; for example, they will access water from a well where a relative is a member, that is, where the relative has contributed to well construction and management. Relatives from another territory are granted access to the well, although they have not contributed and are not members of the group. Mostly, elders facilitate and negotiate the decision to grant access, which is then collectively binding. However, when this influx of nonmembers with kin relations becomes extraordinarily common, it reduces the incentives of the members to contribute their share to the maintenance of the well. However, when the well is located far away from the settlement area, it is used only randomly and exclusion is difficult. Collective herding, that is, several households pooling their livestock for herding, further exacerbates the pressure on water wells (extraction labor largely surpasses surcharge rates), because even households that have not contributed can water their livestock as part of the larger pool of animals, thereby gaining access to water wells that are managed by others.

Broadly speaking, it is almost impossible to exclude nonmembers from using well water, either because the resource location entails greater cost of monitoring or because of clan and kinship relations. It is considered to violate commonly accepted cultural norms to exclude someone who is related to a member, even remotely. Furthermore, especially among Somali clans, entitlements to use water are often based on multiple clan relations and social obligations, which persist over generations. Contributions from nonmembers that date back several decades or generations may continue to entitle the family and clan members to access rights even though the current generation has not contributed. In effect, this creates a system of customary rules whereby even nonmembers gain rights of access to well water (see also Unruh 2005; Devereux 2006; Hagmann 2007). Among Somali clans it is not deemed appropriate to exclude someone in need, in particular in times of crisis. This means, on the other hand, that incentives for members to contribute to well management decline the more often crisis situations prevail and multiple users from different clans make use of communal water wells. Well water is thereby transformed from common property to an open-access resource, because the sanctions and enforcement rules for members cannot be applied to nonmembers, but nonmembers can still use the resource.

Cisterns

Cisterns or *birkas* are water collection reservoirs dug into the ground. They are either covered or remain open, because both options permit inflow of the surface runoff, but most cisterns are cemented and covered. In the study area, cisterns are constructed only in Kebribeyah and Harshin, the two sites in Somali Region. They are normally cemented. At these locations, *birkas* are often the main sources of water for livestock and humans (Boku 2000). The construction of *birkas* started in the 1960s but increased significantly after the 1970s due to increasing competition for water from communal wells between pastoralists and refugees from neighboring Somalia. Communal wells tended to deteriorate because of neglect; the massive in-migration of refugees weakened the ability of user groups to enforce their traditional rules (Sugule and Walker 1998). In addition, several aid agencies constructed *birkas,* but many of those have been abandoned due to poor maintenance. For example, many *birkas* in Kebribeyah disappeared due to conflicts over ownership and control after the South East Rangelands Project, the aid program that had constructed the cistern, left the location. Property rights disputes around communal *birkas* are widespread. The core question that interests us here is why clan elders fail to enforce user rights and duties, although water from *birkas* is essential for pastoralist livelihoods.

PHYSICAL ATTRIBUTES. Because *birkas* are cemented, infiltration and leakage are reduced. Evaporation can also be limited by covering the cistern. In Harshen, communal cisterns can be quite large and deep, with dimensions of $30 \times 40 \times 4$ meters, but private ones are typically smaller. The most expensive part of the investment is paying for skilled labor (masons) and the purchase of cement. Private *birka* owners either pay those skilled laborers in cash or transfer user rights to them in return for labor contributions. In the case of communal cisterns, all users contribute labor and other inputs, but often construction is subsidized by aid agencies (which distorts investment costs).

RIGHTS AND DUTIES. There are marked differences between private and communal cisterns. In Kebribeyah, private cisterns are dominant, whereas in Harshen, there are both private and communal cisterns. The owners of private *birkas* use them to generate revenue and thus are seen as profit-seeking entrepreneurs. Water users have to pay for water. Prices may vary from 5 birr per barrel in the rainy season to 20 birr per barrel in the dry season.[4] In some places, there are fixed rates for each animal species. Private owners normally allow their relatives to use *birkas* freely or levy a lower price. In the case of communal cisterns, those who contributed labor gain access and user rights. Moreover, revenue generated from water sales to nonmembers, such as livestock traders crossing the area and neighboring clan members, is shared among group members.

---

4. US\$1.00 ~ 8.60 birr (May 2007).

SOCIAL PRACTICES.   The proliferation of private cisterns in the 1980s and 1990s, in particular in Kebribeyah, brought water prices down and reduced incentives to maintain communal cisterns and wells because it was more convenient to buy water at low prices from private *birkas*. However, with the gradual decline of communal water points, private *birka* owners realized their strategic importance in supplying water. They subsequently increased the water prices. Because of a decline in technologies providing access to water, water became unaffordable during prolonged dry seasons, when it is scarce and prices are higher.

The move of wealthier clan members to construct private cisterns was a turning point in collective action for the joint management of communal water resources. Wealthier segments of the clan did not have further incentives to contribute to the maintenance of communal water points (cisterns, wells, ponds). In other words, it was the potential leadership group, the elite of the clans, who failed to deliver their share of collective action and thereby weakened the organizational capacities of the remaining clan members to act collectively for resource management. In effect, communal *birka* maintenance was considered an issue not for the whole clan but for the remaining clan members, who are often politically less influential and/or economically less powerful. This transformation of intraclan responsibilities and duties toward the pastoralist commons effectively changed the genealogical and social networks and connections that balance the rights–duties relationship inherent in customary rules.

Cistern owners have gained strong power over a strategic resource in the pastoralist economy, which potentially disfavors the poor and vulnerable clan members who depend on buying water from their cisterns (because communal water points have declined). Clan elders have often tried to negotiate with cistern owners in times of acute water scarcity to keep water prices at affordable levels for less wealthy clan members, but their action has not always been successful or only temporarily so. In Kebribeyah, clan elites have also tried to establish rules that forbid the construction of new private cisterns. Cistern owners stated that they were worried that additional cisterns would further disturb the grazing patterns and reduce the availability of grazing land, increasing the pressure on the remaining pastureland and leading to its eventual degradation. Cisterns also compete for watershed space, because they require a long water inflow channel. Those wishing to build new cisterns argued that the current cistern owners wanted to keep potential competitors out of the water market in order to be able to uphold water prices and secure oligopolistic gains from a limited number of cisterns.

Interestingly, in neighboring clan areas, similar agreements (not to allow establishment of new cisterns) can be found: in 1996, members of the Habr Yoonis clan in Gashamo District south of Kebribeyah made agreements not to establish new cisterns, as was done in the Ogaden and Isaaq controlled territories (Sugule and Walker 1998). The rapid spread of this rule has put pressure on clan elders in Kebribeyah to follow suit. In effect, this rule may increase wealth disparities at the expense of more vulnerable clan members, because those who in earlier years established the rule to allow construction of private cisterns now exclude potential newcomers who wish to join the club. The bargaining power of poor and vulnerable clan members to influence the elites in rule making is thereby limited. The individualization and commercialization of water as a commodity rather than as a common (club = clan) good has increased not only wealth disparities but also power differentials within the clan. It is a case of elite capture.

Ponds

In the study area, ponds are shallow earthen reservoirs dug to capture and store rainwater runoff. Compared to cisterns, they have a lower water retention capacity and are normally not cemented. Pond construction is a low-cost water-harvesting technique propagated by the central government in various campaigns and regional programs of community-based water management. This type of water-harvesting technique is tailored toward increasing farm productivity and encouraging the production of high-value crops. Pond construction was a traditional water-harvesting technique of agropastoral groups even prior to the government's intervention, but the government programs reinforced those traditions.

PHYSICAL ATTRIBUTES.   User groups need to provide labor for the construction of ponds as well as for maintenance (silt removal, fence construction and renewal, channel clearing). The capacity of ponds varies, on average, a communal pond contains up to 5,000 cubic meters of water, while privately constructed ones range from 150 to 200 cubic meters. If effectively managed, such ponds can retain water up to six months after the end of the major rainy season and the water availability from them is quite predictable and reliable. At the same time, infiltration losses are large because the walls and surfaces of the reservoirs are generally not cemented. Even cemented ponds experience water losses because the poor soil quality leads to cracks in the cement and resulting seepage. These technical limitations are site specific and predominant in Mieso. To reduce infiltration losses, the government propagated plastic sheets that were supplied for user groups on loan basis. However, most plastic sheets are used in private ponds rather than communal ones, because the sheets are not sufficiently large to cover larger communal ponds.

USER RIGHTS AND DUTIES.   A communal pond is a common property of *kebele* residents.[5] The Ethiopian government has made great efforts to encourage the construction of communal ponds as a means of water harvesting. According to the specifications of most government-initiated programs, user groups have the duty to contribute labor during construction and for maintenance.

---

5. A *kebele* is the lowest formal administrative unit, also termed a peasant association.

Noncontribution will result in oral warnings and financial fines. When a user remains absent during a day of communal labor, a warning is issued after the first day of absence. If he or she fails to contribute repeatedly, a fine will be imposed. The amount of fines is set in advance to avoid bias and ensure fairness. But it is subject to revision depending on a defector's health, physical ability, and wealth; the rich pay higher fines. Enforcement is exercised through the "team leader"—a person selected from among the users—with the support of elders. The team leader reports about payment of fines at village meetings. Poor users who cannot pay fines may compensate by providing double amounts of labor in the future. These are the kind of rules that exist "on paper"; they provide some flexibility in meeting the specific needs of poorer group members, but enforcement is often difficult due to other social obligations and reluctance to punish.

In principle, all members who have contributed have the right to use water from communal ponds, but access to water may be prioritized among users according to certain criteria, such as the numbers and types of animals to be watered or human versus livestock consumption. The rules (or enforcement of rules) for those who fail to contribute differ from place to place. In some locations, those who do not contribute will be excluded from water use. In other places, rather than excluding defectors, users collectively push defectors to contribute because exclusion is difficult to enforce due to the organizational challenge of monitoring water use and social obligations that may make it difficult to refuse water use to a member in need. Many communal ponds are located at considerable distances from places of residence, often in the middle of crop fields. Most of them are not fenced off, so stray animals can water in the ponds and exclusion is difficult to enforce without guards, making rule enforcement costly.

SOCIAL PRACTICES.   In our sample, ponds were constructed by agropastoralists only in Mieso and Kebrebeyah. Pond water allows some intensive farming and livestock-keeping activities but only in locations with good market access and natural conditions conducive to water harvesting. A number of agropastoralist households have started cultivating high-value crops (vegetables, fruits, *k'hat*) using water from the ponds. Other agropastoralist households use water for livestock fattening in conjunction with intensive feeding (using stalks and a cut-and-carry system), because the road to Addis Ababa provides good market access for livestock. Where pond water is used for crop farming, oxen ownership serves as an incentive to contribute labor during pond construction. However, those (asset-poor) households without oxen often rent oxen from wealthier farmers in order to ensure their contribution to pond construction. However, not all asset-poor households are able to pay for the rental, and those who cannot are potentially unable to derive benefit streams from their rights to use water; they are effectively excluded from these entitlements.

Government-led programs, such as those for water harvesting, tend to construct an additional organizational level (for example, the "team leader") and layer of rules that coexist with the established clan rules. Users prioritize clan rules and clan relations over rules and structures developed in the state-driven programs, because those programs are present for a short period of time only, whereas the clan, clan rules, and genealogical relations will prevail. This makes enforcement of rules difficult, because it requires the consent and tacit or explicit support of clan elders. Where the economic benefits that can be appropriated from ponds is significant, for instance, due to good market access, clan elders have a greater incentive to support the construction and management of ponds.

Multiple Technologies, Multiple Uses, Multiple Rules

In the (agro-)pastoralist economies of eastern Ethiopia, we found different tech-nologies with their own sets of rules and practices to make water available for human consumption, livestock watering, and irrigation purposes. Differential sets of rules in use have emerged around these different technologies depending on physical attributes, social relations, and economic incentives. Table 10.2 summarizes the attributes of the three technologies (ponds, cisterns, wells) in use among (agro-)pastoralists across the study sites.

Our research suggests that incentives for collective action in managing water technologies depend on economic cost–benefit considerations as well as on social norms. In the cases of all three technologies discussed here, exclusion of nonmembers is difficult to enforce, either because it is impossible to monitor water access or because it is socially unacceptable to exclude nonmembers. This reduces the incentives to contribute to collective action in maintaining those infrastructures, a problem particularly pertinent in the case of communal wells. Although in the case of ponds reciprocal and social obligations instill a kind of inclusive access practice, it is the opposite in the case of cisterns, where wealthy clan members have appropriated the technology of water use and estab-lished an oligopoly of cistern owners that has imposed new rules that forbid others to construct their own cisterns. This results in a form of elite capture of former common property through individualization of rights that comes at the expense of poorer segments of the clan and increases economic inequalities within clans.

Our research has shown that poor households may also practice enclosure, which offers them control over some types of benefit streams (such as cultiva-tion, charcoal burning). Overall, however, the enclosure and privatization pro-cess excludes many poor households from access to resources that are essential for livestock keeping (for example, access to water from private cisterns, for which they have to pay high prices). Some of the practices linked with priva-tized benefit streams are environmentally and economically unsustainable in the medium term. For example, many poor households use their enclosed land to sell its charcoal resources to private traders. This promises a short-term wind-

TABLE 10.2 Comparison of artifacts for water management at the three study sites

Artifacts	Ponds	Cisterns	Wells
Sites	Mieso, Kebribeyah	Kebribeyah, Harshin	All sites
Uses	Livestock, irrigation	Livestock, water sales	Livestock, drinking water
Resource location	On farm	Communal and enclosed land, close to settlement	Communal land, far away from settlements
Labor inputs	Constructing channels, silt removal, fencing, planting perennial trees	Digging, cementing, maintaining cracked walls, sharing costs of skilled labor	Digging, covering, and opening; preventing inflow of runoff; fencing
Physical attributes	Poor water retention capacity, water loss through evaporation; require a watershed to capture water inflow	High investment costs, lower amount of seepage; require a large water-shed to capture water inflow	High investment costs (digging) but durable if well maintained; point source
Access rules	Members only; unclear or under-specified user rules	Members only, reciprocal use for nonmembers, water sales to nonmembers	Members; nonmembers on a reciprocal basis; first-come, first-served rule; priority given to small herds
Enforcement	Enforcement through fines but exclusion difficult in practice	Exclusion relatively easy to monitor (close to settlement)	Exclusion from water use nearly impossible due to cultural norms and kinship obligations
Property rights	Club good but exclusion difficult to enforce	Private or communal	Attenuated due to reciprocity obligations
Management challenges	Large water losses	Conflict of interest between established cistern owners and potential new ones	High extraction costs, poor maintenance, disputes over who comes first
Effects on livelihoods	Incentives for crop production	Elite capture of water resources	Domination of reciprocity principle

SOURCE: Focus group discussions and interviews with elders and district experts.

fall gain but degrades the pasture basis and deprives users from future benefit streams.

Reciprocity and Social Obligation

The literature on pastoralism in the Greater Horn of Africa generally emphasizes clan membership as a precondition for access rights to pasture resources, which are confined to a clan's territory (Lewis 1999; Gebre 2001; Getachew 2001; Hagmann 2005). Access to pasture resources beyond a clan's territory requires negotiation and interclan cooperation (Unruh 2005). Interclan cooperation is based on kinship relations and reciprocal resource access; that is, access to clan territories and their resources is granted in the expectation that similar treatment will be returned by the receiving clan or another clan in similar conditions (this mostly occurs during dry season). A complex customary set of rules regulates access to grazing land and pasture resources for secondary users, that is, neighboring clans that ask for permission to use the communal grazing resources of another clan. Interclan kinship relations that exist because clan members have relatives within other clans with distinct territories are crucially important in these negotiations. These lineages and networks across clans or subclans have played an essential role in establishing the reciprocity principle (Lewis 1999; see also Unruh 1995). Somali pastoral society is organized on a genealogical basis, with lineages and their segmented units forming the basis for defining rights to clan territories and their communal grazing (and water) resources. Access to communal grazing is based on membership in a lineage responsible for and capable of defending such rights against competitors. Based on interclan genealogical linkages, co-users from other clans in the clan territory can therefore hold primary user rights and become important agents in negotiating secondary access rights for their fellow clan members who lack those genealogical linkages (Gebre 2001; Hagmann 2005, 2007; Unruh 2005; Beyene 2009).

Our research suggests that the spread of private enclosures in Kebribeyah and Harshen undermines the reciprocal system of granting access to grazing resources. At many places in our study area, clans have subdivided their territory and distributed the land to individual private rights holders or influential clan members have violated clan rules and created "facts on the ground" by unmaking the commons and constructing enclosure fences for cisterns or pastures. This reduces the overall availability of communal resources (pastureland and water) that could be subject to reciprocal exchange in negotiations with other clans over reciprocal sharing.

This situation becomes clear when considering the process of negotiating interclan reciprocal access arrangements. In our study area, each clan possesses primary user rights over its own clan territory and is expected to confine herd movement within the boundaries of this clan territory under "normal" conditions. Secondary user rights, that is, the right to use the communal grazing resources of a neighboring clan's territory, are considered adequate only in times of crisis when the clan's own pasture resources are insufficient due to drought or are inaccessible due to violent conflict with other clans. In our research, clan elders explained that interclan negotiation rituals encompass discussions of the rights to use communal water points, the length of stay in a clan's territory (the extent of grazing rights), the number of livestock to be admitted, agreements not to trespass enclosed lands of hosting clan members, complete payment of "blood money" (*mag*), and assurances that the livestock entering the clan territory is healthy (to avoid the spread of disease).[6] Clans usually grant access rights in prolonged dry seasons when grazing reservoirs have been used up. Enclosed pastureland and privatized water sources (such as cisterns) are not subjected to these interclan negotiations but require individual market-based transactions (rental contracts) between individual households of different clans. This reduces the leverage of clan elders in negotiations, makes mobility patterns across seasons and years more complicated and restricted, and decreases the options for adapting to and coping with drought conditions.

The problem of enclosure is not confined to our study areas. Indeed, a significant part of clan territories in northern Somali Region has become enclosed, that is, privately owned, and therefore is not subjected to interclan negotiations (Hagmann 2007). Other studies conducted in the Ethiopian context similarly suggest that changes in land tenure regimes favoring privatization and individualization, mostly of land, have discouraged mobility and undermined reciprocal sharing arrangements (Helland 1997, 1999, 2006; Tache 2000; Gebre 2001; Getachew 2001; Abdul, Swallow, and Kirk 2004; Hagmann 2006; Hundie 2008; Mulugeta and Hagmann 2008; Bogale and Korf 2009; Beyene 2010a, 2010b). Further, Mulugeta and Hagmann (2008) suggest that enclosure, individualization of tenure, and privatization of access rights—the unmaking of the commons—was significantly reinforced by the administrative decentralization of the Ethiopian state. Physical violence is the result of individual and group attempts to increase a clan's territorial boundaries in order to become less dependent on interclan reciprocal arrangements.

Our research suggests another problem emerging from the unmaking of the commons that is less discussed in the literature: access to grazing land is effective only if granted in combination with access to water. Through privatization of water resources, access to grazing land and to water becomes subject to negotiations on different levels. In interclan negotiations, the right to communal grazing land is generally granted in combination with access to communal water sources but not in combination with access to private water sources, which requires individual contractual arrangements with the owners. Where

---

6. Blood money is compensation for persons killed or wounded in interclan strife and is paid in cash or in kind to the relatives and kinship group of the victim (Hagmann 2007).

water is not available from communal sources, secondary users have to negoti-ate individual access to private water sources (and pay for the water). This means that the granting of grazing rights (including the right to use communal water sources) on an interclan level may not be sufficient for poor pastoral households to transform their access rights to pasture into economically viable user rights because of inadequate access rights to water. In our research area, this situation triggered a differentiation of secondary users between those wealthy enough to buy water from private cistern owners and those poorer clan members who could not afford to buy water from private cisterns.

Conclusions

Regimes of property rights to pastoral resources have undergone dynamic changes in eastern Ethiopia. Our research has shown a pertinent trend toward privatizing and individualizing benefit streams to resources, whereby rights to those benefits are individualized but the duties—for instance, to maintain com-munal resources—are externalized. This process of privatization, individual-ization, and enclosure, or the subdividing of the pastoralist commons (Mwangi 2007), has become a widely observed phenomenon in pastoralist societies in eastern Africa and in the literature is often attributed to the commoditization and diversification of resource use, governmental interventions, unclear tenure legislation, and ambivalent clan rule (Niamir-Fuller 1999; Manger 2000; Salih, Dietz, and Ahmed 2001; Unruh 2005; Abdulahi 2007; Mwangi 2007; Beyene 2008, 2009; Hagmann and Mulugeta 2008; Homewood 2008; Hundie 2008). This literature generally suggests that the individualization and privatization of pasture regimes disturbs reciprocal resource sharing between different clans and also herd mobility. In our case study in eastern Ethiopia, we found similar problems, but our focus was on the effects of individualization and privatization on customary practices of collective action and intraclan social obligations in managing pasture resources.

Our research has shown that property rights to land and its multiple resources (for example, pastureland, water, wood) are central in defining incen-tives for collective action. Even genealogical rights–duties relationships of reciprocal obligations—the "clan" factor in Somali society—come under scru-tiny when privatization and individualization of property rights take place. In our study area, private cistern construction has reduced incentives to maintain communal wells and water points, as has land enclosure. Both patterns of individualizing access rights have disturbed the reciprocal resource-sharing arrangements between different clans and have also induced interclan disputes and restricted mobility patterns and thereby coping strategies in times of re-source scarcity. The de facto privatization and individualization of property rights has provided some clan members with secure access to resources and addi-tional income, for instance, by selling production inputs to other users. In many instances, poor households have been excluded from such benefit streams or have been burdened with additional costs to access pasture resources. For example, in some places in our study area, poor households were increasingly forced to buy water at private cisterns because communal water points were dilapidated. Owners of private cisterns did not have an incentive to contribute to collective action in managing these communal resources.

The broader conclusions that can be drawn from our case study are therefore that the unmaking of the pastoral commons unravels patterns of reciprocity and social obligation, both intraclan and interclan. In some cases, unmaking the commons may lead to entitlement failures. On the interclan level, the use of reciprocal customary mobility patterns as a strategy of risk coping is becoming more difficult, increasing the risk that marginal pastoralist households are experiencing in the face of climatic variability. Although wealthier households are able to pay for access to privatized resources (for example, water, contract grazing), asset-poor households cannot afford to do so and experience entitlement failures and a shrinking of their coping capabilities. In particular, although interclan negotiation may entail access to pasture commons, asset-poor households may fail to capture the associated benefit streams when water access is privatized and prohibitively priced. In such cases, clan members may have endowments to some commons resources (here pasturelands) but will not enjoy entitlement to actual benefit streams because of exclusion from others (in this case, water).

Policy Implications

Any kind of policy recommendation needs to be read within the context of the Ethiopian state's politics of pastoralist development and "ethnic federalism." Past and present land tenure policies have tended to discriminate against the communal interests of pastoralist communities (Helland 2006; Abdulahi 2007; Hagmann 2007). The federal government's policy has not yet resulted in a balanced land tenure policy on regional levels that would account for both customary modes of communal land use and emerging trends in privatized land use (Helland 2006). The latest version of the federal Rural Land Administration and Land Use Proclamation 456/2005 reinstates the doctrine that all land is state property with ambivalent effects on the communal rights of pastoralists: "The Government being the owner of rural land, communal rural landholdings can be changed to private holdings as may be necessary" (para. 5, 3). This means that communal land can be easily appropriated for private purposes and user rights be individualized, thereby substantially weakening communally held rights.

Collective action on a local scale—cooperation among a group of users of communal resources—is insufficient to counter the unmaking of the commons. It needs to be complemented by a land tenure policy that ensures the rights of communal users. Privatization and individualization of property rights to pastoral resources often comes at the expense of less endowed pastoralist households that lack access to clan power and financial resources to even out the diminishing returns from communally managed resources. Externally funded programs for collective action to manage communal resources are often insufficient to effectively support the poor, especially when they are paralleled by such a trend of privatizing water (and subsequently pasture) access by influential, wealthy clan members. The Ethiopian government's program that supports the construction of communal ponds for water harvesting is a good example of this dilemma. This program addresses poorer households but often fails to provide them with viable access to water. Ponds suffer from technological deficiencies (high seepage rates). In our study area, ponds have been economically viable only in a few places with good market access where vegetable production has been possible.

The Somali Regional State in Ethiopia has given the powers to define communal versus private user rights to clan rulers. Our study shows that this has had ambivalent effects; elite capture has encouraged some clan elites to drive forward a politics of enclosure, which excludes asset-poor households from benefit streams, encourages unsustainable land use practices (for instance, charcoal production as windfall gain), and disturbs customary reciprocity patterns among and between clans. The disturbance of these patterns has triggered violent disputes over resource access, as Hagmann and Mulugeta (2008) have shown. This indicates that clans and customary rule systems are not "innocent" or best adapted to environmental and social requirements, nor has the state found a constructive role yet in the encounter between pastoralism and clan societies. It is the redefinition of this relationship that is needed most urgently to deal with the unmaking of the commons.

References

Abdul, K., B. Swallow, and M. Kirk. 2004. Policies, interventions and institutional change in pastoral resource management in Borana, Southern Ethiopia. *Development Policy Review* 22 (4): 381–403.

Abdulahi, M. 2004. Pastoral development strategies/policies in Ethiopia: A critical analysis and evaluation. In *Proceedings of the Third National Conference on Pastoral Development in Ethiopia: Pastoralism and Sustainable Pastoral Development*. Addis Ababa, Ethiopia: Ethiopia Pastoralist Forum.

———. 2007. The legal status of the communal landholding system in Ethiopia: The case of pastoral communities. *International Journal on Minority and Group Rights* 14 (1): 85–125.

Agarwal, R. J. 2000. Possibilities and limitations to cooperation in small groups: The case of group-owned wells in Southern India. *World Development* 28 (8): 1481–1497.

Banerjee, A., D. Mookherjee, K. Munshi, and D. Ray. 2001. Inequality, control rights and rent seeking: Sugar cooperatives in western Maharashtra. *Journal of Political Economy* 109 (1): 138–190.

Bardhan, P. K. 2000. Irrigation and cooperation: An empirical analysis of 48 irrigation communities in South India. *Economic Development and Cultural Change* 48 (4): 847–865.

Beyene, F. 2008. *Challenges and options in governing common property: Customary institutions among (agro-)pastoralists in Ethiopia.* Aachen, Germany: Shaker.

———. 2009. Property rights conflict, customary institutions and the state: The case of agro-pastoralists in Mieso District, eastern Ethiopia. *Journal of Modern African Studies* 47 (2): 213–239.

———. 2010a. Customary tenure and reciprocal grazing arrangements in eastern Ethiopia. *Development and Change* 41 (1): 107–129.

———. 2010b. Locating the effects of rangeland enclosure among herders in eastern Ethiopia. *Land Use Policy* 27 (2): 480–488.

Bogale, A., and B. Korf. 2007. To share or not to share? (Non-)violence, scarcity and resource access in Somali Region, Ethiopia. *Journal of Development Studies* 43 (4): 743–765.

———. 2009. Resource entitlement and mobility of pastoralists in Yerer and Daketa Valleys, Eastern Ethiopia. *Human Ecology* 37 (4): 453–462.

Boku, T. 2000. Changing patterns of resource control among the Borana pastoralists of southern Ethiopia: A lesson for developing agencies. In *Pastoralists and environment: Experiences from the greater Horn of Africa,* ed. L. Manger and A. G. M. Ahmed. Addis Ababa: Organisation for Social Science Research in Eastern and Southern Africa.

Bromley, D. W. 1991. *Environment and economy: Property rights and public policy.* Cambridge, Mass., U.S.A.: Blackwell.

Cleaver, F. 2000. Moral ecological rationality: Institutions and the management of common property resources. *Development and Change* 31 (2): 361–383.

Cousins, B. 1996. Conflict management for multiple resource users in pastoralist and agro-pastoralist contexts. *IDS Bulletin* 27 (3): 41–54.

Dayton-Johnson, J. 2000. Determinants of collective action on local commons: A model with evidence from Mexico. *Journal of Development Economics* 62 (1): 181–208.

Devereux, S. 2006. *Vulnerable livelihoods in Somali Region, Ethiopia.* IDS Research Report 57. Brighton, U.K.: Institute of Development Studies.

FDRE (Federal Democratic Republic of Ethiopia), Ministry of Federal Affairs. 2002. *Statement on pastoral development policy.* Addis Ababa.

———, Ministry of Finance and Economic Development. 2003. *Rural development policy and strategies.* Addis Ababa.

Gächter, S., B. Herrmann, and C. Thoni. 2004. Trust, voluntary cooperation, and socioeconomic background: Survey and experimental evidence. *Journal of Economic Behavior and Organization* 55 (4): 505–531.

Gadamu, F. 1994. The post-revolutionary rethinking of arid land policy in Ethiopia. *Nomadic Peoples* 34–35: 69–79.

———. 2000. *Arid land and the role of pastoral nomads in the economic and political integration of the Horn of Africa with particular reference to Ethiopia.* Occasional Paper 15. Addis Ababa: Ethiopian International Institute for Peace and Development.

Gebre, A. 2001. *Pastoralism under pressure: Land alienation and pastoral transformations among the Karrayu of eastern Ethiopia, 1941 to present.* Aachen, Germany: Shaker.

Gebremedhin, B., J. Pender, and G. Tesfay. 2004. Collective action for grazing land management in crop–livestock mixed systems in the highlands of northern Ethiopia. *Agricultural Systems* 82 (3): 273–290.

Getachew, K. 2001. Resource conflicts among the Afar of north-east Ethiopia. In *African Pastoralism: Conflict, institutions and government,* ed. M. A. Mohamed Salih, T. Dietz, and A. G. M. Ahmed. London: Pluto.

Hagmann, T. 2005. Beyond clannishness and colonialism: Understanding political disorder in Ethiopia's Somali Region. *Journal of Modern African Studies* 43 (4): 509–536.

———. 2006. Pastoral conflict and resource management in Ethiopia's Somali Region. Ph.D. dissertation, Institut de hautes études en administration publique, Université de Lausanne, Switzerland.

———. 2007. Bringing the sultan back in: Elders as peacemakers in Ethiopia's Somali Region. In *A new dawn for traditional authorities? State recognition and democratization in Sub-Saharan Africa,* ed. L. Buur and H. M. Kyed. New York: Palgrave.

Hagmann, T., and A. Mulugeta. 2008. Pastoral conflicts and state-building in the Ethiopian lowlands. *Afrika Spectrum* 43 (1): 19–37.

Halderman, M. 2004. *The political economy of pro-poor livestock policy-making in Ethiopia.* Pro-Poor Livestock Policy Initiative Working Paper 19. Rome: Food and Agriculture Organization of the United Nations.

Helland, J. 1997. Development interventions and pastoral dynamics in southern Ethiopia. In *Pastoralists, ethnicity and the state in Ethiopia,* ed. R. Hogg. London: Haan.

———. 1999. Land alienation in Borana: Some land tenure issues in a pastoral context in Ethiopia. *Eastern African Social Science Research Review* 15 (2): 1–19.

———. 2006. Land tenure in the pastoral areas of Ethiopia. Paper presented at the International Workshop on Property Rights, Collective Action and Poverty Reduction in Pastoral Areas of Afar and Somali National Regional States, Ethiopia, October 30–31, in Addis Ababa.

Hogg, R. 1996. Government policy and pastoralism: Some critical issues. In *Conference on Pastoralism in Ethiopia, 4–6 February 1993,* ed. S. Edwards and Tafesse Mesfin. Addis Ababa: Ministry of Agriculture.

———. 1997. Introduction. In *Pastoralists, ethnicity and the state in Ethiopia,* ed. R. Hogg. London: Haan.

Homewood, K. 2008. *Ecology of African pastoralist societies.* Oxford: James Currey.

Hundie, B. 2008. *Pastoralism, institutions and social interaction: Explaining the co-existence of conflict and cooperation in pastoral Afar, Ethiopia.* Aachen, Germany: Shaker.

Kandel, E., and E. D. Lazear. 1992. Peer pressure and partnerships. *Journal of Political Economy* 100 (4): 801–817.

Kassa, B., F. Beyene, and W. Manig. 2005. Coping with drought among pastoral and agro-pastoral communities in eastern Ethiopia. *Journal of Rural Development* 28 (Winter): 185–201.

Lane, C. R., ed. 1998. *Custodians of the commons: Pastoral land tenure in East and West Africa.* London: Earthscan.

Lewis, I. M. 1999. *A pastoral democracy: A study of pastoralism and politics among the northern Somali of the Horn of Africa,* 3rd ed. Hamburg, Germany: LIT.

Little, P. D., K. Smith, B. A. Cellarius, D. L. Coppock, and C. Barrett. 2001. Avoiding disaster: Diversification and risk management among east African herders. *Development and Change* 32 (3): 401–433.

Manger, L. 2000. East African pastoralism and underdevelopment: An introduction. In *Pastoralists and environment: Experiences from the Greater Horn of Africa,* ed. L. Manger and A. G. M. Ahmed. Addis Ababa: Organisation for Social Science Research in Eastern and Southern Africa.

Marshall, G. 1998. *A dictionary of sociology.* New York: Oxford University Press.

McCarthy, N., C. Dutilly-Diane, and B. Drabo. 2004. Cooperation, collective action and natural resource management in Burkina Faso. *Agricultural Systems* 82 (3): 233–255.

Moris, Jon R. 1999. *Under three flags: The policy environments for pastoralism in Ethiopia and Kenya.* SR/GL–CRSP Pastoral Risk Management Project Technical Report 04/99. Logan, Utah, U.S.A.: Utah State University.

Mulugeta, A., and T. Hagmann. 2008. Governing violence in the pastoralist space: Karrayu and state notions of cattle raising in the Ethiopian Awash Valley. *Africa Focus* 21 (2): 71–87.

Mwangi, E. 2007. Subdividing the commons: Distributional conflict in the transition from collective to individual property rights in Kenya's Maasiland. *World Development* 35 (5): 815–834.

Ngaido, T. 1999. Can pastoral institutions perform without access options? In *Property rights, risk and livestock development in Africa,* ed. N. McCarthy, B. Swallow, M. Kirk, and P. Hazell. Washington, D.C.: International Food Policy Research Institute.

Niamir-Fuller, M., ed. 1999. *Managing mobility in African rangelands.* London: Intermediate Technology Publications.

Ostrom, E. 1998. A behavioral approach to the rational choice theory of collective action. *American Political Science Review* 92 (1): 1–22.

Place, F., G. Kariuki, J. Wangila, P. Kristjanson, A. Makauki, and J. Ndubi. 2004. Assessing the factors underlying differences in achievement of farmer groups: Methodological issues and empirical findings from the highlands of central Kenya. *Agricultural Systems* 82 (3): 257–272.

Runge, F. C. 1986. Common property and collective action in economic development. *World Development* 14 (5): 623–635.

Salih, M. A. M., T. Dietz, and A. G. M. Ahmed. 2001. *African pastoralism: Conflicts, institutions and government.* London: Pluto.

Samatar, A. I. 2004. Ethiopian federalism: Autonomy versus control in the Somali Region. *Third World Quarterly* 25 (6): 1131–1154.

Samuel, B., and J. Pender. 2006. Collective action in community management of grazing lands: The case of the highlands of northern Ethiopia. *Environment and Development Economics* 11: 127–149.

Scoones, I., and O. Graham. 1994. New directions for pastoral development in Africa. *Development Practice* 14 (4): 188–198.

Singleton, S., and M. Taylor. 1992. Common property, collective action and community. *Journal of Theoretical Politics* 4 (3): 309–324.

Sugule, J., and R. Walker. 1998. *Changing pastoralism in the Ethiopian Somali National Regional State.* Survey Report. Addis Ababa, Ethiopia: South East Rangelands Project and United Nations Development Programme Emergencies Unit for Ethiopia.

Tache, B. 2000. Changing patterns of resource control among the Borana pastoralists of southern Ethiopia: A lesson for development agencies. In *Pastoralists and environment: Experiences from the Greater Horn of Africa,* ed. L. Manger and A. G. M. Ahmed. Addis Ababa: Organisation for Social Science Research in Eastern and Southern Africa.

Thébaud, B., and S. Batterby. 2001. Sahel pastoralists: Opportunism, struggle, conflict and negotiation: A case study from eastern Niger. *Global Environmental Change* 11 (1): 69–78.

Unruh, J. D. 1995. Pastoralist resource use and access in Somalia: A changing context of development, environmental stress and conflict. In *Disaster and development in the Horn of Africa,* ed. J. Sorennson. London: Macmillan.

———. 2005. Changing conflict resolution institutions in the Ethiopian pastoral commons: The role of armed confrontation in rule-making. *GeoJournal* 64 (3): 225–237.

Vanderlinden, J. P. 1999. Conflicts and co-operation over the commons: A conceptual and methodological framework for assessing the role of local institutions. In *Property rights, risk and livestock development in Africa,* ed. N. McCarthy, B. Swallow, M. Kirk, and P. Hazell. Washington, D.C.: International Food Policy Research Institute.

Vedeld, T. 1994. *The state and rangeland management: Creation and erosion of pastoral institutions in Mali.* Dryland Networks Programs. IIED Paper 46. London: Institute for Environment and Development.

Wade, R. 1987. *Village republics: Economic conditions for collective action in south India.* Cambridge, U.K.: Cambridge University Press.

Watkins, B., and M. L. Fleisher. 2002. Tracking pastoralist migration: Lessons from the Ethiopian Somali National Regional State. *Human Organization* 61 (4): 328–338.

Watson, E. 2003. Examining the potential of indigenous institutions for development: A perspective from Borana, Ethiopia. *Development and Change* 34 (2): 287–310.

Yacob, A. 2000. Pastoralism in Ethiopia: The issues of viability. Conference paper, National Conference on Pastoral Development in Ethiopia, February 2, in Addis Ababa, Ethiopia.

11 Escaping Poverty Traps? Collective Action and Property Rights in Postwar Rural Cambodia

ANNE WEINGART AND MICHAEL KIRK

Collective action and property rights are able to shape people's livelihoods. The conceptual framework presented in Chapter 2 shows that property rights shape people's claims to benefit streams out of their owned resources and have an impact on their asset base. When property rights are suited to address people's needs, they have a better chance to shape their livelihoods and to escape poverty traps. Secure access to resources increases a household's capital base and broadens (poor) people's capacities to engage in activities to improve their well-being. Effective collective action increases or secures people's access to resources and can also enable households to improve their livelihoods. Thus, collective action also becomes part of people's strategies to shape property rights and increase their well-being.

Both property rights and collective action were severely challenged in Cambodia by the Khmer Rouge regime. After democratic consolidation, attempts to (re-)create a legal framework that secures access to land and natural resources were made by the Royal Government of Cambodia (RGC) and strongly supported by major donors. Nevertheless, the introduction of laws and decrees created new uncertainties among the rural poor and advantaged the more powerful (Global Witness 2007). Resource degradation and conversion of natural resources into arable land has left Cambodia's rural poor with ever fewer options to derive income from these resources. Furthermore, a relatively slow rate of land titling in rural areas or unclear parcel boundary demarcations have left less powerful people vulnerable to land grabbing and excluded them from the benefits of common property (Catalla 2001; Sovannarith et al. 2001; Törhönen and Palmer 2004). Collective action also still suffers from the Khmer Rouge legacy, because large segments of traditional social ties such as mutual help networks, religious institutions, and even family ties have been destroyed (Mehmet 1997). Collectivization under the communist regime also left marks on the willingness of the Cambodians to cooperate in agriculture to a larger extent.

The objective of the case study reported in this chapter was to identify effective practices and policy interventions at a local level that enhance the way in which cooperation or collective action and property rights have been used and shaped to build up secure assets and income streams for the rural poor in Cambodia. In order to provide policymakers, community groups, civil society organizations, and researchers with a better understanding of the property regimes in place, we assess existing property rights systems in rural Cambodia to identify what benefit streams poor people can rely on for their livelihood. We identify existing forms and mechanisms of economic and social cooperation, how they influence property rights systems, and to what extent the rural poor are part of village networks that contribute to resource protection. Based on this assessment, concrete linkages and feedback mechanisms among property rights, collective action, and poverty are analyzed at a village level. In concrete terms, we show what (common) resources poor households can use, what property rights systems govern these resources, and whether collective action, which is re-emerging after the genocide, helps poor people to address their needs. From these findings some policy implications can be drawn.

In terms of the conceptual framework explained in Chapter 2, we focus on three key aspects of the context: the lack of assets and weak asset accumulation for the poor, the vulnerability of people to both natural and political risks, and the legal structures and power relations that disadvantage the poor. A major part of empirical data from the exploratory study on property rights and collective action in rural Cambodia concentrates on the effects of these contextual factors. The action arena in this case is postconflict rebuilding, in which local resource users and the state are key actors that make use of institutions of property rights and collective action, as well as changing these institutions. Education, social groups, and land rights are key action resources, but lack of these prevents many rural Cambodians from engaging in this action arena effectively. The patterns of interaction that emerge indicate that mutual help networks, religious activities, and small-scale associations are regaining ground in Cambodia. However, these types of associations, though they aim to help the rural poor, actually cannot reach them properly. Poor people lack confidence (a key action resource) to take part in associations and sometimes are unable to use their services. In addition, collective action to secure natural resources is not yet successful in addressing ongoing resource degradation. Formal, legally backed institutions still lack local recognition and are thus unable to enforce rules set up to protect rice fields, forests, or fish ponds. Villages that manage their resources on traditional principles tend to cooperate better across village boundaries and are thus more successful in natural resource management, leading to positive feedback to the asset base. Nevertheless, they too are unable to protect their base against increasing interventions from outsiders. Observed low degrees of cooperation in natural resource management are an outcome of low degrees of mutual trust. This lack of trust will have to be considered when implementing grassroots development projects on the ground.

The theme of risk and vulnerability to shocks is prominent in Cambodia, where both natural resource fluctuations and major political upheavals have pushed millions into poverty and created the need for individual and collective coping mechanisms. Although market development is not much advanced, natural resource governance and access to resources shape the interactions within communities and with the state. Conflict and postconflict development are major themes in this case; the Pol Pot terror regime and civil war have left scars in the social fabric. Our case study also examined the extent of elite capture as the outcome of interactions between different groups within communities and with outsiders.

The Background of Cambodia

Cambodia is a Southeast Asian country with a gross national income per capita of US$380 (World Bank 2006). Its main income source is agriculture (19.1 percent of gross domestic product at 2005 current prices), growing at a below-average rate. Around 80 percent of the Cambodian population lives in rural areas, where 72.5 percent are employed in the agricultural sector. In 2004, 35 percent of the Cambodian population lived below the national poverty line of US$0.45 per capita per day, with the highest poverty incidence in rural areas. Cambodians living in rural areas account for nearly 91 percent of the country's poor (World Bank 2006). This high poverty incidence has largely resulted from high population pressure on the limited natural resources in the rainfed lowlands, inadequate job opportunities and low capabilities, the insecurity of access to land and other productive assets, continuing exclusion of poor communities from economic growth, and high vulnerability due to natural disasters, violence, and economic shocks (World Bank 1999; Acharya et al. 2001; EIC 2005).[1] Although more than 70 percent of Cambodia's population is employed in agricultural production, large shares do not have access to arable land. Landlessness among rural households rose from 12.6 percent in 1997 to 19.6 percent in 2004 (Sophal, Saravy, and Acharya 2001; RGC 2002b; World Bank 2006).

Because Cambodia is a rural economy, most of the Cambodian population lives in low, arable plains, where natural resources are crucial in securing livelihoods for the poor because they contribute a large share to household incomes (Turton, 2000; Acharya and Sophal 2002; Marschke 2004; World Bank 2006). Such resources are able to contribute to poverty reduction given secure access and sustainable use (Hach and Sothea 2004). Furthermore, natural resources

---

1. According to the United Nations Population Fund (UNFPA 2005), Cambodia's population growth rate is 2.4 percent, which is relatively high compared with neighboring countries where the populations are growing by 1.4 percent (Vietnam) and 1.0 percent (Thailand). Furthermore, Cambodia's population is less concentrated in the cities than are its neighbors' populations.

have multiple uses for income generation by multiple users, ranging from the collection of nontimber forest products for subsistence to additional income generation through logging at different scales and fishery operations (Degen et al. 2000; Fraser and Department of Forestry and Wildlife 2000; McKenney and Tola 2002; Baran 2005). Access to resources, however, is defined by multiple and often overlapping rights, both private and common, which are in turn governed by formal and informal patterns of cooperation. Therefore, the ability of people to decide and act together plays an important role in improving rural livelihoods (see Chapter 2 of this volume). As an outcome of the process of political stabilization and re-establishment of government institutions in the country from the mid-1990s on, cooperative management approaches were recognized (or even reinvented) by the government, civil society organizations, and the private sector as potentially successful governance patterns not only for individual livelihood generation but also to achieve more sustainable resource use.

To understand the sensitivity of those recent initiatives and the high risk of failure in their implementation, it is important to take Cambodia's recent history of civil war into account. In 1975 the Khmer Rouge came into power and introduced a totalitarian agrarian communism (Chandler 1996) whereby Cambodians had to provide forced labor. The Khmer Rouge abolished private ownership; destroyed existing infrastructure, including written evidence of land ownership or use rights; and systematically killed intellectuals, government employees, and monks. In 1979, Vietnamese troops overcame the Khmer Rouge regime and introduced a centrally planned economy and state-owned rural producer cooperatives. Currently Cambodia superficially appears to be a peaceful country; however, the years of unrest left marks on Cambodia's physical, human, and social capital, and a painful reconstruction process is ongoing.

Due to Cambodia's recent history, legal pluralism exists there (Simbolon 2002). Property rights have developed under the different regimes that Cambodians have faced over time: the traditional Khmer regime (with property rights similar to usufruct), French colonization (introducing private property and individual land ownership), the Khmer Rouge regime (abolition of any private property), and the Vietnamese-supported People's Republic of Kampuchea (collectivization of property with different levels of individually secured use rights). Restricted private ownership was reintroduced in 1989, when Cambodia started to transform its socialist system to a market economy (Williams 1999). Constant changes in property-related law created a legal plurality, with traditional and statutory rights coexisting (for example, the Land Law of 2003, a vast body of legislation on natural resources together with reacknowledged unwritten indigenous rights [RGC 2001]). Today the legal framework is still weak, with different components developing at different speeds and discrepancies in the level of implementation (van Acker 2003).

Cambodian Case Study: Research Methodology

We employed a mixture of methods of empirical research for our case study during the field research phases, which were conducted between April 2005 and February 2007. In the first step, we conducted interviews and group discussions with local to national nongovernmental organizations (NGOs), donor agencies, and ministerial staff in order to identify research sites. We selected these sites with regard to criteria reflecting different experiences with formalized institutions for cooperation, their natural resource endowments, and their accessibility to the research team in the rainy season. The selected research sites are situated in central Cambodia in the provinces of Kampong Thom and Kampong Cham, both located in the major floodplains of the country. With the support of collaborating organizations, in the final step we chose four villages: Chrang Krohom and Leuk in Kampong Thom and Krorsang and Svay Teap in Kampong Cham. These villages differ in terms of the kinds of resources available to the population; their accessibility, income sources, and natural resource management institutions and practices; and the degree to which these villages receive external support, such as that from NGOs.[2] None of the villages is equipped with electricity or sanitation infrastructure, but all have access to a primary school.[3] Table 11.1 gives an overview of village characteristics as stated above.

Empirical data collection at the four sites included (1) semistructured interviews with key informants to gather information on village structure and development; (2) a household survey; (3) group discussions and the drawing of resource maps to identify changes in the resource base and to assess the property rights of different user groups; and (4) the collection of economic experimental evidence to asses trust levels in the villages.[4] We employed secondary data analysis at the provincial and national capitals to fill gaps that the field research could not address.

---

2. Accessibility is restricted by temporary isolation during the rainy season, lack of roads for four-wheeled vehicles, distance to the main marketplaces, and poor availability of public transportation.

3. The village of Svay Teap cannot provide education to its villagers currently; it has established a self-organized school for which no teacher is available at the moment.

4. The information on village structure and development included data on the villages' socioeconomic backgrounds, histories, demographics, and infrastructure. The household survey included information on income sources, past and current engagement in collective action, participation in village decisionmaking processes, and asset endowments. The sample was randomly chosen by the researchers based on a household list obtained from the village authorities or with their assistance. Trust games based on Berg, Dickhaut, and McCabe (1995) were played in all four villages. On the role of field experiments, see Cardenas and Ostrom (2004).

TABLE 11.1 Characteristics of the research sites in rural Cambodia

Province	Village	Main income source (percent)	Resource	Resource use	External support
Kampong Thom	Chrang Krohom	Rice cultivation (97.1)	Forest	Subsistence: nontimber products (NTP)	Strong external support
			Lake	Subsistence: fishing, water plant harvesting	
	Leuk	Rice cultivation (97.1)	Forest	Subsistence and religious customs and services	Strong external support
			Lake	Subsistence: fishing, water plant harvesting	
Kampong Cham	Krorsang	Cash cropping (88.6)	Forest	Subsistence: NTP	Low external support
	Svay Teap	Rice cultivation (78.1)	Forest	Subsistence: NTP and religious customs and services	No external support
			Lake	Subsistence: fishing, water plant harvesting	

SOURCE: Authors' data.

Research Results

Household and Village Characteristics

In the household survey we compiled data from 146 households in all four villages, randomly chosen by the researchers based on a household list obtained from the village authorities or with the village authorities' assistance. At least one-fifth of each village's households were included in the survey. All villages are similar in their household characteristics. Table 11.2 provides an overview of these household characteristics. The average size of the households interviewed was six persons, and their average educational level was 1.6 years in school. On average, 46.5 percent of the villagers engaged in different forms of collective action.

A very large share of the households diversified their income over more than one source. The households also relied on natural resources for livelihood generation.[5] Table 11.3 provides an overview of income diversification at the study sites.

In Kampong Thom Province, the villages of Chrang Krohom and Leuk use adjacent forest and water resources for subsistence and have been supported by international donors and NGOs in the past. At least seven formal associations exist in Chrang Krohom, offering credit and religious services, natural resource management, and advisory services to village authorities.

In order to improve forest resource management, village authorities established a community forest organization that is already in place but still lacks legal recognition. The goal of this forest organization is to protect the local forest against overexploitation and, where necessary, to start reforestation. Water resources are traditionally managed by the villagers themselves. However, there are efforts to further formalize existing water resource management: at the moment, the village committee manages the resource and takes action when problems arise.[6] Water resource management is mainly meant to guarantee the water needed for agriculture but also to keep the fish stock at sustainable levels to ensure continuous income during the dry season. Chrang Krohom has been supported by donor agencies, NGOs, and a major Cambodian political party. Agricultural extension services, infrastructure improvement, and assistance to establish credit associations have been provided to supplement the work of the existing community forest organization.

In contrast to the situation at Chrang Krohom, at the village of Leuk both the communal forest and the local pond are managed in common by the village

---

5. These natural resources include the resources that people use for income-generating activities, such as commercial fishing. Activities to support livelihoods are also included. Examples of these are collecting mushrooms, catching crabs, or harvesting water lilies.

6. The Village Committee consists of the village leader, who is appointed by the government; the vice village leader; and some elders who are respected and trusted by most villagers.

TABLE 11.2 Overview of households surveyed

Characteristic	*n*	Share	Percentage
Female-headed households	146	26	17.8
Land poor (0–1 hectare)	146	60	41.1
Illiteracy rate	146	42	28.8
Dependence on natural resources for income generation	146	87	59.6

SOURCE: Authors' data.

TABLE 11.3 Income diversification at the research sites

Village	Share of households that diversify their income (percent)	Income sources (percent)	Natural resource on which the village is most dependent (percent)
Chrang Krohom	97.1	Rice cultivation (97.1)	Forest (25.7)
		Cash cropping (91.2)	Water (20.0)
		Fishing (41.0)	
Leuk	97.2	Rice cultivation (97.1)	Forest (25.7)
		Cash cropping (67.7)	Water (11.4)
		Small businesses (23.0)	
Krorsang	88.1	Rice cultivation (42.9)	Forest (34.3)
		Cash cropping (88.6)	Water (not available)
		Small businesses (22.9)	
Svay Teap	74.3	Rice cultivation (78.1)	Forest (51.4)
		Cash cropping (71.9)	Water (37.1)

SOURCE: Authors' data.

authorities of all three neighboring villages that use these resources jointly. The forest serves not only as an important income source but also as a social space for religious festivities that are jointly celebrated with neighboring villages. Four formal associations are active in Leuk. They provide credit and religious services and advise the village authorities. Leuk received support from donor agencies and NGOs for agricultural extension and to establish rice banks. Funds are raised to finance common activities to improve infrastructure.

In Kampong Cham Province, we studied the villages of Krorsang and Svay Teap. Krorsang faced major in-migration, with the village population increasing by about 50 percent during the five years before our study. It depends only on forest resources for livelihood generation. The local forest is allocated to the commune and is hence used by several villages jointly. One association guarantees its members' access to credit. At the commune level a community forest organization is in place that aims to protect the forest against illegal deforestation and to provide subsistence income for poor villagers in particular. Krorsang was supported by NGOs and government programs in establishing its community forest organization and a credit association, and it received support to improve its accessibility.

In contrast to all other villages, Svay Teap only recently began to receive government support to improve its accessibility. It uses forest and water resources that have both been managed traditionally by village elders. The forest area is also used for religious festivities shared with surrounding villages. There is one association in Svay Teap, which was established to support women against domestic violence.

The villages thus differ in the ways they manage their natural resources and the extent to which people act collectively within them. The following section will present more detailed findings on the role of property rights in natural resource management at the local level.

Property Rights, Natural Resource Use, and Cooperation:
Processes and Actors

Secured access to land and other resources is of major importance for sustaining livelihoods in Cambodian rural areas. Rice cultivation and cash cropping (for instance, raising soybeans and yams) are the main income sources of the rural population. Natural resources are mainly used by the rural poor to complement their small income. Therefore, this section first focuses on access to and use of natural resources and then gives an overview of the effects of resulting conflicts on livelihoods.

Natural resources such as forests and lakes, ponds, and other water units are, as the Land Law (RGC 2001) states, owned by the state as either "public" or "private" state domain. Privatization of these resources is endorsed by the Land Law under very restricted conditions only (Kirk 2004). Complementary to property rights legislation, resource management is regulated by different laws, decrees, and regulations executed by different government departments on provincial and district levels. In all four villages we studied (illegal) conversion of natural resources has been detected.[7] In Cambodia natural resources are in fact already degraded, with most conversions having started in the late 1970s during the Pol Pot regime or right after its end.[8]

Relatively new tools to address forest resource degradation are community forest organizations and fishery communities, which have been introduced by the RGC to hand over resource rights to local people and to initiate sustainable

---

7. There are, for example, activities to fill up lakes to grow more rice or to clear remaining forests for cropping purposes.

8. One exception is Krorsang, where clearing began only in 2000 with immigration and completely changed the traditional pattern of fallow cropping systems, where the forest was cleared for cropping and then left alone for three years to recover.

natural resource management.[9] These new tools have been established or are being set up in two of the villages we studied, whereas the other two still manage their resources traditionally. According to the Land Law, each village can decide whether it wants to apply for such a formalized community or not. The establishment of these organizations depends on whether legal knowledge of the existence of community forest organizations or fishery communities has already been disseminated, whether human and financial resources are available, whether the communes go through the registration process, and whether the resource is part of a natural reserve or an economic concession. At the research sites where local authorities chose to set up fishery communities or community forest organizations, the problems that arise during implementation are similar: (1) the procedures required to register the community organizations, as stated by village members involved in their establishment, are very time consuming and impossible for the applying villages or communes to monitor; (2) there are uncertainties about exact community boundaries, which have to be jointly identified, clarified, and settled before registration can be finalized; and (3) the level of cooperation with other villages or communes is rather low and makes it difficult to include all user groups. As a result, there are no clear responsibilities during the time span between the application for a fishery community or community forest organization and the finalization of the registration process. As a consequence, administration officers sometimes stop the ongoing processes arbitrarily on inspection tours, leaving community members in uncertainty as to whether they are allowed to enforce rules not yet officially approved.

The villages of Krorsang and Chrang Krohom decided to establish community organizations for natural resource management. In Krorsang forest resources are rapidly decreasing even though a community forest organization is in place. The first clearings were done or tacitly protected by higher-ranking people from the military who were in clandestine contact with some villagers. Villagers opposing logging were threatened, even with arms. These patterns of pushing deforestation by mere force are still widespread in rural Cambodia (AHRCHK 2006). The cleared land was then sold to immigrants, resulting in a remarkable population increase of more than 50 percent in the village during the five years before our study. In 2003, the village authorities of Krorsang established the community forest organization, but registration was finalized only in 2006. During the three years of unclear responsibilities to protect the forest against illegal logging, around 50 new houses were built within the area of the community forest organization, and large parts of the forests had already been turned into farmland. Clearings took place even though all parties involved knew that damaging the forest resource was forbidden and the community forest area had already been provisionally marked as a protected area by the com-

---

9. The Forestry Law states the possibility for local groups to manage their forests (RGC 2002a, Article 5/8). These local user groups are often simply named forest communities.

munity forest organization. During the registration process, migrants who settled within the forest turned it into agricultural and homestead land.[10] These settlements hindered the original villagers from continuing their traditional fallow cropping.[11] It further aggravated the existing pressure on local resources.

The ever-shrinking forest units continued to be of major importance to the original villagers, who rely on them for income generation. Even though the community forest organization immediately reports to the local forest administration whenever rules are broken, no impact on halting logging or the conversion of forests to agricultural land has been observable. Settling in the community forest area remains unpunished. Krorsang is unable to cooperate with other villages that also heavily rely on the forest, because the Krorsang authorities feel unable to inhibit the abuse of forestlands or in-migration by other villages' inhabitants. As community forest organization members point out, punishment of intruders is the right of the intruders' "home" authorities. In addition, newly settled villagers invite their kin and neighbors to Krorsang because their experience in acquiring land through forest conversion has been positive and they assume that more land is available. This indicates that newcomers expect not to be punished in the short run.[12] As a result, Krorsang is still unable to keep migrants from settling in the forest and is still unable to prevent anyone from logging. As a consequence, the community forest organization has failed to protect the village's forest and to accomplish a shift to a more sustainable forestry system.

In Chrang Krohom the institutional settings offered under the new legislation also fail to preserve forest resources. Here, too, the main threat to forest areas is their conversion into agricultural land. However, in contrast to Krorsang, this conversion is not due to in-migration but a direct consequence of the scarcity of arable land in the village. During two years prior to our study, floods destroyed parts of the rice harvest, encouraging people to look for new fields in locations that are less flood prone and more reliable for income generation. Experiencing higher returns on the crops grown in the former forest area, more and more villagers made an effort to gain access to parcels of this fertile land. They thus started with slash-and-burn agriculture and over time shifted from raising rice to cash cropping. However, some differentiation is necessary, because poor people are not even able to invest time in slash-and-burn activities while still crucially depending on forest products. They spend ever more time

---

10. The term *migrants* refers to people coming from neighboring villages and communes as well as to people from other districts and provinces.

11. The original villagers are understood as members of households that have been living in Krorsang since they were born and are still familiar with fallow cropping traditions.

12. In this context, the work of the community forest organization is further complicated if user groups are actively in-migrating from other communes or districts, because neither community members nor local administrative staff feel entitled to inhibit exploitation by "foreign" people from other communes and districts.

generating the minimum amount needed for subsistence, which was easily provided by the products of the forests in the past. The benefit streams from the forest decrease the scarcer the resource becomes. Our study found that the people in Chrang Krohom who relied mainly on forest products for their livelihoods were the only ones whose well-being had deteriorated over the previous five years. In order to address the issue of deteriorating forests, local authorities applied for a community forest organization in order to preserve the remaining forest in the area.[13] As in Krorsang, the community forest organization in Chrang Krohom suffers from a lack of responsibility and from unclear local boundaries. In addition, authorities fail to cooperate with neighboring villages using the same forest.

Altogether, in turn, the conditions we have described result in an institutional setup that does not allow communities to effectively exclude anyone from extracting goods from their natural resource base or to convert forests. Even in cases in which user communities have already been established and are setting rules, only rarely have trespassers been detected. Even rarer occasions can be identified in which they have been held responsible for their actions. Altogether, the institutional setting is close to an open-access situation.

This rather disappointing sketch of the current situation, however, does not preclude the continued operation of traditional mechanisms in Cambodia to manage common resources effectively. In all four of the villages we studied, traditional resource management institutions have been in place historically. However, in Krorsang and Chrang Krohom indigenous responsibility has been handed over to an institution that replaces traditional mechanisms. Cambodian traditional natural resource management mechanisms also aim to achieve sustainable use of natural resources: local authorities elaborate solutions to resource threats and develop, revitalize, and try to enforce sets of rules that aim to overcome problems that arise. Traditional management also results in regular common activities such as lake excavations or dam building and maintenance, in which all villagers are asked and expected to take part. Religious tradition is another norm and a rule-creating and -enforcing mechanism that brings people together to prepare for festivities, allocate sacred sites, set up or renovate temporary huts, and clear the forest from shrub.

Once a rule is set, it applies to villagers as well as outsiders. Trespassers, when caught, are told the rules as well as the reasons they have been applied. The monitoring of compliance is done by all villagers, and the village leader is expected to take action if a trespasser does not refrain from breaking these local rules. Action means mainly reporting the incident to the commune council. There are no further enforcement mechanisms in place, with the result that a number of trespassers do not abide by the rules. However, respect for village

---

13. The registration process was not finished until June 2007.

elders and religious beliefs hinders most local people from breaking jointly formulated rules.[14]

The villages of Leuk and Svay Teap manage their resources based only on these traditional, endogenous mechanisms. These villages still have a traceable history of cooperation among neighbors, because they traditionally cultivate rice and are thus dependent on support from fellow villagers to transplant seedlings or for animal traction. Village authorities respond to changes in the resource base and when problems occur. On all lands surrounding the villages, people have access rights to extract products for subsistence, no matter whether the land is privately or commonly owned.[15] In Leuk, rules are in place to limit extraction rates with the aim of keeping the forest its current size. Plans are under way to increase the quality of the resource base by enlarging the local pond to contribute additional income for subsistence through fishing. In Svay Teap, local rules prohibit the use of certain fishing gear and the conversion of forests into arable land. Villagers act collectively to protect their resource base when resources are used as common property.

These examples describe different setups for natural resource management institutions and property rights enforcement mechanisms, including their different outcomes. Leuk and Svay Teap are still traditionally managed, whereas Chrang Krohom and Krorsang have established external institutions (fishery communities and community forests) in an attempt to make traditional use rights legally enforceable. Nevertheless, all village authorities feel vulnerable to the interventions of higher-ranking authorities. They are unable to oppose plans interfering with their local management strategies, leaving formalized and traditional institutions vulnerable to external intervention and thus undermining the local authorities' ability to enforce rules at the local level.

Because agriculture remains the main income source in rural Cambodia, scarce arable land, together with rapid population growth, has put increasing pressure on natural resources as many farmers seek to transform so-called unproductive land and add it to their existing landholdings.[16] Because laws, decrees, and other legal texts set different prerequisites and incentives for establishing private property rights and have been implemented and communicated to the local population incompletely, conflicts arise over common pool resources.[17]

---

14. There are strong beliefs that a person disrupting "Neak Ta," the forest spirits, will suffer from ill health or bad harvests.

15. Collecting fuelwood, catching crabs in rice fields, and so on are allowed as long as these activities do not affect the harvest. After harvesting, the fields usually become common grazing grounds for livestock.

16. Land is often left unused when the household that owns the land lacks capital, labor force (for instance, through illness or temporary migration), or seeds for planting. Forested land is also considered unproductive once valuable woods have been logged.

17. There are conflicts about agricultural and homestead lands, too, but the focus here will be on other natural resources.

These conflicts have different impacts on people's livelihoods depending on the amount of land and the actors involved.

In the absence of cadastral records, land is often assumed to be state owned and is sold on a large scale without consulting local-level administrators about its current uses, correct location, or extent (Zimmermann and Kruk 2002; Bliss 2005). This lack of communication opens the door to speculation, often involving government officials, the military and the Khmer, or expatriate businessmen. This speculation is facilitated by villagers' unawareness of state laws, causing conflicts between villagers and government bodies at all administrative levels. Villagers often do not know that resources are owned by the state and must not be converted to arable land.

The most severe consequence of such practices is a loss of these resources as productive assets for households or the community as a whole. Such a loss might be temporary, lasting only until the conflict is resolved. However, it might also result in a complete loss of land due to decisions by local authorities or courts or the exertion of power by local elites (for instance, when forests are converted into rubber plantations). In addition, conflict resolution processes tie up the labor force and often substantial financial assets.[18]

Conflicts over natural resources can usually be solved only at the district, provincial, or even national level. Local villagers on their own are often unable to enforce their rights. Nevertheless, because quite a number of local resource users are usually affected by a conflict, they can pool their resources and lobby their local authorities or civil-society organizations to take action on their behalf. Collective action might help not only to overcome resource management problems but also to enforce rights against opponents. In the following section we identify forms of collective action in rural Cambodia and analyze factors that influence engagement in collective action.

Collective Action in Rural Cambodia

Even after the Pol Pot terror regime and civil war, people in Cambodia continue to cooperate in many ways, ranging from agricultural activities such as transplanting rice to building social infrastructure such as schools to membership in other associations, not necessarily with an economic focus. In all four villages we studied, a wide range of activities was identified in which collective action is practiced in an effort to improve rural livelihoods and deliver local public goods.[19] In this study we defined *collective action* broadly. We understood it as

---

18. Costs of conflict resolution include fees for administration and transportation costs. Both usually rise when conflicts are resolved at higher administrative levels. In addition, conflicts also affect parties' self-esteem and threaten their physical well-being when they turn violent.

19. Such activities range from spontaneously offering help after a house burns down (to build a shelter and provide clothes), engaging in bilateral livestock-sharing arrangements (to provide animal traction for plowing), and participating in informal natural resource management to the activities of more formalized associations with written rules and constitutions.

the voluntary engagement of a group of people to reach a common goal. Villagers planned for and executed activities that served not only their household but also the village as a whole.

Figure 11.1 provides an overview of the different domains of collective action and the frequency with which help was given to fellow villagers as a percentage of households engaging in different activities. Patterns of help went beyond lines of kinship, especially in cases in which help was needed due to illness, for funerals, and for communal work. Help for house construction or fieldwork rather followed lines of affinity but still went beyond the extended family.

Although a wide range of collective action issues could be identified, quite different factors influenced individuals' readiness to engage in activities that were in the common interest. What are the household characteristics that may have influenced their engagement in activities in the common interest? Using Cramer's V coefficients we have measured the strength of association between households' characteristics and their engagement in common activities.

The strongest association was found for the variable "years spent in the village" (Cramer's V coefficient = 0.495). The longer a household lives in a village, the longer the household receives benefits from public goods provided by its fellow villagers; social ties improve, and commitment to the village increases. People taking part in village meetings might be more committed to the village and thus inclined to take part in collective action (Cramer's V coefficient = 0.320). Even the meetings themselves may help motivate people, because development projects are normally announced at these meetings and financial needs and labor requirements are discussed. The variable "household size" shows a strong association with participation in communal work (Cramer's V coefficient = 0.317). A larger household is better able to spare a member to participate in collective projects.[20] Smaller households' participation in common activities can be costly, especially if a household depends on daily wage labor and cannot afford to take part in collective action that generates no direct payoffs. Education has the weakest association with participation (Cramer's V coefficient = 0.260).

Simple correlations (Table 11.4) also indicate that being landless and land poor is strongly associated with engagement in formalized institutions for collective action. The same is true of being less educated. It can be assumed that the landless and the land-poor as well as less educated households are less likely to engage in formalized institutions for collective action, such as cash associations or rice banks.

Table 11.5 illustrates that less educated households were less likely to engage in associations. It plots the shares for each category of school education

---

20. In most villages at least one member per household is expected to take part in common activities.

FIGURE 11.1 Reasons that help is given to other villagers

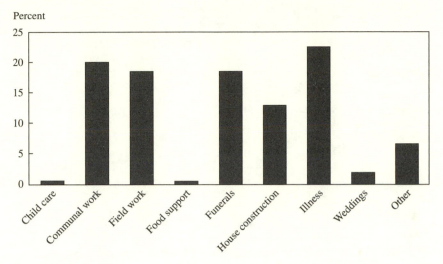

SOURCE: Authors' findings.

TABLE 11.4 Membership in associations and schooling of household heads at the research sites

Expected engagement in village associations	Schooling of household head (percent)			
	None (illiterate)	1–3 years	3–6 years	>6 years
Less	1.4	0.0	0.0	0.0
Same	8.1	14.3	9.1	25.0
More	56.8	57.1	72.7	62.5
No information on association	33.8	28.6	18.2	12.5
Total	100.0	100.0	100.0	100.0

SOURCE: Authors' findings.

against whether households expected to engage less, at the same level, or more in associations. At our research sites, 56.8 percent of the illiterate households and 57.1 percent of households with one to three years' schooling expected to become more engaged in associations, whereas 72.7 and 62.5 percent of the households with higher levels of education expected more engagement. Illiterate or poorer people frequently felt that they were "only ordinary villagers" who were not worthy of taking part in associations unless they were explicitly invited by association leaders. One of the main reasons people did not become members of an association was mistrust and a lack of confidence. People often

TABLE 11.5 Matrix of correlation between education and exercising power to influence local decisionmaking at the research sites

Characteristic		Power to influence village decisions	Years in school	Wealth
Power to influence	Pearson's correlation	1.000	0.259**	0.184*
village decisions	Significance (two-sided)		0.002	0.027
	n	146	146	146
Years in school	Pearson's correlation	0.259**	1.000	0.400**
	Significance (two-sided)	0.002		0.000
	n	146	146	146
Wealth	Pearson's correlation	0.184*	0.400**	1.000
	Significance (two-sided)	0.027	0.000	
	n	146	146	146

SOURCE: Authors' findings.

NOTES: * means significant at the 0.05 percent level; ** means significant at the 0.01 percent level; blank cells mean not applicable.

did not take part when the association leaders supported a political party or belonged to an informal network of kinship and affinity that was different from the one with which the potential member was affiliated.

In addition, landless and land-poor villagers were afraid that their financial assets would not be sufficient to pay back loans when they became members of cash associations or rice banks or to pay regular membership fees. People who owned middle-sized land parcels were strongly engaged in these associations. They were also more likely to engage in more than one association, establishing more complex networks through cooperation with a stronger impact on local well-being. However, every second household owning more than 4 hectares of land did not take part in any association. There were two reasons that they opted out. First, people with large landholdings were not dependent on rice banks or cash associations. Their harvests guaranteed enough income for consumption as well as for investments to crop in the next season. The second reason was time restrictions. Agricultural activities are labor intense, time consuming, and time sensitive. The larger the landholdings, the more time household members spend in caring for crops. Therefore, households especially opted out when association membership required that they engage in time-consuming activities (guarding natural resources, for example).

However, there were exceptions. Research in Krorsang village shows that low levels of engagement of middle-sized landowners in associations were due to the fact that a large number of immigrants had purchased middle-sized parcels without integrating completely into the village. As immigrants contribute to an ever-increasing share of the total village population, they can be expected to establish their own associations in the future. In the village of Svay Teap, no association is operating, even though a women's association formally exists.

Households with a small human capital base are less likely to shape their livelihoods by taking part in collective decisionmaking processes. Though they do take part in collective action, less educated people do not feel free to participate if they are not explicitly included by authorities due to their low self-confidence. The same is true of poorer people. They will not take part in decision-making processes unless local authorities include them. Table 11.5 illustrates the strong positive correlation of educational level, wealth, and power to influence village decisionmaking. Nevertheless, contentedness with decisions made for the village was evenly distributed among all households.

The differences between households that participate in communal activities and those that do not lie in household variables as well as village characteristics. All villages investigated planned for and executed common activities that served not only the household itself but the village as a whole (for example, road construction). Cross-sectional data from the 2005 survey give some insights as to what particular household characteristics influenced a household's decision to take part in collective action. Based on the results of the measures of association, a binary logistic regression was employed with the aim of analyzing what characteristics (village or household related) were likely to increase a household's participation in collective action. Thus, the regression should show how strong and in what direction household and village characteristics influenced a household's readiness to engage in collective action. The results of the associations and correlations discussed earlier should be confirmed by the regression (see Appendix 11A for the variables in the regression). The regression should also include village characteristics to explain how these characteristics influenced the probability that a household would take part in collective action. The dependent variable in the regression is dichotomous: it is one if a household took part in collective action, zero if it did not. An overview of the regression results is given in Table 11.6. The classification table highlights that the model successfully predicts 79.5 percent of the cases. The variables have also been tested for collinearity (see Appendix 11B for the correlation matrix and Appendix 11C for parameter estimates), and all of the correlations are below the level critical to cause collinerarity problems.

Because the sample size was relatively small, the prediction quality is low. Still, important insights can be derived. In order to explain the results, qualitative data collected during semistructured interviews and group discussions have been taken into account to underline the regression's outcomes. Household size and access to information on village matters positively influenced a household's participation in village activities, whereas an increase in wealth might have added to the probability of not taking part in common activities. This would be consistent with the observation that wealthier households buy themselves out of obligatory community work by hiring poorer villagers to do their part in the

TABLE 11.6 Binary logistic regression on participation in common activities at the research sites

Observed		Predicted participation in communal work		Percentage correct
		No	Yes	
Participation in activities	No	9	22	29.0
for the common good	Yes	8	107	93.0
Overall percentage				79.5
Omnibus test	Chi-squared: 37,794	df: 5		
Model summary	−2 log-likelihood: 113,178	Cox and Snell R^2: 0.354		
Variables in the regression	B	Standard error	Wald	p
Household size	0.388	0.313	8.739	0.003
Satisfaction with village decisionmaking	−0.650	0.884	0.541	0.462
Wealth	−0.394	0.238	2.746	0.034
Market access	−2.378	0.643	13.653	0.000
Village institutions	1.972	0.589	11.189	0.001
Access to information on village affairs	0.940	0.534	3.103	0.078
Constant	−0.607	1.159	0.247	0.600

SOURCE: Authors' findings.

NOTE: If Exp (B) > 1, the explaining variable increases the probability of a household to switch to "yes" (that is, taking part in common activities); if Exp (B) < 1, the explaining variable increases the probability of an individual's "no" (that is, no engagement in common activities).

required activities. Village characteristics that have been included in the regression seem to have an impact on the probability that a household would take part in common activities: households in a village with traditional institutions tended to act more collectively than those in villages without such institutions.

A village's market access was expected to lower the probability that a household would take part in collective action. On the one hand, villages with better market access were also more accessible to government agencies and NGOs, whose activities in the villages might have crowded out collective action because they often employ villagers to build up common goods. On the other hand, because main elements of collective action in rural Cambodia are concerned with road construction and accessibility of the village in general, villages with good market access might not have needed as much effort to maintain physical infrastructure compared to those with poor accessibility. Only a small and nonsignificant effect was found for the variable "satisfaction with village decisionmaking." Other explanatory variables, such as "years lived in the village" and "education," have been tested for their influence on households' willingness to participate in village activities. But the results have been non-significant and did not add much to the explanation of what influenced households to participate in village activities.

As described earlier, poorer and less educated households reported not feeling capable of taking part in decisionmaking processes or engaging in formal institutions. Often a certain mistrust also kept villagers from engaging in these activities. In order to substantiate these results from descriptive data analysis, economic field experiments on trust in the form of a trust game have been conducted in the villages (a detailed description of the game is given in Appendix 11D). The experiment's results are shown in Table 11.7. People in all villages trusted their fellow villagers only to some degree (as indicated by the fractions sent). People's level of trust (represented in the fractions returned) was low, and return ratios varied across villages.[21]

Postgame interviews indicated that players' sending larger fractions of their endowments to their counterparts might have been due to religious attitudes of solidarity, because most individuals gave fairness or fear of punishment as the main reason to send money.[22] Only a few respondents mentioned the opportunity of extra gains as their predominant intention in sending money to their counterparts. These attitudes would be expected to lead to similar levels in the fractions of the endowments returned, because religious attitudes of solidarity or fear of punishment should also have applied to players in Group B who returned the money to the players in Group A. Again, the postgame questionnaire sheds some light on the reasons behind the lack of reciprocity. People who did not return the endowments or returned only small fractions assumed that their counterparts were wealthier and thus took the amount received as a gift. Religious attitudes were not controlled for, because all participants were Buddhist.

On an individual level, household size had a significant negative impact on an individual's trust level; that is, individuals living in large families tended to send less money to their counterparts than did those from smaller households. Looking at the research villages separately, Chrang Krohom shows the lowest level of trust and Leuk the highest. In Chrang Krohom the trust level decreased

---

21. The return ratio was calculated as the share of the amount sent back by Player B to the amount sent by Player A (players in Group A who sent nothing are not included, because division by zero is not defined). Return ratios smaller than 1.0 indicate that people who trusted their fellow villagers with money did lose part of the amount they sent. Return ratios higher than 1.0 show that the players in Group B shared the surplus received through the design of the game.

22. This might be due to religious beliefs about punishment in the next life but might also be due to fear that their behavior will come to light after the game (torture during the Khmer Rouge regime included the threat that the Angka (the Communist Party) knows everything and would find out each and every lie). Another explanation might be the recent history of forced collectivization, where villagers were forced to contribute to common goals whereas free riding has not been punished (Colletta and Cullen 2000).

TABLE 11.7 Trust levels in the research villages demonstrated by a trust game

Village	Fractions sent (average)	Fractions returned (average)	Return ratio
Chrang Krohom	0.150000	0.159200	1.416670
Leuk	0.546875	0.285600	1.546880
Krorsang	0.236110	0.128200	1.000000
Svay Teap	0.403846	0.124700	0.772730
Average, all villages	0.334210	0.174400	1.184070

SOURCE: Authors' data.

NOTE: For the rules of the game and an explanation of the terms that head the columns in the table, see Appendix 11D.

the more common activities an individual engaged in during a year's time. This was due to the fact that most of the common activities available to improve the local physical infrastructure were still perceived as forced labor.[23] It is noteworthy that in both villages with formal community forest organizations or fishery communities (Chrang Krohom, Krorsang) the level of trust was lower than in the two traditionally managed villages (Leuk, Svay Teap). The measure of the strength of association between an individual's trust level and traditional village institutions (Cramer's V) took the value of 0.536.

Discussion of Research Results

In all villages studied, natural resource degradation is observable and negatively affects the rural poor. Van Acker (1999) and others (World Bank 2003) have already noted that resource degradation is severe, requiring a "total harvest approach" (van Acker, 1999, 5). Thus the outcomes of the patterns of interaction deplete the natural capital assets of the communities for the future—a negative feedback loop. Incomplete regulation and, in particular, weak enforcement at all levels of jurisdictions were the major causes of resource degradation identified by Hach and Sothea (2004). In addition, traditional succession schemes together with high levels of population growth put significant pressure on natural resources.[24] The RGC tries to address resource degradation through community forest organizations and fishery communities. However, these ap-

---

23. The term *common activities* is used here to differentiate these activities from the voluntary collective action discussed earlier.

24. Traditionally, children "inherit" part of their parents' land when they get married to start their own households. With the high level of population growth, the sizes of the land plots that young couples receive are becoming smaller and are often not sufficient to sustain the new families. Thus, new strips of land are cleared to generate sufficient income.

proaches face several obstacles. For example, slow registration processes lead to uncertainties as to how to apply rules for community organizations. Most of the forests are difficult to assess, thus complicating an exact definition of the boundaries of the resource unit. Because the forest administration is reported to lack sufficient human and financial resources, it is unable to react quickly and effectively to requests of the communes (EIC 2005). Van Acker (1999) and Calavan, Briquets, and O'Brien (2004) have found that corruption is one of the factors that slows the registration process at the local level. Commonly reported examples of corruption include administrative staff's demanding extra payments for "express services" (to speed up administrative processes) or gasoline expenditures for staff who need to travel to the villages. On a larger scale, Global Witness (2007) reported that corruption is a major obstacle to sustainable resource management throughout Cambodia.

Low levels of cooperation between villages leaves communities unable to enforce rules applied by different villages. This might be due to the low levels of trust observed in the villages during our field experiments in 2006.[25] Different studies (for example, Colletta and Cullen 2000; Pellini and Ayres 2005) have found that bridging and linking social capital is rather low in Cambodia. According to Uphoff's (2000, 227) definition of trust as the "essential 'glue' of society," trust is necessary to build up and sustain long-term cooperation. Given the low degrees of trust in the villages of our case study (especially in those with community forest organizations and fishery communities), we can assume that if villagers do not even consider their fellow villagers trustworthy, they would be even less likely to trust those from neighboring villages. Observed differences in the ability to coordinate within the village (as opposed to among villages) can be attributed partly to a strict top-down leadership. An important issue for further research is whether religion influences attitudes and what kind of religious attitudes influence the differences in trust and trustworthiness among members of the Cambodian rural population.

Unsuccessful natural resource management can also be attributed to the lack of trust, which hinders people from cooperating in order to protect their resources. In a cross-country study Zak and Knack (2001) found low trust levels in countries where the political environments are unstable and the level of social heterogeneity is high. Experimental evidence from the villages we studied shows lower levels of trust in those villages where authorities have chosen to establish new property rights–related institutions. In fact, there is a strong positive association between an individual's trust level and the presence of traditional village institutions.

---

25. There is some experimental evidence that people in Chrang Krohom are less trustful than villagers in the other villages.

Conclusions and Policy Implications

In rural Cambodia, property rights to natural resources such as local forests, fish ponds, lakes, water streams, or harvested fields are normally commonly owned, used, and managed. This makes effective collective action a precondition for sustainable resource management as well as income generation and asset accumulation for the rural poor. In a country that has been disrupted for decades by war, genocide, and forced collectivization and is still characterized by fragile or even weak government institutions that put pressure on the rule of law, legal security, and human rights enforcement, it is not surprising that neither property rights systems nor collective action fulfill the requirements and expectations of them by researchers, civil society organizations, or donors. Here the theme of natural resource governance and access to resources intersects with the theme of postconflict development; many of the institutions for governance, including those for property rights and formal collective action, have been undermined by the conflict, and the trust that is necessary to rebuild them has been eroded. Looking at the theme of elite capture, we see that village decisionmaking is dominated by those with more human capital, but the greater threats to resource access and control come not from elites within the villages but from government officials and well-connected outsiders who acquire land in the villages and reduce local people's incentives and ability to guard and govern their common resources.

The ongoing process of devolution of natural resource management in Cambodia might be considered premature and shortsighted in terms of its immediate impact on collective action and can inhibit or even undermine expected sustainable use patterns. Under current devolution policies, important monitoring and enforcement mechanisms executed by a still weak though existent local forest administration are abruptly removed after the responsibility for resource management is handed over to local community forest organizations or fishery communities. Yet these organizations are neither officially acknowledged by the government nor able to execute the whole spectrum of responsibilities assigned to them. The result is that an institutional vacuum emerges, which does not favor the poor.

For formal institutions to be efficient in managing the local commons, the concrete procedures and sequencing required to formulate and enforce bylaws and statutes integrating both the guiding principles of a devolving state and traditional local rules and enforcement mechanisms should be given more consideration. Uncertainties on the part of both the government and the local user groups will have to be diminished. An important first step will be to reduce existing uncertainties about village or commune boundaries, responsibilities, and the procedures to be used in case of violation of rules. However, this will be successful only if different line agencies responsible for forestry and fisheries, such as a decentralized Ministry of Land or Ministry of Agriculture, support villagers in identifying their boundaries, demarcating them and documenting the results in a joint effort. Enforcement will work only at the interface of old established informal institutions and newly developed formal ones if administrative procedures are transparent regarding how to fine violators of common property rules.

An immediate transfer of the tasks and power to monitor and enforce sustainable resource use from line ministries and other state agencies to local users cannot be accomplished overnight in a country that has been ridden by mistrust, forced settlement in the villages, and a long period of interruption of the development of social cohesion and capital. To enhance local users' efforts to enforce their rights, those ministries should not remove their officers from their responsibilities but rather should redefine their tasks as cooperating with and supporting local community organizations.

For the rural poor, in particular, any participation in organizations to foster collective action and to govern the commons is quite costly; the activities are time consuming, direct compensation cannot be expected, and unbalanced reciprocity has often proved not to work for them. Although the poor in rural Cambodia might profit most from protecting their local commons, they often lack the action resources necessary to effectively defend their interests within village organizations. They remain dependent on more affluent villagers to initiate and continue cooperation to protect their interests. Because the poor are often those with no formal education, a weak human capital base, and very little land or none, they are less likely to become involved in formalized groups that have mostly been externally established to support agricultural activities. Nevertheless, they participate in informal gatherings and groups in their villages as entry points for further cooperation. There are indications that the poor are not "lost" to collective action and that different ties and links exist that offer them the potential to be strengthened by external temporary support from NGOs or other initiatives. However, empirical results show that in the rural setting the poor are more likely to simply comply with rules and mechanisms but not to take deliberate action to shape them or to defend them actively.

Complementary to the typical role of collective action, the role of religious festivities and Buddhist values and norms needs further consideration. Jointly exercised religious activities can be instruments to enhance cooperation in and between villages and are explicitly used by political entrepreneurs and local leaders as a means to protect natural capital and to foster social cohesion and trust. On the basis of religious initiatives and the overall imperative of harmony, people start to communicate experiences in which collective action has been successful in protecting their interests against the government, the military, large-scale investors, or others. They do not actively protest and demonstrate but begin by formulating petitions and memoranda to raise awareness of their problems, address conflicts, and ask for external support. Although these activities might be assessed as rather defensive and "shy," they can be seen as part of a new action arena with different rules that may be more beneficial to the poor, and they should be regarded as a starting point to encourage the poor to rely more on collective action to protect their property rights and to make use of reformed property rights systems, which would allow for new forms of collective action to combat poverty in rural areas.

Appendix 11A: Variables in the Regression

TABLE 11A.1 Variables in the regression

Variable in the regression	Type of variable	Value of variable
Household size	Interval	Number of persons
Satisfaction with village decisionmaking	Binary	0: I am not satisfied with village decisionmaking 1: I am satisfied with village decisionmaking
Wealth	Interval	Standardized (derived from money available per month in Riel)
Market access	Interval	Measured in kilometers
Village institutions	Binary	0: No traditional institution existent 1: Traditional institution(s) existent
Access to information on village affairs	Binary	0: I feel uninformed about village affairs 1: I feel informed about village affairs

Appendix 11B: Correlation Matrix of Regression Coefficients

In order to check for collinearity, the correlations of the regression coefficients have been plotted in Table 11B.1. According to Menard (1995), correlations between regression coefficients should not be higher than 0.8. In the sample the highest correlation between satisfaction with village decisionmaking and the constant was identified as −0.599.

TABLE 11B.1 Correlation matrix

Variable	Constant	Household size	Village institutions	Market access	Access to information on village affairs	Wealth	Satisfaction with village decision-making
Constant	1,000	426	161	408	171	206	599
Household size	426	1,000	182	226	22	320	128
Village institutions	161	182	1,000	260	139	471	107
Market access	408	226	260	1,000	204	207	10
Access to information on village affairs	171	22	139	204	1,000	30	32
Wealth	206	320	471	207	30	1,000	57
Satisfaction with village decisionmaking	599	128	107	10	32	57	1,000

NOTE: A Huber–White test was conducted that corrects for suspected correlations among the error terms of observations.

Appendix 11C: Parameter Estimates

TABLE 11C.1 Parameter estimates

		B	Standard error	95 percent confidence interval		Hypothesis test		
Parameter				Lower	Upper	*t*	df	Significance	Lower	Upper
Threshold	[Participation in common activities = 0]	−1.460	1.140	−6.365	3.446	−1.280	2.000	0.329
Regression	Household size	0.183	0.111	−0.293	0.659	1.654	2.000	0.240
	Satisfaction with village decisionmaking	−0.398	1.095	−5.108	4.311	−0.364	2.000	0.751
	Village institutions	−0.978	0.211	−1.887	−0.069	−4.632	2.000	0.044
	Market access	2.053	0.292	3.310	0.796	−7.026	2.000	0.020
	Wealth	0.022	0.176	−0.735	0.779	0.125	2.000	0.912

NOTE: All numbers in the table have been converted to the U.S. system of notation (for instance, 0.66 for decimals). If Exp (*B*) > 1, the explaining variable increases the probability of a household to switch to "yes" (that is, taking part in common activities); if Exp (*B*) < 1, the explaining variable increases the probability of an individual's "no" (that is, no engagement in common activities).

Appendix 11D: Rules of the Trust Game

For the experiment the group of players was divided into two subgroups: the "first movers," here referred to as Group A, and the "responders," here referred to as Group B. Each Player A was coupled with a Player B, but the exact match was unknown to the players; that is, no Player A knew who was the Player B with whom he or she was playing the game. To start the game, each Player A received an amount of money as an initial endowment. Player A could decide to keep the endowment or send part or all of it to his or her unknown counterpart in Group B. The amount sent by Player A was tripled and given to Player B on top of his or her initial endowment, which was identical to that of Group A. Now the player from Group B owned the tripled fraction that Player A sent plus his or her initial endowment. Player B had to decide whether to send any amount back or keep the whole sum. After Player B had made this decision, the money he or she sent back was given to Player A and the game ended. The players in Group A had thus to decide whether to trust their counterparts in Group B: the higher the fraction of money sent, the higher the trust in their counterpart that their investment (the fraction sent) would pay off. The Nash equilibrium for selfish preferences is to pass on nothing, because a self-interested person would return none of the amount received.

References

Acharya, S., and C. Sophal. 2002. *Facing the challenge of rural livelihoods: A perspective from nine villages in Cambodia.* CDRI Working Paper. Phnom Penh, Cambodia: Cambodia Development Resource Institute.

Acharya, S., B. Ballard, S. Rathmony, R. Sopheap, S. Sovannarith, and U. Utey. 2001. *Social assessment of land in Cambodia: A field study.* CDRI Working Paper. Phnom Penh, Cambodia: Cambodia Development Resource Institute.

Asian Human Rights Commission–Hong Kong (AHRCHK). 2006. *Cambodia: The situation of human rights in 2006.* Hong Kong.

Baran, E. 2005. *Cambodian inland fisheries: Facts, figures and context.* Phnom Penh, Cambodia: World Fish Center and Inland Fisheries Research and Development Institute.

Berg, J., J. Dickhaut, and K. McCabe. 1995. Trust, reciprocity and social history. *Games and Economic Behavior* 10 (1): 122–142.

Bliss, F. 2005. *Preventing corruption in resource allocation: Land reform, forestry management, agriculture irrigation.* Division 42: Sector Project Development and Testing of Strategies and Instruments for the Prevention of Corruption. Eschborn, Germany: GTZ.

Calavan, M. M., S. D. Briquets, and J. O'Brien. 2004. *Cambodia corruption assessment.* Washington, D.C.: U.S. Agency for International Development.

Cardenas, J. C., and E. Ostrom. 2004. What brings people experiments in the field about cooperation in the commons? *Agricultural Systems* 82 (3): 307–326.

Catalla, R. F. 2001. *Small-scale land distribution in Cambodia: Lessons from three case studies.* ADI Project. Phnom Penh, Cambodia: Cooperation Committee for Cambodia.

Chandler, D. 1996. *A history of Cambodia.* Boulder, Colo., U.S.A.: Westview.

Colletta, N., and M. Cullen. 2000. *Violent conflict and the transformation of social capital: Lessons from Cambodia, Rwanda, Guatemala and Somalia.* Washington, D.C.: World Bank.

Degen, P., F. Van Acker, N. Van Zalinge, N. Thuok, and L. Vuthy. 2000. Taken for granted conflicts over Cambodian's freshwater fish resources. Contribution to the 8th IASCP Conference, May 31–June 4, in Bloomington, Ind., U.S.A.

EIC (Economic Institute of Cambodia). 2005. *Cambodia economic watch.* Phnom Penh, Cambodia.

Fraser, T., and Department of Forestry and Wildlife. 2000. *Forest concession management planning manual.* Phnom Penh, Cambodia: World Bank and Asian Development Bank.

Global Witness. 2007. *Cambodia's family trees: Illegal logging and the stripping of public assets by Cambodia's elite.* London.

Hach, S., and O. Sothea. 2004. *Cambodia economic watch.* Phnom Penh, Cambodia: Economic Institute of Cambodia.

Kirk, M. 2004. State land economics in Cambodia. Policy discussion paper. Ministry of Land Management, Urban Planning, and Construction, Phnom Penh, Cambodia. Mimeo.

Marschke, M. 2004. Learning and adapting with change: An examination of two Cambodian villages' level of resource management. Paper presented at the Tenth Conference of the International Association for the Study of Common Property, The Commons in an Age of Global Transition: Challenges, Risks and Opportunities, August 9–13, in Oaxaca, Mexico.

McKenney, B., and P. Tola. 2002. *Natural resources and rural livelihoods in Cambodia: A baseline survey.* CDRI Working Paper 23. Phnom Penh, Cambodia: Cambodia Development Research Institute.

Mehmet, O. 1997. Development in a war torn society: What next in Cambodia? *Third World Quarterly* 18 (4): 673–686.

Menard, S. 1995. *Applied logistic regression analysis.* London: Sage.

Pellini, A., and D. Ayres. 2005. *Social capital and village governance: Experiences with village networks.* Discussion paper. Phnom Penh, Cambodia: Community Based Rural Development Project GTZ.

RGC (Royal Government of Cambodia). 2001. *Land law.* Phnom Penh.

———. 2002a. *Forestry law.* Phnom Penh.

———. 2002b. National poverty reduction strategy paper. National Assembly, Phnom Penh.

Simbolon, I. 2002. *Access to land of highland indigenous minorities: The case of plural property rights in Cambodia.* Working Paper 42. Halle/Saale, Germany: Max Planck Institute for Social Anthropology.

Sophal, C., T. Saravy, and S. Acharya. 2001. *Land tenure in Cambodia: A data update.* CDRI Working Paper 19. Phnom Penh, Cambodia: Cambodia Development Resource Institute.

Sovannarith, S., R. Sopheap, U. Utey, S. Rathmony, B. Ballard, and S. Acharya. 2001. *Social assessment of land in Cambodia: A field study.* CDRI Working Paper 20. Phnom Penh, Cambodia: Cambodia Development Resource Institute.

Törhönen, M., and D. Palmer. 2004. Land administration in post conflict Cambodia. In Symposium on land administration in post conflict areas. http://www.fig.net/commission7/geneva_2004/index.htm. Accessed August 10, 2011.

Turton, C. 2000. *The sustainable livelihoods approach and program development in Cambodia.* Working Paper 130. London: Overseas Development Institute.

UNFPA (United Nations Population Fund). 2005. *Country profiles for population and reproductive health policy developments and indicators.* New York.

Uphoff, N. 2000. Understanding social capital: Learning from the analysis and experience of participation. In *Social capital: A multifaceted perspective,* ed. P. Dasgupta and I. Serageldin. Washington, D.C.: World Bank.

van Acker, F. 1999. *Hitting a stone with an egg? Cambodia's rural economy and land tenure in transition.* Centre for ASEAN Studies Discussion Paper 23. Antwerp, Belgium: International Management and Development, University of Antwerp.

———. 2003. *Cambodia's commons: Changing governance, shifting entitlements?* Centre for ASEAN Studies Discussion Paper 42. Antwerp, Belgium: Centre for International Management and Development, University of Antwerp.

Williams, S. 1999. Land policy and institutional involvement in land issues in Cambodia. Cambodia Land Study Project, Oxfam Great Britain, Phnom Penh, Cambodia.

World Bank. 1999. *Cambodia poverty assessment.* World Bank Report 19858-KH. Washington, D.C.: Poverty Reduction and Economic Management Sector Unit and Human Development Sector Unit, East Asia and Pacific Region.

———. 2003. *Cambodia environment monitor 2003.* Washington, D.C.

————. 2006. *Cambodia, halving poverty by 2015?* Poverty assessment 2006. Washington, D.C.

Zak, P. J., and S. Knack. 2001. Trust and growth. *Economic Journal* 111 (April): 295–321.

Zimmermann, W., and G. Kruk. 2002. Der Weg Kambodschasals: Post-conflict country in transition. *Land Reformen in Transformationsländern Südost-Asiens Entwicklung und ländlicher Raum* 36 (5): 22–25.

PART IV

Synthesis and Conclusions

This section contains the synthesis and conclusions. Parts I and IV can be thought of as mirror-image "bookends" to this volume. Whereas Chapter 1 introduces the themes of the volume, Chapter 13 recaps the findings of the case studies under these themes. Chapter 2 presents the conceptual framework, and Chapter 12 uses the framework to review the findings of the nine case studies and draw out broader lessons.

Chapter 12 goes back over each element of the conceptual framework, drawing out the lessons learned from the case studies about how that element relates to collective action and property rights for poverty reduction. In reviewing the contextual factors, the chapter emphasizes how different types of assets, risks, and governance structures affect the likelihood that collective action or equitable property rights will emerge. In discussing the action arena, it gives examples of the different ways in which collective action and property rights can strengthen the action resources of the poor or shape rules to be more in their favor. Patterns of interaction and outcomes then identify whether these result in increases in welfare, especially for poor households and communities. By reviewing the various elements of the conceptual framework, the chapter draws out the immense diversity and complexity of contexts that contribute to poverty reduction.

Chapter 13 presents conclusions and implications for policy, practice, and research. It draws together and highlights findings on the major themes of the book and the contributions of the volume to the confluence between the literature on natural resource management and that on poverty reduction. The discussion under each theme looks back on what has been learned from the case studies, as well as looking forward to how these lessons can be applied in policy and practice. These findings are not definitive, however, so the chapter also reviews the key questions that are open for further research that can contribute to improved understanding as well as action to enable poor women and men to claim their rights to resources and move out of poverty.

12 Collective Action and Property Rights for Poverty Reduction: A Synthesis

ESTHER MWANGI, HELEN MARKELOVA,
AND RUTH MEINZEN-DICK

The major theoretical enterprise of this book is to understand how the institutions of collective action and property rights influence rural poverty and livelihoods. Their links to sustainable natural resource management (NRM) are relatively well established, but this does not necessarily translate into poverty reduction. To address this question, we also need to look at the inclusiveness of these institutions; how they are influenced by (lack of) assets, risks, and governance structures that favor or disfavor poor people; and how these institutions shape the resources and strategies that poor and nonpoor actors use to further objectives of meeting basic needs and increasing income, security, social and political inclusion, or sustainability. We do this through a series of case studies that applies an extended version of the Institutional Analysis and Development (IAD) framework; the IAD framework was originally developed to isolate and understand the function of institutions in NRM. In this chapter we reflect on the findings from the nine case studies presented in this volume.

No single case study covered all aspects of the framework, and not all relationships hypothesized in Chapter 2 were covered by the case studies. Rather, each case study examined portions of the framework that were most relevant to that situation (Table 12.1).

Although all studies touched on assets, they differed in the types of assets addressed and the degree of emphasis. For example, the Ethiopia–*iddir* (burial societies) and Philippines case studies treated financial, physical, and social assets comprehensively, while the Ethiopia–Afar, African Highlands Initiative, Indonesia, and Ethiopia–Somali studies placed much emphasis on natural and social assets, with relatively less emphasis on financial and physical assets. On the other hand, the India study emphasized natural and social assets but also considered the role of financial and physical assets. Risk was the starting point for the Ethiopia–*iddir* and Philippines studies and was important in the African Highlands Initiative, Ethiopia–Somali and –Afar, and Cambodia studies. The governance context was a focus of the Kenya, Indonesia, Ethiopia–Somali, Ethiopia–Afar, and Cambodia studies.

TABLE 12.1 Case studies and the parts of the conceptual framework they explored

Case study	Context		Governance	Institutions		Action arena		Patterns		Outcomes
	Assets	Risks or shocks		Collective action	Property rights	Internal	External	Co-op	Non-co-op	
Ethiopia *iddir* (burial societies: groups for risks or shocks)	+	+		+		+		+		Maintenance of consumption levels with exclusion of those without assets; ineffectiveness with covariate shocks
Philippines (groups and familial networks for risks or shocks)	+	+		+		+		+		Increased expenditures; maintenance of consumption; spatially diversified networks effective for covariate shocks
Kenya (marketing groups)	+		+	+		+		+		Improved incomes; restriction of group participation to those with assets; constraint of access to credit by legal framework
India (watershed management)	+					+		+		Resource sustainability, restriction of benefits to those with assets

Case study	C1	C2	C3	C4	C5	C6	C7	C8	Outcomes
African Highlands Initiative (facilitation of collective action in natural resource management [NRM])	+	+	+	+	+		+		Sustainable land management; equitable access to resource benefits; strengthened access to natural resources
Indonesia (facilitation of collective action in NRM)	+	+	+	+	+		+		Increased bargaining power of local actors; prevention of elite capture; strengthening of property rights; increased involvement in policy processes
Ethiopia–Afar (Property rights and collective action in NRM)	+	+	+	+	+	+	+	+	Tensions in state–pastoral–farming interface; property rights conversion; collective action for farming
Ethiopia–Somali (Property rights and collective action in NRM)	+	+	+	+	+	+	+	+	Resource privatization; rent monopolization by elites; exclusion of poorer individuals from resources
Cambodia (Property rights and collective action in NRM)	+	+	+	+	+		+		Localized cooperation; pressures on land leading to expropriation and degradation; decentralization

SOURCE: Authors.

NOTE: A plus sign in a cell means that the given case study explores the part of the conceptual framework indicated.

Linkages among context, institutions, and poverty outcomes are inherent in all of the case studies because all focused extensively on the effects of collective action on poverty outcomes. Property rights were a major element of the Indonesia, Ethiopia–Somali, and Ethiopia–Afar case studies and to some extent of the African Highlands Initiative study but were given less emphasis in the Ethiopia–*iddir* and Philippines studies. The Indonesia and Ethiopian pastoralism case studies stand out for their exploration of the interactions between collective action and property rights.

The action arenas in the case studies ranged from subcommunity groups (for instance, *iddir* in Ethiopia) to formal marketing organizations (as in Kenya) to interactions over resource management within the community (for example, in the African Highlands Initiative study), among communities, or between the communities and the state (as in India, Ethiopia–Afar, Ethiopia–Somali, Indonesia, and Cambodia). Four of the case studies (that is, the Ethiopia–*iddir,* Philippines, India, and Kenya studies) involved interactions in the action arena comprised solely of actors internal to the system, who have a direct stake and interest in the relevant action arena and are, in turn, directly affected by the outcomes of their interactions. The other five studies (the African Highlands Initiative, Indonesia, Ethiopia–Afar, Ethiopia–Somali, and Cambodia studies) involved both internal and external actors. The capacities in which external actors were involved, however, differed markedly, with the external actors in the African Highlands Initiative and Indonesia acting to aid negotiations among actors with different action resources and types of bargaining power in contrast to external actors that work to implement government policy, sometimes in a top-down fashion that impedes cooperation among actors.

Diverse poverty outcomes are explored, from direct impacts on incomes (that is, consumption and expenditures) in the Ethiopia–*iddir,* Philippines, Kenya, India, and Ethiopia–Afar studies to impacts on personal security (illness in the Ethiopia–*iddir* and Philippines studies) to more indirect impacts such as strengthened property rights for local resource users (Indonesia, African Highlands Initiative), improved coordination among officials and resource users (African Highlands Initiative, Indonesia), and resource privatization and extinguished rights for some resource users (Ethiopia–Somali), among other outcomes listed in Table 12.1.

Taken together, the case studies form a mosaic from which a broader, complex picture emerges. In this chapter we examine the patterns of this mosaic first by tracing how various contextual factors (assets, risks, and governance arrangements) shape collective action and property rights and how these, in turn, affect the poverty outcomes as reported in the case studies, linking these back to hypotheses suggested by the framework presented in Chapter 2. We then revisit the action arena component of the framework for additional insights on how consideration of the different actors and their action resources can help to identify strategies that are likely to help (or harm) poor and marginalized groups, as well as the likely patterns of interaction for which we should be looking. The final section discusses emerging insights from the framework and the case studies on the role of collective action and property rights for poverty reduction.

Context

Assets

As Chapter 2 highlights, assets, both tangible and intangible, are crucial for the livelihoods of the poor, not only as the means of income generation but as instruments of accumulating other assets. The sustainable livelihoods approach (SLA) highlights the importance of different types of assets in the "asset pentagon": human, physical, financial, natural, and social capital (DfID 1999; Mwangi and Markelova 2009). Public and political capitals are also often added as important assets in the portfolios of the poor (Winters, Davis, and Corral 2002; Birner and Wittmer 2003). The creators of the SLA framework highlight that assets should be viewed and examined in relation to the vulnerability context and the institutions and policies that condition the socioeconomic environment (Bebbington 1999; Hulme and Shepherd 2003); the framework in this volume undertakes this approach as well. In the collection of case studies here, most of the households at the study sites are asset poor in terms of the natural, physical, financial, human, and public capitals. The African Highlands Initiative and Indonesia studies were the exception; there multistakeholder negotiations facilitated by the research teams through the participatory action research methodology brought communities together with the representatives of authorities at various levels. The rest of the studies revealed that the poor are significantly disadvantaged in terms of political capital. In fact, the Somali and Afar cases highlighted the antipastoralist policies of the Ethiopian state, which prevented the pastoralists from acquiring such assets. The stocks of other assets across the studies varied, and the poor quality of public assets (roads, infrastructure) was visible in most of the studies.

Table 12.2 lists the key assets that were addressed by each case study and their relationships to the institutions of collective action and property rights, as well as their influence on various poverty outcomes. Bebbington (1999) identifies several functions of the assets: instrumental (allowing households to make a living), hermeneutic (making living meaningful), and emancipatory (challenging power structures). These functions are illustrated by the case studies in this volume, especially that of social capital, which creates the basis for collective action. The findings from all research sites show that social capital is one type of asset that even the poor possess and in which they are able and willing to invest. These findings confirm the notion in poverty literature that social capital is indeed a vital asset (and action resource) for the resource poor, which

TABLE 12.2 Key assets by case study and links to institutions and poverty reduction

Case study	Key assets	Links to collective action, property rights, and poverty reduction
Ethiopia–*iddir* (burial societies)	Social: *Iddir*; other formal and informal groups	Local groups enabled the poor to smooth incomes, prevented loss of human capital, and provided for basic needs in times of shock but were unable to deal with wider shocks.
Philippines	Social: Formal (cooperatives or associations) and informal (lending, burial, wedding) groups Physical: Land, other productive assets Human	Intrafamilial networks and formal groups helped households deal with shocks by smoothing consumption. Wealthier households belonged to more and "better" groups. Daughters (with education) were expected to contribute more in times of need (through migrant networks) than sons.
Kenya	Social: Producer marketing groups (PMGs) Political: Legal status of PMGs as self-help societies	Collective marketing groups enabled smallholder producers to enter markets to increase incomes and create a sustainable source of income. The legal status of PMGs limited their effectiveness in facilitating market access.
India	Social: Self-help groups, watershed user groups Natural: Land, water	Watershed associations enabled communities to sustainably manage their natural resources but have not yet led to higher incomes. Collective watershed management contributed to improved resource conditions.
African Highlands Initiative	Natural: Land, forests Social: Local natural resource management (NRM) groups Political: External intervention	Sustainable resource management required collective action between community members and with other stakeholders. Local collective action was a foundation for effective and equitable NRM. Multistakeholder negotiations and participatory bylaw reforms ensured social or political inclusion of the poor in local decisionmaking, increasing equity in benefits from NRM and access to technology.

Country	Capital / Type	Description
Indonesia	Natural: Forests	Resource-dependent communities faced competition in accessing resources because of the ambiguity in property rights arrangements.
	Social: Various formal and informal groups	Local forms of collective action formed a basis for income generation from resources and served as a platform for negotiation with other actors.
	Political: Decentralization reforms, multi-stakeholder workshops	Decentralization reforms created space for multistakeholder workshops that fostered vertical cooperation in clarifying access rights that would secure the livelihoods and political inclusion of the poor.
Ethiopia–Afar	Natural: Communal and private grazing lands	Unclear tenure arrangements limited the livelihood sources of poor pastoralists.
	Political: Marginalization of pastoralists	Unfavorable government policies led to uncertainty in property rights that would jeopardize the personal and property security of the poor.
	Social: Cooperation around farming	Social capital in the form of cooperation around livelihood activities enabled the poor to overcome their low stocks of natural and political capital.
Ethiopia–Somali	Physical: Livestock	Wealthier pastoralists had better access to water sources and greater ability to limit poorer households' access to them.
	Social: Cooperation around water sources maintenance and access	Cooperation based on traditional norms of reciprocity clarified the rules for access to essential resources but offered only limited enforcement.
Cambodia	Social: "Forestry communities," "fishery communities," formal and informal groups and associations	Local forms of cooperation enabled the poor to overcome low stocks of natural, human, and political capital and contributed to resource sustainability and both personal and property security.

SOURCE: Authors.

enables them to deal with the lack or difficulty of access to other assets (Groot-aert 1999; Uphoff and Wijayaratna 2000). The bases for these groups and networks are the institutional arrangements that help to enhance their liveli-hood options. These range from the kinship ties used for various purposes (such as to access water resources in the Somali study) to insurance schemes (such as *iddir* in Ethiopia) to conflict resolution mechanisms based on the traditional authority structures in the Cambodia study. Individuals and households belong to numerous groups and networks that allow them to compensate, to some extent, for the lack of other resources and allow disadvantaged households to reach certain poverty outcomes by serving as a valuable action resource. For example, in the Kenya study area the smallholder farmers have formed pro-ducer marketing groups (PMGs) to overcome market failures and difficulty in accessing financial markets, enabling them to make a better living (the instru-mental function of social capital). In the Afar and Somali study areas, the norms of trust and reciprocity not only fulfill a livelihoods (that is, instrumental) func-tion but also serve as a culturally important way of life (the hermeneutic func-tion of social capital). In Indonesia, forest-dependent households have relied heavily on social capital by forming groups not only to engage in income-generating activities but also to lobby the authorities for change in forest access rights thus coping with deficiencies in other assets (instrumental and emancipa-tory functions).

However, the case studies also reveal that asset endowments and asset accumulation processes are not the same for all, and the poor may be disadvan-taged even with respect to social capital. For example, the Philippines study shows that the wealthier households belong to more productive (formal) net-works from which the poorer households are excluded. The Ethiopia–*iddir* study demonstrates that households with larger landholdings (that is, greater endowments of natural capital) are part of larger and "better-quality" burial societies. Both of these studies highlight that the poor are disadvantaged in terms of accruing social capital. The Cambodia study shows that the land-less or nearly landless and those with lower educational levels are less likely to participate in formalized groups such as cash associations and rice banks. Additionally, the African Highlands Initiative study points out that wealthier households have more influence on local authorities, or larger amounts of political capital, positioning them for easier accumulation of other assets and especially enabling them to gain greater access to natural resources. However, even resource-poor households are able to participate in groups and networks, even though the "quality" or the number of such memberships may be lower than in better-off families.

Of special importance to this volume are the institutions of collective action and property rights and their role in mediating poverty. These institutions figure prominently in the livelihood arrangements of the households at the research sites. As mentioned in Chapter 2, collective action can be understood as an outcome of social capital (Uphoff and Wijayaratna 2000); therefore, when examining the interaction between assets and collective action, it is clear that asset endowments affect households' ability and incentives to participate in collective activities. Better-endowed households are more likely to engage in collective action. By contrast, the Ethiopia–Afar and Ethiopia–Somali studies show the opposite effect of assets on participation in collective activities: they show that pastoralists with greater livestock endowments have fewer incentives to engage in groups for watershed and pasture management. Therefore, the effect of assets on collective action is variable and context dependent: it is clear that participation in groups and networks often provides a valuable fallback option for the asset poor, whereas wealthier households may use their asset base either to "opt out" of group ventures or as a means to participate in and influence the outcomes of collective activities.

The studies show that collective action can contribute to asset accumulation, thus increasing the action resources of the poor and leading to better poverty outcomes. For example, the Kenyan farmers studied are able to access financial and product markets via their participation in the action arena of PMGs. Indonesian forest-dependent communities are able to negotiate their rights to the forests and forest products because of their engagement in the collective negotiation and lobbying activities catalyzed by the Center for International Forestry Research (CIFOR). The Ethiopia–*iddir* study shows that through collective action the poor are able to prevent the loss of human capital in times of shocks, illustrating the links between assets (social capital in this case) and risks. The Philippines case reveals that remittances from migrant networks, a form of intrafamilial collective action, enable households to build up stocks of both physical and human capital that may be negatively affected by a shock. The Ethiopia–Afar study reveals similar findings for collective farming, which is used by the pastoralists to compensate for the diminished amounts of natural and political capitals in the context of unfavorable government policies (which could be classified as sociopolitical shocks). In the India study, participation in collective watershed management institutions has been seen to improve the stock of natural capital.

Property rights are fundamental for tangible assets. These rights determine who can benefit from "natural capital," be it forests in the Indonesia study or grazing lands and water sources in the Afar and Somali studies. The literature on property rights shows that they are not just about ownership (individual or communal) but cover all aspects of resource tenure from access rights to management rights to the ability to derive an income from access to a resource (see Schlager and Ostrom 1992; Ribot 1998; Meinzen-Dick and Mwangi 2009). The case studies collected in this volume provide a strong illustration of this point. The Indonesia study shows that the poor are organizing to obtain not just access to the forest but also the right to harvest and sell nontimber forest products, that is, to secure a source of income. The Ethiopia–Afar case shows that rights to grazing lands are complicated and intertwined with many other institutions such as kinship ties and interclan reciprocity. In Cambodia the entire structure of individual and communal property rights is in flux as a result of the country's sociopolitical background and the ambiguity in the current land laws; in this case, property rights are understood as different levels of access arrangements ranging from using lands in common to land grabbing to formal private land titling.

What impact does the assets–institutions nexus have on poverty reduction? The case studies show that although many of the poor may lack natural, physical, financial, public, and human capitals, most of them are endowed with social capital through membership in various groups and networks. Even though the distribution of social capital is not equal among the poor, many households are able to engage in various collective action institutions, ranging from insurance schemes to resource management arrangements, which allow them to cope with disadvantages faced in the accumulation of other types of assets. Thus, collective action enables them to avoid falling deeper into poverty (Ethiopia–*iddir*, Philippines) and even improve their livelihoods (Kenya). However, in several cases poor men and women face certain barriers to participation in collective activities (Cambodia, Philippines, African Highlands Initiative); in other situations, collective action is an institution used more by poorer families than by their better-off cohorts (Afar, Somali). On the other hand, the India case shows that collective action does not directly lead to improvements in welfare. Improvements in resource conditions may have an indirect effect on welfare with longer gestation periods, but unless the poor have rights to the benefit streams, they will not share in the direct benefits, because the landless are left out in India.

Property rights institutions fulfill an important function in the lives of the poor: they provide a means to obtain other assets and determine households' access to other assets, thus serving as valuable action resources and paving the way to acquire other action resources. Here again the wealthier households are able to take greater advantage of these institutions. The Ethiopia–Somali and Ethiopia–Afar studies show that households with larger livestock herds and more political connections were able to secure rights to individual pastures and water sources and thus exclude the poorer pastoralists (or charge them user fees). The Indonesia study mentions that private companies gained rights to large parts of forest areas. In all these cases, communal rights proved to be of great importance to the poor (see Wily 2006). Therefore, the findings of the case studies show that what happens with the assets in the action arena can lead to different patterns of interaction; depending on how assets are used and transformed in the action situation, cooperation, elite capture, or even conflict can occur and influence poverty outcomes in different ways.

Risks and Shocks

Chapter 2 highlights that vulnerability to risks is an important element of the multidimensional reality of the poor, or the context in which they live. It has a direct impact on poverty outcomes (lowering incomes, leading to greater social exclusion, adversely impacting personal and property security, and so on), which makes it necessary for any poverty-related study to examine the impact of shocks on the poor and the mechanisms used to deal with various uncertainties. The case studies presented in this volume confirm the findings in the literature that the poor are very vulnerable to risks from various sources (Jalan and Ravallion 1999; Dercon 2002) and illustrate how assets as well as the institutions of collective action and property rights are used to mitigate the effect of shocks. This section highlights lessons learned from the studies on the interaction between poverty and vulnerability and examines how vulnerability influences collective action and property rights and what institutional arrangements the poor employ to deal with risk.

As discussed in Chapter 2, three types of shocks are usually identified in the literature: natural, economic, and sociopolitical shocks (Little et al. 2001; Dercon 2002). Earlier studies on the interaction between vulnerability and poverty also revealed that health shocks, primarily death and illness, are identified by the poor as the most harmful (Krishna et al. 2004). In addition, risks occur with varying frequency and predictability, which affects households' ability to prepare for them. Both of these characteristics of the nature of shocks are important because they demand different coping strategies and affect the institutions of collective action and property rights in different ways. The studies reported in this volume show that certain risks are not specific to any region; the poor in both East Africa and South Asia face droughts, which have devastating consequences for their agricultural production. Similarly, households in both Asia and Africa have to cope with economic shocks such as seasonal price changes, market risks, and increasing oil prices. In addition, the Indonesia, Ethiopia–*iddir,* and Kenya studies show that the poor are adversely affected by health shocks, such as the spread of HIV and malaria as well as the incipient epidemic of avian flu. Political instability and conflicts over resources also appear in several of the case studies (Ethiopia–Afar and Ethiopia–Somali, Cambodia, Indonesia, and the Philippines).

Table 12.3 presents the most prominent shocks encountered in each of the case studies, along with their frequency or predictability and their links with institutions of collective action and property rights that influence poverty outcomes. Alderman and Paxson (1994) identify two general types of strategies that the poor use in dealing with shocks: risk-coping mechanisms, which include self-insurance through assets, savings, and informal group-based risk-sharing, and risk management strategies, which mainly involve income diversification. The case studies presented in this volume provide examples of both. In the discussion of assets earlier in this chapter we mentioned the linkages between various types of assets and the ability to withstand shocks (and, conversely, the effects of shocks on fluctuations of assets).

The case studies reported in this volume show that shocks and their perceived consequences provide incentives for people to engage in collective action.

TABLE 12.3 Key risks or shocks by case study and links to institutions and poverty reduction

Case study	Shock	Frequency	Links to collective action, property rights, and poverty reduction
Ethiopia–*iddir* (burial societies)	Death in the family; illness or hospitalization	High	Local forms of collective action enabled households to deal with health shocks and other individual shocks but were limited in their ability to mitigate widespread shocks.
Philippines	Death in the family; illness or hospitalization	High	Intrafamilial networks and other formal and informal groups enabled families to overcome a lack of financial assets in times of need to prevent loss of income.
Kenya	Fluctuation in commodity prices	High	Collective marketing groups enabled small producers to deal with economic shocks and secure livelihood sources.
India	Seasonal rainfall	High	Collective natural resource management (NRM) enabled households to cope with natural shocks.
African Highlands Initiative	Pests and weeds	High	Participatory negotiation processes (vertical cooperation) allowed households to deal with natural shocks by providing equitable access to agricultural technologies and collective NRM.
Indonesia	Conflicts over forest rights	High	Vertical cooperation enabled resource-dependent communities to negotiate access to resources essential to their livelihoods.
Ethiopia–Afar	Sedentarization policies, other government actions	Medium	Cooperation around farming enabled pastoral households to overcome risks posed by unfavorable government policies in accessing grazing lands.
Ethiopia–Somali	Contraband trade	Medium	Collective action enabled pastoralists to withstand various sociopolitical shocks, including contraband trade and violent conflicts.
Cambodia	Shifts in property rights	Medium	Changes and uncertainty in tenure arrangements led to conflict and loss of livelihoods.

SOURCE: Authors.

People form networks and groups, both formal and informal, to cope with shocks as they realize their inability to deal with these shocks on an individual basis and have experienced the benefits of joint action in their economic and other activities. Collective action is an effective and widely used risk-mitigating method among the poor in the absence of well-functioning credit and insurance markets. Several of the studies show that membership in formal and informal groups and networks is a crucial element in the risk-smoothing portfolios of the poor by serving as both an ex ante (Ethiopia–*iddir*) and an ex post mechanism (African highlands, Ethiopia–Afar, Philippines). However, they also provide evidence supporting the hypothesis presented in Chapter 2 that collective action has limitations in dealing with covariate shocks compared with idiosyncratic shocks. Collective action also has limitations in ensuring equitable participation opportunities for both the better off and the poor, as demonstrated in the Ethiopia–*iddir* and Philippines case studies.

The findings also support the hypothesis stated in Chapter 2 that the frequency of shocks influences these incentives for organizing, with collective action a more common response to frequent, relatively predictable risks than to rarer, less predictable shocks. On the one hand, the Ethiopia–*iddir* and Philippines studies show that health shocks were identified by respondents themselves as among the most damaging shocks affecting household well-being; therefore, these risks provided a greater incentive for people to form *iddir* and familial networks. This finding confirms the results of other studies in these and other countries (see Dercon 2002; Krishna et al. 2004; Fafchamps and Gubert 2007). Similarly, in the African Highlands Initiative case study it was the persistent natural resource problems (pests and soil degradation) that provided an impetus for organizing and collectively finding solutions to these problems. Climatic variations that resulted in price fluctuations for agricultural products led to the formation of PMGs in Kenya and watershed associations in India. These studies show that in addition to often being the only viable risk-coping options for the asset-poor households, groups and networks help deal with the information asymmetries in the formal insurance markets (Udry 1994). On the other hand, where the shocks were less frequent and therefore less predictable (for example, in the case of climatic distress), there was less incentive to organize. The literature on collective action in NRM shows that there are both tangible and intangible costs of cooperation (Meinzen-Dick et al. 2002). These costs, observed in the Kenya and India case studies, show that risks that occur less frequently do not force people to prepare for them ex ante by forming or joining groups with the purpose of risk sharing. Furthermore, these less frequent but drastic events, such as policy shifts in the Ethiopia–Afar case, can undermine local collective action by destroying trust among the community members. Even if rare, such major events as civil war have long-term repercussions, as seen in Cambodia.

As for the interaction between vulnerability and property rights, the Indonesia case study shows that large-scale sociopolitical shocks, such as decentralization, can create ambiguity around rights to resources and thus lead to conflict and deteriorating welfare. In this case, however, it was this uncertainty of access to and ownership of resources that created fertile ground for local collective action around property rights issues. In the Afar and Somali studies, unpredictable government policies of privatizing common pastoral lands produced uncertainty around rights to land, which led to the breakdown in social capital (trust) and the decline of some collective action institutions. In Cambodia, shifts in property rights arrangements as a result of changing political regimes also created ambiguity, which led to conflicts over resources and greater income inequality. All these cases demonstrate that property rights themselves can become a source of sociopolitical risk, which in some cases can provide incentives to collectively deal with it, either through organizing around lobbying for greater access to resources (Indonesia) or through forming groups to diversify income from a risky activity (Ethiopia–Afar).

Risk management strategies are well illustrated in the Afar and Somali cases, where farming (versus the traditional livestock herding) is used to diversify climate-related and sociopolitical risks by way of collective farming (that is collective action as an instrument of income diversification). However, although the poor employ multiple strategies to deal with risk, the poverty outcomes are heterogeneous and are based on their asset portfolios and other coping strategies available to them. Earlier studies have shown that even informal mechanisms seem to be less effective for the poor than for their better-off counterparts (Jalan and Ravallion 1999; Dercon and Krishnan 2000). The findings in the Ethiopia–*iddir* and Philippines studies demonstrate the interactions among assets, ability to withstand shocks, and the role played by the institutions of collective action in mitigating risks. These studies show that the poor are disadvantaged in terms of joining groups: better-off households belong to a greater number and "higher-quality" groups as well as to more productive networks than do poorer families. Similarly, in Afar the poorer families cannot mitigate shocks well with just livestock because it is a lumpy asset, while the wealthier rely on accumulating and diversifying livestock (in terms of both species and location of herding) and thus have more reliable risk management options.

Property rights to land and other resources are necessary for people to be able to use their assets during shocks. Both pastoral cases in Ethiopia (Afar and Somali) also show that flexible property rights arrangements are also a response to highly fluctuating environments, enabling people to reduce their risk of not having water for their animals, supporting the hypothesis offered in Chapter 2 that infrequently occurring risks about which there is an imprecise knowledge of their probability are likely to lead to flexible property rights arrangements. These studies also show that those with a larger asset base prefer fixed, in most cases individual (versus communal), property rights for their risk-smoothing portfolios. Unclear property rights can also be a source of risk: as the Indonesia and Cambodia case studies show, the ambiguity of access to vital resources can generate shocklike conditions (conflicts), which were dealt with in these cases via various forms of collective action.

In sum, the case studies reveal the twofold link between vulnerability and the institutions of collective action and property rights: susceptibility to risk creates incentives for the creation of these institutions, and these institutions serve as instruments of coping with risks. Most important, these examples highlight that the poor are not passive recipients of their "fate" who have no resources to use in the action arena. On the contrary, the case studies show that in the context of a complex and uncertain environment, the poor have become skillful managers of their portfolios, employing multiple strategies to cope with shocks even though they may still be somewhat limited in the options they have to reduce their vulnerability. Collective action institutions, such as *iddir* or familial networks that emerge from the existing stocks of social capital, serve as valuable action resources that result in cooperation (pattern of interaction) to mitigate the negative impacts of shocks and prevent losses in income and the provision of basic needs. Unclear property rights to resources (natural capital), as in the Ethiopia–Afar and Ethiopia–Somali studies, become a source of risk, prevent the poor from using their assets in the action arena, and may lead not only to cooperation but also to elite capture and even conflicts (other types of patterns of interaction), resulting in negative poverty outcomes. Which pattern of interaction emerges from the action arena in this case is greatly influenced by the governance structures in place, which are discussed in the next section.

Governance Structures

This section reflects on the legal, political, and power structures that conditioned the collective action and property rights of the poor in the case studies presented in this volume. The conceptual framework introduced in Chapter 2 suggests that the governance structures in which poor people are embedded exert a major influence on their abilities to organize to improve their income streams or resource access or to take advantage of opportunities. These initial conditions also determine the substantive rights of individuals and their ability to access or exploit those rights in order to improve their well-being.

In the case studies reported in this book, the governance structures in which people were embedded included the following:

- Norms and customs endogenous to communities (in the Ethiopia–Somali and Ethiopia–Afar studies), including other structural attributes of communities such as ethnic heterogeneity.
- Formal rules external to communities, often introduced by governments, with varying state capacity. These included decentralization reforms (Indonesia, Ethiopia–Afar), sedentarization or modernization reforms (Somali and Afar), and market liberalization (Kenya).
- Project rules and norms generated by nongovernmental actors such as

CIFOR (Indonesia) and the African Highlands Initiative, which actively support community organizing and rights through projects and also constitute the context for communities.
* Formal organizational practices, for example, strategies for the delivery of agricultural extension services that left out women farmers (African Highlands Initiative) or charged membership fees to PMGs (Kenya).

Although many programs and policies focus on the formalized rules introduced by governments, these are not the only relevant legal and political structures that shape people's lives. A range of customary norms are also important, and it is crucial to understand how these interact with formal external legal structures. This legal pluralism has implications for both property rights and collective action. Finally, organizational practices are also relevant, because these practices will shape how formal rules are implemented, and how people can interact with the organizations, internal or external to the community. Table 12.4 presents a summary of how governance structures encountered in each case study interacted with collective action and property rights to influence outcomes. The remainder of this section discusses how these factors play out in the case studies in this volume.

In the Ethiopia–Somali study (Chapter 10) customary rules and practices provided a basis for collective access to and management of water in a dry, semiarid environment. These rules determined group membership, the nature of rights, responsibility for facility maintenance, and sanctions for noncompliance. Customary rules also defined conditions of access by nonmembers. These rules coordinated the use of sparsely distributed and highly variable resources by multiple users. Their inclusiveness and flexibility allowed both the poor and the less poor group members and recognized nonmembers to use water for their needs, even during times of scarcity (Niamir-Fuller 1999; Meinzen-Dick, Mwangi, and Dohrn 2006).

However, an influx of refugees and a series of government projects undermined the coordinating function of customary rules and sanctions. These acted as disincentives to group participation, especially of wealthier herders, who withdrew their support and instead sought to privatize water resources and concentrate the benefits of a previously communal resource among themselves. Because wealthier members often play a critical role in collective action, providing leadership and sometimes even underwriting collective action when it is in their interest (Olson 1965), their withdrawal from the group particularly undermines group efforts. These findings are supportive of the hypothesis in Chapter 2 that in legal systems where statutory systems are dominant, collective action among local communities may not only be crowded out but repressed altogether. This was also true in the Ethiopia–Afar case study, as we see in the next paragraph.

Rules and practices that are imposed from the outside also affect whether poor people can exercise existing resource rights or self-organize to improve their lives and livelihoods without retribution. Repeated government policies and interventions aimed at modernizing pastoralists in Ethiopia (see the Ethiopia–Afar study in Chapter 9) forcibly appropriated communal lands, circumscribed access to critical pastoral resources, and weakened traditional clan-based rules and norms for the collective use and management of pasture and resources. This is not far afield from Scott's (1999) observations that powerful states in different parts of the world, in their attempts at political control, forced through ambitious, large-scale schemes that disregarded or destroyed local knowledge and institutions built up over generations. This imposition and enforcement of rules from the outside in Ethiopia–Afar has been found to restrict within-group cooperation, resulting in the dominance of individual strategies, such as privatization. By weakening the mutual dependence that provided the incentive to cooperate in the first place, privatization undermined collective action (Runge 1986; Seabright 1993).

Similarly, in Uganda (see the African Highlands Initiative study in Chapter 7) the state's desire to fully control protected areas resulted in the eviction of ethnic minorities and loss of access to a major livelihood source. The Indonesia case study (Chapter 8) also documents a sociopolitical setting that has undermined the rural peoples' access to resources. By devolving forest management to district authorities without clarifying rights, roles, and responsibilities or providing budgetary support, the reforms created ambiguities and revenue deficits that resulted in the conversion of forests to "profitable" plantations, the allocation of concessions to state and private firms, and insecurities for indigenous communities that lived and farmed in the forests. It also heightened conflict between communities, district and central governments, and private concessionaires. Power asymmetries among state agents, concessionaires, and the rural poor are vast, posing difficulties for local-level organizing to reclaim rights.

The outcomes of Indonesia's forestry devolution program (and of other top-down reforms) are consistent with the discussion of decentralization in Chapter 2 and echo the findings of other scholars and practitioners who suggest that where the legal framework in support of decentralization is ambiguous as to the rights, roles, and responsibilities of relevant actors (such as local communities, local governments, central governments, and other private entrepreneurs), opportunities for the capture of benefits by local and national elites abound, often to the exclusion of the poorer communities that inhabit forests and forest margins (Manor 1999; Larson 2005). Such ambiguities are also associated with the increased insecurity of the customary rights of resource users (McCarthy 2004). The Cambodia case (Chapter 11) represents an extreme example of state terror's decimating existing local forms of social capital that inhered in customary and religious systems and forcibly appropriating resources by evicting people from forests. Current decentralization reforms in the natural resources and land sectors are further redistributing resources away from the rural poor to military and urban elites.

TABLE 12.4 Links among governance structures, collective action, property rights, and poverty reduction by case study

Case study	Key governance structures	Links to collective action, property rights, and poverty reduction
Kenya	Market liberalization policies	High transactions costs, coordination failure, pervasive market imperfections, and a lack of market-enabling institutions kept the benefits of liberalization policies from reaching small-scale farmers.
	State regulations for producer associations	Collective marketing by producer marketing groups linked farmers to markets, increased the adoption of productivity-enhancing technologies, and generated higher prices for participating smallholders. The scope of participatory marketing groups was limited by their lack of legal recognition.
African Highlands Initiative	Project with external facilitation by state and nonstate actors	Extension strategies encouraged individual strategies for the use of shared resources, which discouraged collective action for sustainable resource use and management.
		Women farmers and poorer resource users were excluded from the benefits of new technologies.
	State policies for protected area conservation	Negotiation support built trust and provided a communication platform among state and community actors; increased cooperation in the management of shared resources, including design and enforcement of bylaws for resource use and management; strengthened property rights for forest dwellers; and led to more inclusive service delivery.
		Ethnic minority groups were evicted from forests and denied access to forest resources.
Indonesia	State decentralization policies in the forestry sector	Implementation of forestry decentralization resulted in ambiguities in roles, rights, and responsibilities. It increased conflict and the insecurity of property rights of forest-dwelling and forest-adjacent communities and encouraged elite capture by private companies.

	Project with external facilitation by state and nonstate actors	Negotiation support and collective action (among community, state, and private actors) created space for strengthening the rights of communities, including them in local budgeting processes, and identifying forest-based income-generating enterprises.
Ethiopia–Afar	Customary systems that regulated pasture access and collective action for use and management of pastures	Customary systems allowed legitimate claimants, regardless of wealth and status, to gain access to resources even during droughts.
	State policies of sedentarization	Sedentarization policies weakened customary systems and promoted land privatization and a change of the production system to cultivation, resulting in elite capture and loss of land or allocation of unviable land to poorer herders and women.
Ethiopia–Somali	Customary systems that regulated water access and collective action for maintenance of water facilities	Customary systems allowed legitimate claimants, regardless of wealth and status, access to resources even during drought. Water privatization and marketization reduced the influence of customary authority, undermined collective action, and resulted in the exclusion of poorer herders from water access.
Cambodia	Customary and religious resource management institutions	Although authority for natural resource management has been devolved to lower-level institutions that rely on traditional and religious rules and norms for shared use and management of resources (forestry and fisheries) by village communities, interference by higher-level authorities undermined the capacity to enforce rules for resource use and management at the village level.
	State decentralization policies in the natural resources sector	Procedures for recognizing, clarifying, and strengthening community rights to resources under decentralization programs were slow and lacked transparency, creating uncertainty and conflict over boundaries.

An absence of state intervention can provide space for community organizing. Market liberalization policies, the removal of state marketing boards, and the promotion of the private sector created opportunities for the formation of participatory marketing groups in semiarid parts of Kenya (see Chapter 5). Moreover, the government's lack of provision of health insurance and its complete absence from intervention in *iddir* in Ethiopia (see Chapter 3) has provided an opportunity for the expansion and diversification of burial groups into a wide range of activities, including the provision of illness and health insurance. It has also provided an opportunity for *iddir* to develop formal rules that are adapted to their ecological environment and membership demographics.

Although governments can affect people's livelihoods through the reforms they pursue, they can also affect people directly through their practices when implementing sectoral activities. In the African Highlands Initiative study, targeting individuals (instead of groups) for the management of common pool resources limited possibilities for joint action to solve common problems. By selectively excluding women from access to new technologies, extension officers systematically undercut women's roles as relevant community actors and constrained their efforts to provide for their livelihoods. The exclusion of women through government practice is also evident in the Indonesia case study, in which women were rarely seen participating in public meetings and decision-making forums prior to CIFOR's intervention. These findings support the hypothesis in Chapter 2 that the poor are disadvantaged by decisionmaking rules—in these cases, even by the rules and approaches of development agencies. These can undermine the potential for collective action among communities and in some cases may actively create conditions that further marginalize the poor.

The previous discussion highlights several issues that are consistent with the governance component of the conceptual framework: the legal and political structures that comprise formal policy and law that is external to communities, as well as customary structures that originate from communities, can and do influence local-level efforts at poverty reduction.[1] Externally enforced solutions, even well-intended ones such as decentralization and devolution, can undermine local-level rights to resources, even if they have built-in provisions and support for community participation and resource management. External solutions that are not attuned to local needs and actively seek to stamp out local forms of organizing and rights through the use of force only increase the vulnerability of the poor. Finally, faulty implementation of government projects can constrain local livelihood efforts.

It is not inevitable for state–society interactions to have negative consequences for communities' collective attempts to provide for their livelihoods

---

1. Note that these external conditions are those in which research projects were embedded. It does not mean that they cannot be changed.

or access resources vital to their production systems. Much depends on the way reforms are structured and, critically, on whether such state-led reforms are animated by local-level needs (Anderson and Ostrom 2008). The back and forth of Indonesia's and Uganda's forestry sector decentralization, in which rules were made, unmade, and remade in rapid succession, affected the patterns of resource distribution and authority between government agencies and authorities at different governance levels and also between them and resource users. It created uncertainties and ambiguities with regard to resource allocation decisions and accountability processes, which in turn allowed for elite capture in which well-connected individuals in positions of advantage directed benefits toward themselves. A better understanding of the effect of such governance changes on the action arena can help societies to anticipate the outcomes of reforms.

Similar processes are evident in the top-down privatization of resources in Ethiopia and Cambodia. In these cases, a disregard for local practices and norms that evolved over many years under conditions of ecological variability weakened customary authority and norms of water access and distribution. It resulted in the privatization of communal resources, the exclusion of legitimate claimants, and the imposition of water fees. Once again, greater attention to the interplay of institutions and environment at the local level (instead of government enforcement and compulsion) and an attempt to complement existing customary practices on the basis of comparative advantage across governance and ecological scales would have had less dramatic consequences in terms of the capacities to organize (Mwangi and Ostrom 2009).

Overall, what can we learn regarding how governance structures interact with the rest of the elements of the conceptual framework, including property rights and collective action, in order to produce outcomes? The case studies in this book support the hypothesis presented in Chapter 2 that governance structures greatly influence poverty outcomes. For example, when reforms are conducted within a governance system that is characterized by weak state institutions that lack enforcement capabilities or clarity, they can increase rather than reduce vulnerability and hence poverty. More specifically, when rule changes occur (in such areas as decentralization, sedentarization, or modernization) and no effort is made to moderate differentials in authority, power, knowledge, and information among societal actors (that is, action resources among actors in the action arena), better-endowed actors will exploit their action resources to advance their gains to the detriment of less endowed actors. Government actors, for example, may manipulate, intimidate, or coerce respected and legitimate (but often weaker) customary authorities into enforcing new rules. Similarly, wealthier, more powerful individuals (or corporate individuals) may use their influence to seek a disproportionate allocation of resources to themselves. These actions in the action arena (that is, patterns of interaction that are characterized by noncooperation and exclusion) may lead to a decline in collective action and sharpen individual strategies, wealth concentration, and loss of access for and exclusion of poorer, less influential individuals. Exclusion and loss of resource access undermine the ability of poorer individuals and groups to provide for their livelihoods (that is, achieve positive poverty outcomes).

The expectation of elite capture of benefits in reform settings can be refined to incorporate further lessons from the case studies in this volume. For example, negotiation support brokered by trusted actors in the action arena can serve to increase the bargaining power of poorer or marginalized individuals or groups (that is, their action resources) and encourage cooperation among actors with vastly different action resources (that is, patterns of interaction) to secure their property rights to resources and their access to decisionmaking processes. Collective action by the poor is an insufficient safeguard, and the brokerage of external actors and champions may be necessary to improve outcomes, especially for the very poor.

The Action Arena

Although contextual factors play an important role in shaping the institutions of collective action and property rights, the action arena is where it all comes together in the interplay among individual or collective actors who have preferences and action resources and are subject to rules that order their interactions. Actors, action resources, and decisionmaking arrangements delimit the space in which actors form strategies, make choices, and take action. Better understanding of the action arena can help us to understand and anticipate how changes in conditions are likely to affect poverty outcomes, but because there is human agency, these outcomes are not deterministic. This section reviews some of the further insights on these processes represented in the case studies in this volume.

Action resources provide the actor with the ability to act in pursuit of his or her preferences. These action resources comprise the tangible assets discussed earlier, as well as intangible assets such as information, information-processing capabilities, power endowments, status, and mental models, among others. Mental models, on the level of knowing things as well as on the normative level, also delimit the capacity of actors to make choices and take action. In this regard, actors may not always make deliberate or conscious choices but often act based on "rules of thumb," "what we have always done," or "what is expected of me." In the scope of this study, agency itself reflects the ability to exercise livelihood choices, to participate in collective action at various levels to affect livelihoods, and to influence other actors' choices, as well as to get involved in political processes, consistent with the role attributed to agency in other poverty-related literature (Hulme and Shepherd 2003).

In the case studies presented in this book, we encounter a range of actors who are broadly representative of actors in any given empirical setting. These include officials in various capacities in government ministries, such as the

Ministry of Forestry in Indonesia or general officials in Ethiopia, each pursuing objectives consistent (or not) with their official mandates and bearing the resources of power, status, information, budgets, and networks that characterize their positions. In addition, we encounter men and women from distinct communities, interacting with each other and, in some cases, with the officials to whom they can gain access. As the framework in Chapter 2 proposes, all these actors are endowed with individual assets or collective resources (such as group organization and networks) critical for pursuing various livelihoods and welfare-enhancing objectives, from marketing produce to coping with illness risks, securing individual and collective access to critical natural resources, enabling collective farming, or even resisting top-down efforts at pastoral sedentarization. Their interactions with each other and with external actors are subject to the assets that they own, their positions and status in their societies, and their networks and connections with political actors within and outside their communities. In some cases these interactions are also influenced by socialized notions of appropriate actions due to individuals' roles and status in their communities.

There is considerable evidence to support the hypothesis stated in Chapter 2 that the poor are disadvantaged by lack of action resources, with natural capital (such as land and water) especially important in the Ethiopia–Somali case study and social capital critical in the Ethiopia–*iddir* and Philippines studies. Political capital, or voice, emerged as a critical action resource in many of the case studies, and lack of political capital left marginalized groups with little ability to shape the decisionmaking rules (as in Ethiopia–Afar and Cambodia studies), unless there was outside facilitation (as in the Indonesia or the African Highlands Initiative study).

As discussed in the earlier sections on governance, assets, and risks, the state and its policies and actions play a prominent role in enabling or hindering poor people's transition in and out of poverty, influencing how these contextual factors affect poverty outcomes. Government agents, whether from the local or the central government, have at their discretion a wide range of resources that can facilitate or encumber people's access to resources, which in turn have implications for livelihoods. In Indonesia, for example, government actors in the Ministry of Forestry, the National Land Agencies, and the provincial and district administrations have various authorities and powers. These include the power to recommend forest conversion to different land uses, to issue permits to private concessionaires, to endorse community property rights to resources (including use and ownership), to enter into social forestry or joint forest management agreements with communities, and to craft and implement development plans and budgets. In addition, they are endowed with privileged knowledge and information of the new decentralization laws and provisions, and also with networks that extend to other actors in society, including local communities, village elites, and private entrepreneurs.

Much as in Indonesia, the government in Ethiopia has proven to be a dominant actor in the reconfiguration of property rights and production systems in the drylands (see the Ethiopia–Afar and Ethiopia–Somali case studies). Not only has it used law, budgets and finances, information, and propaganda to appropriate pastoral land and convert it to agricultural state farms; it has also exploited ideological discourses of modernization to push through its sedentarization policies. By characterizing pastoralism as a primitive and inefficient use of scarce resources, it has legitimized the use of institutions (including decrees), budgets, and even the military to coerce pastoralists to adopt its sedentarization program. The introduction of ethnicity-based federalism, a state-led reform, reverted power to clan elders, while at the same time introducing a new set of actors (local government as well as NGOs), and a new process for completing the farming and sedentarization project of earlier years. The power of persuasion, through provision of information on farming techniques and the provision of capital and farming implements, was a key action resource employed by external actors. In the Ethiopia–Somali case study, the central government has been a key factor in the provision of water resources, seeking to construct low-cost water-harvesting technologies to supplement community sources. As in the Ethiopia–Afar case study, such state-led programs have relied on their capacity to mobilize community labor for construction and maintenance through the imposition of financial penalties enforced by co-opted team leaders drawn from the traditional leadership. Nonetheless, users are more responsive to clan rules and leadership that is rooted in community ideology and history, which provide a historical basis for stable and recognized reciprocal access and negotiation across a vast territory (see also the Cambodia case study).

Individuals and communities with lower stocks of assets, including political capital, have leveraged their resources, individual and collective, in their efforts to construct and sustain their livelihoods. In Indonesia, for example, local actors, both women and men, had available to them the capacity to organize, but often they did so along narrow gendered lines. This ability to organize with considerable facilitation and information about alternative options from NGOs proved valuable in increasing their bargaining power, to the extent that they were able to make demands of government officials, pursue land certification through government-sponsored programs, create space for their views and needs to be reflected in local planning priorities, bargain with government-sponsored private concessionaires to recover and sustain their claims to forest resources, and obtain additional information and access to different government-supported community development programs and grants. However, bargaining power can also be used to resist state action (as opposed to making demands of the state), as did the numerous pastoralists in the Ethiopia–Afar case study, who used their sheer numbers to sabotage and frustrate state-led efforts to sedentarize them.

Community actors on their own also draw on their own self-organizing capacities to achieve mutual benefits. In the Kenya case, for example, which also involved NGO facilitation through the provision of information and improved crop varieties, individuals contributed their own resources to the group effort by paying annual membership fees, attending meetings, and providing cash capital. There were no ideological barriers to women's participation. Individual assets such as land, livestock, and education enabled participation but were not exclusionary. Similarly, reciprocal social networks, including burial societies, were valuable action resources for coping with illness and drought shocks in the Ethiopia–*iddir* and Philippines case studies. These studies have shown how social capital can be turned into a valuable action resource to obtain certain poverty outcomes. Yet the extent of access to such social resources is, in turn, predicated on an individual's access to material wealth such as landholdings or livestock holdings or to nonmaterial resources such as status or connections within the village. In the Philippines, in particular, wealth and education are important action resources that allow better-endowed individuals to belong to more groups and networks, enhancing their abilities to insure themselves against economic losses. Membership in groups assumes even more significance as an action resource because it has a positive impact on the number of networks that individuals can access.

Alternatively, group membership can determine whether individuals gain property rights to critical resources for their livelihoods. Among the Somali and Afar of Ethiopia, reciprocal access to water resources, a limiting production factor in the dryland environment, is dependent on kinship and clan membership, even though operational access is predicated on the contribution of labor to construction and maintenance of water facilities. However, in certain circumstances the authority and local legitimacy of clan elders have been subverted by state actors and instead used to mobilize community participation and to enforce sanctions through fines and capital punishment. Also, with changing socioeconomic conditions and community differentiation, wealth became an important resource that allowed community elites, including clan elders, to privatize land and water resources and to extract rents from previously communal resources.

Although a lack of livestock wealth may have mitigated against some pastoralists in Afar making use of the rights to resources, the availability of suitable land opened up alternative livelihoods options, such as farming. Provision of information on farming possibilities, farm machinery, and irrigation equipment by external actors further boosted the tendency toward adopting collective action for farming. Land ownership after subdivision of state farms provided bargaining power to pastoralists to enter into sharecropping arrangements and also to derive incomes from lease contracts with cultivating communities. However, the pastoralists' inability to read and write, their lack of accounting skills, and their poor farming skills undermine the nature of the contracts they can enter into with the cultivating highlanders, who have these resources and skills. After subdivision a larger share of state farms went to clan elites and wealthier individuals with political connections, to the disadvantage of poorer cattle herders. This situation is similar to Mwangi's (2007) findings on the subdivision and privatization of Maasai group ranches in Kenya.

The role of ideology, captured in the account of forced sedentarization by government agencies in Ethiopia, is also reflected in the marginalization of women in the distribution of land after the subdivision of state farms. Culturally, women are generally regarded as minors and thus have no rights to own property. In the Filipino society, by contrast, gendered roles and expectations influence the action resources exploited by men and women. Daughters, socialized to have a responsible, nurturing role, often migrate to urban areas and send remittances home, while sons, engaged in agricultural production, are a source of information on agricultural production technologies. The functioning of the networks, however, is diminished by ideological notions of embarrassment, especially of the very poor, who feel ashamed to seek support from their friends and neighbors.

Based on the discussion of the action arena in Chapter 2, if particular categories of actors are disadvantaged because the rules in that arena call for action resources that those actors lack, there are two strategies that can help them: strengthening their action resources to enable them to operate more effectively within the existing rule structures or changing the rules to valorize the action resources that they do possess. The African Highlands Initiative case study illustrates the strategy of changing the rules, with intervention by the African Highlands Initiative helping to demonstrate the value of local knowledge as opposed to "scientific" approaches to resource management. Collective action provides a mechanism for these scientific approaches to build on the social capital that many of the case studies report as an asset of the poor. Although individuals are able to use their human and physical assets to enhance their own welfare, they are also able to band together in groups and networks to improve access to resources and services they would otherwise not be able to access as individuals. Yet this is not a panacea for redressing poverty and inequality: those with less human capital and fewer physical assets have limited access to collective enterprises; gendered roles in society can also constrain such access. It is important to note that where groups are successfully mobilized, either from within themselves or through access to external actors with information and resources, they are able to make demands of state actors that have welfare-enhancing implications. Collective action can be a source of power. On the other hand, state power and resources can be successfully deployed to undermine and even demobilize community action.

Patterns of Interaction

As described in Chapter 2, patterns of interaction are observable, regularized behavior patterns that result from the bargaining processes that occur between the actors in the action situation, depending on their action resources. They are both suboutcomes of the action arena and in turn determine the final outcomes of the action situation. These regularized behaviors are conditioned by various rules, norms, strategies, and conventions (that is, institutions) that emerge in the action arena. This section looks at the observable mechanisms by which the interactions between the actors occur and discusses how these particular patterns influence outcomes.

Actions by individuals and groups and their interactions lead to diverse outcomes that can affect well-being directly or indirectly. Outcomes can comprise direct improvements in welfare indicators such as incomes, consumption, nutrition, and health. Outcomes can also be intermediate by way of changing institutions that are anticipated to improve well-being over the longer run.

From all the studies in this volume, the patterns of interaction that emerge during the processes occurring in the action arena can be grouped into several common categories. Even though these do not account for all observable behaviors among the actors in the case studies, they show that despite the differences in context (or initial conditions), some repeated interactions between actors mediated by the institutions of collective action and property rights are similar across settings.

- *Cooperation and collective activities:* All the case studies highlighted that in the context of poverty, the livelihoods of households within and across communities are interdependent. Collective action emerged as a potent tool in poor peoples' struggles to sustain or improve their livelihoods. The poor rely on help from their kin, neighbors, and friends in the context of scarce vital resources, vulnerability to shocks, and limited opportunities for productive activities. As a result, their interactions are guided by the principles of reciprocity and mutual trust. Based on such reciprocal exchanges is the pattern of acting collectively around various challenges. Such interactions are usually based on some delineated rules or bylaws and manifest themselves in formal and informal institutions of collective action. All studies in this volume present ample evidence of cooperation, which in turn usually leads to positive poverty-related outcomes such as increased incomes, resource sustainability, fulfillment of basic needs, and enhanced property and personal security. For example, the Kenya case study spotlights various joint activities related to the functioning of the PMGs (elections, meetings) as well as the marketing of chickpea and pigeon pea crops (bulking, grading, sorting, and selling), leading to higher returns from marketing. The Afar study tells of collective management of pastures and cooperation around farming activities, insuring personal and property security among other things. The Ethiopia–*iddir* and Philippines studies provide examples of collective action in the form of membership in groups and networks for the purpose of risk mitigation, allowing households to prevent dips in welfare.

- *Negotiations:* Although negotiations usually imply bargaining processes that occur in the action arena and lead to the appearance of a particular pattern of interaction, the studies reported here show that in many settings, negotiations have become repeated behavior patterns (based on the action resources of the actors) that are in themselves an outcome of the action situation. The Indonesia and African Highlands Initiative case studies, both of which relied heavily on participatory action research methodology, demonstrate that multistakeholder negotiations can be catalyzed or facilitated; they become an important pattern of interaction through which poverty-related outcomes such as equitable NRM or access to vital resources are achieved. The Indonesia case study shows that these negotiations do not cease when the immediately desired changes are realized; they continue by engaging different actors and their action resources (for instance, various levels of government) to reach yet other outcomes. Unlike in the Indonesia case study, the negotiations over water resource use in the Ethiopia–Somali study are not emergent: such interactions have become regularized in this case due to the need to renegotiate and re-establish the rules of water use, which keep changing as a result of various climatic shocks, population pressures, and government policies. Overall, the negotiation processes recounted in this volume have been seen to improve the social and political inclusion of marginalized groups, which is difficult to achieve via other mechanisms. Moreover, the rules created in the negotiation processes have a potential to contribute to resource sustainability and increased incomes. For example, effective porcupine control in one of the African Highlands Initiative case studies has reduced crop destruction and freed up valuable time otherwise spent by communities in controlling the pest, while the equitable distribution of improved crop varieties has increased food security and incomes.
- *Elite capture:* Disparity in action resources such as wealth, gender, or political connections can cause more advantaged individuals to benefit more from interactions. Such unequal interactions can, in turn, lead to an unequal distribution of benefits. For example, the better-off members of the watershed user associations in India tended to reap more benefits from the collective management activities. In the Ethiopia–Somali example, the local pastoral elites were able to construct private water sources, which positioned them not only to have a stable water supply for their livestock but also to charge others a fee for using these water sources. The African Highlands Initiative study shows that the local leaders and others with connections to authorities have better access to agricultural research and extension, while women, for example, do not. The Indonesia study demonstrates the misuse of revolving funds and profiteering on unfair land sales by corrupt local elites. In Cambodia, less educated community members are less likely to participate in collective decisionmaking processes.

When interactions that advantage one set of actors at the expense of others are repeated over time, they lead to greater gaps in income and power outcomes for the elites vis-à-vis everyone else. This pattern of interaction actually hinders the fulfillment of certain positive poverty outcomes, especially social or political inclusion, as demonstrated by the case studies in this volume.

- *Conflict:* The case studies reviewed here show that in the context of limited resources, increasing population pressures, changing government policies, and vulnerability to shocks, interactions between individuals and groups can turn into conflict (cf. Buckles 1999; Homer-Dixon 1999). Both the Afar and the Indonesia case studies show that scarcity of vital natural resources and ambiguity over rights and access to these resources carry a potential to turn into confrontations (of varying degrees) between various resource-dependent actors. The Cambodia case study echoes these findings: conflicts over land have been increasing as a result of the national policies (both past and present), the scarcity of arable land, and the ongoing process of land titling and demarcation. The Ethiopia–Somali study demonstrates how one-sided government policies can lead to the marginalization of one group and hence a violent conflict between that group and the state. These conflicts have a negative impact on people's livelihoods, with the worst consequences for the poorest.

- *Interactions with the state:* The ability of the poor to enhance their livelihoods is also affected by external political and legal structures (as shown in earlier sections). These case studies show interactions with the state that were often unfavorable to the poor. National policies and programs tend to overlook the reality on the ground, such as power dynamics and socioeconomic differentiation. They also disregard or misunderstand the needs of the poor. The Ethiopia–Somali and Ethiopia–Afar studies show that the sedentarization and privatization policies carried out by the Ethiopian state only exacerbated the pastoralists' vulnerability to shocks and gave more ground for elite capture by the better-off households, negatively affecting the pastoralists' inclusion in the political processes and their personal and property security. The Indonesian case study shows that the see-saw of forest management policies, some of which have a potential to benefit the poor, created ambiguity around access to forest-based resources and led to conflict between the forest communities and the private sector. The Cambodia study gives an example of a repeated bargaining process through petitions and protests between communities and local authorities. On the other hand, the African Highlands Initiative and Indonesia studies also give examples of interactions with local authorities (during the negotiation processes) that create conditions for positive outcomes for the poor, resulting in improvements in their "power" status (social and political inclusion), higher incomes, and greater tenure security.

Overall, the case studies show that the bargaining processes that occur in the action arena condition the behavior patterns that guide the interactions between the actors. These patterns are influenced by the action resources that the actors bring into the action situation and, in turn, directly impact poverty-related outcomes. Although these patterns are not meant to serve as an entry point for any poverty program or policy, they are uniquely positioned for "tracking" the production of desired outcomes from the context through the action arena.

Linking It All Together

This chapter illustrates how the conceptual framework from Chapter 2 could be used for poverty research by using the examples of our case studies to connect the dots between the elements of the framework to show their relationship with collective action and property rights and their influence on poverty outcomes. Many of the findings of the case studies confirm hypotheses outlined in Chapter 2. Contextual factors influence how the institutions of collective action and property rights are formed, which in turn influences the action arena, where patterns of interaction lead to both positive and negative poverty outcomes. Even though most of the studies in this volume did not provide illustrations of the feedback loops from the outcomes to the context due to the limited time duration of the research projects, it is important to remember that the newly created outcomes are fed back into the context to eventually produce new action situations and new outcomes.

The case studies also show the strong links between collective action and property rights and why these two types of institutions were chosen to be part of the same framework, the same research project, and the same volume. The fifteen years of research findings collected by the Systemwide Program on Collective Action and Property Rights (CAPRi) of the Consultative Group on International Agricultural Research have shown the connection between the two, mentioned in Chapter 1. In Chapter 2 we proposed that looking at the two institutions together as the prism for understanding poverty may reveal some new lessons and insights for poverty reduction efforts and tie together the elements of a new conceptual framework derived from the "original" IAD framework.

The African Highlands Initiative, Indonesia, Ethiopia–Afar, Ethiopia–Somali, and Cambodia case studies all explicitly demonstrate that collective action is an essential tool for securing greater access to resources, clarifying tenure arrangements, and promoting greater equity and sustainability of access. In many of these studies, property rights were precisely the reason that actors invested in organizing to engage with more powerful actors and authority structures. For example, in Indonesia the threat of losing access to forests and the need to have those claims recognized and protected was a primary reason for communities to organize. In the African Highlands Initiative case study, by organizing, groups that had been evicted from forests gained sufficient bargaining power to reclaim access and management rights to the forest. In both case studies, groups started investing in various forest-based income-generating activities. Even in the Kenya case study, which focused on collective action, PMG members are all landowners, demonstrating the importance of secure property rights in providing a launching pad from which to pursue collective income-generating opportunities. Breaking the link between the two institutions is shown to have negative consequences for the poor. In the Ethiopia–Afar case study, for instance, the conversion of communal property regimes (managed collectively) to state property withdrew resources from herders, including critical survival resources such as dry-season pastures. This transformation later created incentives for resource privatization, which saw wealthier and more influential individuals acquiring larger portions, squeezing the poorer and female-headed households into much smaller, less productive units. In this volume this interconnectedness between collective action and property rights is seen to play a role in achieving better outcomes for the poor, be they higher incomes, greater resource sustainability, enhanced property security, or increased social or political inclusion.

The studies also produced findings regarding poverty outcomes that had not been foreseen by the conceptual framework. We learned that collective action contributes to investments in and management of jointly held natural assets (as proposed in the framework), but these do not necessarily lead to identifiable effects on the asset endowments of the poor. Although collective action can result in improvements in resource management, the direct poverty outcomes of such improvements require longer time horizons to be realized, and it is possible that low levels of asset endowments may lock poorer households out of the benefits of resource improvements.

Three more lessons for poverty outcomes can be extracted from these case-specific findings:

1. Communities can organize on their own to resolve the challenges confronting their well-being, but they often do so imperfectly, leaving out those among them who stand to gain the most from joint action. There are thus limits to collective action, and researchers, policymakers, and practitioners need to be aware of this gap and to design research practices and policy interventions that actively identify and target those excluded from the benefits of group action.

2. External actors who are trusted (that is, whose interests are not contrary to or in direct competition with those of interested internal or external actors) and who have resources (such as time, money, or reputation) can motivate

collective action that may lead to favorable implications for community well-being, including the alleviation of the elite capture of resources or the expansion of the access rights of poorer, less powerful actors.

3. Well-functioning collective action, regardless of whether it is mediated by external entities, is important for secure property rights. This is seen particularly in the case studies in which collective action was weak; resources are subject to elite capture or acquisition by outsiders.

Because poverty is a complex condition, these propositions and findings are by no means exhaustive, nor are they meant to be; they are, rather, illustrative of some of the factors that researchers, policymakers, or practitioners seeking a better understanding of poverty can explore. We take these up in the context of the themes of the volume in the concluding chapter.

References

Alderman, H., and C. Paxson. 1994. Do the poor insure? A synthesis of the literature on risk and consumption in developing countries. In *Economics in a changing world*. Vol. 4, *Development, trade and the environment,* ed. D. Bacha. London: Macmillan.

Anderson, K., and E. Ostrom. 2008. Analyzing decentralized natural resource governance from a polycentric perspective. *Policy Sciences* 41 (1): 1–23.

Bebbington, A. 1999. Capitals and capabilities: A framework for analyzing peasant viability, rural livelihoods and poverty. *World Development* 27 (12): 2021–2044.

Birner, R., and H. Wittmer. 2003. Using social capital to create political capital: How do local communities gain political influence? A theoretical approach and empirical evidence from Thailand. In *The commons in the new millennium: Challenges and adaptation,* ed. N. Dolsak and E. Ostrom. Cambridge, Mass., U.S.A.: MIT Press.

Buckles, D., ed. 1999. *Cultivating peace: Conflict and collaboration in natural resource management.* Ottawa: International Development Research Centre.

Dercon, S. 2002. Income risk, coping strategies, and safety nets. *World Bank Economic Observer* 17 (2): 141–166.

Dercon, S., and P. Krishnan. 2000. In sickness and health: Risk sharing within households in rural Ethiopia. *Journal of Political Economy* 108 (4): 688–727.

DfID (Department for International Development). 1999. Sustainable livelihoods guidance sheets. London. <www.ennonline.net/resources/667>. Accessed February 8, 2011.

Fafchamps, M., and F. Gubert. 2007. The formation of risk sharing networks. *Journal of Development Economics* 83 (2): 326–350.

Grootaert, C. 1999. *Social capital, household welfare, and poverty in Indonesia.* World Bank Policy Research Working Paper 2148. Washington, D.C.: World Bank.

Homer-Dixon, T. 1999. *Environment, scarcity and violence.* Princeton, N.J., U.S.A.: Princeton University Press.

Hulme, D., and A. Shepherd. 2003. Conceptualizing chronic poverty. *World Development* 31 (3): 403–423.

Jalan, J., and M. Ravallion. 1999. Are the poor less well insured? Evidence on vulner-ability to income risk in rural China. *Journal of Development Economics* 58 (1): 61–81.

Krishna, A., P. Kristjanson, M. Radeny, and N. Wilson. 2004. Escaping poverty and becoming poor in 20 Kenyan villages. *Journal of Human Development* 5 (2): 211–226.

Little, P., K. Smith, B. Cellarius, D. L. Coppock, and C. Barrett. 2001. Avoiding disaster: Diversification and risk management among East African herders. *Development and Change* 32 (3): 401–433.

Larson, A. 2005. Democratic decentralization in the forestry sector: Lessons learned from Africa, Asia and Latin America. In *The politics of decentralization: Forests, power and people,* ed. C. J. Pierce Colfer and D. Capistrano. London: Earthscan.

Manor, J. 1999. *The political economy of democratic decentralization.* Washington, D.C.: World Bank.

McCarthy, J. F. 2004. Changing to gray: Decentralization and the emergence of volatile socio-legal configurations in Central Kalimantan, Indonesia. *World Development* 32 (7): 1199–1223.

Meinzen-Dick, R., and E. Mwangi. 2009. Cutting the web of interests: Pitfalls of formal-izing property rights. *Land Use Policy* 26 (1): 36–43.

Meinzen-Dick, R., E. Mwangi, and S. Dohrn. 2006. *Securing the commons.* CAPRi Policy Brief 4. Washington, D.C.: International Food Policy Research Institute.

Meinzen-Dick, R., A. Knox, B. Swallow, and F. Place, eds. 2002. *Innovation in natural resource management: The role of property rights and collective action in devel-oping countries.* Baltimore: Johns Hopkins University Press.

Mwangi, E. 2007. *Socioeconomic change and landuse in Africa: The transformation of property rights in Kenya's Maasailand.* New York: Palgrave Macmillan.

Mwangi, E., and H. Markelova. 2009. Collective action and property rights: A review of methods and approaches. *Development Policy Review* 27 (3): 307–331.

Mwangi, E., and E. Ostrom. 2009. Top down solutions: Looking up from East Africa's rangelands. *Environment* 51 (1): 35–44.

Niamir-Fuller, M. 1999. Managing mobility in African rangelands. In *Property rights, risk and livestock development in Africa,* ed. N. McCarthy, B. Swallow, M. Kirk, and P. Hazell. Washington, D.C.: International Food Policy Research Institute.

Olson, M. 1965. *The logic of collective action: Public goods and the theory of groups.* Cambridge, Mass., U.S.A.: Harvard University Press.

Ribot, J. 1998. Theorizing access: Forest profits along Senegal's charcoal commodity chain. *Development and Change* 29 (2): 307–341.

Runge, C. F. 1986. Common property and collective action in economic development. *World Development* 14 (5): 623–635.

Schlager, E., and E. Ostrom. 1992. Property rights regimes and natural resources: A conceptual framework. *Land Economics* 68 (3): 249–262.

Seabright, P. 1993. Managing local commons: Theoretical issues in incentive design. *Journal of Economic Perspectives* 7 (4): 113–134.

Scott, J. C. 1999. *Seeing like a state: How certain schemes to improve the human condi-tion have failed.* New Haven, Conn., U.S.A.: Yale University Press.

Udry, C. 1994. Risk and insurance in a rural credit market: An empirical investigation in Northern Nigeria. *Review of Economic Studies* 61 (3): 495–526.

Uphoff, N., and C. M. Wijayaratna. 2000. Demonstrated benefits from social capital: The productivity of farmer organizations in Gal Oya, Sri Lanka. *World Development* 28 (11): 1875–1890.

Wily, L. A. 2006. The commons and customary law in modern times: Rethinking the orthodoxies. In *Land rights for African development: From knowledge to action*. CAPRi policy brief. Washington D.C.: International Food Policy Research Institute.

Winters, P., B. Davis, and L. Corral. 2002. Assets, activities, and income generation in rural Mexico: Factoring in social and public capital. *Agricultural Economics* 27 (2): 139–156.

13 Conclusions and Implications for Policy, Practice, and Research

ESTHER MWANGI, HELEN MARKELOVA,
AND RUTH MEINZEN-DICK

This book began by proposing that institutions of collective action and property rights can play a valuable role in facilitating poverty reduction. As discussed in Chapter 1, there is a disconnect between the natural resource management (NRM) and non-NRM poverty research: each has its own strengths, but to date, there have not been many attempts to cross-fertilize the two with lessons learned from each for poverty reduction. This volume bridges this gap by connecting institutional research, which is strong in the NRM literature, with the poverty analysis better covered by other poverty studies to apply the knowledge on institutions to poverty reduction research across sectors, countries, and methods. Four of the five main themes that are spotlighted in this volume (risk and vulnerability to shocks, market access for smallholders, natural resource governance and access to resources, and conflict and postconflict development) serve as venues for this cross-pollination, each focusing on a particular poverty area to show how institutions, especially those of collective action and property rights, can enable the poor to improve their condition. The fifth theme, power, is woven through the whole volume as relevant across all themes and settings when dealing with poverty.

Our case studies have highlighted how collective action and property rights enhance the abilities of the poor to increase their stock of assets, mitigate the harmful impact of shocks, negotiate equitable resource governance rules, effectively deal with market imperfections, interact with government authorities and local elites, and negotiate access to land, water, and forests. They also show the limitations of these institutions to overcome poverty in the context of certain forms of asset disparities, risks, and governance or power relations. Findings were obtained from commonalities drawn across somewhat disparate sociopolitical and historical contexts and sectors from among a set of countries whose annual gross national incomes per capita (which vary from US$110 in Ethiopia to US$1,170 in the Philippines) place them in the mostly lower-income category.[1] The power of these findings derives from their application across

---

1. See the World Bank's *Little Green Data Book* (World Bank 2006).

sectors, especially among NRM, risk and vulnerability, conflict management, and market access. Recognizing that each situation must be sufficiently contextualized, what are the policy actions and practices that can help strengthen the roles of collective organizing and property rights in improving the well-being of the poor? How can policy and practice be improved so as to encourage, strengthen, and not undermine the self-organizing efforts of the poor and their rights and access to diverse assets?

In this concluding chapter we turn from a detailed analysis of the findings from the studies collected here to the contributions they make to the literature on their respective themes in terms of the way that collective action and property rights can facilitate poverty reduction. Recognizing that conducting these nine studies was just one step in this task, we also consider the open questions that the studies have brought forth for future research and propose the implications that these findings can have for policy and practice. We first discuss the findings in terms of the five themes of the volume and then highlight some contributions that the studies make to the broader literature on collective action and property rights, then end with broader implications for policy, practice, and research.

Revisiting the Themes of the Volume

Risk and Vulnerability to Shocks

The literature on risk mitigation by the poor has shown that in the face of imperfect credit and insurance markets, the poor rely on various types of assets, including social capital, mostly in the form of mutual assistance groups and credit and savings associations (Dercon 2002). The Ethiopia–*iddir* (burial societies) and Philippines studies show that other forms of collective action, such as burial societies and familial networks, are now being used as risk-mitigating mechanisms by the poor. These studies describe how these innovative approaches to insurance deal with the traditional problems of informational asymmetries and how their composition contributes to their effectiveness and sustainability. The Ethiopia–Afar study makes a contribution to the existing work on the vulnerability of pastoral groups (see Little et al. 2001) by examining the collective action–based responses to climatic and sociopolitical shocks, as well as the negative impact that collective shock mitigation has on customary property rights institutions. Even though the breakdown in the traditional pastoralists' institutions has been mentioned in other studies on pastoralism, this chapter uniquely shows how these transformations, in the forms of both cooperation and property rights arrangements, are results of shocks coming from various sources (droughts, government policies, and so on). Even though these studies did not explicitly set out to study the dynamic nature of poverty (see Barrett

2005), they inevitably exposed this aspect by showing how vulnerability to shocks adversely affects the well-being of those who are already asset poor.

These findings have important implications for policy and practice, especially because it has been widely acknowledged in the literature that shocks and the low resilience of poor households to deal with them are some of the primary drivers of chronic poverty (Hulme and Shepherd 2003; Krishna 2004). First of all, highlighting the potential of existing local institutions to enhance the ability of the poor to withstand various shocks should signify to policymakers and practitioners the need to account for the importance of these institutions; acknowledging their effectiveness and financial and organizational sustainability, programs and policies should aim not to interfere but rather to support them. For example, the Philippines study suggests that investing in telecommunications is a means to enable easier and faster remittance transfers to households in need. The Afar study calls for improvements in the information systems available to the pastoralists as well as innovative insurance schemes that would enable them to continue livestock production as a viable livelihood option, especially in the face of increasing droughts. Second, the limited ability of local collective action to deal with widespread shocks should be recognized, especially because the number of drastic climatic events and even widespread economic shocks is increasing. Here governments, donors, and practitioners can play an important role in preventing households from going further into poverty as a result of shocks by providing safety nets, creating food banks, and organizing other relief programs.

The findings of these studies also provide suggestions for future research on collective action for risk mitigation. For example, given that local collective action is not able to deal with covariate shocks, can vertical links be built up between local groups and other actors (collective action at various scales) to enable these groups to serve as a base for dealing with such shocks? And if so, how will the involvement of outsiders affect these groups' norms of trust and reciprocity? Are there ways to make these autonomous groups more inclusive of the very poor? On the other hand, how will emerging global trends (demographic shifts, climate change, and so on) affect the operation and sustainability of these groups, and will these groups be able to provide "coverage" in the face of these new shocks? Finding answers to some of these questions will be challenging because it may require expensive longitudinal studies, but the benefits of finding ways to build on the effective local cooperation to contribute to poverty reduction and prevent chronic poverty may prove more cost efficient than coming up with new top-down insurance schemes.

Market Access for Smallholders

Chapter 5 (Kenya) fits well with the recently renewed interest in collective action to increase market access for smallholders. Other studies have found that there are few incentives for smallholders to organize around marketing staples (Coulter 2007; Markelova et al. 2009). However, in semiarid Kenya, producer groups were an effective mechanism to deal with poor provision of market infrastructure and motivate farmers to cooperate around marketing their staple goods. This chapter goes a step further from analyzing the economic benefits of the groups to showing what makes a non-NRM group, such as a marketing group, function in an organizationally and financially sustainable way, especially highlighting the role of bylaws in ensuring such durability and effectiveness. There are some studies on bylaws in the NRM literature (Wily 1999; Agrawal and Ostrom 2001), and this chapter contributes to this literature by showing how bylaws serve as organizational rules that can be used in both the NRM and non-NRM studies on collective action.

The chapter also has clear implications for policy, especially because there is growing attention from policymakers and donors who are eager to invest in bringing smallholders into markets. Providing new market-relevant infrastructure (roads, telecommunications) and improving the quality of existing infrastructure, along with making business development services (training, credit) available to smallholders, can create more incentives to organize around marketing and enable smallholders to participate in more profitable marketing chains. Providing initial start-up funding and access to other financial services in the context of credit constraints is another practical intervention to support group marketing, especially where there are delays in payment through groups, as in this case. As the study mentions, in Kenya some of these things can be achieved by changing the legal status of smallholder marketing groups. This recommendation can be relevant to other countries that recognize groups at higher scales as elements of agribusiness, with certain services available, but do not give the same status to groups at the local level. Alternatively, organizing these smallholder groups into federated structures may enable them to reach this desirable legal status as well as to increase production and marketing volumes. However, as this chapter shows, new rules, or bylaws, for effective cooperation at larger scales must be created.

Further research is needed to see if collective marketing is a viable way out of poverty for smallholders. The Kenya study mentions the "middle-class" effect of these groups, which have certain membership requirements that preclude poorer households from joining. Many studies of commercialization have indicated that men are more likely to be involved and benefit, which can increase gender inequality in control of income (World Bank 2009). Thus, it is important to investigate what types of rules and procedures ensure that women also benefit. Another question has to do with the aforementioned federated structures, or collective action at larger scales. How can these federations be organized so that the benefits are distributed in a fair and equitable way? There are examples of successful federations of cocoa-growing farmers in Bolivia (Bebbington 1996), but these were organized around cash crops with significant external funding and linkages to international markets; whether this would work with staples producers remains to be seen.

Natural Resource Governance and Access to Resources

Chapters 6–11 all deal with the governance of natural resources, including land, water, pastures, and forests. They use a variety of quantitative and qualitative techniques (including action research) to assess the factors affecting collective action for natural resource governance. In this they contribute to the burgeoning literature on factors affecting the management of private and common-pool resources. However, the major contribution of the case studies reported in these chapters has been to look beyond the condition of the resources to the condition of the poor people who depend on those resources.

Broadly speaking, these studies have found that collective action is necessary for resource governance but in itself is not sufficient to improve the welfare of the poor. Two additional conditions are needed to translate effective resource governance into welfare gains for the poor: equitable distribution of benefits from the natural resources and possibilities to use the resources for profitable livelihood activities. This was clearly shown in the Indian watershed management case study, in which collective action indexes were significantly related to resource-improving investments, especially water-harvesting structures and good management of these resources, but not significantly related to the index of poverty parameters. In this case study the distribution of property rights played a key intervening role: many of the poor were landless and therefore did not have a direct claim to the benefit stream generated by improved water harvesting used in irrigation, and additional livelihood-creation activities are recommended for the landless. Similarly, in Cambodia or the pastoral case studies in Ethiopia, collective action to manage the resources was insufficient to insure the welfare of poor communities when the resources to which they had customary rights were subject to expropriation from outsiders or the state. In the Afar case study, collective action for farming did not deliver poverty reduction because of the risky nature of farming in that environment and the pastoralists' lack of knowledge about farming. However, the effects of collective action on poverty may be underestimated if we do not account for the many examples (for instance, from Cambodia, Afar, and the African Highlands Initiative) in which *lack* of collective action in managing resources has led to greater immiseration. As Krishna (2004) has shown, preventing vulnerable people from falling into poverty is as important as helping the poor to move out of poverty.

All NRM case studies reported in this volume address, to some extent, factors that affect the likelihood that people will cooperate for managing common-pool resources. The India, Afar, and Cambodia studies used quantitative approaches to test for the effect of factors identified in theory, including characteristics of the biophysical environment, the user groups, and the governance characteristics (for example, Ostrom 1990; Bardhan 1993; Baland and

Platteau 1996; Agrawal 2001). In all these case studies, some, but not all, factors were found to have a significant effect on cooperation. This is not surprising, given the complexity involved and the difficulty of measuring some of even the basic concepts such as market access. But, more important, human agency and decisionmaking are involved in collective action, so we cannot expect deterministic outcomes. The action research approaches used in the African Highlands Initiative and Indonesia case studies allowed them to deal more with process than with structural factors, finding that (again, consistent with theory) participatory decisionmaking is an important contributor to collective action in resource management.

Looking beyond environmental outcomes to poverty impacts sheds new light on one of the fundamental theoretical principles of collective action in NRM: the role of exclusion. Ostrom's (1990) first "design principle" for long-enduring management of the commons is clearly defined boundaries, and this was borne out in the Somali and Cambodia case studies: communities that cannot exclude outsiders have little incentive or ability to regulate the use of their resources, which become degraded. But, at the same time, excluding some people from rights to use critical natural resources (in a context in which there are few livelihood alternatives) can result in poverty. This is seen in the case study of watershed management in India, where the landless did not benefit from improvements in the resource base. This tension between exclusion to preserve resources and inclusion to reduce poverty may not be resolved within the NRM sector itself. A key policy implication is that, along with equitable distribution of property rights, alternative livelihoods less dependent on natural resources are needed where population densities are high or increasing, as suggested by the India study.

All of the NRM case studies dealt with property rights in some manner. In the pastoral studies in Ethiopia, flexible land tenure offered a means of coping with the risky biophysical environment, whereas in Indonesia and Cambodia, ambiguous property rights were a disincentive to invest. In India, land rights played a crucial role in accessing the benefits from collective watershed activities. But the studies also show that property rights are dynamic, shaped by the action arenas discussed in these chapters. Indian and African Highlands Initiative watershed programs negotiate changes in use rights and benefit streams. In the Ethiopia–Afar and Cambodia cases, state actions changed property rights to land, often to the detriment of customary users, whereas in the Ethiopia–Somali case the changes in rights to water sources and enclosure of the commons came more from within the groups (a local action arena). Positive changes in property rights for the poor are more difficult to achieve (as the record of land reforms has shown), but the Indonesia case study indicates that there is scope for negotiated approaches to secure collective rights.

Because of the great diversity of resource conditions, there remains considerable scope for research to document and share lessons on effective governance approaches. Key questions remain: How can these be made inclusive of the poor and of women? How can property rights be flexible enough to deal with climatic risks without being a source of insecurity themselves? What can be done to increase the returns to the natural resources that poor people do have without creating conditions such that they lose those resources as they become more valuable?

Conflict and Postconflict Development

The links among collective action, property rights, and conflict are discussed in Chapters 9 (Ethiopia–Afar), 10 (Ethiopia–Somali), and 11 (Cambodia). Central to the Afar and Somali studies is the emergence of the state as the perpetrator of conflictive situations by impinging on traditional institutions and attempting to change them coercively, which evoked resistance from the pastoralists. These findings contribute to the literature on natural resource conflicts by showing that property rights systems rooted in norms of trust, reciprocity, and cooperation (typical of pastoral societies) can lie at the root of longstanding conflicts between the state and its citizens. These findings also point out that although conflict can transform one institution (communal rangelands to individual plots in the Afar case, for example), it can also lead to the emergence of another institution (collective farming in the Afar case). These studies bring a new angle into the literature on conflict by highlighting its impacts on local institutions, as well as pointing out the dynamic and resilient nature of such institutions.

One central policy implication that arises from these studies is that because traditional institutions have proven effective in mediating conflicts and aiding in postconflict rebuilding, these institutions should be supported to make them even more effective in this role. Identifying which institution to build upon is a first step; in Cambodia, many customary institutions were eroded by years of war and repression, but religious and neighborhood institutions that survived offered a basis for rebuilding trust. Additionally, some type of reconciliation between customary and statutory rights to land and partner resources (such as water) has to be considered in order to not divest communities that are heavily dependent on resources held under the customary tenure of their livelihood sources. If poverty reduction is the goal, especially in "fragile" areas undergoing conflict or postconflict rebuilding, a careful assessment of the potential impact of policies and programs on existing local institutions is crucial; as the Ethiopia–*iddir* study points out, trust is always easier to destroy than to build.

Research on conflict and postconflict situations is dangerous because it may pose threats as researchers try to unveil sensitive issues. However, because conflicts always affect institutions, this research is much needed. Our studies point to a few other questions whose answers can provide more insight into the interaction between conflict and local institutions. For example, in the context of coercive and noncoercive transformation of property rights, will collective action institutions formed in response provide lasting solutions, or will this cooperation end with another shift in rights? Where conflicts have destroyed trust (as in Cambodia), what mechanisms are needed to rebuild collective action? One intriguing possibility is to use experimental games not just as research tools (as in the Cambodia case) but also as entry points to discussions with communities as a means of strengthening collective action (Cárdenas 2009).

Power and Poverty

As discussed in Chapter 1, the case studies in this volume show that understanding the poverty–institutions nexus requires attention to nuanced issues of power and inclusiveness. Most of the case studies highlighted that the distribution of power is an important determinant of the institutions that are adopted and implemented. They also shed light on how power and power relations, including elite capture, are manifested in the daily reality of the poor and especially on how these relations interact with the institutions of collective action and property rights. Even though not all the case studies began with an explicit aim to study power, in their analysis of varying issues affecting the poor most ultimately ran into the problem of power differentials that became incentives or hindrances in creating or sustaining the institutions and improving the well-being of the poor. Property rights, and especially security of tenure, become major factors in power relations in the hands of both the poor (Indonesia) and other actors such as local elites, government agencies, and the private sector (Ethiopia–Somali, Ethiopia–Afar, Indonesia, Cambodia). Collective action is seen as a way to acquire and access assets (a tangible aspect of power), as in the Kenya and Ethiopia–Afar case studies, as well as to shift power relations in favor of the poor (an intangible aspect of power), as in the African Highlands Initiative and Indonesia studies. On the other hand, the Cambodia and Ethiopia–Somali studies show that the local resource users (Cambodia) and pastoralists (Somali) are disadvantaged in terms of power because they are excluded from participating in decisionmaking processes that shape their livelihoods. Collective action by the poor alone may help, but it is often not enough to offset unequal power relations, which often play out within the local collective action institutions as well. External facilitation can help, but we should not assume that they will create a "level playing field" (Edmunds and Wollenberg 2002).[2]

Elite capture is an important aspect of power relations. The chapters in this volume present various accounts of elite capture, but perhaps none are more illustrative than those that are set in the context of decentralization reforms. Many developing countries are actively undertaking decentralization reforms in which authority for the management of natural resources is progressively being ceded to lower levels of governance (see Gibson and Lehoucq 2003;

---

2. These examples are discussed in more detail under "The Action Arena" in Chapter 12, highlighting the applicability of the framework that guides this volume to a comprehensive analysis of power and power relations.

Colfer and Capistrano 2005). Many scholars and practitioners recognize elite capture as a central dilemma in decentralization processes and call for research to develop effective strategies for avoiding or countering it (Bardhan 1997; Larson and Ribot 2005; Meynen and Doornbos 2005). The African Highlands Initiative and Indonesia case studies make important contributions to the growing body of literature on decentralization by showing that such reforms can be chaotic, involving rapid and often contradictory rule changes and with consequences that negate the very objectives of the reform processes, including the creation of insecurities through evictions and elite capture of benefits. Indeed, the Cambodia case study shows that when collective action institutions are weak, decentralization and abrupt removal of state administration can leave an institutional vacuum that leads to resource degradation and negative effects on the poor (see also Meinzen-Dick, Knox, and Di Gregorio 2001). Barrett, Mude, and Omiti (2007) have found that in order to avoid elite capture, transparency of the processes of decisionmaking is not necessarily desirable, especially where such openness provides information that can be used by negatively affected parties to punish decisionmakers. The results of the studies in this volume are inconsistent with this finding. Transparency of the processes of decisionmaking and resource allocation (including land use planning and budget allocation) are vital for avoiding elite capture. However, it can be added that the presence of a disinterested third-party broker, such as the Center for International Forestry Research in the Indonesia case, which creates opportunities for aligning opposing interests and provides a platform for negotiated problemsolving and trust-building over repeated face-to-face interactions, can be one way of avoiding the elite capture of benefits.

The most obvious implication of this theme for policy and practice that arises out of the volume is the need to recognize that power issues on the ground are real and that no policy or intervention targeting poverty reduction can be implemented in isolation from the influence of power relations. Those policies and programs that aim to work through the institutions of collective action need to be cognizant that groups are subject to elite capture or may not be open to all the poor, which can skew the distribution of benefits. On the other hand, strengthening existing groups and networks of the poor, such as insurance groups and marketing associations, can help them to obtain more leverage and bargaining power by increasing their incomes and a number of their other assets, including social capital. Moreover, secure property rights constitute assets that can be increased via collective action and give the poor leverage, especially as land becomes a more valuable and scarce resource attractive to foreign and domestic investors.

As for the implications for future research, this volume offers examples of how to incorporate power into poverty studies in both the NRM and non-NRM arenas. Although many of the case studies have addressed gender inequalities as part of the work on elite capture, valuable synergies could result from strengthening linkages to analyses of gendered power relations, for understanding both common factors at play and the possibilities to overcome cultural as well as economic barriers to resource control. More research on power relations and their effects on various poverty-related outcomes is needed. For instance, what assets (action resources) would give the poor enough leverage to preserve their traditional property rights arrangements in the face of more powerful actors, such as the state or the private sector, as in the study of the Ethiopian pastoralists or the Cambodia study? What is the scope for increasing their action resources or changing the rules to favor the resources that they have? Can collective action in the form of multistakeholder negotiations (African Highlands Initiative and Indonesia studies), together with the support of other more powerful stakeholders, be the most viable way of ensuring equitable outcomes for the poor? If so, are there ways to multiply and scale up such intensive processes, or is time for negotiation and trust-building an inherent requirement?

New Insights on Collective Action and Property Rights

In addition to contributing to the literature on the topics outlined in the previous section, the case studies together add interesting and valuable insights to the broader literature on collective action and property rights.

Collective Action and the Marginalization of Poorer Actors

To summarize the empirical chapters, collective action, by way of group organizing and networks at multiple levels, can serve a variety of purposes, including defending or gaining rights to productive resources and assets, mitigating resource degradation, undertaking sustainable land management, improving access to product markets, reducing vulnerability to idiosyncratic illness and drought shocks, and accessing critical information. The quantitative studies demonstrate that organizing can yield income gains or protect people from losing out due to shocks. Across all case studies, however, it was seen that organizing can actively exclude poorer, more marginalized members of society and those without connections to local elites. Sometimes wealthier individuals who have other options may also abstain from participating in groups (see the Ethiopia–Somali and Ethiopia–Afar studies). In other cases, such as in the Ethiopia–*iddir* and Philippines studies, it is the better-endowed households that belong to more groups and networks and to more economically beneficial ones. The Kenya study also shows that local collective action institutions can exclude those below a certain asset threshold.

The primary message here is that institutions of collective action, regardless of the problem arena in which they operate, are faced with the nontrivial challenge of ensuring the inclusion of less powerful individuals. The limits to collective action by poorer groups have been identified in the literature (Cleaver 2005; Thorpe, Stewart, and Heyer 2005). The case studies in this volume provide a window into the specific mechanisms by which such exclusions occur, which include biases against women rooted in cultural institutions, the inability of even poorer individuals to make reciprocal contributions in cash or in kind to group enterprises, the invisibility of women farmers and their circumvention by the providers of extension services, a lack of networks and connections to influential elites, a culture of shame that constrains poorer individuals from participating in groups, and power differentials that allow some to shape the rules of resource access in their favor or to flout existing rules.[3]

Thus, the beneficial effects of local organizing are limited by the structural characteristics of the social, cultural, and political contexts within which groups are embedded. The action research studies (African Highlands Initiative and Indonesia) demonstrate that these structural constraints can be lessened modestly where credible external actors are ready and willing to invest time and resources in leveling the playing field and supporting negotiation. Such negotiations can result in altering the structural conditions (such as power differentials with government officials or among individuals in communities). Well-structured dialogues are thought to be a promising avenue because they provide information (Dietz, Ostrom, and Stern 2003). Policies and formal rules that specify procedural mandates for the participation of women, ethnic minorities, and other marginalized groups in public policy are increasingly important in creating the policy and political spaces for their inclusion, as illustrated by the Indonesia study and new Indian government guidelines for watershed management projects (GOI 2008), but implementation of such policies and procedures is equally critical. Ultimately, researchers and practitioners must self-consciously seek to establish the extent to which structural constraints limit full and meaningful participation of relevant actors in order to at least not reinforce inequalities and, preferably, seek to moderate them.

Collective Action and External Actors

The case studies presented in this volume also portray an aspect of collective action that, in addition to making the point on inclusiveness, has important implications for both research and practice and contributes to the existing literature on collective action. This point has to do with whether collective action that emerged endogenously without the involvement of outsiders can be as effective for poverty reduction as collective action catalyzed or supported by external actors, especially the state. From the first two case studies (the Ethiopia–*iddir* and Philippines studies) we see that these endogenously created groups, such as burial societies and intrafamilial networks, help the poor deal with certain shocks but are unable to protect them against widespread shocks, for which the involvement of the state is necessary. The next chapter, on Kenya, shows that the producer marketing groups are created with the help of nonstate

---

3. For application of this conceptual framework to issues of the gender inclusiveness of collective action, see Pandolfelli, Meinzen-Dick, and Dohrn (2007).

actors (the International Crops Research Institute for the Semiarid Tropics and others), but the success of the groups in accessing various services, such as credit, is still limited because of legal structures that do not grant them a certain status. This case study points out that various actors in the external environment of the poor can be instrumental in supporting their collective action, but the role of the state in creating favorable political and legal mechanisms is critical for the success of this type of collective action.

The studies in Part III on NRM show that groups created with external facilitation can lead not only to positive welfare outcomes for the poor but also to their empowerment and the sustainability of these outcomes. However, the India case study also shows that people do not always engage in collective action for resource management, and even when they do, it does not always result in poverty reduction, especially if the poor are landless, with very little stake in the improvement of the natural resources. The action research studies (African Highlands Initiative and Indonesia) describe the way that collective action can be catalyzed by outsiders in such a way that the poor are able to negotiate with various stakeholders, make demands on the state, and ensure equitable distribution of the rights and resources that come out of the negotiations. The chapters in the section on conflict and postconflict rebuilding go back to the endogenously emerging collective action. The collective action institutions in the two case studies on Ethiopian pastoralists actually appeared as a response to unfavorable state policies, and although this cooperation is effective in protecting the poorer pastoralists against more powerful actors (the state, wealthier peers), these institutions appear to be somewhat fragile, susceptible to changes in the face of pressure from external actors. The Cambodia case shows collective action institutions that are developing based on the existing norms and forms of local cooperation without being recognized or acknowledged by the state, indicating the resilience and adaptability of endogenously created institutions.

Therefore, the case studies present an interesting progression, from cooperation that is driven by the poor themselves at a purely local level to collective action that is catalyzed by nongovernmental agencies with some involvement from local government officials, then back to institutions of the poor that emerge as a response to unfavorable policies. The outcomes of the studies highlight the benefits and limitations of all these types of collective action as well as their sustainability and inclusiveness based on how they were created and "treated" by external actors. The studies also stress that there are cases in which external interventions via collective action institutions can lead to empowerment and other situations in which such interventions undermine the foundations (such as trust) and sustainability of cooperation. We find that there are opportunities for outsiders to get involved and build or support local collective action, but the way in which this engagement occurs and who participates (the state, civil society, other actors such as research and extension groups) can dictate whether collective action can help move people out of poverty. Further review and synthesis are needed to identify the characteristics of each.

Property Rights

The studies in this volume underscore the important effect of property rights on whether individuals and groups can draw benefits and incomes from natural resources, but they also show how property rights mitigate the effects of drought and other shocks as individuals with recognized rights are able to exploit the resources. Property rights mediate access to safety nets and influence the extent to which individuals can leverage other assets such as finances, infrastructure, and groups and networks to improve their well-being. The articulation of customary and statutory regimes, a tight spot in the implementation of current land tenure reform, is well captured by the case studies in dryland Ethiopia (Afar and Somali). They show that customary arrangements for resource access and management ensure broad access to resources, especially for poorer and marginal groups, and that privatization cuts off access, increasing inequality (Peters and Kambewa 2007; Meinzen-Dick and Mwangi 2009).

In many parts of the world, privatization processes were largely the offshoots of state modernization programs (see Scott's 1999 analysis of state-run "legibility" schemes). The consequences of such programs have been the loss of pre-existing capacities for collective decisionmaking, resource allocation, and access under customary authority. Privatization provides more power to those who are allocated private rights and less to those who are not, and it undermines the mutual dependence that initially served as the incentive to cooperate (Seabright 1993 and the Somali case study in this volume). The tradability of private property rights also undermines the reliability of informal cooperation mechanisms such as reputation. Gaps between customary and state rules create uncertainty in decisionmaking, prompting actors to forum-shop (Meinzen-Dick and Pradhan 2001) and create loopholes through which elite actors can grab resources (see the Somali, Afar, and Cambodia case studies). These case studies confirm the need for introduced property regimes to be informed by the cultural attributes of resource users (Runge 1986; Bromley 1991; Mwangi 2007). Indeed, they strengthen the call for more formal recognition of customary systems of landholding by government authorities and assurance that their structures and functions will be supported and complemented rather than superseded by alternative authorities.

Conversely, the Indonesia case study shows how external intervention and state action can strengthen the collective property rights of poor people. However, this was accomplished not by one simple legislative reform or "policy lever" but through negotiation and the finding of common interests between the state and forest communities. This reinforces the importance of adapting property rights to the local conditions of both the resource base and the users, taking account of both the assets (including human capital) of local people and the types of risks that they face.

Both biophysical and sociopolitical risks shape property rights in Cambodia, consistent with the framework developed in Chapter 2 of this volume. This highlights the need to address the nature and capacity of the state to understanding, let alone intervene to strengthen, property rights for the poor. This need is compounded in postconflict settings, where records have often been destroyed and human capital, especially education levels, is low. External interventions are likely to be needed in such cases to help poor people secure their property rights (such as through boundary demarcation for communities), but action research accompanying such interventions can help to identify processes that can be expanded to other areas, as the Indonesia study has done.

Broader Implications for Policy, Practice, and Research

Over the past decade, programs of NRM and a range of community-driven development programs have given increasing attention to group-based approaches, using some form of collective action as a supplement to state or external assistance for poverty reduction. The case studies reported in this volume provide indications that there is no simple prescription for such programs, but an understanding of the existing institutions of collective action and property rights and how they are used (or not) by poor people can contribute to more effective programs. One major concern is that policymakers and practitioners must exercise caution, because trust, which is at the heart of effective collective organization, is fragile and easier to destroy than to create (as indicated in the Ethiopia–*iddir* and Cambodia case studies). Development actors should take into account the long-run nature of the poverty reduction enterprise. Strengthening collective action and expanding property rights are both long-term ventures that require significant effort on the ground to be effective. They are not universal remedies but rather important dimensions to consider when structuring interventions and are most effective when applied in conjunction with other complementary investments in infrastructure, information on markets, telecommunications, and so on, and when governmental and nongovernmental actors assume supportive roles.

New arrangements are necessary to provide a supportive framework for local-level activities and efforts. These new arrangements, whether formal institutions (such as producer marketing groups in Kenya) or changes in organizational practices (such as the Ethiopian *iddir* taking on health insurance), will be necessary to perform functions such as providing guidance in linking insurance groups and marketing groups to different sources and mechanisms of financing and to formal insurance schemes. Not many farmers can raise the collateral often demanded in exchange for financing, and community-designed insurance schemes often need backups when shocks are widespread. At the same time, when developing public intervention programs it is important to consider whether they are "crowding out" or displacing important forms of property rights or collective action on which the poor depend. Dercon (2005) notes that transfers associated with formal social protection programs may crowd out transfers from traditional institutions and even undermine those institutions. Even though crowding out in itself may not be a problem if the formal schemes provide superior coverage in terms of wider geographic spread and larger scale of shocks, the informal institutions may perform other social and economic functions in the community. It is important to ask whether programs to formalize property rights exclude the poor from important access or use rights (Wily 2006; Peters and Kambewa 2007). In the natural resources sector, new policies and laws are necessary to safeguard against the concentration of the benefits of critical survival resources such as water and dry-season grazing lands among an elite few while excluding a majority of poorer individuals.

However, there is hardly a shortage of policies and laws, especially in NRM, in which many countries around the world have passed decentralization reforms either as part of broader governance reforms or specific to the sector. The enforcement of these institutions, including the clarification of ambiguities that arise from their enforcement, is critical to whether they will achieve the stated outcomes of improved livelihoods and environmental sustainability. Much support is required in the form of capacity-building and training of officials for a new and inclusive mandate, the interpretation of the new rules to a wide range of stakeholders, and an overall political commitment to the principle of equity. These are dimensions that require consideration when translating policies and laws into viable practices that advance a more equitable distribution of benefits and ultimately empower communities.

Although creating new rules and norms is often necessary, it can sometimes be less costly to recognize and strengthen existing local-level institutions that are valued and have been proven to contribute to livelihood goals at the local level. Such institutions are likely viewed as legitimate and will thus be resisted less and trusted more and have built-in monitoring, sanctioning, and conflict resolution procedures. Local institutions are not always benign and can have built-in biases against certain groups and individuals. Any effort at working with pre-existing institutions must explore distributional issues and negotiate special provisions and safeguards that will adjust any discrepancy.

For local-level actions or efforts to be effective, the chapters in this volume have demonstrated a need for coordination with other actors beyond the local. These can be both government and nongovernmental actors who can provide information (including examples of good practices), resources, and conflict resolution and can also link isolated communities to others with shared interests and needs and ultimately increase their bargaining power. As an example, producer marketing groups can federate, providing a much larger amount of product volume and increasing market share. Similarly, examples of good practice of *iddir* can be disseminated across space, helping create associations of associations. Examples of conflict resolution mechanisms whereby property rights are flexible and negotiated may also have broader applicability. This kind of dissemination of lessons can be provided by government actors, whose mandate covers large spatial scales and wider jurisdictions. It can be provided by non-governmental organizations (NGOs), as CIFOR and the African Highlands Initiative have shown. The general point is that coproduction provides a fertile avenue for exploiting synergies between actors with complementary responsibilities and resources, but it takes time to establish.

In sum, the implications for policy and practice can be separated into three broad categories. A first category proposes a minimal set of reforms that can embed current successes and, by so doing, provide a mechanism for scaling up. A second category encourages the use of existing institutions and norms as building blocks, and a third strongly recommends better coordination among actors to exploit complementarities in mandates and capabilities. These three implications are planted within an overall recognition that collective action and property rights are not *the* solutions to rural poverty but are invaluable components of broader programs. Although collective action and property rights do not always result in immediate transformation of consumption, expenditures, or institutions, attention to these key institutions draws attention to the role of poor people as central actors rather than as passive recipients of poverty reduction programs.

In this volume we did not attempt to provide all the answers on how institutions contribute to poverty reduction. In addition to going across sectors, themes, and methods in analyzing the roles that collective action and property rights play in improving people's livelihoods, we aimed to pave the way for future research of this kind, especially by showing how the Institutional Analysis and Development (IAD) framework can be adapted and used across poverty-related arenas. Although the IAD framework has been used extensively in the NRM literature, it is less extensively applied in other areas of collective action (for exceptions see Devaux et al. 2009; Kirsten et al. 2009). Indeed, the literatures on collective action in resource management, community-driven development, risk mitigation, and cooperative marketing have not often been brought together (cf. Meinzen-Dick et al. 2009). Yet the findings from studying collective action in one context may provide insights into other domains, just as insights from one type of natural resource (such as water) have cross-fertilized studies of other types of resources (for example, forests or rangelands).

Finally, research is faced with the enduring challenge of understanding the conditions under which (including incentive systems) wealthier community members will work with the poorer or public officials will invest effort in building partnerships with communities and NGOs. What are effective ways to institutionalize procedures that demand partnerships and accountability among partners? The effectiveness of pro-poor policies or their likelihood of implementation can be better enhanced with a nuanced understanding of these questions.

Concluding Thoughts

The studies collected in this volume have demonstrated that poverty is a multi-faceted phenomenon that manifests itself in diverse ways such as levels of income, expenditures, access to valued natural resources and services, and vulnerability. They have also demonstrated that poverty is "produced" in different ways: through illness and climatic shocks and via poorly implemented governmental reforms, including modernization projects. By using a mix of methodologies, including longitudinal quantitative studies, qualitative studies, participatory action research, and experimental games, the studies in this volume have collectively exposed these multiple facets and provided insights into the production of poverty and steps that can be taken to reduce it. Although quantitative studies provide a sense of the intensity of poverty, how it varies over time and space, and correlations between indicators, qualitative studies provide insights into how poverty comes to be and, in the case of action research, some preferred actions that can be taken by communities and external actors. Methodological pluralism gives us a more complete understanding of movement in and out of poverty.

An adapted version of the IAD framework was used to assemble key analytical variables and hypothesize relationships among those variables. This framework helped us to order and organize the large number of variables across the different contextual settings. However, the framework is broad; none of the projects reported addressed all the elements of the entire framework, though each project did tackle parts of it. The IAD provided a basis for teasing out relationships among actors, which are at the heart of poverty. Asymmetries in relationships and interactions were approximated by considering the material and nonmaterial assets that both individuals and groups held, as well as their positions (that is, their action resources), which subsequently influenced their ability to participate in collective action (or not) or to influence property rights. The action arena, a component of the framework, isolates the specific problem-solving situation in which actors are caught up as well as the resources and positions that they hold. It provides scope for a nuanced analysis of poverty. However, the power of such a framework is enhanced when case studies use it consistently.

Through the case study and synthesis chapters we not only tried to show the complexity that surrounds institutions, be it their inclusiveness or exclusiveness, adaptability, or response to outside influence; we also tried to show that the poor are deeply embedded in this complex institutional environment. We hope that the tools (our framework) and approaches to studying poverty described in this volume will motivate other researchers to grapple with this complexity. We also hope that both the global research project that laid the foundation for this book and the written findings of the project captured here will induce policy changes in the project countries and around the world that would contribute to poverty reduction. We recognize that the findings of the case studies in this volume do not show drastic increases in poor people's income levels or radical improvements in their political representation. However, putting a spotlight on institutions of collective action and property rights as lenses for poverty analysis and the means of achieving poverty reduction is an important step in accounting for the messy and multifaceted reality of the poor and moving closer to providing effective and lasting solutions.

References

Agrawal, A. 2001. Common property institutions and sustainable governance of resources. *World Development* 29 (10): 1649–1672.

Agrawal, A., and E. Ostrom. 2001. Collective action, property rights, and decentralization in resource use in India and Nepal. *Politics and Society* 29 (4): 485–514.

Baland, J. M., and J. P. Platteau. 1996. *Halting degradation of natural resources: Is there a role for rural communities?* New York, and Oxford, U.K.: Food and Agriculture Organization of the United Nations and Clarendon Press.

Bardhan, P. 1993. Analytics of the institutions of informal cooperation in rural development. *World Development* 21 (4): 633–639.

———. 1997. Corruption and development: A review of issues. *Journal of Economic Literature* 35 (3): 1320–1346.

Barrett, C. 2005. Rural poverty dynamics: Development policy implications. *Agricultural Economics* 32 (1): 43–58.

Barrett, C. B., A. G. Mude, and J. M. Omiti. 2007. Decentralization and the social economics of development: An overview of concepts and evidence from Kenya. In *Decentralization and the social economics of development: Lessons from Kenya,* ed. C. B. Barrett, A. G. Mude, and J. M. Omiti. Cambridge and Wallingford, U.K.: CABI.

Bebbington, A. 1996. Organizations and intensifications: Campesino federations, rural livelihoods and agricultural technology in the Andes and Amazonia. *World Development* 24 (7): 1161–1177.

Bromley, D. W. 1991. *Environment and economy: Property rights and public policy.* Cambridge, U.K.: Basil Blackwell.

Cárdenas, J. C. 2009. Experiments in environment and development. *Annual Review of Resource Economics* 1 (24): 157–182.

Cleaver, F. 2005. The inequality of social capital and the reproduction of chronic poverty. *World Development* 33 (6): 893–906.

Colfer, C. J. P., and D. Capistrano, eds. 2005. *The politics of decentralization: Forests, people and power.* London: Earthscan.

Coulter, J. 2007. *Farmer groups enterprises and the marketing of staple food commodities in Africa.* CAPRi Working Paper 81. Washington, D.C.: International Food Policy Research Institute.

Dercon, S. 2002. Income risk, coping strategies, and safety nets. *World Bank Economic Observer* 17 (2): 141–166.

———. 2005. *Insurance against poverty.* Policy brief. Helsinki, Finland: United Nations University World Institute for Development Economics Research.

Devaux, A., D. Horton, C. Velasco, G. Thiele, G. López, T. Bernet, I. Reinoso, and M. Ordinola. 2009. Collective action for market chain innovation in the Andes. *Food Policy* 34 (1): 31–38.

Dietz, T., E. Ostrom, and P. C. Stern. 2003. The struggle to govern the commons. *Science* 302 (5652): 1907–1912.

Edmunds, D., and E. Wollenberg. 2002. *Disadvantaged groups in multistakeholder negotiations*. Bogor, Indonesia: Center for International Forestry Research.

Gibson, C., and F. Lehoucq. 2003. The local politics of decentralized environmental policy. *Journal of Environment and Development* 12 (1): 28–49.

Hulme, D., and A. Shepherd. 2003. Conceptualizing chronic poverty. *World Development* 31 (3): 403–423.

GOI (Government of India). 2008. *Common guidelines for watershed development projects*. New Delhi.

Kirsten, J. F., A. R. Dorward, C. Poulton, and N. Vink, eds. 2009. *Institutional economics perspectives on African agricultural development*. Washington, D.C.: International Food Policy Research Institute.

Krishna, A. 2004. Escaping poverty and becoming poor: Who gains, who loses, and why? *World Development* 32 (1): 121–136.

Larson, A., and J. Ribot. 2005. Democratic decentralization through a natural resources lens: An introduction. In *Democratic decentralization through a natural resource lens,* ed. J. C. Ribot and A. M. Larson. London and New York: Routledge.

Little, P., K. Smith, B. Cellarius, D. L. Coppock, and C. Barrett. 2001. Avoiding disaster: Diversification and risk management among East African herders. *Development and Change* 32 (2001): 401–433.

Markelova, H., R. Meinzen-Dick, J. Hellin, and S. Dohrn. 2009. Collective action for smallholder market access. *Food Policy* 34 (1): 1–7.

Meinzen-Dick, R., and E. Mwangi. 2009. Cutting the web of interests: Pitfalls of formalizing property rights. *Land Use Policy* 26 (1): 36–43.

Meinzen-Dick, R., and R. Pradhan. 2001. Implications of legal pluralism for natural resources management. *IDS Bulletin* 32 (4): 10–17.

Meinzen-Dick, R., A. Knox, and M. Di Gregorio, eds. 2001. *Collective action, property rights, and devolution of natural resource management: Exchange of knowledge and implications for policy*. Feldafing, Germany: Zentralstelle für Ernährung und Landwirtschaft.

Meinzen-Dick, R., H. Markelova, J. Hellin, and S. Dohrn. 2009. Collective action for smallholder market access. *Food Policy* 34 (1): 1–7.

Meynen, W., and M. Doornbos. 2005. Decentralizing natural resource management: A recipe for sustainability and equity? In *Democratic decentralization through a natural resource lens,* ed. J. C. Ribot and A. M. Larson. London and New York: Routledge.

Mwangi, E. 2007. *Socioeconomic change and land use in Africa: The transformation of property rights in Kenya's Maasailand.* New York: Palgrave Macmillan.

Ostrom, E. 1990. *Governing the commons: The evolution of institutions for collective action.* Cambridge, U.K.: Cambridge University Press.

Pandolfelli, L., R. Meinzen-Dick, and S. Dohrn. 2007. *Gender and collective action: A conceptual framework for analysis.* CAPRi Working Paper 64. Washington, D.C.: International Food Policy Research Institute.

Peters, P., and D. Kambewa. 2007. Whose security? Deepening social conflict over "customary" tenure in the shadow of land tenure reform. *Journal of Modern African Studies* 45 (3): 447–472.

Runge, C. F. 1986. Common property and collective action in economic development. *World Development* 14 (5): 623–635.

Scott, J. C. 1999. *Seeing like a state: How certain schemes to improve the human condition have failed.* New Haven, Conn., U.S.A.: Yale University Press.

Seabright, P. 1993. Managing local commons: Theoretical issues in incentive design. *Journal of Economic Perspectives* 7 (4): 113–134.

Thorpe, R., F. Stewart, and A. Heyer. 2005. When and how far is group formation a route out of chronic poverty? *World Development* 33 (6): 907–920.

Wily, L. A. 1999. Moving forward in African community forestry: Trading power, not use rights. *Society and Natural Resources* 12 (1): 49–61.

———. 2006. The commons and customary law in modern times: Rethinking the orthodoxies. In *Land rights for African development: From knowledge to action.* CAPRi policy brief. Washington, D.C.: International Food Policy Research Institute.

World Bank. 2006. *Little green data book.* Washington, D.C. <http://siteresources.worldbank.org/INTEEI/936214-1146251511077/20916989/LGDB2006.pdf>. Accessed February 8, 2011.

———. 2009. *Gender in agriculture: Sourcebook.* Washington, D.C.: World Bank, Food and Agriculture Organization of the United Nations, and International Fund for Agricultural Development.

Contributors

Kassahun Aberra was a community facilitator with the Southern Agricultural Research Institute of Ethiopia at the time he contributed to this work. He is currently working at the Agricultural Technology Vocational Training College (ATVAT), Wolayta Soddo, Ethiopia.

Francis Alinyo was a program officer with ActionAid International Uganda and chairman of the Kapchorwa District Landcare Chapter, Uganda, at the time he contributed to this work. He is currently a district coordinator for the National Agricultural Advisory Services of the Ministry of Agriculture, Uganda.

Shenkut Ayele is an early warning assessment and response manager with Catholic Relief Services in Addis Ababa, Ethiopia.

Kiflu Bedane was a senior researcher with the Ethiopian Agricultural Research Organization (now the Ethiopian Institute of Agricultural Research) at the time he contributed to this work. He is currently working as a freelance consultant based in Addis Ababa, Ethiopia.

Leulseged Begashaw is a researcher in plant pathology at the Southern Agricultural Research Institute, Hawassa, Ethiopia.

Fekadu Beyene was a doctoral candidate at Humboldt University of Berlin at the time he contributed to this work. He is currently an assistant professor at the College of Agriculture and Environmental Sciences, Haramaya University, Ethiopia.

Sarah Charamila was a research assistant with the African Highlands Initiative, Lushoto, Tanzania, at the time she contributed to this work.

Awadh Chemangeni was a senior environment officer in Kapchorwa District, Uganda, and a part-time lecturer in the Department of Biological Sciences of the Islamic University in Uganda at the time he contributed to this work. He

413

also worked as a project coordinator for the International Union for Conservation of Nature's Livelihoods and Landscape Strategy for the Mount Elgon Ecosystem. He is currently the natural resources coordinator for the Ministry of Water and Environment in Kapchorwa and chairperson of the Kapchorwa District Landcare Chapter.

William Cheptegei was a member of the Kapchorwa District Landcare Chapter secretariat, Uganda, at the time he contributed to this work and formerly worked as an extension agent for the Ministry of Agriculture. He is currently an independent farmer and serves as a district counselor in Kapchorwa.

Carol J. Pierce Colfer was principal scientist in the Forests and Governance Programme of the Center for International Forestry Research, Bogor, Indonesia, at the time she contributed to this work. She is currently a senior research associate at the Center and a visiting fellow at the Cornell International Institute for Food, Agriculture, and Development, Ithaca, N.Y., U.S.A.

Stefan Dercon is a professor of development economics at the University of Oxford, U.K.

Monica Di Gregorio was a research analyst in the Environment and Production Technology Division of the International Food Policy Research Institute, Washington, D.C. She is currently a fellow in the Department of International Development of the London School of Economics and Political Science.

Mesfin T. Gebremikael was a research assistant at the Ethiopian Agricultural Research Organization (now the Ethiopian Institute of Agricultural Research), Holetta, at the time he contributed to this work. He is currently a doctoral candidate in the Soil Management Department of the Faculty of Bioscience Engineering of Ghent University, Belgium.

Laura German was a scientist and the acting regional coordinator of the African Highlands Initiative at the time she contributed to this work. She is currently a senior scientist in the Forests and Governance Programme of the Center for International Forestry Research, Bogor, Indonesia.

Marie Godquin was a research assistant at the Institut National de la Recherche Agronomique, Paris, and a doctoral candidate at the University of Paris I–Pantheon–Sorbonne at the time she contributed to this work. She is currently head of quantitative and market risk audit at Deutsche Bank, London.

Konrad Hagedorn is a professor in the Division of Resource Economics, Department of Agricultural Economics, Faculty of Agriculture and Horticulture of Humboldt University of Berlin, and director of the Institute of Cooperative Studies at Humboldt University of Berlin.

John Hoddinott is deputy division director in the Poverty, Health, and Nutrition Division of the International Food Policy Research Institute, Washington, D.C.

Bekele Hundie was a doctoral candidate in the Division of Resource Economics of Humboldt University of Berlin at the time he contributed to this work. He is currently an assistant professor in the Department of Development Economics of the Ethiopian Civil Service College, Addis Ababa.

Zewdie Jotte was a research and community development assistant with the Ethiopian Agricultural Research Organization (now the Ethiopian Institute of Agricultural Research) at the time he contributed to this work.

Menale Kassie is an agricultural and resource economist at the International Maize and Wheat Improvement Center, Mexico City, and is based in the Center's regional office in Nairobi, Kenya.

Tewodros A. Kebede is a researcher at the Fafo Institute for Applied International Studies, Oslo, Norway.

Michael Kirk is a professor of development economics at the Institute for Cooperation in Developing Countries at Philipps-Universität Marburg, Germany.

Heru Komarudin is a researcher in the Forests and Governance Programme of the Center for International Forestry Research, Bogor, Indonesia.

Benedikt Korf is an assistant professor in the Department of Geography of the University of Zurich, Switzerland.

Pramila Krishnan is a senior lecturer in the Faculty of Economics and a fellow of Jesus College, University of Cambridge, U.K.

Helen Markelova was a research analyst in the Environment and Production Technology Division of the International Food Policy Research Institute, Washington, D.C., at the time she contributed to this work. She is currently pursuing a doctoral degree in the Department of Applied Economics of the University of Minnesota, St. Paul, U.S.A.

Waga Mazengia is a researcher in agronomy at the Southern Agricultural Research Institute in Areka, Ethiopia.

Nancy McCarthy was a research fellow in the Environment and Production Technology Division of the International Food Policy Research Institute, Washington, D.C., at the time she contributed to this work. She is currently president of LEAD Analytics, Washington, D.C.

Scott McNiven was a research analyst in the Food Consumption and Nutrition Division of the International Food Policy Research Institute, Washington, D.C., at the time he contributed to this work. He is currently a doctoral candidate in agricultural and resource economics at the University of California at Davis, U.S.A.

Ruth Meinzen-Dick is a senior research fellow in the Environment and Production Technology Division of the International Food Policy Research Institute, Washington, D.C., and coordinator of the Systemwide Program on Collective Action and Property Rights (CAPRi) of the Consultative Group on International Agricultural Research.

Ashenafi Mekonnen was a junior researcher with the Southern Agricultural Research Institute of Ethiopia at the time he contributed to this work. He is currently a master of science student in Natural Resource Economics at the Hawassa University College of Forestry, Ethiopia.

Geoffrey Muricho is a research associate at the International Maize and Wheat Improvement Center, Mexico City, and is based in the Center's regional office in Nairobi, Kenya.

Esther Mwangi was a postdoctoral fellow in the Environment and Production Technology Division of the International Food Policy Research Institute, Washington, D.C., at the time she contributed to this work. She is currently a scientist in the Forests and Governance Programme of the Center for International Forestry Research, Bogor, Indonesia.

Simon Nyangas is an extension officer and organizing secretary for Kapchorwa District Land Care Chapter, Kapchorwa, Uganda.

Gideon Obare is a professor of agricultural economics in the Department of Agricultural Economics and Agribusiness Management of Egerton University, Kenya.

Martina Padmanabhan was a research fellow in the Division of Resource Economics, Faculty of Agriculture and Horticulture of Humboldt University of Berlin, at the time she contributed to this work. She is currently leader of the

BioDIVA research group at the Institute of Environmental Planning at Leibniz Universität Hannover, Germany.

Agnes R. Quisumbing is a senior research fellow in the Poverty, Health, and Nutrition Division of the International Food Policy Research Institute, Washington, D.C.

V. Ratna Reddy was a professor at the Centre for Economic and Social Studies, Hyderabad, India, at the time he contributed to this work. He is currently the director of the Livelihoods and Natural Resource Management Institute, Hyderabad.

Bekele Shiferaw is currently director of the Socioeconomics Program of the International Maize and Wheat Improvement Center (CIMMYT), Mexico City, and is based at the Center's regional office in Nairobi, Kenya. Before joining CIMMYT in 2009, he was a senior and principal scientist, Resource and Development Economics, at the International Crops Research Institute for the Semi-Arid Tropics (ICRISAT), based initially at Patancheru, India, and later at the regional office in Nairobi, Kenya. The data collection and analysis for this work were carried out during his tenure at ICRISAT.

Yuliana L. Siagian was a research assistant in the Forests and Governance Programme of the Center for International Forestry Research, Bogor, Indonesia, at the time she contributed to this work. She is currently an independent consultant.

Brent Swallow is a professor in and chair of the Department of Resource Economics and Environmental Sociology of the University of Alberta, Edmonton, Canada.

Joseph Tanui was a regional research fellow with the African Highlands Initiative, Kampala, Uganda, at the time he contributed to this work. He is currently a doctoral candidate in the Environmental Economics and Natural Resources Group of Wageningen University, the Netherlands.

Hailemichael Taye was a development evaluation specialist working for an African Development Bank–funded agricultural project in Addis Ababa, Ethiopia, at the time he contributed to this work. He is currently a research officer on the Innovation in Livestock Systems team, Market Opportunities Theme, of the International Livestock Research Institute, Nairobi, Kenya, and is based in the Institute's office in Addis Ababa.

Zenebe A. Teferi was a researcher with the Ethiopian Agricultural Research Organization (now the Ethiopian Institute of Agricultural Research) at the time he contributed to this work. He is currently a doctoral candidate at Wageningen University and Research Center, the Netherlands.

Wilberforce Tirwomwe was a community facilitator/research assistant with the African Highlands Initiative in Kabale, Uganda, at the time he contributed to this work. He is currently a program coordinator with the African International Christian Ministry, Kabale.

Tessema Tolera was a research and community development assistant with the Ethiopian Agricultural Research Organization (now the Ethiopian Institute of Agricultural Research) at the time he contributed to this work. He is currently working as a freelance consultant in Addis Ababa, Ethiopia.

Anne Weingart was an economist and doctoral candidate at the Institute for Cooperation in Developing Countries at Philipps-Universität Marburg, Germany, at the time she contributed to this work. She is currently a referent in the Ministry of Economics and European Affairs of Brandenburg State, Potsdam, Germany.

Tassew Woldehanna is an associate professor at the School of Economics, Addis Ababa University, Ethiopia.

Index

Page numbers for entries occurring in boxes are followed by a *b;* those for entries in figures, by an *f;* those for entries in notes, by an *n;* and those for entries in tables, by a *t.*